Professional Selling

A Trust-Based Approach

Professional Selling

A Trust-Based Approach

Thomas N. Ingram
Colorado State University

Raymond W. LaForge
University of Louisville

Ramon A. Avila
Ball State University

Charles H. Schwepker Jr.
Central Missouri State University

Michael R. Williams
Illinois State University

Harcourt College Publishers

Fort Worth   Philadelphia   San Diego   New York   Orlando   Austin   San Antonio
Toronto   Montreal   London   Sydney   Tokyo

Publisher	Mike Roche
Acquisitions Editor	Bill Schoof
Market Strategist	Charles Watson
Developmental Editor	Jana Pitts
Project Editor	Jim Patterson
Art Director	April Eubanks
Production Manager	James McDonald

Cover image © Guy Crittenden, www.getphoto.com

ISBN: 0-03-026701-3
Library of Congress Catalog Card Number: 00–104766

Address for Domestic Orders:
Harcourt, Inc., 6277 Sea Harbor Drive, Orlando, FL 32887-6777
800-782-4479

Address for International Orders:
International Customer Service
Harcourt, Inc., 6277 Sea Harbor Drive, Orlando, FL 32887-6777
407-345-3800
(fax) 407-345-4060
(e-mail) hbintl@harcourtbrace.com

Address for Editorial Correspondence:
Harcourt College Publishers, 301 Commerce Street, Suite 3700, Fort Worth, TX 76102

Web Site Address:
http://www.harcourtcollege.com

Printed in the United States of America

0 1 2 3 4 5 6 7 8 9   043   9 8 7 6 5 4 3 2 1

Harcourt College Publishers

To Jacque
        —Thomas N. Ingram

To Susan, Alexandra, Kelly, my Dad, and in memory of my Mom
        —Raymond W. LaForge

To Terry, Sarah, Anne, Ryan, Laura, Kate, and my parents
        —Ramon A. Avila

To Laura, Charlie III, and my parents
        —Charles H. Schwepker Jr.

To Marilyn, Aimee, Kerri, my Mom, and in memory of my Dad
        —Michael R. Williams

The Harcourt Series in Marketing

Assael
Marketing

Avila, Williams, Ingram, and LaForge
The Professional Selling Skills Workbook

Bateson and Hoffman
Managing Services Marketing:
Text and Readings
Fourth Edition

Blackwell, Blackwell, and Talarzyk
Contemporary Cases in Consumer Behavior
Fourth Edition

Blackwell, Miniard, and Engel
Consumer Behavior
Ninth Edition

Boone and Kurtz
Contemporary Marketing
Tenth Edition

Boone and Kurtz
Contemporary Marketing 1999

Churchill
Basic Marketing Research
Fourth Edition

Churchill
Marketing Research: Methodological
Foundations
Seventh Edition

Czinkota and Ronkainen
Global Marketing

Czinkota and Ronkainen
International Marketing
Sixth Edition

Czinkota and Ronkainen
International Marketing Strategy:
Environmental Assessment and
Entry Strategies

Dickson
Marketing Management
Second Edition

Dunne and Lusch
Retailing
Third Edition

Ferrell, Hartline, Lucas, and Luck
Marketing Strategy

Futrell
Sales Management: Teamwork,
Leadership, and Technology
Sixth Edition

Ghosh
Retail Management
Second Edition

Hoffman
Marketing: Best Practices

Hoffman and Bateson
Essentials of Services Marketing
Second Edition

Hutt and Speh
Business Marketing Management:
A Strategic View of Industrial and
Organizational Markets
Seventh Edition

Ingram, LaForge, Avila, Schwepker,
and Williams
Professional Selling: A Trust-Based
Approach

Ingram, LaForge, Avila, Schwepker,
and Williams
Sales Management: Analysis and
Decision Making
Fourth Edition

Krugman, Reid, Dunn, and Barban
Advertising: Its Role in Modern Marketing
Eighth Edition

Lindgren and Shimp
Marketing: An Interactive Learning System

Oberhaus, Ratliffe, and Stauble
Professional Selling: A Relationship Process
Second Edition

Parente
Advertising Campaign Strategy: A Guide
to Marketing Communication Plans
Second Edition

Reedy
Electronic Marketing

Rosenbloom
Marketing Channels: A Management View
Sixth Edition

Sandburg
Discovering Your Marketing Career
CD-ROM

Schaffer
Applying Marketing Principles Software

Schaffer
The Marketing Game

Schellinck and Maddox
Marketing Research: A Computer-
Assisted Approach

Schnaars
MICROSIM

Schuster and Copeland
Global Business: Planning for Sales
and Negotiations

Sheth, Mittal, and Newman
Customer Behavior: Consumer Behavior
and Beyond

Shimp
Advertising and Promotion:
Supplemental Aspects of Integrated
Marketing Communications
Fifth Edition

Stauble
Marketing Strategy: A Global Perpsective

Talarzyk
Cases and Exercises in Marketing

Terpstra and Sarathy
International Marketing
Eighth Edition

Watson
Electronic Commerce

Weitz and Wensley
Readings in Strategic Marketing
Analysis, Planning, and Implementation

Zikmund
Exploring Marketing Research
Seventh Edition

Zikmund
Essentials of Marketing Research

Harcourt College Outline Series

Peterson
Principles of Marketing

PREFACE

The basic objective of *Professional Selling: A Trust-Based Approach* is to provide students with comprehensive coverage of contemporary professional selling in an interesting and challenging manner. This objective is achieved by integrating recent sales research with leading personal selling practice in an effective, time-tested pedagogical format. The major professional selling topics are addressed in separate modules. These modules are then presented in a logical sequence from the perspective of a professional salesperson. Each module contains similar pedagogical approaches to facilitate student learning.

Key Features

Professional Selling: A Trust-Based Approach has several key features that differentiate it from existing texts:

- The complete text consists of 9 modules. These modules contain the important content for a personal selling course. However, it is much easier to schedule 9 modules into a semester or quarter course than the many chapters available in most personal selling textbooks. This makes it possible for professors to cover the entire text, but to also have sufficient time to use the role-playing and other active learning exercises so popular in personal selling classes.

- The text is available in a low-cost format, so the price to the student will be much less than for typical hard-cover books. The modular format also facilitates custom publishing. Thus, professors can use the entire book or can order customized versions with only the modules desired. Professors who teach personal selling and sales management in one course have an additional option. These professors can create a customized text for their course by selecting specific modules from *Professional Selling: A Trust-Based Approach* and from the fourth edition of *Sales Management: Analysis and Decision Making*. The same author team wrote both texts and both texts have similar pedagogical features.

- Incorporating leading personal selling practice is a hallmark of this text. One of the ways we accomplish this is by assembling a Professional Selling Panel. This panel consists of sales executives and salespeople from different types of companies. Each panel member prepared comments for the text. These comments are presented in the "Professional Selling in the 21st Century" boxes in each module.

Text Organization

Professional Selling: A Trust-Based Approach is targeted to the undergraduate student enrolled in a one-semester or one-quarter personal selling class. However, it is sufficiently rigorous to be used at the MBA level, if supplemented with additional materials. The text contains nine separate modules. Modules 1-5 provide the knowledge and skill foundation for successful professional selling. Modules 6-9 focus on using this knowledge and skills within the different stages of the professional selling process.

MODULE 1: OVERVIEW OF PERSONAL SELLING   This module introduces the student to the exciting field of professional selling. It begins with a historical review of the sales function from ancient times up to the modern era in which professionalism is essential for success. The contributions made by salespeople to society, employers, and customers are discussed, and different types of sales jobs are explained. The module concludes with a discussion of sales careers and the qualifications and skills necessary for sales success.

MODULE 2: UNDERSTANDING BUYERS   Following a discussion of different types of buyers, this module introduces students to the activities of buyers common to each phase of the buying decision process and the corresponding roles and activities practiced by successful salespeople. The needs gap, a primary driver of buyers' purchasing behaviors, is explained, and different forms of buyer needs are catalogued and illustrated. This is followed by an explanation of the different types of purchasing decisions and their implications for salespeople. The growing incidence of multiple buying influences and buying teams is also demonstrated along with their impact on selling strategy. Finally, emergent trends such as relationship strategies, supply-chain management, target pricing, and the growing importance of information and technology are discussed from the perspective of the salesperson.

MODULE 3: BUILDING TRUST   This module introduces the concept of trust and why it is important to a salesperson. The distinguishing characteristics of trust-based selling and how to earn trust are covered. Five trust-builders are discussed and how they can be used by a salesperson to gain credibility. Knowledge bases are covered and why it is important for a salesperson to bring knowledge to the buyer. This module concludes with a discussion of sales ethics and three important areas of unethical behavior salespeople may encounter.

MODULE 4: COMMUNICATION SKILLS   This module builds students' understanding and mastery of collaborative, two-way communication. First, the process of relational sales communication is explained along with the important role it plays in successful selling. Each dimension of relational sales communication is explained from the salesperson's perspective, and examples are provided to further enhance mastery and application. The verbal dimension is first examined with an emphasis on its three sub-components: (1) developing effective questioning methods for use in uncovering buyers' needs and expectations; (2) utilizing active listening skills to facilitate the interchange of ideas and information; and (3) maximizing the responsive dissemination of information to buyers in order to explain and bring alive the benefits of proposed solutions. The nonverbal dimension is also examined with an emphasis on its application and meaningful interpretation in selling. Finally, the written dimension of communication is explored with an emphasis on how to develop quality sales proposals.

MODULE 5: SELF LEADERSHIP AND TEAMWORK SKILLS   This module familiarizes students with the concepts and processes of self leadership and provides an effective framework for developing and enhancing selling skills and abilities. First, a methodology for setting effective selling goals and objectives is discussed and integrated with techniques for territory analysis and account classification. This is followed by a discussion of how the objectives and information from the territory and account analysis become inputs for generating and implementing effective, multi-level sales planning. Finally, the importance of assessing performance results and goal attainment is reviewed. Wrapping up the module is an examination of internal and external team-work as vehicles for expanding the capabilities of an individual salesperson, increasing customer value, and creating sustainable competitive advantage for salespeople.

MODULE 6: STRATEGIC SELLING PROCESS   This module provides an introduction to the sales process as described in three steps: initiating, developing, and enhancing customer relationships. Key topics include adaptive selling, sales presentation planning, approaching the customer, gaining customer commitment, and building the relationship after the sale. Alternative selling models such as need satisfaction and consultative selling are also detailed in this module.

MODULE 7: INITIATING THE RELATIONSHIP   Following a discussion of the importance of strategic prospecting, this module introduces why prospecting can be a challenging task for a salesperson. This is followed by an explanation of where salespeople can find prospects. The importance of gathering and studying pre-call information and planning the initial sales call is then discussed. This module then builds students' understanding of how to approach and initiate contact with each prospect. Finally, the importance of questioning skills and discovering buyer needs is emphasized.

MODULE 8: DEVELOPING THE RELATIONSHIP   This module familiarizes students with the methods salespeople use to select appropriate customer offerings by assessing customer needs. First, different types of sales presentations and what goes into their planning are covered. This is followed by a discussion of different tools that can be used to customize a sales presentation. An explanation of how salespeople can link solutions to needs by using features, potential benefits, and confirmed benefits is discussed. Why prospects raise objections and the different types of objections are explained. Next, the LAARC method is introduced as a method to overcome buyer resistance and earn commitment. Finally, a presentation checklist is reviewed as to its importance in getting ready for the presentation with the buyer.

MODULE 9: EXPANDING CUSTOMER RELATIONSHIPS   This module builds students' understanding of how to follow-up to assess customer satisfaction. First, using technology to enhance follow-up is discussed. This is followed by a discussion of how to maintain open, two-way communication. Next, an explanation is given as to why it is important for a salesperson to encourage critical encounters and to expand collaborative involvement between the buyer and seller. Finally, how to add value and enhance mutual opportunities is discussed from the perspective of the salesperson.

Module Pedagogy

The following pedagogical format is used for each module to facilitate the student learning process.

LEARNING OBJECTIVES.   Specific learning objectives for the module are stated in behavioral terms so that students will know what they should be able to do after the module has been covered.

OPENING VIGNETTES.   All modules are introduced by an opening vignette that typically consists of a recent, real-world company example addressing many of the key points to be discussed in the module. These opening vignettes are intended to generate student interest in the topics to be covered and to illustrate the practicality of the module coverage.

KEY WORDS.   Key words are highlighted in bold type throughout each module and summarized in Understanding Professional Selling Terms at the end of the module to alert students to their importance.

BOXED INSERTS.   Each module contains two boxed inserts titled "Professional Selling in the 21st Century." The comments in these boxes are provided by members of our Professional Selling Panel and were made specifically for our text.

FIGURE CAPTIONS.   Every figure in the text includes a summarizing caption designed to make the figure understandable without reference to the module discussion.

MODULE SUMMARIES.   A module summary recaps the key points covered in the module by restating and answering questions presented in the learning objectives at the beginning of the module.

DEVELOPING PROFESSIONAL SELLING KNOWLEDGE.   Ten discussion questions are presented at the end of each module to review key concepts covered in the module. Some of the questions require students to summarize what has been covered, while others are designed to be more thought provoking and extend beyond module coverage.

BUILDING PROFESSIONAL SELLING SKILLS.   Application exercises are supplied for each module, requiring students to apply what has been learned in the module to specific personal selling situations. Many of these exercises allow students to record responses directly in the book. This encourages active learning in a workbook format.

MAKING PROFESSIONAL SELLING DECISIONS.   Each module concludes with two short cases. Most of these cases represent realistic and interesting professional selling situations. Many are designed so that students can role play their solutions.

Supplements

Instructor's Manual, Test Bank.   A comprehensive package of supplementary materials is available to make it easy for professors to teach a rigorous and interesting sales course. The *Instructor's Manual, Test Bank* contains a separate section for each module as well as teaching notes for all of the cases. Each section includes a summary; examples, exercises, and materials not covered in the book that could be incorporated into class discussion; and answers to review questions and application exercises. The manual also contains sample course outlines. The *Test Bank* contains multiple-choice and true-false questions and is available in a computerized version for Windows.

MICROCOMPUTER SOFTWARE.   The SPREE (Salesperson Review and Evaluation) software has been very popular with professors and students in the past. The software is designed to be very easy for students to use, and everything necessary to incorporate the microcomputer analysis into a sales management class is provided in the *Instructor's Manual.* The software has been revised and improved by updating to a Windows environment.

VIDEOS.   A video package has been prepared to provide a relevant and interesting visual teaching tool for the classroom. Two distinct selling series headline this video package. *Direct Selling on the Global Frontier* presents an overview of the global sales operation of direct selling companies and has a specific case situation for a particular company. *Inc. Magazine* videos show portrayals of "real" salespeople and sales calls with "real" clients in a variety of occupations. Companies represented include: Shearson-Lehman, 3M Health Care, and Ben & Jerry's.

INTERNET SUPPORT.   Visit the Harcourt Web site at http://www.harcourtcollege. com for the latest support material for the Harcourt series in marketing. These resources include annotated articles, resource links, and other pedagogical aids which will be constantly updated.

The update will include the latest company examples, new research findings, and other teaching aids geared to each module, making it easy for professors to incorporate this current information into their class sessions.

NEW! **POWERPOINT PRESENTATION.**   This enables professors to customize their own multimedia instruction. Organized by modules, this presentation includes highlights of important concepts, figures from the text, and footage from the video package to help illustrate the text discussion. Slides for both Sales Management and Professional Selling are included.

Acknowledgments

The writing of a book is a long and arduous task that requires the dedicated efforts of many individuals. The contributions of these individuals are greatly appreciated and deserve specific recognition. We are especially grateful for the efforts of the 98 instructors who participated in the market survey.

A great deal of credit for this book should go to all of the wonderful people at Harcourt. Their expertise, support, and constant encouragement turned an extremely difficult task into a very enjoyable one. We would like to recognize specifically the tremendous efforts of the following professionals and friends: Bill Schoof, Lisé Johnson, Jana Pitts, Jim Patterson, James McDonald, April Eubanks, Linda Blundell, Lisa Kelley, and Beverly Dunn. Without their efforts this edition would not have seen the light of day. However, we also want to thank the many individuals with whom we did not have direct contact but who assisted in the development and production of this book. We have been treated superbly by everyone at Harcourt during this project.

We are also very appreciative of the support provided by our colleagues at Colorado State University, the University of Louisville, Central Missouri State University, Ball State University, and Illinois State University.

Thomas N. Ingram
Raymond W. LaForge
Ramon A. Avila
Charles H. Schwepker Jr.
Michael R. Williams

June 2000

Module Format

Professional Selling: A Trust-Based Approach was written for students. Therefore, its aim is to provide comprehensive coverage of professional selling in a manner that you will find interesting and readable. Each module blends recent research results with current professional selling practice in a format designed to facilitate learning.

At the beginning of each module, "Learning Objectives" highlight the basic material that the student should expect to learn. These learning objectives are helpful in reviewing modules for future study. An opening vignette then illustrates many of the important ideas to be covered in the module, using examples of companies in various industries to illustrate the diversity and complexity of professional selling. Most of the companies described in the vignettes are well known, and most of the situations represent recent actions by these firms.

Key words in the body of each module are printed in bold letters, and figures and exhibits are used liberally to illustrate and amplify the discussion in the text. Every figure contains an explanation so that it can be understood without reference to the text.

Each module contains two boxed inserts entitled **Professional Selling in the 21st Century.** The examples in both boxes have been provided specifically for this textbook by sales executives from various companies whom we recruited to serve as a **Professional Selling Panel.** To ensure that the textbook includes the latest practices from leading sales organizations, each executive was asked to provide specific examples of "best practices" in their company. Backgrounds of each executive are provided at the end of this section.

Sales managers are confronted with various ethical issues when performing their job activities. Many of these ethical issues are addressed in **An Ethical Dilemma** boxes that appear throughout the modules. You will be presented with realistic ethical situations faced by sales managers and asked to recommend appropriate courses of action.

A module summary is geared to the learning objectives presented at the beginning of the module. **Understanding Professional Selling Terms** lists the key words that appear in bold throughout the module. **Developing Professional Selling Knowledge** presents 10 questions to help you develop an understanding of important professional selling issues and relationships. **Building Professional Selling Skills** consists of three exercises in which you can apply the professional selling knowledge learned in the module. **Making Professional Selling Decisions** includes two interesting case situations that allow you to make important professional selling decisions. If you understand professional selling terms, develop professional selling knowledge, and build professional selling skills, you will be prepared to make successful professional selling decisions.

Professional Selling Panel

Tom Avila's title of sales engineer for Davis and Davis has him representing approximately 20 different companies in protected territories in the process-control industry. Based in Denver, Colorado, Tom holds a B.S. in business with a focus in finance, management, and marketing from Ball State University.

Darrell Beaty is manager of business development for Ontario Systems. In his position, he provides leadership and direction to members of the business development group. The primary responsibility of the group is to build strong relationships with strategic clients and assist with strategic goals of Ontario Systems. Darrell attended Ball State University.

Jennifer Blessin is a marketing representative for Caterpillar. She graduated from Illinois State University as a marketing major with a concentration in professional selling and sales management. Jennifer was awarded the distinguished honor of Outstanding Marketing Senior at Illinois State University. At Caterpillar, Jennifer works directly with the dealer network and is part of a marketing team charged with the responsibility for the introduction, sales, and marketing of a new line of products.

Greg Burchett is a district sales manager for Wallace Computer Services in Ft. Wayne, Indiana. He supervises four salepeople who sell commercial printing and supplies to businesses and organizational customers. Greg has a B.S. in marketing from Indiana University, Bloomington.

Fielding Cagle is currently key account manager for Progressive Foods, Inc. Based in Oklahoma, Fielding has an extensive background in selling and sales management with over 26 years of experience in the institutional and retail food industries. An avid writer, he attended the University of Oklahoma as an English major. Fielding has received numerous honors and much recognition for his selling and business related accomplishments including serving as an executive board member for the National Board of Directors of the National Correctional Food Service Association.

Brett Carrington is a sales representative for Wallace Computer Services in Ft. Wayne, Indiana. Brett manages a territory in northeast Indiana and northwest Ohio. He sells commercial printing, business forms, labels, and other various printed materials. Brett has a B.S. in marketing from Ball State University.

Phil Clark is a district agent for Northwestern Mutual Financial Network. Based in Carmel, Indiana, Phil has represented the company for 15 years, concentrating in business and estate planning. He is also active in the development of career agents and manages an office of 10 producers. He is a graduate of Indiana University school of business with a major in finance.

Kim Davenport is a senior district sales manager for Shering-Plough Labs. He manages 16 pharmaceutical sales representatives in Arizona and New Mexico. Kim holds a B.S. in marketing and general business administration from Ball State University.

Jennifer DeMarco has achieved a solid record of success in sales and marketing at Chicago-based CDW Computer Centers. As a salesperson, Jennifer distinguished herself as a top performer in selling computer technology solutions to a diverse account list of business customers. This record of achievement has propelled her into sales management where she currently serves as sales recruiting supervisor. She graduated from Illinois State University.

Jay Deragon is director of strategy for Nashville-based Discover eHoldings. Jay manages a business consulting group specializing in organizational assessment, strategic planning, marketing, sales, and process improvement. In addition to his initial work as a business administration student at the University of Southern Maine, Jay has also studied advanced business management at Wharton College and the University of California and has completed certification courses at the Deming Institute and the Juran Institute.

John Haack is the senior vice president of sales and marketing for Ball Foster Glass. He has held various sales and marketing management positions in the packaging industry throughout his career. John holds a B.S. in business from Ball State University.

Jerry Heffel started with The Southwestern Company as a college student salesperson in 1965, and has been president of the company since 1980. He is responsible for current profitability and setting the future direction for the company. Jerry has a B.A. in history from Oklahoma State University, and an M.B.A. from the University of Oklahoma.

John Jenkins, technical sales executive for STL Technology Partners, graduated from Illinois State University with a degree in applied computer science. In his sales management position, John works directly with the organization's salesforce and a broad range of corporate clients. He is charged with the strategic responsibility for marketing and customer fulfillment and has just been honored as the recipient of *The Commitment to Excellence Award,* STL Technology Partners' distinguished award for sales and service achievement.

L.A. Mitchell is sales planner, business management, for Lucent Technologies. She works with the sales team as a strategic financial partner with the sales directors which involves financial analysis, forecasting, and the identification of sales opportunities. L.A. has B.S.B.A. in marketing and an M.S. in marketing from Colorado State University.

Todd Reffett is director of sales and marketing for the Market Driven Quality Group, LLC. Todd has accumulated a rich background of sales and marketing experience in the business services industry. In his position, Todd works with a diverse mixture of clients ranging from established Fortune 500 companies to small business start-ups. Todd holds a B.B.A. in marketing and management and an M.B.A. from Illinois State University.

Aaron Simmons is an agent for State Farm Insurance. He has succeeded in establishing and building a highly successful insurance and financial services business. With full responsibility for all sales and marketing strategies and activities related to his central Illinois-based agency, Aaron works closely with a wide variety of consumer as well as business clients. Prior to joining State Farm, Aaron was a top performing salesperson and dis-

trict manager with Wallace. His combined experiences in sales and marketing provide him with a rich background of valuable business experience, which he readily shares with others in training programs and university level classes. Aaron is a graduate of Illinois State University.

Missy Harbit Rust is an executive sales representative for Glaxo Wellcome, Inc. Her pharmaceutical accounts territory is in central Indiana. Missy attended Ball State University and has a B.S. in marketing and fashion merchandising.

Stephanie Urich is an area manager for Hormel Foods Corporation. Her unit is responsible for food-service sales to institutional customers in the Chicago area. Stephanie has a B.S. in marketing from Ball State University.

ABOUT THE AUTHORS

Thomas N. Ingram (Ph.D., Georgia State University) is department chair and professor of marketing at Colorado State University. Before commencing his academic career, he worked in sales, product management, and sales management with Exxon and Mobil. Tom is a recipient of the Marketing Educator of the Year award given by Sales and Marketing Executives International (SMEI). He was honored as the first recipient of the Mu Kappa Tau National Marketing Honor Society recognition award for Outstanding Scholarly Contributions to the Sales Discipline. On several occasions, he has been recognized at the university level for outstanding teaching. Tom has served as the editor of *Journal of Personal Selling and Sales Management,* chair of the SMEI Accreditation Institute, and as a member of the Board of Directors of SMEI. He is the editor of *Journal of Marketing Theory and Practice.* Tom's primary research is in personal selling and sales management. His work has appeared in the *Journal of Marketing, Journal of Marketing Research, Journal of Personal Selling and Sales Management,* and *Journal of the Academy of Marketing Science,* among others. He is the co-author of *The Professional Selling Skills Workbook* and *Marketing Principles and Perspectives,* and co-editor of *Emerging Trends in Sales Thought and Practice.*

Raymond W. (Buddy) LaForge (DBA, University of Tennessee) is the Brown-Forman Professor of Marketing at the University of Louisville. He founded the *Marketing Education Review,* served as editor for eight years, and is currently executive editor. Buddy has co-authored *Marketing: Principles & Perspectives, Sales Management: Analysis and Decision Making, The Professional Selling Skills Workbook,* and co-edited *Emerging Trends in Sales Thought and Practice.* His research is published in many journals including the *Journal of Marketing, Journal of Marketing Research, Journal of the Academy of Marketing Science,* and *Journal of Personal Selling and Sales Management.* Buddy currently serves on the Direct Selling Education Foundation Board of Directors and Executive Committee, DuPont Corporate Marketing Faculty Advisory Team for the Sales Enhancement Process, Family Business Center Advisory Board, as Vice President of Conferences and Research for the American Marketing Association Academic Council, and as Vice President/Marketing for the Academy of Business Education. He is developing the Sales Program at the University of Louisville and establishing the Sales Professional Network (http://cbpa.louisville.edu.salesnetwork) linking sales faculty, students, and executives to improve sales careers, education, research, and practice. Buddy and his wife, Susan, and daughters, Alexandra and Kelly, enjoy tennis, golf, and thoroughbred racing in Louisville, Kentucky.

Ramon A. Avila (Ph.D., Virginia Tech University) is the George and Frances Ball Distinguished Professor of Marketing at Ball State University. Before coming to Ball State, he worked in sales with the Burroughs Corporation. He has also held two visiting professorships at the University of Hawaii. Ramon was presented the 1999 Mu Kappa Tau's Outstanding Contributor to the Sales Profession. He is only the third recipient of this award. Ramon has also received the University's Outstanding Junior Faculty award, the University's Outstanding Service award, the College of Business Professor of the Year, and the Dean's Teaching award every year since its inception in 1987. Ramon also sits on six editorial review boards. Ramon's primary research is in personal selling and sales management. His work has appeared in the *Journal of Marketing Research, Journal of Personal Selling and Sales Management, Industrial*

Marketing Management, Journal of Marketing Management, and the *Journal of Marketing Theory and Practice,* among others. He is the co-author of *The Professional Selling Skills Workbook.*

Charles H. Schwepker Jr. (Ph.D., University of Memphis) is professor of marketing at Central Missouri State University. He has experience in wholesale and retail sales. His research interests are in sales management, personal selling, marketing ethics and consumer behavior. His articles have appeared in the *Journal of the Academy of Marketing Science, Journal of Public Policy and Marketing, Journal of Personal Selling and Sales Management* and *Journal of Business Ethics,* among other journals, various national and regional proceedings, and books, including *Marketing Communications Classics.* He is co-author of *Sales Management: Analysis and Decision Making.* He is on the editorial review boards of the *Journal of Personal Selling and Sales Management, Journal of Marketing Theory and Practice, Journal of Business & Industrial Marketing* and *Southern Business Review,* and has won awards for outstanding reviewer.

Michael R. Williams (Ph.D., Oklahoma State University) is associate professor of marketing at Illinois State University. Coinciding with his successful academic and research career, Mike brings with him a rich experience of more than 20 years' work in industrial sales, sales management, and marketing research. Mike's research has been published in a variety of journals, including the *Journal of Personal Selling and Sales Management, International Journal of Purchasing and Materials Management, Journal of Business and Industrial Marketing, Quality Management Journal, Competitiveness Review, Journal of Industrial Technology, Journal of Marketing Theory and Practice,* and *Simulation and Gaming: An International Journal of Theory, Design, and Research.* His work has also received numerous honors, including Outstanding Article for 1998 in the *Journal of Business and Industrial Marketing,* the AACSB's Leadership in Innovative Business Education Award, and the Marketing Science Institute's Alden G. Clayton Competition. Mike has also been honored with numerous university and college research and teaching awards, and his work in the field of corporate and university education has resulted in his being named to *Who's Who in American Education.* Recognition of his work in the areas of sales and organizational performance, customer orientation, and corporate culture have further resulted in Mike's being honored in *Who's Who in the South and Southwest,* and *Who's Who in America.* Mike is currently national director for the National Conference in Sales Management, faculty advisory board member for the Fisher Institute of Personal Selling at the University of Akron, and co-director of the Market-Driven Quality Group.

BRIEF CONTENTS

CONTENTS

Professional Selling

A Trust-Based Approach

Overview of Personal Selling

Sales Team Drives Auto Dealer's Profits

A well-coordinated sales team from Reynolds & Reynolds Automotive Products Group has a simple message for auto dealers such as American Ford in Bloomington, Minnesota: we can help you make more money. The Reynolds & Reynolds sales team has two key strengths that allow them to make such a claim. First, they have expertise in database marketing for automotive clients. Second, they have sufficient time to implement direct marketing incentive programs. These strengths match up well with American Ford's needs, as busy dealer personnel lack expertise in database analysis and in the implementation of direct marketing incentive programs.

Working from American Ford's database, Reynolds & Reynolds determined which customers were returning for service work. The Reynolds team then recommended marketing programs designed to increase the frequency of return visits and to encourage visits from new car buyers who had not returned to the dealership for service work. American Ford expects to gain approximately $30,000 per month in additional service department revenue by adopting the recommendations of the Reynolds team.

To gain the American Ford account, Reynolds deployed a three-person sales team comprising a regional sales manager, a sales associate, and a marketing specialist. Sales associate Bob Sherman made initial contact with American Ford. After two sales calls, Sherman brought in his sales manager, Tim O'Neil, an expert in service reminder programs. Sherman and O'Neil succeeded in getting approval from American Ford's Carol Bemis, new parts and service director, to analyze the American database. This analysis served as the basis for Reynolds' proposal to American. The proposal was made by Sherman, O'Neil, and marketing specialist Chuck Wiltgen, each of whom played specific roles in developing and delivering the proposal. Sherman provided findings from Reynolds' analysis of the American Ford database analysis, pointing out several opportunities for improving the profit picture for American through the service department. Wiltgen handled the details of implementing direct marketing programs to take advantage of these opportunities. O'Neil provided support at each step in the sales process and took the lead in gaining a commitment from the American management team.

After the sale was made, Carol Bemis noted the professionalism of the Reynolds team and described the meeting as very productive. She observed that Reynolds had developed a customized solution for American, rather than "having to squeeze into something prefabricated." She added, "I also didn't feel pressured . . . I didn't feel they were selling something just for the sake of selling something. I left the meeting with the confidence that no matter what we ended up with it would be the best decision made with the most accurate information."

Source: Malcolm Fleschner, "Anatomy of a Sale," *Selling Power* (January/February 1999): 78.

Learning Objectives

After completing this module, you should be able to

1 Describe the evolution of personal selling from ancient times to the modern era.

2 Explain the contributions of personal selling to society, business firms, and customers.

3 Describe different types of personal selling jobs.

4 Discuss the characteristics of sales careers.

5 Describe the skills and characteristics required for success in most sales positions.

Evolution of Personal Selling

The successful professional salesperson of today and the future is likely a better listener than a talker, is more oriented toward developing long-term relationships with customers than placing an emphasis on high-pressure, short-term sales techniques, and has the skills and patience to endure lengthy, complex sales processes. In earning the American Ford account, the Reynolds & Reynolds sales team displayed these qualities of sales professionals.

Personal selling has evolved into a different activity than it was just a decade ago. Throughout this course, you learn about new technologies and techniques that have contributed to this evolution. This module provides an overview of personal selling, affording insight into the operating rationale of today's salespeople and sales managers. In the highly competitive, complex environment of the world business community, personal selling and sales management have never played more critical roles.

Origins of Personal Selling

Ancient Greek history documents selling as an exchange activity, and the term *salesman* appears in the writings of Plato.[1] However, true salespeople, those who earned a living only by selling, did not exist in any sizable number until the Industrial Revolution in England, from the mid-eighteenth century to the mid-nineteenth century. Prior to this time, traders, merchants, and artisans filled the selling function. These predecessors of contemporary marketers were generally viewed with contempt because deception was often used in the sale of goods.[2]

In the latter phase of the Middle Ages, the first door-to-door salesperson appeared in the form of the peddler. Peddlers collected produce from local farmers, sold it to townspeople, and, in turn, bought manufactured goods in town for subsequent sale in rural areas.[3] Like many other early salespeople, they performed other important marketing functions—in this case, purchasing, assembling, sorting, and redistributing of goods.

Industrial Revolution Era

As the Industrial Revolution began to blossom in the middle of the eighteenth century, the economic justification for salespeople gained momentum. Local economies were no longer self-sufficient, and as intercity and international trade began to flourish, economies of scale in production spurred the growth of mass markets in geographically dispersed areas. The continual need to reach new customers in these dispersed markets called for an increasing number of salespeople.

It is interesting to note the job activities of the first wave of salespeople in the era of the Industrial Revolution. The following quotation describes a salesperson who served the customer in conjunction with a producer:

> Thus, a salesman representing the producing firm, armed with samples of the firm's products, could bring the latter to the attention of a large number of potential customers—whether buying for sale to others or for their own production requirements—who might not, without the salesman's visit, have learnt of the product's existence, and give them the opportunity of examining and discussing it without having to go out of their way to do so. . . . Even if the salesman did not succeed in obtaining an order, he frequently picked up valuable information on the state of the market, sometimes the very reasons for refusal. . . . This information could be very useful to the producer.[4]

Post–Industrial Revolution Era

By the early 1800s, personal selling was well established in England but just beginning to develop in the United States.[5] This situation changed noticeably after 1850, and by the latter part of the century, salespeople were a well-established part of business practice in the United States. For example, one wholesaler in the Detroit area reported sending out 400 traveling salespeople in the 1880s.[6]

At the dawning of the twentieth century, an exciting time in the economic history of the United States, it became apparent that marketing, especially advertising and personal selling, would play a crucial role in the rapid transition of the economy from an agrarian base to one of mass production and efficient transportation.

Glimpses of the lives of salespeople in the early 1900s, gained from literature of that period, reveal an adventuresome, aggressive, and valuable group of employees often working on the frontier of new markets. Already, however, the independent maverick salespeople who had blazed the early trails to new markets were beginning to disappear. One clear indication that selling was becoming a more structured activity was the development of a **canned sales presentation** by John H. Patterson of the National Cash Register Company (NCR). This presentation, a virtual script to guide NCR salespeople on how to sell cash registers, was based on the premise that salespeople are not "born, but rather they are made."[7]

Sales historians noted the changes occurring in personal selling in the early twentieth century. Charles W. Hoyt, author of one of the first textbooks on sales management, chronicled this transition in 1912, noting two types of salespeople:

> The old kind of salesman is the "big me" species. . . . He works for himself and, so far as possible, according to his own ideas. . . . There is another type of salesman. He is the new kind. At present he is in the minority, but he works for the fastest growing and most successful houses of the day. He works for the house, and the house works for him. He welcomes and uses every bit of help the house sends to him.[8]

Hoyt's observations about the "old" and the "new" salesperson summed up the changing role of personal selling. The managements of firms in the United States were beginning to understand the tremendous potential of personal selling and, simultaneously, the need to shape the growth of the sales function. In particular, a widespread interest arose in how to reduce the cost of sales. According to Hoyt, this did not mean hiring lower-cost salespeople, but instead called for "distributing much larger quantities of goods with less motion."[9]

War and Depression Era

The 30-year span from 1915 to 1945 was marked by three overwhelming events—two World Wars and the Great Depression in the United States. Because economic activity concentrated on the war efforts, new sales methods did not develop quickly during those periods. During the Great Depression, however, business firms, starved for sales volume, often employed aggressive salespeople to produce badly needed revenue. Then, with renewed prosperity in the post–World War II era, salespeople emerged as important employees for an increasing number of firms that were beginning to realize the benefits of research-based integrated marketing programs.

Professionalism: The Modern Era

In the middle 1940s personal selling became more professional. Not only did buyers begin to demand more from salespeople, but they also grew intolerant of high-pressure, fast-talking salespeople, preferring instead a well-informed, customer-oriented salesperson. In 1947, the *Harvard Business Review* published "Low-Pressure Selling,"[10] a classic article followed by many others that called for salespeople to increase the effectiveness of their sales efforts by improving their professional demeanor.

An emphasis on **sales professionalism** is the keynote of the current era. The term has varied meanings, but in this context we use it to mean a customer-oriented approach that uses truthful, nonmanipulative tactics to satisfy the long-term needs

EXHIBIT 1.1	Continued Evolution of Personal Selling

Change	*Salesforce Response*
Intensified competition	More emphasis on developing and maintaining trust-based, long-term customer relationships
More emphasis on improving sales productivity	Increased use of technology (e.g., laptop computers, electronic mail, fax machines)
	Increased use of lower-cost-per-contact methods (e.g., telemarketing for some customers)
	More emphasis on profitability (e.g., gross margin) objectives
Fragmentation of traditional customer bases	Sales specialists for specific customer types
	Multiple sales channels (e.g., major accounts programs, telemarketing, electronic networks)
	Globalization of sales efforts
Customers dictating quality standards and inventory/shipping procedures to be met by vendors	Team selling
	Salesforce compensation sometimes based on customer satisfaction and team performance
Demand for in-depth, specialized knowledge as an input to purchase decisions	Team selling
	More emphasis on customer-oriented sales training

of both the customer and the selling firm. The effective salesperson of today is no longer a mere presenter of information but now must stand equipped to respond to a variety of customer needs before, during, and after the sale. In addition, salespeople must be able to work effectively with others in their organizations to meet or exceed customer expectations.

The current stage in the evolution of the sales professional is aptly illustrated in a *Selling* magazine interview with Stephen E. Heiman, a leading sales consultant and trainer:

> The future will call increasingly for non-manipulative sales skills. Twisting a customer's need to fit our product or service is "yesterday's way of selling," says Heiman. The new way requires an ability to "ask, listen, and understand the issues behind the product need," he says. Forget the notion that your job is to tell the customer why your product is better than all the rest. "The major job you have is understanding the customer's concept," Heiman maintains. "Unless you're perceived to be making a contribution to your customer's success," Heiman says, "you're not ready for selling in the 21st century."[11]

Future evolution is inevitable as tomorrow's salesperson responds to a more complex, dynamic environment. Also, increased sophistication of buyers and of new technologies will demand more from the next generation of salespeople. Exhibit 1.1 summarizes some of the likely events of the future.[12]

Contributions of Personal Selling

Although advertising has traditionally captured most of the attention of students and researchers, personal selling is actually the most important part of marketing communications for most business firms. This is particularly true in firms that engage in business-to-business marketing. More money is spent on personal selling than on any other form of marketing communications, whether it be advertising, sales promotion, publicity, or public relations.

The sizable investment in personal selling is reflected in the estimated costs of employing a salesperson. A common denominator of this investment is the **cost per sales call index** as calculated by various organizations. For example, *Sales and Marketing Management* magazine, a well-known source, estimates an approximate cost range of $80–242 for a single sales call.[13] Multiply this estimate by multiple sales calls per day for each salesperson, and extend the mathematics for an entire year, and the conclusion is clear—personal selling is expensive. A sales manager's response is to ask, how can we make such an investment pay off? Indeed, this may be the most crucial question a sales manager deals with, at both strategic and tactical levels. We now take a look at how this investment is justified by reviewing the contributions of personal selling to society in general, to the employing firm, and to customers.

Salespeople and Society

Salespeople contribute to their nations' economic growth in two basic ways. They act as stimuli for economic transactions, and they further the diffusion of innovation.

SALESPEOPLE AS ECONOMIC STIMULI   Salespeople are expected to stimulate action in the business world—hence the term **economic stimuli.** In a fluctuating economy, salespeople make invaluable contributions by assisting in recovery cycles and by helping to sustain periods of relative prosperity. As the world economic system deals with issues such as increased globalization of business, more emphasis on customer satisfaction, and building competitiveness through quality improvement programs, it is expected that salespeople will be recognized as a key force in executing the appropriate strategies and tactics necessary for survival and growth.

SALESPEOPLE AND DIFFUSION OF INNOVATION   Salespeople play a critical role in the **diffusion of innovation,** the process whereby new products, services, and ideas are distributed to the members of society. Consumers who are likely to be early adopters of an innovation often rely on salespeople as a primary source of information. Frequently, well-informed, specialized salespeople provide useful information to potential consumers who then purchase from a lower-cost outlet. The role of salespeople in the diffusion of industrial products and services is particularly crucial. Imagine trying to purchase a companywide computer system without the assistance of a competent salesperson or sales team!

While acting as an agent of innovation, the salesperson invariably encounters a strong resistance to change in the latter stages of the diffusion process. The status quo seems to be extremely satisfactory to many parties, even though, in the long run, change is necessary for continued progress or survival. By encouraging the adoption of innovative products and services, salespeople may indeed be making a positive contribution to society.

Salespeople and the Employing Firm

Because salespeople are in direct contact with the all-important customer, they can make valuable contributions to their employers. Salespeople contribute to their firms as revenue producers, as sources of market research and feedback, and as candidates for management positions.

SALESPEOPLE AS REVENUE PRODUCERS   Salespeople occupy the somewhat unique role of **revenue producers** in their firms. Consequently, they usually feel the brunt of that pressure along with the management of the firm. Although accountants and financial staff are concerned with profitability in bottom-line terms, salespeople are constantly reminded of their responsibility to achieve a healthy "top line" on the profit and loss statement. This should not suggest that salespeople are concerned only with sales revenue and not with overall profitability. Indeed, salespeople are increasingly responsible for improving profitability, not only by producing sales revenues, but also by improving the productivity of their actions.

MARKET RESEARCH AND FEEDBACK   Because salespeople spend so much time in direct contact with their customers, it is only logical that they would play an important role in market research and in providing feedback to their firms. For example, on a weekly basis, regional sales managers from the Discovery Channel discuss details of the past week's activity with each of their sales representatives. On an ongoing basis, Discovery Channel sales managers encourage new ideas from the salesforce and actively seek input while working with salespeople in the field. This regular solicitation of ideas helps to improve sales performance, formulate future strategies, and build a sales culture based on communication and cooperation.[14]

Some would argue that salespeople are not trained as market researchers, or that salespeople's time could be better used than in research and feedback activities. Many firms, however, refute this argument by finding numerous ways to capitalize on the salesforce as a reservoir of ideas. It is not an exaggeration to say that many firms have concluded that they cannot afford to operate in the absence of salesforce feedback and research.

SALESPEOPLE AS FUTURE MANAGERS   In recent years, marketing and sales personnel have been in strong demand for upper management positions. Recognizing the need for a top management trained in sales, many firms use the sales job as an entry-level position that provides a foundation for future assignments. As progressive firms continue to emphasize customer orientation as a basic operating concept, it is only natural that salespeople who have learned how to meet customer needs will be good candidates for management jobs. For more on salespeople as future managers, see "Professional Selling in the 21st Century: The Value of Sales Experience."

Salespeople and the Customer

Extensive research by Learning International, a large training and consulting firm, reveals the expectations that buyers have of salespeople. According to respondents of a Learning International survey, buyers like to deal with salespeople who

- are honest

PROFESSIONAL SELLING IN THE 21ST CENTURY

The Value of Sales Experience

Jerry Heffel, president of The Southwestern Company, comments on the importance of sales experience as preparation for upper management positions:

Peter Drucker wrote many years ago that the purpose of business can be stated succinctly: The purpose of business is to create a customer. In well-managed businesses, every level of management—from the CEO to the first-line supervisor—should be oriented toward creating and retaining customers. Salespeople are the crucial spark that ignites a prospect into a customer, and having that firsthand experience is enormously important at higher levels of management. Here at Southwestern, every single person in sales and marketing management started as a direct salesperson, making between 4 and 10 thousand one-on-one presentations before moving into their present positions. For more than 130 years, our effectiveness in helping college students in our summer program has been directly related to the emotional intelligence that each of us gained from those firsthand experiences in selling.

- understand general business and economic trends, as well as the buyer's business
- provide guidance throughout the sales process
- help the buyer to solve problems
- have a pleasant personality and a good professional appearance
- coordinate all aspects of the product and service to provide a total package[15]

The overall conclusion is that buyers expect salespeople to contribute to the success of the buyer's firm. Buyers value the information furnished by salespeople, and more than ever before, they value the problem-solving skills of salespeople. See "An Ethical Dilemma" for a scenario in which the salesperson must think about where to draw the line in sharing information with customers.

An Ethical Dilemma

Terry Kelly, sales representative for EFAX, a computer software company, has just concluded a sales call with Landnet, one of his distributors. During the call, purchasing agent Linda Meyer mentioned that Ron Hawkins, Landnet's top salesperson, had suddenly resigned and moved out of the state. Ms. Meyer said that this unexpected resignation could not have come at a worse time, as several key customer contracts were pending renewal, and Landnet had no candidates to replace Hawkins. On his way to his next sales call with Netserve, his largest distributor, Terry debated whether or not he should share the news of Hawkins' resignation. After all, the buyer at Netserve viewed Terry as a great source of market information, and Terry figured that the Netserve buyer would hear the news anyway before the day was over. What should Terry do?

As salespeople serve their customers, they simultaneously serve their employers and society. When the interests of these parties conflict, the salesperson can be caught in the middle. By learning to resolve these conflicts as a routine part of their jobs, salespeople further contribute to developing a business system based on progress through problem solving. An important part of resolving potential conflict between customers and salespeople is to have a customer-oriented code of ethics for salespeople. An example of such a code is shown in Exhibit 1.2.

EXHIBIT 1.2	Code of Ethics for Professional Salespeople

As a Certified Professional Salesperson, I pledge to the following people and organizations:

The Customer. In all customer relationships, I pledge to

Maintain honesty and integrity in my relationships with customers and prospective customers.

Accurately represent my product or service to place the customer or prospective customer in a position to make a decision consistent with the principle of mutuality of benefit and profit to the buyer and seller.

Keep abreast of all pertinent information that would assist my customers in achieving their goals as they relate to my product(s) or service(s).

The Company. In relationships with my employer, coworkers, and other parties whom I represent, I will

Use their resources that are at my disposal for legitimate business purposes only.

Respect and protect proprietary and confidential information entrusted to me by my company.

The Competition. Regarding those with whom I compete in the marketplace, I promise to

Obtain competitive information only through legal and ethical methods.

Portray my competitors and their products and services only in a manner that is honest and truthful and that reflects accurate information that can be or has been substantiated.

Classification of Personal Selling Jobs

Because there are so many unique sales jobs, the term *salesperson* is not by itself very descriptive. A salesperson could be a flower vendor at a busy downtown intersection or the sales executive negotiating the sale of Boeing aircraft to the People's Republic of China.

We briefly discuss six types of personal selling jobs:

- sales support
- new business
- existing business
- inside sales (nonretail)
- direct-to-consumer sales
- combination sales jobs

Sales Support

Sales support personnel are not usually involved in the direct solicitation of purchase orders. Rather, their primary responsibility is dissemination of information and performance of other activities designed to stimulate sales. They might concentrate at the end-user level or another level in the channel of distribution to support the overall sales effort. They may report to another salesperson, who is responsible for direct handling of purchase orders, or to the sales manager. There are two well-known categories of support salespeople: missionary or detail salespeople and technical support salespeople.

Missionary salespeople usually work for a manufacturer but may also be found working for brokers and manufacturing representatives, especially in the grocery industry. There are strong similarities between sales missionaries and religious missionaries. Like their counterparts, sales missionaries are expected to "spread the word" with the purpose of conversion—to customer status. Once converted, the customer receives reinforcing messages, new information, and the benefit of the missionary's activities to strengthen the relationship between buyer and seller.

In the pharmaceutical industry, the **detailer** is a fixture. Detailers working at the physician level furnish valuable information regarding the capabilities and limitations of medications in an attempt to get the physician to prescribe their product. Another sales representative from the same pharmaceutical company will sell the medication to the wholesaler or pharmacist, but it is the detailer's job to support the direct sales effort by calling on physicians.

Technical specialists are sometimes considered to be sales support personnel. These **technical support salespeople** may assist in design and specification processes, installation of equipment, training of the customer's employees, and follow-up service of a technical nature. They are sometimes part of a sales team that includes another salesperson who specializes in identifying and satisfying customer needs by recommending the appropriate product or service.

New Business

New business is generated for the selling firm by adding new customers or introducing new products to the marketplace. Two types of new-business salespeople are pioneers and order-getters.

Pioneers, as the term suggests, are constantly involved with either new products, new customers, or both. Their task requires creative selling and the ability to counter the resistance to change that will likely be present in prospective customers. Pioneers are well represented in the sale of business franchises, in which the sales representatives travel from city to city seeking new franchisees.

Order-getters are salespeople who actively seek orders, usually in a highly competitive environment. Although all pioneers are also order-getters, the reverse is not true. An order-getter may serve existing customers on an ongoing basis, whereas the pioneer moves on to new customers as soon as possible. Order-getters may seek new business by selling an existing customer additional items from the product line. A well-known tactic is to establish a relationship with a customer by selling a single product from the line, then to follow up with subsequent sales calls for other items from the product line.

Most corporations emphasize sales growth, and salespeople operating as pioneers and order-getters are at the heart of sales growth objectives. The pressure to perform in these roles is fairly intense; the results are highly visible. For these reasons, the new-business salesperson is often among the elite in any company's salesforce.

Existing Business

In direct contrast to new-business salespeople, other salespeople's primary responsibility is to maintain relationships with existing customers. Salespeople who specialize in maintaining existing business include **order-takers.** These salespeople frequently work for wholesalers, and as the term *order-taker* implies, they are not too involved in creative selling. Route salespeople who work an established customer base, taking routine reorders of stock items, are order-takers. They sometimes follow a pioneer salesperson and take over the account after the pioneer has made the initial sale.

These salespeople are no less valuable to their firms than the new-business salespeople, but creative selling skills are less important to this category of sales personnel. Their strengths tend to be reliability and competence in assuring customer convenience. Customers grow to depend on the services provided by this type of salesperson. As most markets are becoming more competitive, the role of existing-business salespeople is sometimes critical to prevent erosion of the customer base.

Many firms, believing that it is easier to protect and maintain profitable customers than it is to find replacement customers, are reinforcing sales efforts to existing customers. For example, Frito-Lay uses 18,000 route service salespeople to call on retail customers at least three times weekly. Larger customers see their Frito-Lay representative on a daily basis. These salespeople spend a lot of their time educating customers about the profitability of Frito-Lay's snack foods, which leads to increased sales for both the retailer and for Frito-Lay.[16]

Inside Sales

In this text, **inside sales** refers to nonretail salespeople who remain in their employer's place of business while dealing with customers. The inside-sales operation has received considerable attention in recent years, not only as a supplementary sales tactic, but also as an alternative to field selling.

Inside sales can be conducted on an active or passive sales basis. Active inside sales include the solicitation of entire orders, either as part of a telemarketing operation or when customers walk into the seller's facilities. Passive inside sales imply the acceptance, rather than solicitation, of customer orders, although it is common practice for these transactions to include add-on sales attempts. We should note that customer service personnel sometimes function as inside-sales personnel as an ongoing part of their jobs.

Direct-to-Consumer Sales

Direct-to-consumer salespeople are the most numerous type. There are more than 4.5 million retail salespeople in this country and perhaps another million selling real estate, insurance, and securities. Add to this figure another several million selling direct to the consumer for such companies as Tupperware, Mary Kay, and Avon.

This diverse category of salespeople ranges from the part-time, often temporary salesperson in a retail store to the highly educated, professionally trained stockbroker on Wall Street. As a general statement, the more challenging direct-to-consumer sales positions are those involving the sale of intangible services such as insurance and financial services.

Combination Sales Jobs

Now that we have reviewed some of the basic types of sales jobs, let us consider the salesperson who performs multiple types of sales jobs within the framework of a single position. We use the case of the territory manager's position with Beecham Products, U.S.A., to illustrate the **combination sales job** concept. Beecham, whose products include Aqua-Fresh toothpaste, markets a wide range of consumer goods to food, drug, variety, and mass merchandisers. The territory manager's job blends responsibilities for developing new business, maintaining and stimulating existing business, and performing sales support activities.

During a typical day in the field, the Beecham territory manager is involved in sales support activities such as merchandising and in-store promotion at the individual retail store level. Maintaining contact and goodwill with store personnel is another routine sales support activity. The territory manager also makes sales calls on chain headquarters personnel to handle existing business and to seek new business. And it is the territory manager who introduces new Beecham products in the marketplace.

Characteristics of Sales Careers

Although individual opinions will vary, the ideal career for most individuals offers a bright future, including good opportunities for financial rewards and job advancement. As you read the following sections on the characteristics of sales careers, you might think about what you expect from a career and whether your expectations could be met in a sales career. The characteristics to be discussed are

- job security
- advancement opportunities
- immediate feedback
- prestige
- job variety
- independence
- compensation
- boundary-role effects

Job Security

Salespeople are revenue producers and thus enjoy relatively good job security compared with other occupational groups. Certainly, individual job security depends on individual performance, but in general, salespeople are usually the last group to be negatively affected by personnel cutbacks.

Competent salespeople also have some degree of job security based on the universality of their basic sales skills. In many cases, salespeople are able to successfully move to another employer, maybe even change industries, because sales skills are largely transferable. For salespeople working in declining or stagnant industries, this is heartening news.

Furthermore, projections by the U.S. Department of Labor indicate strong demand for salespeople in all categories in the future (see Exhibit 1.3). And growth in the number of salespeople should bring a corresponding growth in the number of sales management positions. According to Exhibit 1.3, there are particularly good opportunities in service industries, including financial services.

Advancement Opportunities

As the business world continues to become more competitive, the advancement opportunities for salespeople will continue to be an attractive dimension of sales careers. In highly competitive markets, individuals and companies that are successful in determining and meeting customer needs will be rewarded. A case in point is Carly Fiorina, CEO of Hewlett-Packard, who began her career as a sales representative for AT&T. She later led the spinoff of Lucent Technologies from AT&T and used her sales skills to raise $3 billion on Wall Street to fund the largest public offering in U.S. history. According to Jo Weiss of Catalyst, Inc., a company that tracks women in business, a sales background was key to Ms. Fiorina's ascent to the top at Hewlett-Packard. Joel Ronning, CEO of Digital River, an e-commerce company in Minneapolis, adds, "Any good CEO has to understand sales. You're constantly selling in all aspects of your life. In my early sales experience, I learned persistence and not to take rejection personally, which made all the difference in the world."[17]

Immediate Feedback

Salespeople receive constant, immediate feedback on their job performance. Usually, the results of their efforts can be plainly observed by both salespeople and their sales mangers—a source of motivation and job satisfaction. On a daily basis, salespeople receive direct feedback from their customers, and this can be stimulating, challenging, and productive. According to a survey conducted by *Purchasing* magazine, business buyers want suppliers to work closely with them to raise performance levels, contain costs, and develop the latest technologies. The same survey indicates a need for salespeople to overcome obstacles and solve problems that inhibit the accomplishment of mutually agreed-on goals. With such buyer expectations, it is readily apparent that seeking and using feedback is an important part of salespeople's careers.[18]

Prestige

Traditionally, sales has not been a prestigious occupation in the eyes of the general public. There is some evidence that as the general public learns more about the activities and qualifications of professional salespeople, the image of salespeople, and

EXHIBIT 1.3	Occupational Outlook for Salespeople	
Job Type	*1996 Employment*	*Projected Growth 1996–2006 Percentage*
Manufacturers and Wholesale	1,557,000	10–20
Services Sales Representative	694,000	36 or more
Real Estate	408,000	0–9
Securities/Financial Services	263,000	36 or more
Insurance Agents	409,000	0–9
Retail	4,522,000	10–20

thus the prestige of selling, is improving. An analysis of the popular press (excluding business publications) reveals that there are more positive than negative mentions of news-making salespeople. In a positive light, salespeople are frequently seen as knowledgeable, well trained, educated, and capable of solving customer problems. The negative aspects of salespeople's image often center on deception and high-pressure techniques.[19]

The struggling, down-and-out huckster as depicted by Willy Loman in Arthur Miller's 1949 classic *Death of a Salesman* is hardly typical of the professional salesperson of today and the future. Professional salespeople destroy such unfavorable stereotypes, and they would not jeopardize customer relationships by using high-pressure sales techniques to force a premature sale.[20] These perceptions are especially true in the business world, where encounters with professional salespeople are commonplace.

Job Variety

Salespeople rarely vegetate due to boredom. Their jobs are multifaceted and dynamic. For a person seeking the comfort of a well-established routine, sales might not be a good career choice. In sales, day-to-day variation on the job is the norm. Customers change, new products and services are developed, and competition introduces new elements at a rapid pace.

The opportunity to become immersed in the job and bring creativity to bear is demonstrated by General Mills, whose salesforce has been named one of the best in America. According to John Maschuzik, vice president of sales in the western United States, salespeople's customization of promotional efforts for their customers is crucial to the company's success. Mr. Maschuzik says that General Mills gives their salespeople a lot of latitude and the opportunity to be creative in spending retail promotion money.[21]

Independence

Sales jobs often allow independence of action. This independence is frequently a by-product of decentralized sales operations in which salespeople live and work away from headquarters, therefore working from their homes and making their own plans for extensive travel.

Independence of action and freedom to make decisions are usually presented as advantages that sales positions have over tightly supervised jobs. College students who prefer sales careers rate freedom to make decisions second only to salary as an important job consideration.[22] Despite its appeal, however, independence does present some problems. New recruits working from their homes may find the lack of a company office somewhat disorienting. They may need an office environment to relate to, especially if their past work experience provided regular contact in an office environment.

The independence of action traditionally enjoyed by salespeople is being scrutinized by sales managers more heavily now than in the past. The emphasis on sales productivity, accomplished in part through cost containment, is encouraging sales managers to take a more active role in dictating travel plans and sales call schedules.

Compensation

Compensation is generally thought to be a strong advantage of sales careers. Pay is closely tied to performance, especially if commissions and bonuses are part of the pay package.

Starting salaries for inexperienced salespersons with a college degree typically average $40,000. Between the extremes of the highly experienced salesperson and the inexperienced recruit, an average salesperson earns approximately $45,000–60,000 per year. More experienced salespersons, including those who deal with large customers, often earn in the $85,000–135,000 range.[23]

Boundary-Role Effects

Salespersons are **boundary-role performers.** That is, they occupy boundary-spanning positions between their employers and their customers. Their loyalties are sometimes torn between customer demand and the expectations of their company or their sales manager. For example, the company may want to sell at list price, whereas the customer demands a discount. The salesperson is caught between the two parties and somehow must resolve the situation. This is but one example of the **role conflict** routinely experienced by salespeople.

Another dimension of boundary-spanning jobs such as sales jobs is **role ambiguity.** It occurs when the salesperson is unsure about what to do in a situation in which no policy or procedure applies. This is not an uncommon event, given the variable nature of sales situations, which sometimes require innovative problem solving.

The uncertainty arising from a lack of direction can contribute to **role stress.** Role conflict may also contribute to role stress, which salespeople, sales managers, organizational psychologists, and sales researchers all agree is strongly associated with sales careers. There is no escaping the conclusion that sales is a high-visibility, "spotlight" position. The revenue-production responsibilities of salespeople create considerable pressure to perform. When customer expectations are at odds with the employer's expectations, the pressure rises. Such a situation is described in "An Ethical Dilemma."

An Ethical Dilemma

Charles Lambert, sales manager for YourWay, a manufacturer of customized furniture, believed in putting his salespeople under pressure to perform. During his 20 years in sales management, Mr. Lambert had always pushed his salespeople to maximize short-run sales volume. Simply put, Mr. Lambert advocated that his salespeople sell as much product as possible, as soon as possible, and at the highest possible price. Recently, the retail buyers of YourWay furniture had begun requesting, even demanding, lower prices and more flexible buying arrangements that would reduce their inventory carrying costs. YourWay salespeople were also asking Mr. Lambert to reconsider his stance on pricing and the maximization of short-term volume. Charles Lambert is unfazed by these developments, even though YourWay recently lost a key retail chain customer. His reaction was to fire the sales representative who, in Lambert's judgment, "lost the account." The remaining salespeople were then urged to increase their sales levels to compensate for the lost volume. Is there anything unethical about Mr. Lambert's approach to sales management? If you were Mr. Lambert's supervisor, would you have any concerns about his management style?

For most salespeople, stress is simply part of the job. It can add an element of excitement to the workday and provide motivation. However, if it becomes excessive, it may produce detrimental results. Successful salespeople are usually driven by a sense of purpose and believe that the opportunities provided by their jobs are worth the efforts required to deal with stress.

Qualifications and Skills Required for Success by Salespersons

Because there are so many different types of jobs in sales, it is rather difficult to generalize about the qualifications and skills needed for success. This list would have to vary according to the details of a given job. Even then, it is reasonable to believe that for any given job, different persons with different skills could be successful. These conclusions have been reached after decades of research that has tried to correlate sales performance with physical traits, mental abilities, personality characteristics, and the experience and background of the salesperson.[24]

Many of the skills and characteristics leading to success in sales would do the same in practically any professional business occupation. For example, the *Occupational Outlook Handbook* published by the U.S. Department of Labor points out the importance of various personal attributes for success in sales, including the following: initiative, tact, patience, good communications skills, motivation, honesty, and maturity.[25] Who could dispute the value of such traits for any occupation?

Success in sales is increasingly being thought of in terms of a strategic team effort, rather than the characteristics of individual salespersons. For example, three studies of more than 200 companies that employ 25,000 salespersons in the United States and Australia found that being customer oriented and cooperating as a team player were critical to salespersons' success.[26] For more on teamwork, see "Professional Selling in the 21st Century: The Importance of Teamwork in Sales."

Being careful not to suggest that sales success is solely a function of individual traits, let us consider some of the skills and qualifications that are thought to be especially critical for success in most sales jobs. Five factors that seem to be particularly important for success in sales are empathy, ego drive, ego strength, verbal communication skills, and enthusiasm. These factors have been selected after reviewing three primary sources of information:

- a study of more than 750,000 salespeople in 15,000 companies (Greenberg and Greenberg)[27]
- two reviews of four decades of research on factors related to sales success (Comer and Dubinsky; and Brown, Leigh, and Haygood)[28]
- surveys of sales executives[29]

PROFESSIONAL SELLING IN THE 21ST CENTURY

The Importance of Teamwork in Sales

Jerry Heffel, president of The Southwestern Company, offers his perspective on teamwork:

Sometimes the salesperson is referred to as the lead car in the business train. But just having a lead car doesn't make a train. For this reason, a salesperson who is effective long-term is also an effective team player—he or she realizes they need coordinated involvement from many different parts of the organization in order to serve the customer. At the same time, whenever they see themselves as part of the customer's team, and that they are both striving for the same outcome, they become an indispensable part of the value chain for that customer. Southwestern's sales training philosophy stresses this team aspect: we tell our salespeople that they are the gas and oil of the free enterprise system, but they also need the tires, the car body, the drive train, and what's in the trunk to get anywhere significant.

Empathy

In a sales context, **empathy** (the ability to see things as others would see them) includes being able to read cues furnished by the customer to better determine the customer's viewpoint. According to Spiro and Weitz, empathy is crucial for successful interaction between a buyer and a seller.[30] An empathetic salesperson is presumably in a better position to tailor the sales presentation to the customer during the planning stages. More important, empathetic salespeople can adjust to feedback during the presentation.

The research of Greenberg and Greenberg found empathy to be a significant predictor of sales success. This finding was partially supported in the review by Comer and Dubinsky, who found empathy to be an important factor in consumer and insurance sales but not in retail or industrial sales. However, Pilling and Eroglu found that retail buyers were more likely to listen to future sales presentations and make purchases from salespeople who displayed empathy.[31] Even though some studies do not find direct links between salesperson empathy and success, empathy is generally accepted as an important trait for successful salespeople.[32] As relationship selling grows in importance, empathy logically will become even more important for sales success.

Ego Drive

In a sales context, **ego drive** (an indication of the degree of determination a person has to achieve goals and overcome obstacles in striving for success) is manifested as an inner need to persuade others in order to achieve personal gratification. Greenberg and Greenberg point out the complementary relationship between empathy and ego drive that is necessary for sales success. The salesperson who is extremely empathetic but lacks ego drive may have problems in taking active steps to confirm a sale. However, a salesperson with more ego drive than empathy may ignore the customer's viewpoint in an ill-advised, overly anxious attempt to gain commitment from the customer.

Ego Strength

The degree to which a person is able to achieve an approximation of inner drives is **ego strength.** Salespeople with high levels of ego strength are likely to be self-assured and self-accepting. Salespeople with healthy egos are better equipped to deal with the possibility of rejection throughout the sales process. They are probably less likely to experience sales call reluctance and are resilient enough to overcome the disappointment of inevitable lost sales.

Salespeople with strong ego drives who are well equipped to do their job will likely be high in **self-efficacy;** that is, they will strongly believe that they can be successful on the job. In situations in which their initial efforts meet resistance, rejection, or failure, salespeople high in self-efficacy are likely to persist in pursuing their goals. For example, Gene Benassi, a sales representative with office furniture supplier Herman Miller, persevered with the Pentagon for more than 10 years, occasionally receiving small contracts. Finally, he landed a large, 15-year contract. As noted by a Herman Miller executive, Mr. Benassi "never gave up on getting a big deal. With teamwork and perseverance and the ability to build a long-term relationship, he finally got the customer to sign."[33]

Interpersonal Communication Skills

Interpersonal communication skills, including listening and questioning, are essential for sales success. An in-depth study of 300 sales executives, salespeople, and customers of 24 major sales companies in North America, Europe, and Japan found that effective salespeople are constantly seeking ways to improve communication skills that enable them to develop, explain, and implement customer solutions. The companies in the study are some of the best in the world at professional selling: Sony, Xerox, American Airlines, Fuji, and Scott paper.[34]

To meet customer needs, salespeople must be able to solicit opinions, listen effectively, and confirm customer needs and concerns. They must be capable of probing customer expectations with open- and closed-end questions and responding in a flexible manner to individual personalities and different business cultures in ways that demonstrate respect for differences.[35] This requires adaptable, socially intelligent salespeople, especially when dealing with multicultural customers.[36]

The importance of communication skills has been recognized by sales managers, recruiters, and sales researchers. These skills can be continually refined throughout a sales career, a positive factor from both a personal and a career development perspective.

Enthusiasm

When sales executives and recruiters discuss qualifications for sales positions, they invariably include **enthusiasm.** They are usually referring to dual dimensions of enthusiasm—an enthusiastic attitude in a general sense and a special enthusiasm for selling. On-campus recruiters have told us that they seek students who are well beyond "interested in sales" to the point of truly being enthusiastic about career opportunities in sales. Recruiters are somewhat weary of "selling sales" as a viable career, and they welcome the job applicant who displays genuine enthusiasm for the field.

Comments on Qualifications and Skills

The qualifications and skills needed for sales success are different today from those required for success two decades ago. As the popularity of relationship selling grows, the skills necessary for sales success will evolve to meet the needs of the marketplace. For example, Greenberg and Greenberg's research has identified what they call an "emerging factor" for sales success, a strong motivation to provide service to the customer. They contrast this **service motivation** with ego drive by noting that, although ego drive relates to persuading others, service motivation comes from desiring the approval of others. For example, a salesperson may be extremely gratified to please a customer through superior postsale service. Greenberg and Greenberg conclude that most salespeople will need both service motivation and ego drive to succeed, although they note that extremely high levels of both attributes are not likely to exist in the same individual. A survey of 28,000 people in 59 major companies by the Forum Corporation reports that a service motivation, along with understanding and respect for customers, is far more effective than aggressive selling tactics in terms of generating sales.[37]

Our discussion of factors related to sales success is necessarily brief, as a fully descriptive treatment of the topic must be tied to a given sales position. Veteran sales managers and recruiters can often specify with amazing precision what qualifications and skills are needed to succeed in a given sales job. These assessments are usually based on a mixture of objective and subjective judgments that is discussed in the module on recruitment and selection later in the book.

Summary

1. **Describe the evolution of personal selling from ancient times to the modern era.** The history of personal selling can be traced as far back as ancient Greece. The Industrial Revolution enhanced the importance of salespeople, and personal selling as we know it

today had its roots in the early twentieth century. The current era of sales professionalism represents a further evolution.

2. **Explain the contributions of personal selling to society, business firms, and customers.** Salespeople contribute to society by acting as stimuli in the economic process and by assisting in the diffusion of innovation. They contribute to their employers by producing revenue, performing research and feedback activities, and comprising a pool of future managers. They contribute to customers by providing timely knowledge to assist in solving problems.

3. **Describe different types of personal selling jobs.** Among the countless number of different personal selling jobs are the following six types: sales support, new business, existing business, inside sales (nonretail), direct-to-consumer sales, and combination jobs. Sales support positions include missionary or detail salespeople and technical support salespeople. Two types of new-business salespeople are pioneers and order-getters. The primary responsibility of existing-business salespeople is to maintain relationships with present customers through routine sales calls and follow-up. Inside sales in nonretail settings is typified in telemarketing operations and is also used to handle walk-in sales transactions. Direct-to-consumer sales include retail selling, as well as the sale of insurance, securities, and real estate. Combination sales jobs are commonplace and may combine new-business selling with sales support and existing-business responsibilities, as shown in the Beecham Products example. Other combinations are also frequently encountered.

4. **Discuss the characteristics of sales careers.** Sales careers are characterized by relatively good job security and reasonable opportunities for advancement. Salespeople get immediate feedback on the job, and this may explain why job satisfaction for salespeople is higher than in many other occupational groups. The prestige of selling seems to be improving gradually. An advantage of sales careers is that they offer the salesperson the chance to become totally involved in a creative, dynamic occupation in which boredom is rare. Sales careers have long been associated with independence of action, although sales managers lately are monitoring sales activities more closely to improve sales productivity. Salespeople are paid fairly well, with those receiving incentive pay such as commissions being paid better than those on a straight salary. Salespeople occupy boundary roles between their customers and their employers. These roles often produce conflict and stress due to pressure to perform well for multiple parties.

5. **Describe the skills and characteristics required for success in most sales positions.** Although no universal profile of the successful salesperson exists, research indicates certain characteristics may be associated with sales success, namely, empathy, ego drive, ego strength, interpersonal communication skills, and enthusiasm.

Understanding Professional Selling Terms

- Canned sales presentation
- Sales professionalism
- Cost per sales call index
- Economic stimuli
- Diffusion of innovation
- Revenue producers
- Sales support personnel
- Missionary salespeople
- Detailer
- Technical support salespeople
- Pioneers
- Order-getters
- Order-takers
- Inside sales
- Combination sales job
- Boundary-role performers
- Role conflict
- Role ambiguity
- Role stress
- Empathy
- Ego drive
- Ego strength
- Self-efficacy
- Interpersonal communication skills
- Enthusiasm
- Service motivation

Developing Professional Selling Knowledge

1. What factors will influence the continued evolution of personal selling?

2. How do salespeople contribute to our society? Are there negative aspects of personal selling from a societal perspective?
3. What are the primary contributions made by salespeople to their employers?
4. Most businesses would have a difficult time surviving without the benefits of the salespeople who call on them. Do you agree?
5. What are the differences in key responsibilities of missionary salespeople and pioneer salespersons? What recurring problems would you expect each type to encounter as they call on their customers?
6. How would you assess sales in terms of the criteria for an ideal career presented in this chapter?
7. How do sales jobs prepare individuals for career advancement?
8. Salespeople enjoy relatively good job security and opportunities for advancement into management. Why is this so, and will these conditions hold true in the future?
9. Explain what is meant by the statement that "salespeople are boundary-role performers."
10. What factors contributed to job stress for salespeople?

Building Professional Selling Skills

1. **a.** An important part of being a sales professional is to practice ethical selling. For the situations that follow, rate each one as A, B, or C, in which

    A = Unethical/unprofessional
    B = Justifiable in some circumstances
    C = No problem, just a good business practice
    Be prepared to defend your responses.
    1. The salesperson exaggerates how quickly orders will be delivered to get a sale.
    2. The salesperson stresses only positive aspects of the product, omitting possible problems the purchasing firm might have with it.
    3. In a shortage situation, the salesperson allocates product shipments to purchasing agents the seller personally likes.
    4. The salesperson attempts to use the economic power of his or her company to obtain concessions from the buyer.
    5. The salesperson gives a purchaser who was one of the best customers a gift worth $50 or more at Christmas or other occasions.
    6. The salesperson gives a potential customer a gift worth $50 or more at Christmas or other occasions.

   b. As a sales manager, how would you encourage your salespeople to sell ethically? (*Source:* Adapted from Ramon A. Avila, Thomas N. Ingram, Raymond W. Laforge, and Michael R. Williams, *The Professional Selling Skills Workbook*, Fort Worth, TX: The Dryden Press, 1996, 31–34.)

2. Assume you are a salesperson for a packaging manufacturing company that supplies retail stores with custom-imprinted shopping bags. The company has manufacturing facilities in Texas, Georgia, New York, and California. There are five functional areas in the company: marketing (includes sales), production, finance and accounting, customer service and shipping, and human resources. You work out of the California plant, which serves the United States west of the Rocky Mountains. Within the marketing department, your key contact is the product manager who routinely interacts with individuals from production, customer service, and shipping to coordinate production runs with promised delivery dates. The product manager has no direct authority over any of the personnel in production or customer service and shipping. For the following situations, explain how you would try to gain the cooperation of the right people to meet customer needs.

   Scenario A: A large customer unexpectedly runs out of shopping bags and is requesting a shipment within 72 hours. Normal lead time for existing customers is 10 working days. Production is fully booked, that is, there is no idle capacity in the California plant.

   Scenario B: A long-time customer buys three different sizes of shopping bags, all shipped in identical corrugated boxes. The smallest size bags are packed 500 to a box, the medium-size bags 250 to a box, and the largest 100 to a box. Black and white labels on one end of the corrugated boxes denote bag sizes. The customer wants brightly colored labels of three different colors to denote bag size. According to the customer, store employees could then tell at a glance if stock for a particular size was running low and thus place prompt requests for reorders. Currently, the black and white labels are applied by a machine as part of the manufacturing process. The colored labels would have to be custom produced and hand-fed into the labeling machine, whereas existing labels are printed inexpensively in large quantities and fed automatically into the labeling machine.

3. Your knowledge of selling can help you get started in a sales career. Landing a job is like making a major sale in that your knowledge, skills, and attitudes must meet the needs of the employer. One way to match up with employer needs is to use the feature-advantage-benefit (FAB) approach to assess yourself relative to employer needs. In selling, a feature is a factual statement about the product or service, for example, "at 10 pounds, it is the lightest electrical motor in its performance category." An advantage describes how the product can be used or help the customer, for example, "it is light enough to be used in portable applications." The benefit is the favorable outcome the customer will experience from the advantage, for example, "your customers no longer will have to come to the repair center for assistance, as service reps will be able to use portable repair kits in the field." To translate this method to the job search, think of yourself as the "product." Select an appropriate company and discover what they are looking for in sales job applicants. You can use classified ads, the college placement center, personal contacts, or other sources to find a sales position that you are interested in. Using the following example as a starting point, complete a FAB worksheet that shows how you are qualified for the job. In a real job search, this information could be translated to your résumé or cover letter requesting an interview.

The FAB Job-Search Matrix (Example)

A *Need*	B *Feature*	C *Advantage*	D *Benefit*
Employer or Problem	Student		Employer
"This job requires . . ."	"I have . . ."	"This means . . ."	"You will . . ."
frequent sales presentations to individuals and groups	taken 10 classes that required presentations	I require limited or no training in making presentations	save on the cost of training; you have ability and confidence to be productive early
	(List additional needs, features, advantages, and benefits.)		

Making Professional Selling Decisions

CASE 1.1   *Concourse Catering Company*

Background

Concourse Catering Company is a leading food supplier to major airports in the United States. Founded in 1968, the company has maintained its leading position in the market by providing high-quality, yet reasonably priced prepackaged meals to the airlines. In recent years, Concourse has branched into the employee cafeteria market for businesses located adjacent to airports in Atlanta, Chicago, Los Angeles, and New York.

The company has a salesforce of 100 that sells directly to the airlines and to the cafeteria customers. Salespersons are paid on a salary-plus-commission basis, which encourages the growth of annual sales volume in each sales territory. Both the airline and cafeteria markets are extremely competitive, and both markets are experiencing slow but fairly steady growth. In such a market environment, Concourse logically emphasizes customer retention as a major focus of its sales strategy.

Current Situation

Courtney Quinn was recently hired to replace retiring veteran Ken Clark as one of the eight Concourse sales representatives in the Los Angeles market. Having graduated from college just 3 months ago, Courtney had joined Concourse as an eager sales trainee. With her sales and sales management courses from college serving as a strong foundation, she had truly enjoyed her initial training. Courtney came out of the training program excited about her first "real" job and anxious to become a top performer.

Following initial sales training, Courtney began a 2-week swing through her future sales territory with Ken Clark. Clark introduced Courtney to the key contacts in each account and provided her with account profiles that detailed their buying history and future sales opportunities. Normally, the district sales manager, Bill Pennick, would accompany the outgoing and incoming salespersons when a territory personnel change was made. However, Pennick was busy preparing for the upcoming annual national sales meeting and left it up to Clark to familiarize Courtney with her new territory.

On their second day of sales calls together, Courtney and Ken were planning to visit Intermodal Container and Shipping, a large freight forwarding company near Los Angeles International Airport. Concourse has been supplying the large Intermodal employee cafeteria for the past year. They would meet with Nelson Gadlage, the cafeteria manager. On the way to visit Intermodal, the following conversation ensued:

Ken: Before we go to Intermodal, I need to stop by Best Buy and pick up a couple of cell phones for Gadlage.

Courtney: [jokingly] . . . Wow! What service! I wish I had someone to run errands for me during the day!

Ken: Well, I'm not exactly running an errand. The phones are not for Gadlage, it's just that I am doing him a favor . . . one of those things you do to keep the customer happy.

Courtney: Sure, I understand. So you are just picking up some phones that Intermodal has in for repair?

Ken: No. These are new phones that I am donating to a good cause. Hey, look, you might as well know the score. Gadlage has been leaning on me to make a contribution to his brother-in-law's campaign for state senator. This goes back several months, and I have been dropping a little cash on him from time to time. Now he wants more, and I agreed to furnish cell phones for two of his brother's staffers during the campaign.

Courtney: But I thought our company policy prohibits us from making contributions to political campaigns through our customers.

Ken: True, but Courtney, you will quickly learn in this business that sometimes you have to grease the wheels. We do a little favor for Gadlage, and he throws the majority of his cafeteria business our way. It's as simple as that.

Courtney: Well, I see it as a political contribution, and I'm not planning on continuing this practice once the territory is mine.

Ken: Fine, do what you've got to do. As for me, I see it as gesture of goodwill. You will find that very few customers expect such gestures, but with Gadlage, I am afraid that we wouldn't do nearly the volume we are without taking care of this request. Besides, nobody really gets hurt. I am paying for the phones out of my own pocket. I win, Concourse Catering wins, and Gadlage wins. One more thing, some of our veteran salespeople who have succeeded in a tough market for many years have told me they do similar things now and then.

After picking up the phones, Courtney and Ken proceeded to meet with Gadlage. During their visit, Courtney got the distinct feeling that Gadlage expected business as usual once she took over the territory. He mentioned several times that he was an avid supporter of his brother-in-law's campaign and thanked both Ken and Courtney for providing the phones. As Courtney and Ken were leaving, Gadlage made it a point to tell Courtney that he "looked forward to working with her to their mutual benefit."

Later that evening on her way home, Courtney began to wonder if she had made the right choice to join Concourse Catering in a sales position. Ken mentioned that some of the company's top performers were doing unethical things to keep their customers happy. Was this true? She explicitly remembered spending the better part of one morning in training discussing ethics and the company's policy on gift-giving, including political contributions. Maybe Ken was just saying that he was not alone in doing customers unauthorized favors. Or if the practice was common, maybe the company's managers were just ignoring it. Courtney recalled that her college had an honor system, yet some students routinely cheated on exams. She thought that maybe she was making a big deal out of the contribution of cell phones and that maybe she should continue the practice. After all, Ken had been successful for many years, and maybe his customers would expect her to follow in his footsteps. Courtney thought, what happens if I don't continue Ken's special favors? Will I make my sales quota and earn what I expected? Then again, she thought that maybe she should report Ken to Bill Pennick. She didn't really want to continue Ken's unauthorized methods, but she hated to ruin his reputation just as he was retiring. Ken was popular with his colleagues, and Courtney didn't want to alienate his friends, her future colleagues.

Questions

1. How would you handle this situation if you were Courtney?
2. What can be done to ensure that this type of situation does not happen again?

CASE 1.2   *Justin Webb's Career Dilemma*

Background

Justin Webb will graduate from the University of Arizona in 4 weeks, and he has been seeking an entry-level sales position. Justin appears to be a prime job candidate. He is an outstanding student. He has been on the Dean's List every semester and will graduate with honors. Justin will receive his bachelor's degree in business with majors in marketing and finance. He is also very active in school. He is a member of the student council, president of the university's American Marketing Association chapter, and a long jumper for the university's track team.

Justin is well liked by both teachers and friends. He has a strong zest for life that seems to permeate those with whom he comes in contact. One of Justin's professors describes him as follows:

Justin is a strong student and exhibits tremendous leadership potential. In class, he's always attentive and asks insightful questions. He is dependable, and other students look to him for advice and support. When working in group projects, his enthusiasm for learning is contagious, and other group members often elect him as the group leader or spokesperson. He has a confident, but not arrogant, attitude. He relates well to his peers but also to the faculty. On many occasions, I have observed his behavior in business settings such as our annual career fair, and I am certain that he is well prepared for the business world. He is mature and knows the value of hard work. He supplemented his track scholarship with part-time jobs to pay for 100 percent of his college education. He has my highest possible recommendation.

Current Situation

Justin's first choice for an employer is Dell Computer Company. He interviewed with a Dell representative who came to campus seeking entry-level sales candidates. Prior to his interview, Justin researched the company and carefully read the information that was available in the campus placement center. Desiring to learn more, he surfed the Web and went to the library to find additional sources of information on Dell. He discovered what he had expected—Dell's training was rated highly and their employee benefits package was generous. After thoroughly researching the company, he was convinced he wanted to work for Dell. His initial interview with Dell went so well he was granted additional interviews. These, too, went well, but Dell has informed Justin that hiring has been suspended for 60 days. Dell management is telling Justin that it is likely he will receive an offer, but there are no guarantees.

Meanwhile, Justin has a firm offer from Coca-Cola to begin work immediately on graduation. Coca-Cola has given Justin a week to decide on its offer, which would involve a relocation to its Atlanta headquarters. Coca-Cola is an attractive company to Justin, but he believes he would be happiest at Dell. At this point, Justin is considering accepting the Coca-Cola offer but switching to Dell if an offer materializes. A week has passed, and Justin is on the phone with the recruiter from Coca-Cola.

Questions

1. What qualifications and skills does Justin possess that would enable him to be a successful salesperson?
2. What would you do if you were Justin Webb?

Understanding Buyers

Fielding Cagle: Uncovering Organizational Buying Motives

Fielding Cagle, the top salesperson for Progressive Foods, Inc., is regularly assigned to the development of new territories and key-accounts such as NTBC, the centralized buying cooperative for a major metropolitan school district. This account represents more than $875,000 in sales potential for meat products produced by Progressive Foods. Successfully acquiring part of the cooperative's meat business was a top priority for Progressive Foods and required Fielding to work with NTBC's buying team for more than three months to build sufficient buying motivation to spur the account into action and gain the sale.

This particular selling situation presented numerous challenges. First, NTBC was located in a new territory and had little or no knowledge of Fielding or his company. Further complicating the situation, purchase decisions were made by a buying team composed of the chief purchasing officer and several head cooks. Possibly the largest difficulty stemmed from NTBC's treatment of meat product purchases as a straight rebuy situation. With NTBC's needs being satisfied by current suppliers, there was no active buying motive that would favor Progressive Foods becoming a new supplier.

Anticipating these challenges, Fielding purposefully included each of the buying team members in his account strategy and made multiple sales calls to each of them. This strategy allowed him to demonstrate his commitment to the account and initiate a trust-based relationship with the various buying team members. Additionally, he was able to gather information regarding NTBC's current situation and new developments that could lead to potential new needs—emerging needs that could present him with the opportunity of winning this account. NTBC's rapid growth had necessitated converting a portion of their storage and freezer space into offices. As a result, storage space had become a significant problem. Kitchen staff also explained how the current packaging of frozen meat products was inefficient for an operation of this size and created a waste-handling problem.

Fielding began to see gaps growing between the schools' needs and what current suppliers were delivering. Armed with the advance knowledge of an emergent buying motive, Fielding set up a sample and cooking show and invited the buying team, staff from the buying office, cooks, kitchen staff members, and school administrators to attend. Fielding passed out product samples and called attention to well-illustrated features and user benefits. As he discussed the different products, he carefully emphasized two specific selling points. First, Progressive Foods' flexibility in shipping, which allows them to economically deliver more frequent and

After completing this module, you should be able to

1 Categorize primary types of buyers.

2 Discuss the distinguishing characteristics of business markets.

3 List the different steps in the business-to-business buying process.

4 Discuss the different types of buyer needs.

5 Describe how buyers evaluate suppliers and alternative sales offerings by using the multiattribute model of evaluation.

6 Explain the two-factor model that buyers use to evaluate the performance of sales offerings and develop satisfaction.

7 Explain the different types of purchasing decisions.

8 Explain the concept of buying teams and specify the different member roles.

smaller-sized shipments. This provides significant benefits to the customer in the form of smaller inventories, which tie up less cash and require less freezer storage space. Second, improved packaging protects the product without having to individually wrap each piece. In addition to cutting waste by two-thirds, the improved packaging also resulted in direct cost savings to the customer approaching 5 percent.

The cooking show was a success and ultimately led to Fielding gaining 60 percent of the cooperative's business. Initially presented with a situation in which existing suppliers had a lock on the business, Fielding did not attempt to manipulate or fast-talk his way to a sale. Instead, he worked with all members of the buying center to gain a more complete understanding of the cooperative's *emerging* and *unarticulated* needs. Although they initially perceived that their needs were being met, Fielding demonstrated that a higher level of attainment was possible and completed a mutually beneficial long-term contract.

Source: Personal interview with Fielding Cagle, April 28, 1999.

Fielding Cagle's experience in working with the members of the NTBC buying center illustrates several fundamentals regarding buyer behavior. Principal among these fundamentals is that purchase decisions result from a purposeful and sequential buying process that begins with the recognition of a need or problem. Successful salespeople know the critical importance of understanding the nature of specific buyers' purchase decisions and how they reached those decisions. Accordingly, effective salespeople allocate a significant portion of their time and effort to gathering specific information and details about a buyer's situation and needs. In turn, this knowledge assists the salesperson in working with the buyer in describing, specifying, and acquiring the buyer's desired solutions. As illustrated by Fielding's experience, multiple buying influences from different individuals in a buying team are common, and the true nature of the needs are often unarticulated or unrealized by buyers. In such selling situations, salespeople become the value-added source of expertise that assists buyers in effectively solving problems and generates long-term buyer-seller relationships and repeat business.

Following a discussion on different types of buyers, this module develops a model of the buying process and the corresponding roles of the salesperson. Buyer activities characteristic to each step of the purchase decision process are explained and related to salesperson activities for effectively interacting with buyers. This is followed by an explanation of different types of purchasing decisions to which salespeople must respond. The growing incidence of multiple buying influences and buying teams is also demonstrated, along with their impact on selling strategy. Finally, emergent trends such as relationship strategies, supply-chain management, target pricing, and the growing importance of information and technology are discussed from the perspective of the salesperson.

Types of Buyers

Salespeople work and interact with many different types of buyers. These buyer types range from heavy industry and manufacturing operations to consumers making a purchase for their own use. These variants of customer types arise out of the unique buying situations they occupy. As a result, one type of buyer will have needs, motivations, and buying behavior that are very different from another type of buyer. Consider the different buying situations and the resulting needs of a corporate buyer for Footlocker compared with the athletic equipment buyer for a major university or Joe Smith, attorney at law and weekend warrior in the local YMCA's basketball league. As illustrated in Exhibit 2.1, each of these buyers may be looking for athletic shoes, but their buying needs are very different. To maximize selling effectiveness, salespeople must understand the type of buyer with whom they are working and respond to their specific needs, wants, and expectations.

The most common categorization of buyers splits them into either (1) **consumer markets** or (2) **business markets.** Consumers purchase goods and services for their own use or consumption and are highly influenced by peer group behavior, aesthetics, and personal taste. Business markets are composed of firms, institutions, and governments. These members of the business market acquire goods and services to use as inputs into their own manufacturing process (i.e., raw materials, component parts, and capital equipment), for use in their day-to-day operations (i.e., office supplies, professional services, insurance), or for resale to their own customers. Business customers tend to stress overall value as the cornerstone for purchase decisions.

EXHIBIT 2.1   Different Needs of Different Athletic Shoe Buyers

	Buyer for Footlocker Shoe Stores	University Athletic Equipment Buyer	Joe Smith—YMCA Weekend Warrior
Functional Needs	• Has the features customers want • Well constructed—minimize returns • Offers point-of-sale displays for store use • Competitive pricing	• Individualized sole texture for different player performance needs • Perfect fit and size for each team member • Custom match with university colors • Size of supplier's payment to coach and school for using their shoes	• Offers the leading edge in shoe features • Prominent brand logo • Highest-priced shoes in the store
Situational Needs	• Can supply stores across North America • Ability to ship to individual stores on a just-in-time basis • Offers 90-day trade credit	• Ability to deliver on time • Provide supplier personnel for team fittings • Make contract payments to university and coach at beginning of season	• Right size in stock, ready to carry out • Takes Visa and MasterCard
Social Needs	• Invitation for buying team to attend trade show and supplier-sponsored reception	• Sponsor and distribute shoes at annual team shoe night to build enthusiasm • Include team and athletes in supplier brand promotions	• Offers user-group newsletter to upscale customers • Periodic mailing for new products and incentives to purchase
Psychological Needs	• Assurance that shoes will sell at retail • Brand name with strong market appeal • Option to return unsold goods for credit	• Brand name consistent with players' self-images • The entire team will accept and be enthusiastic toward product decision • Belief that the overall contract is best for the university, team, and coaches	• Reinforces customer's self-image as an innovator • Product will deliver the promised performance • One of only a few people having purchased this style of shoe
Knowledge Needs	• Level of quality—how the shoe is constructed • How the new features impact performance • What makes the shoe unique and superior to competitive offerings • Product training and materials for sales staff	• What makes the shoe unique and superior to competitive offerings • Supporting information and assurance that the contracted payments to university and coaches are superior to competitive offerings	• What makes the shoe unique and superior to competitive offerings • Assurance that everybody on the court will not be wearing the same shoe

Distinguishing Characteristics of Business Markets

Although there are similarities between consumer and business buying behaviors, business markets tend to be much more complex and possess several characteristics that are in sharp contrast to those of the consumer market. These distinguishing characteristics are described below.

BUYERS ARE LARGER BUT FEWER IN NUMBER   Business markets typically exhibit high levels of consolidation in which a smaller number of large buyers account for most of the purchases. A salesperson selling high-grade industrial silicon for use in manufacturing computer chips will find that his or her fate rests on acquiring and nurturing the business of one or more of the four to five major chip makers around the world. For example, Intel remains the leader in this industry, with $25.8 billion in 1999 chip sales. NEC, the second largest, is much smaller, at $8.6 billion in chip sales, followed by Samsung and Texas Instruments at approximately $7.1 billion. The concentration and size gap are even more apparent after the top four companies, with AMD rating in ninth place, at $2.58 billion in chip sales.

DERIVED DEMAND   **Derived demand** denotes that the demand in business markets is closely associated with the demand for consumer goods. When the consumer demand for new cars and trucks increases, the demand for rolled steel also goes up. Of course, when the demand for consumer products goes down, so goes the related demand in business markets. The most effective salespeople identify and monitor the consumer markets that are related to their business customers so they can better anticipate shifts in demand and assist their buyers in staying ahead of the demand shifts rather than being caught with too much, too little, or even the wrong, inventory. Republic Gypsum's salespeople accurately forecast a boom in residential construction and the pressure it would put on the supply of sheetrock wallboard. Working closely with their key customers, order quantities and shipping dates were revised to prevent those customers from being caught with inadequate inventories to supply the expanded demand. This gave those customers a significant competitive advantage over their competitors who were surprised and suddenly out of stock.

HIGHER LEVELS OF DEMAND FLUCTUATION   Closely related to the derived demand characteristics, the demand for goods and services in the business market is more volatile than that of the consumer market. In economics, this is referred to as the **acceleration principle.** As demand increases (or decreases) in the consumer market, the business market reacts by accelerating the buildup (or reduction) of inventories and increasing (or shifting and possibly reducing) plant capacity. A good example would be the rapidly growing demand for digital portable phones. In response to higher consumer demand, wholesalers and retailers are increasing their inventories of digital phones while decreasing the number of analog phones they carry. In response, manufacturers are shifting their production away from analog phones to increase their production of digital models. Salespeople are the source of valuable information and knowledge enabling their customers to anticipate these fluctuations and assisting them in developing more effective marketing strategies. As a result, both the buying and selling organizations realize mutual positive benefits.

PURCHASING PROFESSIONALS   Buyers in the business markets are trained as purchasing agents. The process of identifying suppliers and sourcing goods and services is their job. This results in a more professional and rational approach to purchasing. As a result, salespeople must possess increased levels of knowledge and expertise to provide customers with a richer and more detailed assortment of application, performance, and technical data.

MULTIPLE BUYING INFLUENCES   Reflecting the increased complexity of many business purchases, groups of individuals within the buying firm often work together as a buying team or center. As a result, salespeople often work simultaneously with several individuals during a sales call and even different sets of buyers during different sales calls. Buying team members come from different areas of expertise and play different roles in the purchasing process. To be effective, the salesperson must first identify, then understand and respond to, the role and key buying motives of each member.

CLOSE BUYER-SELLER RELATIONSHIPS   The smaller customer base and increased usage of supply chain management, characterized by buyers becoming highly involved in organizing and administering logistical processes and actively managing a reduced set of suppliers, has resulted in buyers and sellers becoming much more interdependent than ever before. This increased interdependence and desire to reduce risk of the unknown has led to an emphasis on developing long-term buyer-seller relationships characterized by increased levels of buyer-seller interaction and higher levels of service expectations by buyers. "Professional Selling in the 21st Century: Buyers' Expectations Shift" describes the emerging change in buyers' expectations from a price emphasis to relationships and problem-solving solutions. This shift requires salespeople to change their focus from quickly selling the buyer and closing the current transaction and, in its place, adapt a longer-term perspective emphasizing continuing multiple exchanges into the future. This perspective often includes making multiple sales calls to develop a better understanding of the buyer's needs and then responding to those needs with a sales offering that solves the buyer's needs and enhances the buyer-seller relationship in favor of future interactions.

PROFESSIONAL SELLING IN THE 21ST CENTURY

Buyers' Expectations Shift

Jay Deragon, director of strategy for the Nashville-based Discover eHoldings, Inc., describes the tremendous changes in buyers' needs and expectations that are reshaping the commercial property and casualty insurance market:

Reflecting a radically changed business environment, the old competitive paradigm emphasizing price has been radically expanded. Today, business buyers of property and casualty insurance emphasize the importance of long-term partnerships, mutual trust, and innovative solutions in their evaluation and choice of vendors. The RIMS-QIC Quality Scorecard evidences this shift in buyer expectations and identifies the four primary supplier performance expectations impacting customer satisfaction with and loyalty to suppliers:

- *Building internal and external partnerships.*
- *Generating and maintaining trust and reliability.*
- *Identifying customer needs and creating innovative solutions.*
- *Engaging in two-way interactive communications.*

The Buying Process

Buyers in both the consumer and business marketplace undergo a conscious and logical process in making purchase decisions. As depicted in Figure 2.1, the sequential and interrelated phases of the **business buyers' purchase process** begin with (1) *Recognition of the Problem or Need,* (2) *Determination of the Characteristics of the Item and the Quantity Needed,* (3) *Description of the Characteristics of the Item and Quantity Needed,* (4) *Search for and Qualification of Potential Sources,* (5) *Acquisition and Analysis of Proposals,* (6) *Evaluation of Proposals and Selection of Suppliers,* (7) *Selection of an Order Routine,* and (8) *Performance Feedback and Evaluation.*

Depending upon the nature of the buying organization and the buying situation, the buying process may be highly formalized or simply a rough approximation of what actually occurs. The decision process employed by General Motors for the acquisition of a new organization-wide computer system will be highly formalized and purposefully reflect each of the above described decision phases. Compared to General Motors, the decision process of Bloomington Bookkeeping, a single office and four-person operation, could be expected to use a less formalized approach in working through their buying decision process for a computer system. In the decision to replenish stock office supplies, both of the two organizations are likely to use a much less formalized routine—but still, a routine that reflects the different decision phases.

As further illustrated by Figure 2.1, there is a close correspondence between the phases of the buyer's decision process and the selling activities of the salesperson. It is important that salespeople understand and make use of the interrelationships between the phases of the buying process and selling activities. Effective use of these interrelationships offers salespeople numerous opportunities to interact with buyers in a way that guides the shaping of product specifications and the selection of sources while facilitating the purchase decision.

Phase One—Recognition of the Problem or Need: The Needs Gap

Needs are the result of a gap between buyers' **desired states** and their **actual states.** Consequently, need recognition results from an individual cognitively and emotionally processing information relevant to his or her actual state of being and comparing it to the desired state of being. As illustrated in Figure 2.2, any perceived difference, or **needs gap,** between these two states activates the motivation or drive to fill the gap and reach the desired state. For example, the SnowRunner Company's daily production capacity is limited to 1,000 molded ski-mobile body housings. Their research indicates that increasing capacity to 1,250 units per day would result in significant reductions in per-unit costs and allow them to enter additional geographic markets—both moves that would have significant and positive impacts on financial performance. The perceived need to expand production activates a corresponding motivation to search for information regarding alternative solutions and acquire the capability to increase production by 250 units.

However, if there is no gap, then there is no need and no active buying motive. It is common for salespeople to find themselves working with buyers who, for one reason or another, do not perceive a needs gap to be present. Possibly they do not have the right information or lack full understanding of the situation and the existence of options better than their current state. It is also possible that their understanding of the actual state might be incomplete or mistaken. For example, SnowRunner's buyers might not understand the cost reduction possibilities and increased market potential that could result from increased capacity. As a result, they perceive no need to increase production—the desired state is the same as their

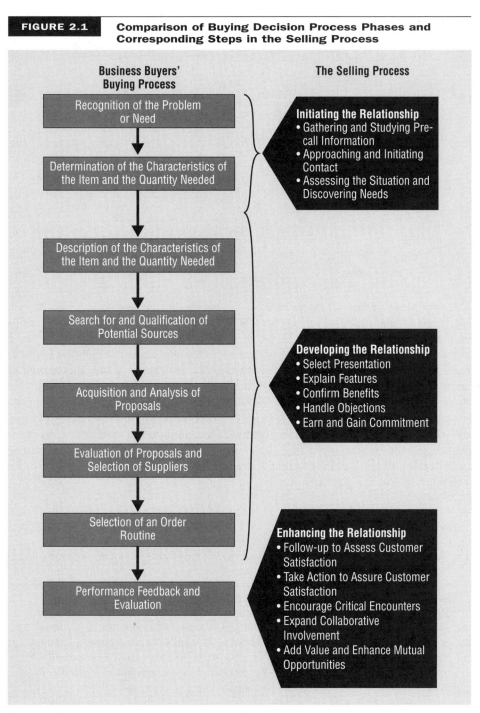

FIGURE 2.1   **Comparison of Buying Decision Process Phases and Corresponding Steps in the Selling Process**

The steps of the selling process correspond with and work to advance the phases of the buying process.

actual state. Similarly, the buyers might be functioning with incomplete information regarding the company's actual state of reduced production capacity due to SnowRunner's existing molding machines requiring increased downtime for maintenance. Properly realized, this lowering of the actual state would result in a needs gap. Successful salespeople position themselves to assist buyers in identifying and

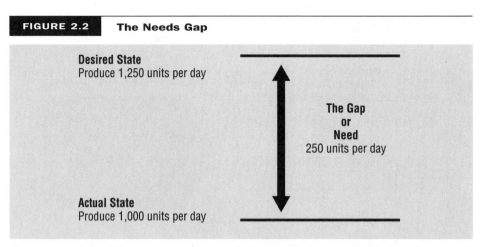

FIGURE 2.2   **The Needs Gap**

Desired State
Produce 1,250 units per day

**The Gap
or
Need**
250 units per day

Actual State
Produce 1,000 units per day

The needs gap is the difference between the buyer's perceived desired state and the buyer's perceived actual state.

understanding needs as a result of their broader expertise and knowledge regarding product use and application. Salespeople can also present buyers with information and opportunities that effectively raise the desired state, generate a need, and trigger the purchase decision process. Like the experience of Fielding Cagle in the opening scenario, top-performing salespeople understand the importance of assisting their buyers in forming realistic perceptions of the actual state and the desired state. In this manner, the salesperson can continue to serve as a non-manipulative consultant to the buyer while affecting buying motives that yield mutual benefits to all parties. However, it should be noted that the persuasive power of assisting the buyer in determining and comparing desired and actual states can also be misused and lead to unethical and manipulative selling behaviors such as those exhibited in "An Ethical Dilemma."

An Ethical Dilemma

The U.S. Supreme Court left intact a $2 billion class action settlement over allegations that insurance agents for Prudential Insurance Company lied to policyholders over a 13-year period. The sales fraud resulted from agents churning current customers. Churning involves a sales agent convincing insured customers to use the built-up cash value of older policies to sell them new and more expensive policies. The allegations against Prudential involve more than 8 million policies sold between 1982 and 1995. Rather than pay fixed salaries, many companies pay large commissions on new sales and significantly reduced commissions for the continued sales to existing customers. Such a compensation system can push sales agents to emphasize new sales over renewals and thus manifest itself in some form of churning. If the company you might work for in the future used a compensation system such as this, how would you handle implicit pressure to emphasize new sales and the potential for higher earnings through churning your customers?

TYPES OF BUYER NEEDS   The total number of potential customer needs is infinite and sometimes difficult for salespeople to grasp and understand on a customer-by-customer basis. Consequently, many salespeople find it helpful to group customer needs into one of five basic types or categories that focus on the buying situation and the benefits to be provided by the product or service being chosen.[1] These five general types of buyer needs are described as follows:

- **Situational needs** are the specific needs that are contingent on, and often a result of, conditions related to the specific environment, time, and place (e.g., emergency car repair while traveling out of town; a piece of customized production equipment to fulfill a customer's specific situational requirements; or providing for quick initial shipment to meet a buyer's out-of-stock status).

- **Functional needs** represent the need for a specific core task or function to be performed—the functional purpose of a specific product or service. The need for a sales offering to do what it is supposed to do (e.g., alcohol disinfects; switches open and close to control some flow; the flow control valve is accurate and reliable).

- **Social needs** comprise the need for acceptance from and association with others—a desire to belong to some reference group. For example, a product or service might be associated with some specific and desired affinity group or segment (e.g., Polo clothing is associated with upper-income, successful people; ISO 9000 Certification is associated with high-quality vendors; leading e-commerce Web sites include discussion groups to build a sense of community).

- **Psychological needs** reflect the desire for feelings of assurance and risk reduction, as well as positive emotions and feelings such as success, joy, excitement, and stimulation. (e.g., a Mont Blanc pen generates a feeling of success; effective training programs create a sense of self-control and determination; selection and use of well-known, high-quality brands provides assurance to buyers and organizations alike).

- **Knowledge needs** represent the desire for personal development, information, and knowledge to increase thought and understanding as to how and why things happen (e.g., product information, newsletters, brochures, along with training and user support group meetings/conferences provide current information on products and topics of interest).

Categorizing buyer needs by type can assist the salesperson in bringing order to what could otherwise be a confusing and endless mix of needs and expectations. Organizing the buyer's different needs into their basic types can help salespeople in several ways. First, as illustrated by Exhibit 2.1 and the example worksheet in Exhibit 2.2, the basic types can serve as a checklist or worksheet to ensure that no significant problems or needs have been overlooked in the process of needs discovery. Organizing what at first might appear to be different needs and problems into their common types also helps the salesperson to better understand the nature of the buyer's needs along with the interrelationships and commonalties between them. In turn, this enhanced understanding and the framework of basic types combine to serve as a guide for salespeople in generating and then demonstrating value-added solutions in response to specific needs of the buyer.

As discussed above, the specific circumstances or types of solution benefits that a buyer is seeking should determine a salesperson's strategy for working with that buyer. Consequently, it should be noted that the needs of business buyers tend to be more complex than consumers' needs. Like consumers, organizational buyers are people and are influenced by the same functional, social, psychological, knowledge, and situational experiences and forces that affect and shape individual needs. However, in addition to those individual needs, organizational buyers must also satisfy the needs and requirements of the organization for which they work. As depicted by Figure 2.3, these organizational needs overlay and interact with the

EXHIBIT 2.2	Example Worksheet for Organizing Buyer Needs and Benefit-Based Solutions

Primary Buyer: *Bart Waits*
Buying Organization: *SouthWest Metal Stampings*
Primary Industry: *Stamped metal parts and sub-components*

Basic Type of Need	*Buyer's Specific Needs*
Buyer's Situational Needs	• Requires an 18% increase in production to meet increased sales • On-hand inventory will not meet production/delivery schedule • Tight cashflow pending initial deliveries and receipt of payment
Buyer's Functional Needs	• Equipment to provide effective and efficient increase in production • Expedited delivery and installation in 6 weeks or less • Equipment financing extending payments beyond initial receipts
Buyer's Social Needs	• Expansion in production transforms them into Top 10 in industry • Belonging to user group of companies using this equipment • Feeling that they are an important customer of the supplier
Buyer's Psychological Needs	• Confidence that selected equipment will meet needs and do job • Assurance that seller can complete installation in 6 weeks • Saving Face—to believe borrowing for equipment is common
Buyer's Knowledge Needs	• Evidence that this is the right choice • Understanding new technology used by the selected equipment • Training program for production employees and maintenance staff

needs of the individual. To maximize selling effectiveness in the organizational or business-to-business market, salespeople must generate solutions addressing both the individual and organizational needs of business buyers.

Phase Two—Determination of the Characteristics of the Item and the Quantity Needed

Coincident to recognizing a need or problem is the motivation and drive to resolve it by undertaking a search for additional information leading to possible solutions. This particular phase of the buying process involves the consideration and study of the overall situation to understand what is required in the form of a preferred solution. This begins to establish the general characteristics and quantities necessary to resolve the need or problem. Consultative salespeople use their knowledge and expertise at this point to assist the buyer in analyzing and interpreting the problem situation and needs. Salespeople offer valuable knowledge of problem situations and solution options that buyers typically perceive as beneficial.

Phase Three—Description of the Characteristics of the Item and the Quantity Needed

Using the desired characteristics and quantities developed in the previous phase as a starting point, buyers translate that general information into detailed specifications describing exactly what is expected and required. The determination of detailed specifications serves several purposes. First, detailed specifications guide

---

FIGURE 2.3   **Complex Mix of Business Buyer Needs**

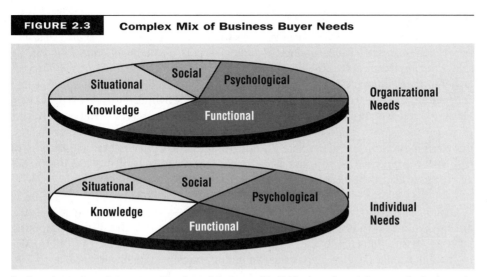

Business buyers' needs are a combination of the buyers' individual needs and the organization's needs.

supplier firms in developing their proposals. Second, these specifications provide the buyer a framework for evaluating, comparing, and choosing among the proposed solutions. Postpurchase specifications serve as a standard for evaluation to ensure that the buying firm receives the required product features and quantities. Trust-based buyer-seller relationships allow salespeople to work closely with buyers and collaboratively assist them in establishing the detailed specifications of the preferred solutions.

Phase Four—Search for and Qualification of Potential Sources

Next, buyers must locate and qualify potential suppliers capable of providing the preferred solution. Although buyers certainly utilize information provided by salespeople to identify qualified suppliers, there is an abundance of information available from other sources such as trade associations, product source directories, trade shows, the Internet, advertising, and word of mouth. Once identified, potential suppliers are qualified on their ability to consistently perform and deliver at the level of quality and quantity required. Due to the large number of information sources available to buyers researching potential suppliers, one of the most important tasks in personal selling is to win the position of one of those information sources and keep buyers informed about the salesperson's company, its new products, and solution capabilities.

Phase Five—Acquisition and Analysis of Proposals

Based on the detailed specifications, **requests for proposals** (known in the trade as an **RFP**) are developed and distributed to the qualified potential suppliers. Based on the RFP, qualified suppliers develop and submit proposals to provide the products as specified. Salespeople play a critical and influential role in this stage of the buying process by developing and presenting the proposed solution to the buyers. In this role, the salesperson is responsible for presenting the proposed features and benefits in such a manner that the proposed solution is evaluated as providing higher levels of benefits and value to the buyer than other competing proposals. Consequently, it is imperative that salespeople understand the basic evaluation procedures used by buyers in comparing alternative and competitive proposals so they can be more proficient in demonstrating the superiority of their solution over the competition.

PROCEDURES FOR EVALUATING SUPPLIERS AND PRODUCTS Purchase decisions are based on the buyers' comparative evaluations of suppliers and the products and services they propose for satisfying the buyers' needs. Some buyers may look for the sales offering that receives the highest rating on the one characteristic they perceive as being most important. Others may prefer the sales offering that achieves some acceptable assessment score across each and every attribute desired by the buyer. However, research into how purchase decisions are made suggests that most buyers use a compensatory, **multi-attribute model** incorporating weighted averages across desired characteristics.[2] These weighted averages incorporate (1) assessments of how well the product or supplier performs in meeting each of the specified characteristics and (2) the relative importance of each specified characteristic.

Assessment of Product or Supplier Performance. The first step in applying the multi-attribute model is to objectively rate how well each characteristic of the competing products or suppliers meets the buyers' needs. Let's use the example of General Motors (GM) evaluating adhesives for use in manufacturing. The buyers have narrowed the alternatives to products proposed by three suppliers: BondIt #302, AdCo #45, and StikFast #217. As illustrated in Exhibit 2.3, the GM buying team has assessed the competitive products according to how well they perform on certain important attributes. These assessments are converted to scores as depicted in Exhibit 2.4, with scores ranging from 1 (very poor performance) to 10 (excellent performance).

As illustrated, no single product is consistently outstanding across each of the eight identified characteristics. Although BondIt #302 is easy to apply and uses the buyer's current equipment, it is also more expensive and has the shortest durability time in the field. StikFast #217 also scores well for ease of application, and it has superior durability. However, it has the longest bonding time and could negatively influence production time.

EXHIBIT 2.3   Important Product Information

Characteristics	BondIt #302	AdCo #45	StikFast #217
Ease of application	Excellent	Good	Very Good
Bonding time	8 minutes	10 minutes	12 minutes
Durability	10 years	12 years	15 years
Reliability	Very Good	Excellent	Good
Non-toxic	Very Good	Excellent	Very Good
Quoted Price	$28 per gal.	$22 per gal.	$26 per gal.
Shelf-life in Storage	6 months	4 months	4 months
Service Factors	Good	Very Good	Excellent

EXHIBIT 2.4   Product Performance Scores

Characteristics	BondIt #302	AdCo #45	StikFast #217
Ease of application	10	5	8
Bonding time	8	6	4
Durability	6	8	9
Reliability	8	10	5
Non-toxic	8	10	8
Quoted Price	5	9	7
Shelf-life in Storage	9	6	6
Service Factors	5	8	10

Accounting for Relative Importance of Each Characteristic. To properly compare these performance differences, each score must be weighted by the characteristic's perceived importance. In the adhesive example, importance weights are assigned on a scale of 1 (relatively unimportant) to 10 (very important). As illustrated in Exhibit 2.5, multiplying each performance score by the corresponding attribute's importance weight results in a weighted average that can be totaled to calculate an overall rating for each product. The product or supplier having the highest comparative rating is typically the product selected for purchase. In this example, AdCo has the highest overall evaluation totaling 468 points compared with BondIt's 430 points and StikFast's 446 points.

EMPLOYING BUYER EVALUATION PROCEDURES TO ENHANCE SELLING STRATEGIES
Understanding evaluation procedures and gaining insight as to how a specific buyer or team of buyers is evaluating suppliers and proposals is vital for the salesperson to be effective and requires the integration of several bases of knowledge. First, information gathered prior to the sales call must be combined with an effective needs-discovery dialogue with the buyer(s) to delineate the buyers' needs and the nature of the desired solution. This establishes the most likely criteria for evaluation. Further discussion between the buyer and seller can begin to establish the importance the buyers place on each of the different performance criteria and often yields information as to what suppliers and products are being considered. Using this information and the salesperson's knowledge of how their products compare with competitors' offerings allows the salesperson to complete a likely facsimile of the buyers' evaluation. With this enhanced level of preparation and understanding, the salesperson can plan, create, and deliver a more effective presentation using the five fundamental strategies that are inherent within the evaluation procedures used by buyers.

• *Modify the Product Offering Being Proposed.* Oftentimes, in the course of preparing or delivering a presentation, it becomes apparent that the product offering will not maximize the buyer's evaluation score in comparison with a competitor's offering. In this case, the strategy would be to modify or change the product to one that better meets the buyer's overall needs and thus would receive a higher evaluation. For example, by developing a better understanding of the adhesive buyer's perceived importance of certain characteristics, the BondIt salesperson could offer a

EXHIBIT 2.5	**Weighted Averages for Performance times Importance and Overall Evaluation Scores**								
Characteristics	**BondIt #302**			**AdCo #45**			**StikFast #217**		
	P	*I*	*PxI*	*P*	*I*	*PxI*	*P*	*I*	*PxI*
Ease of application	10	8	80	5	8	40	8	8	72
Bonding time	8	6	48	6	6	36	4	6	24
Durability	6	9	54	8	9	72	9	9	81
Reliability	8	7	56	10	7	70	5	7	35
Non-toxic	8	6	48	10	6	60	8	6	48
Quoted Price	5	10	50	9	10	90	7	10	70
Shelf-life in Storage	9	6	54	6	6	36	6	6	36
Service Factors	5	8	40	8	8	64	10	8	80
Overall Evaluation Score			430			468			446

different adhesive formulation that is not as easy to apply (low perceived importance) but offers improved durability (perceived high importance) and more competitive price (perceived high importance).

- *Alter the Buyer's Beliefs about the Proposed Offering.* Provide information and support to alter the buyer's beliefs as to where the proposed product stands on certain attributes. This is a recommended strategy for cases in which the buyer underestimates the true qualities of the proposed product. However, if the buyer's perceptions are correct, this strategy would encourage exaggerated and overstated claims by the salesperson and should be avoided. In the instance of BondIt #302's low evaluation score, the salesperson could offer the buyer information and evidence that the product's durability and service factors actually perform much better than the buyer initially believed. By working with the buyer to develop a more realistic perception of the product's performance, BondIt #302 could become the buyer's preferred choice.

- *Alter the Buyer's Beliefs about the Competitor's Offering.* For a variety of reasons, buyers often mistakenly believe that a competitor's offering has higher level attributes or qualities than it actually does. In such an instance, the salesperson can provide information to evidence a more accurate picture of the competitor's attributes. This has been referred to as **competitive depositioning** and is carried out by openly comparing (not simply degrading) the competing offering's attributes, advantages, and weaknesses. As an illustration, the BondIt salesperson might demonstrate the *total* cost for each of the three product alternatives, including quoted price, ease of application, and bonding time. BondIt is much easier to apply and has a faster bonding time. Consequently, less of it must be applied for each application, which results in a significantly lower total cost and a much improved evaluation score.

- *Alter the Importance Weights.* In this strategy, the salesperson uses information to emphasize and thus increase the importance of certain attributes on which the product offering is exceptionally strong. In the case of attributes on which the offering might be short, the strategy would be to de-emphasize their importance. Continuing the adhesive purchase decision, BondIt's salesperson might offer information to influence the buyer's importance rating for ease of application and storage shelf-life—two characteristics in which BondIt is much stronger than the two competitors.

- *Call Attention to Neglected Attributes.* In the case in which it becomes apparent that significant attributes may have been neglected or overlooked, the salesperson can increase the buyer's evaluation of the proposed offering by pointing out the attribute that was missed. For instance, the BondIt #302 adhesive dries to an invisible, transparent, and semi-flexible adhesive compared with the two competitors, which cure to a light gray color that could detract from the final product in cases in which the adhesive flowed out of the joint. The appearance of the final product is a significant concern, and this neglected attribute could substantially influence the comparative evaluations.

Phase Six—Evaluation of Proposals and Selection of Suppliers

The buying decision is the outcome of the buyer's evaluation of the various proposals acquired from potential suppliers. Typically, further negotiations will be conducted with the selected supplier(s) for the purpose of establishing the final terms regarding product characteristics, pricing, and delivery. Salespeople play a central role in gaining the buyer's commitment to the purchase decision and in the subsequent negotiations of the final terms.

Phase Seven—Selection of an Order Routine

Once the supplier(s) has been selected, details associated with the purchase decision must be settled. These details include delivery quantities, locations, and times along with return policies and the routine for re-orders associated with the purchase. For cases in which the purchase requires multiple deliveries over a period of time, the routine for placing subsequent orders and making deliveries must be set out and understood. Is the order routine standardized on the basis of a pre-arranged time schedule, or is the salesperson expected to monitor usage and inventories in order to place orders and schedule shipments? Will orders be placed automatically through the use of electronic data interchange or the Internet? Regardless of the nature of the order routine, the salesperson plays a critical role in facilitating communication, completing ordering procedures, and settling the final details.

Phase Eight—Performance Feedback and Evaluation

The final phase in the buying process is the evaluation of performance and feedback shared among all parties for the purpose of improving future performance and enhancing buyer-seller relationships. Research supports that salespeople's customer interaction activities and communication at this stage of the buying process become the primary determinants of customer satisfaction and buyer loyalty. Consequently, it is critical that salespeople continue working with buyers after the sale. The salesperson's follow-up activities provide the critical points of contact between the buyer and seller in order to assure consistent performance, respond to and take care of problems, maximize customer satisfaction, and further enhance buyer-seller relationships.

UNDERSTANDING POST-PURCHASE EVALUATION AND THE FORMATION OF SATISFACTION   Research shows that buyers evaluate their experience with a product purchase on the basis of product characteristics that fall into a **two-factor model of evaluation** as depicted in Figure 2.4.[3] The first category, **functional attributes**, refers to the features and characteristics that are related to *what* the product actually does or is expected to do—its functional characteristics. These functional characteristics have also been referred to as **"must-have attributes,"** features of the core product that are taken for granted by the customer. These are the attributes that must be present for the supplier or product to even be included among those being considered for purchase. Consequently, they tend to be fairly common across the set of suppliers and products being considered for purchase by a buyer. Characteristics such as reliability, durability, conformance to specifications, competitive pricing, and performance are illustrative of functional attributes.

Psychological attributes make up the second general category. This category refers to *how* things are carried out and done between the buyer and seller. These supplier and market offering characteristics are described as the **"delighter attributes"**—the augmented features and characteristics included in the total market offering that go beyond buyer expectations and have a significant positive impact on customer satisfaction. The psychological or delighter characteristics are not perceived as being universal features across the evoked set of suppliers and market

FIGURE 2.4.	The Two-Factor Model of Buyer Evaluation

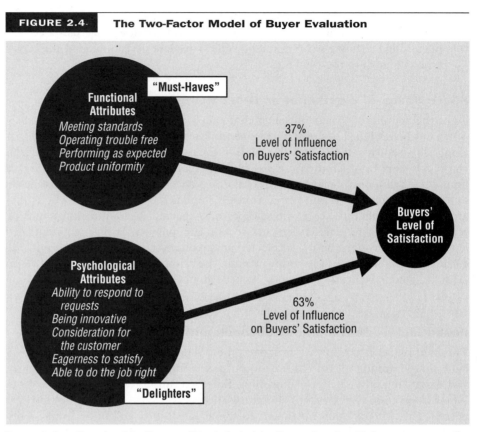

Buyers evaluate Functional Attributes and Psychological Attributes of a sales offering to assess overall performance and satisfaction.

offerings being considered. Rather, these are the differentiators between the competitors. The competence, attitudes, and behaviors of supplier personnel with whom the buyer has contact, as well as the salesperson's trustworthiness, consideration for the customer, responsiveness, ability to recover when there is a problem, and innovativeness in providing solutions are exemplary psychological attributes.

THE GROWING IMPORTANCE OF SALESPEOPLE IN BUYER'S POST-PURCHASE EVALUATION　Understanding the differential impact of functional (must-haves) and psychological (delighters) attributes is important for salespeople. Functional attributes possess a close correspondence to the technical and more tangible product attributes whereas the psychological attributes are similar to the interpersonal communication and behaviors of salespeople and other personnel having contact with customers. Numerous research studies across a variety of industries evidences psychological attributes as having two times more influence on buyer satisfaction and loyalty than functional attributes. This observation underscores special implications for salespeople, as it is their interpersonal communication and behaviors—what they do—that make up the psychological attributes. Although both categories of product characteristics are important and have significant influences on buyer satisfaction, the activities and behaviors of the salesperson as she or he interacts with the buyer have more impact on that buyer's evaluation than the features of the product or service itself.

Types of Purchasing Decisions

Buyers are learners in that purchase decisions are not isolated behaviors. Buyer be-havior and purchase decisions are based on the relevant knowledge that buyers have accumulated from multiple sources to assist them in making the proper choice. Internally, buyers reflect on past experiences as guides for making purchase decisions. When sufficient knowledge from past experiences is not available, buyers access external sources of information: secondary sources of information (e.g., trade journals, product test reports, advertising) and other individuals the buyer perceives as being trustworthy and knowledgeable in a given area.

The level of experience and knowledge a buyer or buying organization pos-sesses relevant to a given purchasing decision is a primary determinant of the time and resources the buyer will allocate to that purchasing decision. The level of a buyer's existing experience and knowledge has been used to categorize buyer be-havior into three types of purchasing decisions: straight rebuys, modified rebuys, and new tasks. As summarized in Exhibit 2.6, selling strategies should reflect the dif-ferences in buyer behaviors and decision-making characteristic of each type of buy-ing decision.

Straight Rebuys

If past experiences with a product resulted in high levels of satisfaction, buyers tend to purchase the same product from the same sources. Comparable with a routine repurchase in which nothing has changed, the **straight rebuy decision** is often the result of a long-term purchase agreement. Needs have been predetermined with the corresponding specifications, pricing, and shipping requirements already es-tablished by a blanket purchase order or annual purchase agreement. Ordering is automatic and often computerized by using electronic data interchange (EDI) and e-commerce (Internet, Intranet, and Extinet). Mitsubishi Motor Manufacturing of America uses a large number of straight rebuy decisions in its acquisition of com-ponent parts. Beginning as a primary supplier of automotive glass components, Vuteq has developed a strong relationship with Mitsubishi Motor Manufacturing of America over a period of several years. As a result, Vuteq's business has steadily in-creased and now includes door trim, fuel tanks, and mirrors in addition to window glass. These components are purchased as straight rebuys by using EDI, allowing Vuteq to deliver these components to Mitsubishi on a minute-to-minute basis, matching ongoing production.

Buyers allocate little, if any, time and resources to this form of purchase deci-sion. The primary emphasis is on receipt of the products and their continued

EXHIBIT 2.6	Three Types of Buying Decisions		
	Decision Type		
	Straight Rebuy	*Modified Rebuy*	*New Task*
Newness of Problem or Need	Low	Medium	High
Information Requirements	Minimal	Moderate	Maximum
Information Search	Minimal	Limited	Extensive
Consideration of New Alternatives	None	Limited	Extensive
Multiple Buying Influences	Very small	Moderate	Large
Financial Risks	Low	Moderate	High

satisfactory performance. With most of the purchasing process automated, straight rebuy decisions are little more than record keeping that is often handled by clerical staff in the purchasing office.

For the in-supplier (a current supplier), straight rebuys offer the advantage of reduced levels of potential competition. Rather than becoming complacent, however, in-salespeople must continually monitor the competitive environment for advances in product capabilities or changes in price structures. They should also follow up on deliveries and interact with users as well as decision makers to make sure that product and performance continue to receive strong and positive evaluations.

Straight rebuy decisions present a major challenge to the out-salesperson. Buyers are satisfied with the products and services from current suppliers and see no need to change. This is a classic case where the buyer perceives no difference or needs gap between their actual and desired state. Consequently, there is no active buying motive to which the out-salesperson can respond. In this case, out-salespeople are typically presented with two strategy choices: First, they can continue to make contact with the buyer so that when there is a change in the buying situation or if the current supplier makes a mistake, they are there to respond. Second, they can provide information and evidence relevant to either the desired or actual states so that the buyer will perceive a needs gap. For example, Vuteq's competitors will find it most difficult to gain this portion of Mitsubishi's business by offering similar or equal products and systems. However, a competitor might adopt future advances in technology that would enable them to offer significant added value over and beyond that being offered by Vuteq. Effectively communicating and demonstrating their advanced capabilities holds the potential for raising the desired state and thus producing a needs gap favoring their solution over Vuteq's existing sales offering.

New Tasks

The purchase decision characterized as a **new task decision** occurs when the buyer is purchasing a product or service for the first time. As illustrated in Figure 2.5, new task purchase decisions are located at the opposite end of the continuum from the straight rebuy and typify situations in which buyers have no experience or knowledge on which to rely. Consequently, they undertake an extensive purchase decision and search for information designed to identify and compare alternative solutions. Reflecting the extensive nature of this type of purchase decision, multiple members of the buying team are usually involved. As a result, the salesperson will be working with several different individuals rather than a single buyer. Mitsubishi buyers and suppliers were presented with new task decisions when the new Mitsubishi four-wheel drive sport utility vehicle was moving from design to production. Moving from their historical two-wheel drive to four-wheel drive powerlines and transmissions presented a variety of new needs and problems.

Relevant to a new task purchasing decision, there is no in- or out-supplier. Further, the buyer is aware of the existing needs gap. With no prior experience in dealing with this particular need, buyers are often eager for information and expertise that will assist them in effectively resolving the perceived needs gap. Selling strategies for new task decisions should include collaborating with the buyer in a number of ways: First, the salesperson can provide expertise in fully developing and understanding the need. The salesperson's extensive experience and base of knowledge is also valuable to the buyer in terms of specifying and evaluating potential solutions. Finally, top salespeople will assist the buyer in making a purchase decision and provide extensive follow-up to ensure long-term satisfaction. By implementing

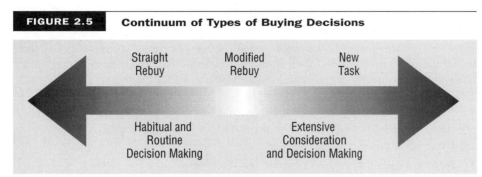

FIGURE 2.5   **Continuum of Types of Buying Decisions**

Straight Rebuy   Modified Rebuy   New Task

Habitual and Routine Decision Making   Extensive Consideration and Decision Making

Buying decisions range from Straight Rebuys (habitual decision making) to New Tasks (extensive decision making).

this type of a consultative strategy, the salesperson establishes a relationship with the buyer and gains considerable competitive advantage.

Modified Rebuys

Modified rebuy decisions occupy a middle position on the continuum between straight rebuys and new tasks. In these cases, the buyer has experience in purchasing the product in the past but is interested in acquiring additional information regarding alternative products and/or suppliers. As there is more familiarity with the decision, there is less uncertainty and perceived risk than for new task decisions. The modified rebuy typically occurs as the result of changing conditions or needs. Perhaps the buyer wishes to consider new suppliers for current purchase needs or new products offered by existing suppliers. Continuing the example of buyer-seller experiences at Mitsubishi, the company's recent decision to reexamine their methods and sources for training and education corresponds to the characteristics of a modified-rebuy decision. Since its beginning, Mitsubishi Motor Manufacturing of America has used a mix of company trainers, community colleges, and universities to provide education and training to employees. Desiring more coordination across its training programs, the company has requested proposals for the development and continued management of a corporate university from a variety of suppliers, including several current as well as new sources.

Often a buyer enters into a modified rebuy type of purchase decision to simply check the competitiveness of existing suppliers in terms of the product offering and pricing levels. Consequently, in-salespeople will emphasize how well their product has performed in resolving the needs gap. Out-salespeople will use strategies similar to those undertaken in the straight rebuy. These strategies are designed to alter the relative positions of the desired and actual state in a way that creates a perceived gap and influences buyers to rethink and reevaluate their current buying patterns and suppliers.

Multiple Buying Influences

A single individual typically makes routine purchase decisions such as straight rebuys and simpler modified rebuys. However, the more complex modified rebuy and new task purchase decisions often involve the joint decisions of multiple participants within a buying center or team. **Buying teams** (also referred to as **buying centers**) incorporate the expertise and multiple buying influences of people from different departments throughout the organization. As the object of the purchase decision changes, the makeup of the buying team may also change to maximize the relevant expertise of team members. The organization's size, as well as the nature and volume of the products being purchased, will influence the actual number and makeup of buying teams. The different members of a buying team will often have varied goals reflecting their individual needs and those of their different departments. Buying team members are described in terms of their roles and responsibilities within the team.[4]

- *Initiators*—**Initiators** are individuals within the organization who identify a need or perhaps realize that the acquisition of a product might solve a need or problem.

- *Influencers*—Individuals who guide the decision process by making recommendations and expressing preferences are referred to as **influencers.** These are often technical or engineering personnel.

- *Users*—**Users** are the individuals within the organization who will actually use the product being purchased. They evaluate a product on the basis of how it will affect their own job performance. Users often serve as initiators and influencers.

- *Deciders*—The ultimate responsibility for determining which product or service will be purchased rests with the role of **deciders.** Although buyers may also be deciders, it is not unusual for different people to fill these roles.

- *Purchasers*—**Purchasers** have responsibility for negotiating final terms of purchase with suppliers and executing the actual purchase or acquisition.

- *Gatekeepers*—Members who are in the position to control the flow of information to and between vendors and other buying center members are referred to as **gatekeepers.**

Although each of these influencer types will not necessarily be present on all buying teams, the use of buying teams incorporating some or all of these multiple influences has increased in recent years. One example of multiple buying influences is offered in the recent experience of an Executive Jet International salesperson selling a Gulfstream V corporate jet to a Chicago-based pharmaceutical company. Stretching over a period of six months, the salesperson worked with a variety of individuals serving different roles within the buying organization:

- **Initiator:** The initiator of the purchase process was the chief operating officer of the corporation who found that the recent corporate expansions had outgrown the effective service range of the organization's existing aircraft. Beyond pointing out the need and thus initiating the search, this individual would also be highly involved in the final choice based on her personal experiences and perceived needs of the company.

- **Influencers:** Two different employee groups acted as the primary influencers. First were the corporate pilots who contributed a readily available and extensive background of knowledge and experience with a variety of aircraft types. Also playing a key influencer role were members from the capital budgeting group in the finance department. Although concerned with documented performance capabilities, they also provided inputs and assessments of the different alternatives using their capital investment models.

- **Users:** The users provided some of the most dynamic inputs, as they were anxious to make the transition to a higher performance aircraft to enhance their own efficiency and performance in working at marketing/sales offices and plants that now stretched over the continents of North and South America. Primary players in this group included the vice presidents for marketing and for production/operations in addition to the corporate pilots who would be flying the plane.

- **Deciders:** Based on the contribution and inputs of each member of the buying team, the ultimate decision would be made by the chief executive officer. Primarily traveling by commercial carriers, her role as decider was based more on her position within the firm rather than her use of the chosen alternative. As the organization's highest operating officer, she was in a position to move freely among all members of the buying team and make the decision on overall merits rather than personal feelings or desires.

- **Purchaser:** Responsibility for making the actual purchase, negotiating the final terms, and completing all the required paperwork followed the typical lines of authority and was the responsibility of the corporate purchasing department with the director of purchasing actually assuming the immediate contact role. The purchasing office typically handles purchasing contracts and is staffed to draw up, complete, and file the related registrations and legal documents.

- **Gatekeepers:** This purchase decision actually involved two different gatekeepers within the customer organization: the executive assistant to the chief operating officer and an assistant purchasing officer. The positioning of these gatekeepers facilitated the salesperson's exchange of information and ability to keep in contact with the various members of the buying team. The COO's executive assistant moved easily among the various executives influencing the decision and was able to make appointments with the right people at the right times. However, the assistant purchasing officer was directly involved with the coordination of each member and bringing their various inputs into one summary document for the CEO. The salesperson's positive dealings and good relationships with each of the gatekeepers played a significant role in Executive Jet getting the sale.

A classic and all-too-common mistake among salespeople is to make repetitive calls on a purchasing manager over a period of several months only to discover that a buying team actually exists and that the ultimate decision will be made by someone other than the purchasing manager. Salespeople must gather information to discover who is in the buying team, their individual roles, and which members are the most influential. This information might be collected from account history files, people inside the salesperson's organization who are familiar with the account sources within the client organization, and even other salespeople. A salesperson should work with all members of the buying team and be careful to properly address their varied needs and objectives. Nevertheless, circumstances sometimes prevent a salesperson from working with all members of the team, and it is important that they reach those that are most influential.

Current Developments in Purchasing

Today's business organizations are undergoing profound change in response to ever-increasing competition and rapid changes in the business environment. The worldwide spread of technology has resulted in intense and increasingly global competition that is highly dynamic in nature. Accelerating rates of change have fragmented what were once mass markets into more micro and niche markets composed of more knowledgeable and demanding customers with ever-increasing expectations. In response, traditional purchasing practices are also rapidly changing.

Increasing Use of Information Technology

Buyers and sellers alike are increasingly using technology to enhance the effectiveness and efficiency of the purchasing process. Business-to-business e-commerce is growing at a rate exceeding 33 percent a year. By 2003, it is forecast that one-fourth of all business-to-business purchasing will be done online. Although EDI over private networks has been in use for some time, nearly all the growth between 1998 and 2003 will be Internet-based transactions.[5]

Information technology electronically links buyers and sellers for direct and immediate communication and transmission of information and data. Transactional exchanges such as straight rebuy decisions can now be automated with Internet- and World Wide Web-enabled programs tracking sales at the point of purchase and capturing the data for real-time inventory control and order placing. By cutting order and shipping times, overall cycle times are reduced, mistakes minimized, and working capital invested in inventories is made available for more productive applications. Further, the automation of these routine transactions allows buyers and salespeople to devote more time to new tasks, complex sales, and post-sale service and relationship-building activities. In addition to facilitating exchange transactions, applications integrating the Internet are also being used to distribute product and company information along with training courses and materials. Several companies have begun publishing their product catalogs online as a replacement for the reams of product brochures salespeople have traditionally had to carry with them. The online catalogs can be easily updated without the expense of obsolete brochures and can be selectively downloaded by salespeople to create customized presentations and proposals.

Relationship Emphasis on Cooperation and Collaboration

More than ever before, the business decisions made by one company directly affect decisions in other companies. Business in today's fast-paced and dynamic marketplace demands continuous and increased levels of interactivity between organizations. As illustrated in "An Ethical Dilemma," more and more buying organizations are adapting by emphasizing longer-term relationships with fewer suppliers to forge stronger and more enduring bonds with a select group of highly capable, trustworthy, and committed suppliers.[6]

An Ethical Dilemma

As a key account manager for Hirsch Production Controls, Jerry had developed a strong relationship with St. Louis-based Forrestor Manufacturing and the members of Forrestor's team of buyers. In place for several years now, this relationship has propelled Jerry into Hirsch Production's top salesperson and transformed Forrestor into Jerry's top customer, accounting for 20 percent of Jerry's annual sales. Working to increase his territory sales, Jerry had been calling on South Chicago-based Dorval Products for the previous seven months. Dorval manufactures a wide assortment of production equipment in plants spread throughout North America and Western Europe and is a direct competitor to Forrestor Manufacturing. Dorval selected Jerry as one of three vendors requested to develop and submit proposals related to a major plant renovation and expansion. While developing the proposal, Jerry had access to a great deal of proprietary information regarding Dorval's new production processes and business plans and had signed the typical confidentiality agreement obligating him to avoid disclosing any of Dorval's plans to any other parties. During his next visit to Forrestor Manufacturing, Clarke Hughley—director of purchasing for Forrestor—began asking Jerry questions about Dorval. It was apparent that Clarke was interested in learning anything he could about Dorval's plant expansion and business plans. All things considered, if you found yourself in Jerry's position, how would you handle the situation?

Rather than competing to win benefits at the expense of one another, leading organizations are discovering that it is possible for all parties to reduce their risk and increase the level of benefits each receives by sharing information and coordinating activities, resources, and capabilities.[7] These longer-term buyer-seller relationships are based on the mutual benefits received by and the interdependence between all parties in this value network. In addition to being keenly aware of changing customer needs, collaborative relationships require salespeople to work closely with buyers to foster honest and open two-way communication and develop the mutual understanding required to create the desired solutions. Further, salespeople must consistently demonstrate that they are dependable and acting in the buyer's best interests.

Supply Chain Management

Having realized that their success or failure is inextricably linked to other firms in the value network, many organizations are implementing **supply chain management** across an extended network of suppliers and customers. Beyond a buyer-seller relationship, supply chain management emphasizes the strategic coordination and integration of purchasing with other functions within the buying organization as well as external organizations including customers, customers' customers, suppliers, and suppliers' suppliers.[8] Salespeople must focus on coordinating their efforts with all parties in the network—end-users and suppliers alike—and effectively work to add value for all members of the network. As described in "Professional Selling in the 21st Century: Using Information Technology to Enhance Personal Selling Performance,"

PROFESSIONAL SELLING IN THE 21ST CENTURY

Using Information Technology to Enhance Personal Selling Performance
Jennifer De Marco, CDW Computer Centers, discusses the innovative use of information technology to enhance continuing customer purchase experiences and generate significant benefits for CDW and the company's customers.

Here at CDW we use the technologies that we sell and have been consistently recognized as an innovator for integrating information technology into a wide range of business practices. This last year, we ranked number 55 on the Information Week 500 and number 11 on FORTUNE's list of the top 100 companies to work for. Prestigious honors such as these evidence that we don't simply use technology for technology's sake. Rather, we use technology to automate our systems and translate the efficiencies into savings and increased levels of service for our customers. Our information technology systems allow customers to benefit from one-on-one relationships with highly trained, knowledgeable account managers; telephone and online purchasing; custom configurations; and lifetime phone and online technical support—benefits that are unmatched by any of our competitors. These benefits are further extended through our CDW@work system that provides personalized Extranet services to our business customers and gives them 24 × 7 access to the company 365 days a year. Customer-centered tehcnological innovations such as these provide high levels of added value for our customers and will continue to set us apart from the competition in the future.

CDW has effectively employed the innovative use of information technology to enhance continuing customer purchase experiences and generate significant benefits for CDW and the company's customers.

Increased Outsourcing

Broader business involvement and expanded integration between organizations is a natural evolution as buyers and suppliers become increasingly confident of the other's performance capabilities and commitment to the relationship. These expanded agreements often involve **outsourcing** to a supplier certain activities that were previously performed by the buying organization. These activities are necessary for the day-to-day functioning of the buying organization but are not within the organization's core or distinct competencies. Outsourcing these activities allows the organization to focus on what it does best. However, these activities are typically among those in which the supplying organization specializes or even excels. As a result of the outsourcing agreement, the relationship gains strength and is further extended in such a way that all parties benefit over the long term. Outsourcing agreements place increased emphasis on the role of the salesperson to provide continuing follow-up activities to ensure customer satisfaction and nurture the buyer-seller relationship. Changes in customer needs must be continually monitored and factored into the supplier's market offering and outsourcing activities.

Target Pricing

Using information gathered from researching the marketplace, buyers establish a **target price** for their final products. For example, buyers determine the selling price for a new printing press should be $320,000. Next, they divide the press into its subsystems and parts to estimate what each part is worth in relation to the overall price. Using such a system, buyers might conclude that the maximum price they could pay for a lead roller platen would be $125 and then use this information when working with potential suppliers. In working with targeted pricing requirements, salespeople find they have two fundamental options. They can meet the required cost level, which often entails cutting their prices, or they can work with the buyer to better understand and possibly influence minimum performance specifications. Certain restrictive specifications might be relaxed as a tradeoff for lower pricing. For example, a salesperson might negotiate longer lead times, fewer or less complex design features, or less technical support in exchange for lower prices. The latter option requires salespeople to have a high level of knowledge regarding their products, organizational capabilities, and customer applications and needs. Just as important is the ability to create feasible options and effectively communicate them to the buyer.

Increased Importance of Knowledge and Creativity

The increased interdependence between buyer and seller organizations hinges on the salesperson's capabilities to serve as a problem solver in a dynamic and fast-changing business environment. Buyers depend on the salesperson to provide unique and value-added solutions to their changing problems and needs. To shape such innovative solutions, salespeople must have broad-based and comprehensive knowledge readily available and the ability to use that knowledge in creative ways. This includes knowledge of one's own products and capabilities, as well as the products and capabilities of competitors. More important, the salesperson must possess a thorough understanding of product applications and the needs of the customer to work with the buyer in generating innovative solutions.

Summary

1. **Categorize primary types of buyers.** Buyers are classified according to their unique buying situations that influence their needs, motivations, and buying behavior. The most common categorization splits buyers into either consumer markets or business markets. Consumers purchase goods and services for their own use or consumption whereas members of the business market acquire goods and services to use them as inputs into manufacturing, for use in the course of doing business, or for resale. Business markets are further divided into firms, institutions, and governments.

2. **Discuss the distinguishing characteristics of business markets.** Business markets have numerous characteristics that distinguish them from consumer markets. Among the more common characteristics are consolidation, which has resulted in buyers being fewer in number but larger in size; demand that is derived from the sale of consumer goods; more volatile demand levels; professional buyers; multiple buying influences from a team of buyers; and increased interdependence and relationships between buyers and sellers;

3. **List the different steps in the business-to-business buying process.** There are eight sequential and interrelated phases that make up the business buyers' decision process. This process begins with (1) Recognition of the Problem or Need, (2) Determination of the Characteristics of the Item and the Quantity Needed, (3) Description of the Characteristics of the Item and Quantity Needed, (4) Search for and Qualification of Potential Sources, (5) Acquisition and Analysis of Proposals, (6) Evaluation of Proposals and Selection of Suppliers, (7) Selection of an Order Routine, and (8) Performance Feedback and Evaluation.

4. **Discuss the different types of buyer needs.** Organizing what might appear to be an endless and confusing mixture of different needs and problems into their common types helps salespeople better understand the nature of the buyer's needs along with their interrelationships. In turn, salespeople are better able to generate and demonstrate value-added solutions that address the different needs. The five general types of buyer needs are described as follows:

   Situational Needs—Needs that are related to, or possibly the result of, the buyers' specific environment, time, and place.
   Functional Needs—The need for a specific core task or function to be performed—the need for a sales offering to do what it is supposed to do.
   Social Needs—The need for acceptance from and association with others—a desire to belong to some reference group.
   Psychological Needs—The desire for feelings of assurance and risk reduction, as well as positive emotions and feelings such as success, joy, excitement, and stimulation.
   Knowledge Needs—The desire for personal development and need for information and knowledge to increase thought and understanding as to how and why things happen.

5. **Describe how buyers evaluate suppliers and alternative sales offerings by using the multiattribute model of evaluation.** Purchase decisions are based on the buyer's comparative evaluation of how well they perceive a supplier or product compares on the basis of specific characteristics that the buyer judges as being important. Using the multiattribute model, buyers establish the attributes they perceive as important and evaluate the degree to which each of the specified attributes is present (or how well each performs) in a proposed solution. Each evaluation is then multiplied by the attribute's relative level of importance to calculate a weighted average for each attribute. These weighted averages are then totaled to derive an overall score for each supplier or product being compared. The product or supplier having the highest score is favored for purchase.

6. **Explain the two-factor model that buyers use to evaluate the performance of sales offerings and develop satisfaction.** The two-factor model is a special type of

multiattribute model in which further analysis of the multiple characteristics results in two primary groupings of factors: functional attributes and psychological attributes. Functional attributes are the more tangible characteristics of a market offering whereas the psychological attributes are primarily composed of the interpersonal behaviors and activities between the buyer and seller. The psychological attributes have been repeatedly found to have higher levels of influence than functional attributes on customer satisfaction and repeat purchase.

7. **Explain the different types of purchasing decisions.** A buyer's level of experience relevant to a given purchasing situation is a primary determinant of the time and resources that the buyer will allocate to a purchasing decision and can be used to categorize buyer behavior into three types of purchasing decisions: straight rebuys, modified rebuys, and new tasks.

   Straight Rebuy. Comparable with a routine repurchase in which nothing has changed, the straight rebuy is often the result of past experience and satisfaction with buyers purchasing the same products from the same sources. Needs have been predetermined with specifications already established. Buyers allocate little, if any, time or resources to this form of purchase decision, and the primary emphasis is on continued satisfactory performance.
   Modified Rebuy. Modified rebuys occupy the middle ground between straight rebuys and new tasks. The buyer has some level of experience with the product but is interested in acquiring additional information regarding alternative products and/or suppliers. The modified rebuy typically occurs as the result of changing conditions or needs. Perhaps the buyer wishes to consider new suppliers for current purchase needs or new products offered by existing suppliers.
   New Task. New tasks decisions occur when a buyer is purchasing a product or service for the first time. With no experience or knowledge on which to rely, buyers undertake an extensive purchase decision and search for information designed to identify and compare alternative solutions. Reflecting the extensive nature of this type of purchase decision, multiple members of the buying center or group are usually involved. As a result, the salesperson often works with several different individuals rather than a single buyer.

8. **Explain the concept of buying teams and specify the different member roles.** In the more complex modified rebuy and new task purchasing situations, purchase decisions typically involve the joint decisions of multiple participants working together as a buying team. Team members bring the expertise and knowledge from different functional departments within the buying organization. Team members may also change as the purchase decision changes. Team members are described by their roles within the team: initiators, influencers, users, deciders, purchasers, and gatekeepers.

Understanding Professional Selling Terms

- Consumer markets
- Business markets
- Derived demand
- Acceleration principle
- Business buyers' purchase process
- Needs
- Actual states
- Desired states
- Needs gap
- Situational needs
- Functional needs
- Social needs
- Psychological needs
- Knowledge needs
- Requests for proposals (RFP)

- Multi-attribute model
- Competitive depositioning
- Two-factor model of evaluation
- Functional attributes
- Must-have attributes
- Psychological attributes
- Delighter attributes
- Straight rebuy decisions
- New task decisions
- Modified rebuy decisions
- Buying teams
- Buying centers
- Initiators
- Influencers
- Users

- Deciders
- Purchasers
- Gatekeepers

- Supply chain management
- Outsourcing
- Target price

Developing Professional Selling Knowledge

1. How might the following characteristic of business-to-business markets affect the relational selling activities of salespeople:
   - Larger, but fewer, buyers?
   - Derived demand?
   - Higher levels of demand fluctuation?
2. How do the three different types of purchasing decisions (straight rebuy, modified rebuy, new task) influence the time and effort a buyer might allocate to the different steps of the purchase decision process?
3. List and compare the probable functional, situational, psychological, social, and knowledge needs of (a) a large financial investment office and (b) a college student who are both looking to purchase a new computer printer.
4. How might a salesperson work with and assist a business buyer in each step of the buying process:
   - Recognition of the problem or need
   - Determination of the characteristics of the item and the quantity needed
   - Description of the characteristics of the item and the quantity needed
   - Search for and qualification of potential sources
   - Acquisition and analysis of proposals
   - Evaluation of proposals and selection of suppliers
   - Selection of an order routine
   - Performance feedback and evaluation
5. Explain the role of functional attributes and psychological attributes in the postpurchase determination of customer satisfaction.
6. How might salespeople use their knowledge of the multiattribute evaluation model to plan and deliver their sales presentation to a buyer?
7. What are the implications for a salesperson if, when making a sales call, they discover that there is no needs gap present? Illustrate your answer with an example.
8. Why has knowledge and the capability to creatively apply that knowledge in creating unique solutions become so important for today's salesperson in the business-to-business marketplace?
9. Under what buying circumstances is it more common to find the multiple buying influences of a buying team? Why?
10. What are the implications of buying teams for a salesperson selling complex production equipment to a manufacturer firm? Develop an example to further explain and illustrate your answer.

Building Professional Selling Skills

1. Respond to each of the following buying situations by describing what you would do as (a) an in-salesperson and (b) an out-salesperson.
   - *Straight Rebuy.* This is a buying situation in which the customer is basically reordering an item already in use. Little or nothing has changed in terms of product, price, delivery, the available sources of supply, or any other aspect. This is a low-risk situation involving little cognitive effort and requiring little information. The purchasing department or a clerical person is most often the key decision-maker and buyer.
     (a) What do you need to do as an in-salesperson to keep this business?
         Explain: _____
         _____
         _____
         _____

(b) What do you need to do as an out-salesperson to get your foot in the door and persuade this company to buy from you?
Explain: _____
_____
_____
_____

- *Modified Rebuy.* A buying situation in which the customer is already purchasing the item but some key aspect has changed. For example, there may be a proposed price change, a new competitive source of supply, a problem with delivery, a change in product specifications, or a newly available product or service. These are moderate-risk situations requiring greater effort and necessitating better information and information sources.

(a) What do you need to do as an in-salesperson to keep this business?
Explain: _____
_____
_____
_____

(b) What do you need to do as an out-salesperson to get your foot in the door and persuade this company to buy from you?
Explain: _____
_____
_____
_____

2. You are a salesperson for Accu-Press Corporation, a regional manufacturer of metal stamping tools used for the shaping (stamping) of small metal component parts. Accu-Press has just introduced a new line of tools featuring several breakthrough design features. The new equipment is faster and easier to use. Tests indicate that it can increase production by 15 percent over conventional tools while simultaneously reducing the rate of defective parts. You are calling on Federal Metal Stampings, a major supplier to the automotive industry, with the objective of selling them the new line of tools. Federal purchases their tools from two of your competitors, and you have been calling on the buyer at Federal for the past six months. In the past, the buyer has seen no need to switch sources and has ended each call by telling you that they are satisfied with their current suppliers.

   Describe how you might use the advanced capabilities of your new tool line to assist the buyer at Federal Metal Stampings to realize a needs gap and thus create an opportunity to sell them the new product.
_____
_____
_____
_____
_____
_____

3. Put yourself in the role of salesperson for National Computer Corporation. You are currently working to sell the College of Business at your university a large number of upgraded personal computers. These computers will be placed in staff and faculty offices for use with a variety of networking, word-processing, spreadsheet, and statistical analysis applications. The committee responsible for the purchase decision includes two faculty members and the director of purchasing for the university. Based on your work with these members of the buying team, you have compiled the following list of buyers' expectations of the salesperson and supplier organization:
   - Coordinate all aspects of the product/service mix to provide a total package.
   - Provide counseling to the customer based on in-depth knowledge of the product, the market, and the customers' needs.
   - Engage in problem solving with a high degree of proficiency so as to ensure satisfactory customer service over extended time periods.
   - Demonstrate high ethical standards and be honest in all communication.
   - Advocate the customer's best interests within the selling organization.
   - Be imaginative in meeting the buyers' needs.

- Be well prepared for sales calls.
- Demonstrate a high level of dependability.

From the perspective of this buying scenario:

(A) Explain what each of the above buyer expectations mean;
(B) Discuss the implications of each expectation and how it might influence your behavior;
(C) Give an example of how a salesperson might fulfill each buyer expectation.

1. Coordinate all aspects of the product/service mix to provide a total package.

_____
_____
_____
_____
_____

2. Provide counseling to the customer based on in-depth knowledge of the product, the market, and the customers' needs.

_____
_____
_____
_____
_____

3. Engage in problem solving with a high degree of proficiency so as to ensure satisfactory customer service over extended time periods.

_____
_____
_____
_____
_____

4. Demonstrate high ethical standards and be honest in all communication.

_____
_____
_____
_____
_____

5. Advocate the customer's best interests within the selling organization.

_____
_____
_____
_____
_____

6. Be imaginative in meeting the buyers' needs.

_____
_____
_____
_____
_____

7. Be well prepared for sales calls.

_____
_____
_____
_____
_____

8. Demonstrate a high level of dependability.

_____
_____
_____
_____
_____

Making Professional Selling Decisions

 CASE 2.1   *Candoo Computer Corporation*

Background

As a salesperson for Candoo Computer Corporation (CCC), you have just received a call from your regional manager regarding a program now under way at one of your key accounts, Farmland Companies. Farmland is a national insurance company with agency offices spread across the United States. The company is in the early stages of designing and specifying a computer system that will place a computer in each agency office. The system will allow each agency to develop, operate, and maintain its own customer database to provide better service to customers. In addition, by linking through the CCC mainframe, agencies, regional offices, and CCC headquarters will be networked for improved internal communications and access to the corporate database.

Current Situation

You have serviced this account for several years, and CCC equipment accounts for the biggest share of computers now in place at Farmland—some 35 to 40 percent of all units. As reflected in your share of this account's business, you and CCC have a good reputation and strong relationship with Farmland. In talking with Aimee Linn, your usual contact in the Farmland purchasing office, you have learned that this agency network system is the brainstorm and pet project of Mike Hughes, a very "hands-on" CEO. Consequently, the probability of the system becoming a reality is high. While faxing a complete set of hardware specs to you, Aimee has also let you know that, although Kerri Nicks, director of the Farmland MIS department, is actually heading up this project, the national agency sales director, Tim Long, is also very active in its design and requirement specification. His interest stems not only from wanting to make sure the system will do what is needed at the corporate, regional, and agency levels but also from the fact that he brainstormed and spearheaded a similar project two years ago that was never implemented. The previous effort did not have the blessing of Nicks in the MIS department, and it became a political football between the two departments. Each department wanted something different, and both sides accused the other of not knowing what it was doing. Primarily because the CEO has commanded that it will be done, both sides seem to be playing ball with each other this time.

Aimee did hint at one concern, however; although corporate is designing and specifying the system, each agency has to purchase its units out of its own funds. Although the agencies exclusively represent only Farmland Insurance products, each agency is owned by the general agent—not Farmland. Some of the agents are not convinced that the system is worth the projected price tag of $3,500 per system, and Farmland cannot force them to buy the systems.

As with other selling opportunities with Farmland, this has all the makings of a decision that will be made as a result of multiple inputs from an assortment of individuals across the company—a buying team of sorts. As the salesperson having primary responsibility for this account, how would you go about identifying the various members of the buying center? Using the worksheet provided, respond to the following activities:

Questions

1. Identify each member of the buying center and the role each participant plays, and estimate the amount of influence (low, medium, high, very high) each has on the final decision.
2. What are the major problems, needs, and expectations that you will need to address for each of these buying center members?

As you complete this assignment, remember that a single individual can perform multiple roles in the center. Furthermore, it is common to find more than one individual playing the same buying center role.

Worksheet for Identifying Buying Team Members and Roles			
Buying Team Role	Team Member Playing This Role	Level of Influence	Team Member's Perceived Needs and Expectations
Initiators			
Users			
Influencers			
Purchasers			
Deciders			
Gatekeepers			

CASE 2.2   *American Seating Company*

Background

You are a salesperson for the American Seating Company (ASC) working with the Seattle Metropolitan Auditorium Authority to replace the seating as part of a major rejuvenation of the auditorium. The remodeling project is being done in response to several private theaters and two universities' entertainment centers that had begun to take major show bookings from the auditorium.

Current Situation

The buyers want the new auditorium seating to be as comfortable as possible and have specified units complete with arms and hinged seats/backs that allow the user to sit upright or slightly recline by leaning back 4 inches. The specifications also specify heavy frames, hardware, and linkage assemblies to yield an expected usable life of 10 years before requiring any form of service or replacement. However, these specifications increased the cost of the chairs by 13 percent. As a result, the buyers are now wanting a lower grade vinyl fabric in hopes of making up for some of the increased hardware costs.

With your expertise of chairs and fabrics, you have recommended the use of higher-grade nylon velvet rather than vinyl. The velvet will not only be much more comfortable but also more durable than the vinyl. Although both fabrics are equally moisture and stain resistant, the velvet comes with a guaranteed usable life of 10 years compared with the vinyl's six-year guarantee.

Question

Use the multi-attribute model of evaluation to develop a strategy for reselling the better-grade fabric as the best choice for the new auditorium seating.

Building Trust

Relationship Building at Darden Accounting

Steve Brady, vice president of T. R. Darden accounting firm, was looking to grow his company's business in the construction industry. His team had identified a large builder (Shear Construction) in the Indianapolis area as a good fit for their services. No one on Steve's team had done business with Shear, and only one member of his team had any connection with Shear's people (i.e., one of Steve's team members belonged to the same country club as Eric Shear, president).

Steve set out a strategy to develop relationships with the Shear people over a six-month period. The initial contact would be to introduce Darden to Shear Construction through their CFO, Tucker Tanley, and invite him to an upcoming seminar. Tucker had attended past Darden seminars and seemed open to a meeting. Steve had his people meet once or twice a month strategizing the Shear account.

After the seminar, the next two months were spent meeting with key players at Shear (i.e., president, accounting department, CEO). Each member of Steve's team was assigned a person and asked to develop the relationship. The member of the country club arranged a round of golf with the president of both companies. A Colts football outing was planned as well as a Pacer basketball game. The accounting department was courted as well as Tucker. It was not until the end of the third month that a thorough needs assessment was started. The first three months were strictly getting to know Shear. Several interesting things were uncovered during the first few months. First, Tucker stated that he thought that their present accounting firm was taking them for granted. New faces were coming and going, and he was not sure who was even in charge of their account. The accounting department was unhappy because they were supposed to get a copy of their completed tax forms for review 10 days before they were due. The day they were to be signed and sent in was the first they were able to see them. A mistake was found, and an extension had to be requested. Mr. Shear told Darden's president, Tom Preston, the time was probably right to look for another agency.

Late in the year, Shear agreed to a full presentation. Steve and his team thought that they understood Shear's needs and had a good relationship with all the key players. During the presentation, Steve introduced the team that would handle Shear's account. Steve would lead the team, along with an experienced group in whom Steve had a great deal of confidence. Steve made it clear that he was only a phone call away if anyone at Shear needed anything from Darden. Another part of their proposal included a date that Shear would receive their completed tax forms each year, two weeks before they were due. This was backed with a penalty that Darden would pay if they missed this deadline. Soon after the presentation, they

Learning Objectives

After completing this module, you should be able to

1 Discuss the distinguishing characteristics of trust-based selling.

2 Explain the importance of trust.

3 Discuss how to earn trust.

4 Explain how knowledge bases help build trust and relationships.

5 Understand the importance of sales ethics.

6 Discuss three important areas of unethical behavior.

received the order, and Darden was commended on their approach. Darden was also told that their competitors sold first and asked questions later. Shear's people felt very comfortable with Steve and his team. Tucker stated they were impressed that all the promises that were made by Darden came true. He also thought that Darden demonstrated that they really knew Shear's business. They were certain this was the start of a great relationship.

Source: Interview with Steve Brady, Darden Accounting, August 28, 1998.

trust reflects the extent of the buyer's confidence that it can rely on the salesperson's integrity. That being said, it is important to note that trust means different things to different people. According to John Newman[1], vice president of Integrated Supply Chains Segment at A. T. Kearney, trust is defined in many ways. Buyers define trust with such terms as **openness, dependability, candor, honesty, confidentiality, security, reliability, fairness,** and **predictability,** as well as other things. For example, in the Kearney study, one manufacturer related trust to credibility and said, "What trust boils down to, in a nutshell, is credibility, and when you say you are going to do something, you do it, and the whole organization has to be behind that decision." Another manufacturer related trust to confidentiality in that "they were afraid that the sales guys were going around and telling account B what account A is doing" and identified this as a violation of trust. Another company related trust to openness in that "we have to share information that traditionally is not shared." One president told how his engineers were sharing manufacturing secrets with their suppliers that would have cost the engineers their jobs if they had held the discussion prior to the past five years.[2]

A salesperson has to determine what trust means to each of his or her buyers, as shown in Figure 3.1. If it is confidentiality, then the salesperson must demonstrate how his or her company handles sensitive information. If credibility is the concern, then the salesperson must demonstrate over time that all promises will be kept. Therefore, trust is whatever it means to the buyer, and it is the salesperson's job through questioning to determine what trust attributes are critical to relationship building for a specific buyer.

FIGURE 3.1   Trust Builders

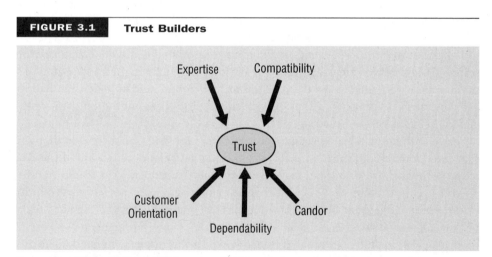

Trust means different things to different people. Trust can be developed by using any of the trust builders. It is the salesperson's job through questioning to determine what trust attributes are critical to relationship building for a specific buyer.

In this module, we first discuss the meaning of trust in the sales context. Next we explore the importance of trust to salespeople. This is followed by a discussion of how to earn trust and what knowledge bases a salesperson can use to build trust in buyer-seller relationships. Finally, the importance of sales ethics in building trust is reviewed.

What Is Trust?

"The essence of trust is that the industrial buyer believes that he can rely on what the salesperson says or promises to do in a situation where the buyer is dependent upon the salesperson's honesty and reliability."[3] One of the keys to a long-term relationship with any client is to create a basis of trust between the sales representative and the client organization.[4]

Thus, gaining credibility in the trust area is imperative to be seen as a reliable salesperson. Long-term sales success in any industry will generally be built on the concept of referral, and trust plays an important role. Clients obviously seek a salesperson they can trust. The problem is, depending on the industry and the situation, they may have had bad experiences that have lowered their hopes of ever finding a trustworthy partner. "An Ethical Dilemma" demonstrates how easy it is for a salesperson to lose the trust of a buyer (even when it is an innocent misunderstanding). Consultative salespeople are in a unique position to capitalize on building credibility with customers who place a high value on trust. Because customers are looking for a trustworthy partner with whom to do business but may have difficulty trusting most salespeople, this equates to an opportunity for the salesperson.

An Ethical Dilemma

Bob Sharpe, account manager for a large computer firm, had been calling on the purchasing manager of an electronics company for more than six months. He thought that the purchasing agent was receptive, but he was not sure the purchasing manager was passing his literature and proposals on to the data processing manager. He had asked several times whether he could approach the data processing manager and the purchasing manager had turned him down, stating company policy. Several weeks later while attending a party, he met one of the data processing managers and they talked about their respective jobs. The data processing manager invited Bob to take a look at their operation, and he did. A few days later, he had a message from the purchasing manager not to call on his company anymore. Did Bob Sharpe do anything wrong? How would you have handled the invitation?

The "trust" described here is beyond the typical transaction-oriented trust schema. Issues—such as, Will the product arrive as promised? Will the right product actually be in stock and be shipped on time? Will the invoice contain the agreed-on price? Can the salesperson be found if something goes wrong?—are only initial concerns. In relationship selling, trust is based on a larger set of factors due to the expanded intimacy and longer-term nature of the relationship. The intimacy of this relationship will result in the sharing of information by both parties that could be damaging should either side leak it or use it against the partner.

Trust answers the questions:

1.   Do you know what you are talking about? — competence; expertise

2. Will you recommend what is best for me? — customer orientation

3. Are you truthful? — honesty; candor

4. Can you and your company back up your promises? — dependability

5. Will you safeguard confidential information that I share with you? — customer orientation, dependability

"Trust" is an integral part of the relationship between customers and suppliers and results in increased long-term revenues and profits.[5]

Why Is Trust Important?

In today's increasingly competitive marketplace, buyers typically find themselves inundated with choices regarding both products and suppliers. In this virtual buyers' market, traditional selling methods that focused on closing the sale have been found to be inefficient and often counterproductive to the organization's larger, longer-term marketing strategy. In this new competitive environment, buyers are demanding unique solutions to their problems—product solutions that are customized on the basis of their particular problems and needs. Additionally, the adversarial, win-lose characteristics so customary in traditional selling are fading fast. In their place, longer-term buyer-seller relationships are evolving as the preferred form of doing business. Although buyers are finding it more effective and efficient to do *more* business with *fewer* suppliers, sellers are finding it more effective to develop a continuing stream of business from the right customers.

This shift toward relationship selling has altered both the roles played by salespeople and the activities and skills they exercise in carrying out these roles—the selling process itself. Today's more contemporary selling process is embedded within the relationship marketing paradigm. As such, it emphasizes the initiation and nurturing of long-term buyer-seller relationships based on mutual trust and value-added benefits. The level of problem-solving activity common to relationship selling requires deliberate and purposeful collaboration between both parities. These joint efforts are directed at creating unique solutions based on an enhanced knowledge and understanding of the customer's needs and the supplier's capabilities so that both parties derive mutual benefits. The nature of this integrative, win-win, and collaborative negotiation relies on augmented communication and interpersonal skills that nurture and sustain the reciprocal trust that allows all parties to fully share information and work together as a strategic problem-solving team.

The skills and activities inherent to relationship selling can be classified according to their purpose as (1) initiation of the relationship (Module 7); (2) development of the relationship (Module 8); and (3) enhancement of the relationship (Module 9). As the activities comprising the selling process have changed, so too have the relative importance and degree of selling effort devoted to each stage of the process.

How to Earn Trust

Trust is critically important to any relationship. Several variables are critical in helping salespeople earn a buyer's trust, such as expertise, dependability, candor, customer orientation, and compatibility. Each is briefly discussed as to its importance.

Expertise

Inexperience is a difficult thing for a young salesperson to overcome. Most recent college graduates will not have the **expertise** to be immediately successful, especially in industrial sales. Companies spend billions of dollars to train new recruits in the hope of speeding up the expertise variable. Training to gain knowledge on company products and programs, industry, competition, and general market conditions are typical subjects covered in most sales training programs. Young salespeople can shadow more experienced salespeople to learn what it takes to be successful. They must also go the extra yard to prove to their customers their dedication to service. For example, Missy Rust, of Glaxo Welcome, had recently spent a few minutes with an anesthesiologist discussing a new product, a neuromuscular blocker. A few days later, the physician called her at 1 A.M. to discuss a patient who he thought was a good candidate for this drug. He was unsure of the correct dosage and needed Missy's expertise in this matter. Missy immediately drove to the hospital and was in the operating room for more than four hours observing the surgery and answering the doctor's questions about this new drug.[6]

Another factor to consider is that many organizations have recently been downsized, thus dramatically cutting the purchasing area in terms of both personnel and support resources. As a result, buyers are having to do more with less and, as such, are thirsty for expertise, be it current insights into their own operations, financial situation, industry trends, or tactical skills in effectively identifying emerging cost cutting and revenue opportunities in their business. Of course, expertise will be even more critical with certain buyers who are technical, detail-driven, and/or just uninformed in a certain area.

Salespeople should be striving to help their clients meet their goals. As an example, individuals or business owners can go online and trade stocks for themselves, but if they think someone else (e.g., financial planner, securities company) is more knowledgeable and brings more expertise to the table, then they will use them.

Today's buyers will respond positively to any attempts to assist them in their efforts to reach bottom-line objectives, be it revenue growth, profitability, or financial or strategic objectives. Thus, "expertise" will take on an even more important role in the customer's assessment of the seller's credibility. For some buyers, especially those with economic or financial responsibilities (e.g., CFO, treasurer, owner-manager), a representative's ability to "contribute" to the bottom line will dominate the perception of a seller's credibility. This is a very important consideration for salespeople, given their pivotal strategy of penetrating accounts at the economic buyer level. Salespeople are seeking to convince clients that they are (1) actively dedicated to the task of positively influencing their bottom-line objectives, and (2) capable of providing assistance, counsel, and advice that will positively affect the ability to reach objectives.[7] This is easier said than done because salespeople frequently do not understand the long-term financial objectives of their client.[8]

Buyers today want recommendations and solutions, not just options. Salespeople must be prepared to help their clients meet their goals by adding value.

Buyers are continually asking themselves: Does the salesperson have the ability, knowledge, and resources to meet his or her prospective customers' expectations? Not only are salespeople selling their knowledge but the entire organization and the support that they bring to the buyer. Does the salesperson display a technical command of products and applications (i.e., is he or she accurate, complete, objective)? During one sales call, a buyer asked about a specific new product that the company was promoting in its advertising. The salesperson responded that the product was launched before he was trained on it. This not only cast doubts on the salesperson's ability but also on the company for failing to train the salesperson.

Expertise also deals with the salesperson's skill, knowledge, time, and resources to do what is promised and what the buyer wants. Small customers must think that they are being treated as well as larger customers and have access to the same resources.

Salespeople must exhibit knowledge generally exceeding that of their customer, not just in terms of the products and services they are selling but in terms of the full scope of the customer's financial and business operations (e.g., products, programs, competitors, customers, vendors). They must bring skills to the table, be it discovery, problem solving, program and systems development, financial management, or planning. These skills must complement those of the customer and offer insight into the best practices in the customer's industry. It is not enough to be an expert. This expertise must translate into observable results and **contributions** for the buyer.

Dependability

Dependability centers on the predictability of the salesperson's actions. Buyers have been heard to say, "I can always depend on her. She always does what she says she is going to do." Salespeople must remember what promises they make to a customer or prospect. Once a promise is made, the buyer expects that promise to be honored. The buyer should not have to call the salesperson to remind them of their promise. The salesperson should take notes during all sales calls for later review. It is harder to forget to do something if it is written down. A salesperson is trying to establish that his or her actions fit a pattern of prior dependable behavior. That is, the salesperson refuses to promise what he or she cannot deliver. The salesperson must also demonstrate an ability to handle confidential information. Buyers and sellers are depending on each other to guard secrets carefully and keep confidential information confidential! "An Ethical Dilemma" demonstrates the importance of trust and the issue of confidentiality.

An Ethical Dilemma

Tom Acres was a sales rep for a large pharmaceutical company. He had been calling on a number of physician offices in the Atlanta area. He had made a number of friendships within these offices. He had even been allowed to observe a number of surgeries as a guest of these physicians. Tom often boasted to his friends that he had seen famous Atlanta athletes and politicians undergo surgery. One night, Tom received a call from a local reporter and was questioned on the seriousness of an athlete's injury. The next day, there was a quote from Tom in the Atlanta Constitution *that he had observed the athlete's surgery and did not think the injury was too serious. The next week Tom received a very cool reception at the physician's office. None of the physicians would see him. What areas of trust may Tom have violated? Why did he get the cool reception?*

Candor

Candor deals with the honesty of the spoken word. One sales manager was overheard telling his salesforce "whatever it takes to get the order." One of the salespeople replied, "Are you telling us to stretch the truth if it helps us get the order?" The manager replied, "Of course!" The trustworthy salesperson understands doing "anything to get an order" will ultimately damage the buyer-seller relationship.

Salespeople have more than words to win over the support of the buyer; they have other sales aids such as testimonials, third-party endorsements, trade publications, and consumer reports. The salesperson must be just as careful to guarantee that the proof is credible. It takes only one misleading (even slightly) event to lose all credibility.

Customer Orientation

Customer orientation means placing as much emphasis on the customer's interests as your own. An important facet of customer orientation is that salespeople work to satisfy the long-term needs of their customers rather than their own short-term goals.

A salesperson who has a customer orientation gives fair and balanced presentations. This includes covering both the pros and cons of the recommended product. The pharmaceutical industry has done a good job understanding this principle, as many firms require their salespeople to describe at least one side effect of their drug for each benefit given. This is done not only because of the legal consideration but also to demonstrate to the physician expertise and trustworthiness. Traditional salespeople often ignored negative aspects of a product, which can turn off many buyers. A customer orientation should also include clear statements of benefits and not overpower the buyer with information overload.

Salespeople with a customer orientation really turn into advisors; that is, they advise rather than "sell." It is critical not to push a product that the buyer does not need to meet a short-term goal. Kim Davenport of Shering-Plough (see "Professional Selling in the 21st Century: In Sync with Your Customers") states, "It is critically important to have a customer orientation. The ultimate goal of any relationship is to transform the personal relationship into a business relationship."

Salespeople must truly care about the partnership, and they must be willing to "go to bat" for the client when the need arises. A warehouse fire left one company without any space to store inventory. The salesperson worked out same-day delivery until the warehouse was rebuilt. This left a lasting impression on the buyer. They knew that if they ever needed any help, their salesperson would come through for them.

Salespeople must be fully committed to representing the customer's interests. Although most salespeople are quick to "talk the talk" about their absolute allegiance

---

PROFESSIONAL SELLING IN THE 21ST CENTURY

In Sync with Your Customers
Kim Davenport, district manager with Shering-Plough Pharmaceutical Company, discusses his philosophy in building relationships. It is critically important that his field reps have the ability to build new relationships, manage relationships, and transform relationships into long-term partnerships. His salespeople call on physicians, hospitals, and pharmacies with the ultimate goal of not only building long-term relationships but also increasing the sales in each of their territories.

At times, all my salespeople are uncomfortable about forming a new relationship with a physician. Salespeople who are reluctant to meet new physicians will never reach their full potential. To achieve a high level of success, salespeople have to manage a multitude of different relationships. Some relationships will be static, some will grow, and some will break down. It is up to the salesperson to set relationship priorities and to decide which relationship to advance and which relationship to put on hold. Some physicians may never allow the relationship to grow. It is each of my salespeople's jobs to transform the relationship from the personal level to the business level. My salespeople avoid advancing the sale for two major reasons: (1) They are stuck in the comfort zone, and (2) they fear rejection. My salespeople cannot be afraid to ask their physicians to write our products. Just chit-chatting with a physician about small talk all the time does not get it done.

to their customers' interests, when it comes to "walking the walk" for their customer on such issues as pricing, production flexibility, and design changes, many lack the commitment and/or skills necessary to support the interests of their clients.

To be an effective salesperson and gain access to a customer's business at a partnership level, the client must feel comfortable with the idea that the salesperson is motivated and capable of representing his or her interests. Exhibit 3.1 overviews some of the questions salespeople need to answer satisfactorily to gain the buyer's trust and confidence.

Compatibility/Likeability

Customers generally like to deal with sales representatives whom they know, they like, and they can feel a bond with. Doug Lingo of Hoechst Marion Roussel Pharmaceutical states that his best friends are his physicians. He goes to Indiana University and Indiana Pacer basketball games with them, he has gone camping with the physicians and their families, and he even had a family vacation shared with one of his physicians. He goes on to state that "compatibility" is critical to his success as a salesperson.[9]

Some salespeople are too quick to minimize the importance of rapport building in this era of the economic buyer. It also may be true that today's buyers are not as prone to spend time discussing personal issues in sales calls as they might have been 10 or 15 years ago. Salespeople today have to be more creative and resourceful when attempting to build rapport. It is not unusual for a pharmaceutical salesperson to take a lunch for the entire staff into a physician's office. These lunches can be for as many as 20–40 persons. The salesperson now has time to discuss his or her products over lunch to a captive audience.

Salespeople have to be aware that their buyers are under considerable time pressure and that some will find it difficult to dedicate time to issues outside of the business. However, remember that buyers are human and do value compatibility, some more, some less.

Compatibility and **likeability** are important to establishing a relationship with key gatekeepers (e.g., receptionists and secretaries). First impressions are important, and a salesperson's ability to find commonalties with these individuals can go a long way in building much-needed allies within the buying organization. Likeability is admittedly an emotional factor that is difficult to pin down, yet a powerful force in some buyer-seller relationships.

If a salesperson has done a good job of demonstrating the other trust-building characteristics, then compatibility can be used to enhance trust building. Buyers do not necessarily trust everyone they like, but on the other hand, it is difficult to trust someone they do not like.

EXHIBIT 3.1	Questions That Salespeople Need to Satisfactorily Answer to Gain a Buyer's Trust

Expertise: Does the salesperson know what they need to know? Does the salesperson and their company have the ability and resources to get the job done right?

Dependability: Can I rely on the salesperson? Does the salesperson keep promises?

Candor: Is the salesperson honest in their spoken word? Is the salesperson's presentation fair and balanced?

Customer Orientation: Does the salesperson truly care about the partnership? Will the salesperson go to bat for the customer? (i.e., wrong order, late delivery)

Compatibility: Will the buyer like doing business with the salesperson? Will the buyer like doing business with the salesperson's company?

Knowledge Bases Help Build Trust and Relationships

The more the salesperson knows, the easier it is to build trust and gain the confidence of the buyer. Buyers have certain expectations of the salesperson and the knowledge that he or she brings to the table. As outlined in Figure 3.2, salespeople may draw from several knowledge bases. Most knowledge is gained from the sales training program and on-the-job training.

Sales training will generally concentrate on knowledge of the industry and company history, company policies, products, promotion, prices, market knowledge of customers, **competitor knowledge,** and basic selling techniques. Exhibit 3.2 summarizes topics generally covered during initial sales training programs.

Industry and Company Knowledge

Every industry and company has a history. The personal computer industry has a short history of 20 years, fax technology even shorter. Other industries have been around for centuries. Some industries change so quickly, such as the pharmaceutical industry through multiple mergers, that it is critical for the salesperson to know their industry to keep physicians informed on new companies, drugs, and procedures. Many buyers are too busy to stay informed and count on their salespeople to help them make sound decisions.

Salespeople should be familiar with their own company's operation and policies. Buyers may ask the salesperson questions such as: How long has their company been in the market? How many people does the company employ? Does the company have a local, regional, national, or international customer base? Who started the company? Who is the president? CEO? What is their market share? What is their market share on this particular product? Salespeople who could not answer such questions would not inspire the trust of the buyer.

Each company initiates policies to ensure consistent decisions are made throughout the organization. An organization implements policies to control factors such as price, guarantees, warranties, and how much money can be spent per week taking clients out to lunch. Knowing the company's policies prevents misunderstanding.

FIGURE 3.2	Knowledge Bases

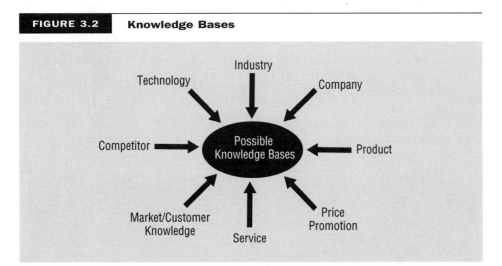

The more the salesperson knows, the easier it is to build trust and gain the confidence of the buyer. Buyers have certain expectations of the salesperson and the knowledge that he or she brings to the table. Most knowledge is gained from the sales training programs and on-the-job training.

For example, if a representative says yes to a customer's request to return goods 60 days after receipt when company policy is 30 days, the shipping department might refuse to accept the returned merchandise. The salesperson looks incompetent to both sales management and the customer. If the customer is not allowed to return the goods to the factory, the angry customers probably will never buy from the salesperson again.

Salespeople must understand their company policies. This includes being familiar with the company's formal structure and key personnel. It is important to work as a team with all company personnel. This helps build team spirit and a willingness to cooperate when a salesperson needs help in meeting a customer's need. It is difficult to provide outstanding service when the sales department is not on good terms with shipping and delivery, for instance.

Product Knowledge

Product knowledge includes detailed information on the manufacture of a product and knowing whether the company has up-to-date production methods. What materials are used when making the products? What quality control procedures are involved? Who are the design engineers?

Salespeople representing their company are expected to be experts on the products they sell. The fastest way to win the respect of a buyer is to be perceived as being an expert. If the buyer truly feels the salesperson knows what he or she is talking about, then the buyer will be more willing to discuss the salesperson's solution to the buyer's problems or opportunities.

EXHIBIT 3.2	**Topics Generally Covered during Initial Sales Training Programs**

- Industry history
- Company history and policies
- Product
  - promotion
  - price
- Market
  - line of business *(know your customer)*
  - manufacturing
  - wholesaling
  - financial
  - government
  - medical, etc.
- Competitive knowledge
- Selling techniques
- Initiating customer relationship
  - prospecting
  - precall
  - approaching the customer
- Developing customer relationships
  - sales presentation delivery
  - handling sales resistance
- Enhancing customer relationships
  - follow-up
  - customer service

The salesperson must know what his or her product can and cannot do. Just knowing product features is insufficient.

Service

> **The effective salesperson must be ready to address service issues such as:**
>
> *Does the company service its products or does the company send them to a third party?*
>
> *Does the company service its products locally or send them off to another state for service?*
>
> *Does the price include service or will there be a service charge when service is needed?*
>
> *What does the service agreement include? Shipping? Labor? Or none of these.*
>
> *How long does the service generally take? Same day? Within a week? Will a loaner be provided until the product is fixed?*
>
> *Are there any conditions that make service not available? After five years? Damage from flood? fire?*

Buyers need to be comfortable with answers to these questions, and a good salesperson will make sure they are answered appropriately.

Darrell Beaty from Ontario Systems in Muncie, Indiana, spends quite a bit of time discussing service with each of his prospects.[10] His company sells collection software (i.e., receivables) that requires support from his field engineers. Ontario Systems also has an 800 support group that takes calls 24 hours a day, seven days a week. Why is this important to Darrell? One of his major competitors also has 800 support, but only 8–5, Monday through Friday. Darrell knows that he has service superiority. Salespeople who can offer the better service have an advantage for generating new business and taking away business from the competition. The salesperson's service mission is to provide added value for the customer. It is important for the salesperson to understand what service dimensions are a concern to the buyer.

For instance, delivery, installation, training, field maintenance, and investing are all issues that a salesperson may be prepared to talk about. Buyers, however, may only be concerned with inventory because their present supplier runs out of stock frequently.

Exhibit 3.3 reviews service dimensions in which a salesperson could demonstrate service superiority. Additions may be made depending on specific customer demands.

Promotion and Price

Promotion and **price knowledge** are other knowledge tools that the salesperson must understand. The ability to use this knowledge often makes the difference between a well-informed buyer who is ready to make a decision and another buyer who is reluctant to move the sales process forward. Hershey Chocolate, USA, supports its retailers with heavy promotions during Halloween, Christmas, and Easter. The promotional programs must be explained properly so the buyer can place the correct order size during the promotion. How many dollars are to be spent? Is it a national program? Is this a co-op program? What will it cost the buyer? If these questions are answered properly, the buyer will be more at ease and ready to make a purchase.

Price can be another area that makes a buyer hesitant if not properly explained. Knowledge of pricing policies is important because the salesperson often

EXHIBIT 3.3	Service Superiority

Dimension	*Potential Superiority*
1. Delivery	Can our company demonstrate speed? Deliver more often?
2. Inventory	Can we meet the demands of our customers at all times?
3. Training	Do we offer training? At our site? At our customers?
4. Field Maintenance	Do we go the field to fix our products? Do our customers have to bring their equipment to us to fix?
5. Credit and Financial Consideration	Do we grant credit? Do we help finance?
6. Installation	Do we send a team to your site for start-up?
7. Guarantees and Warranties	What are our guarantees? How long? What do we cover?
8. Others	Do we offer anything unique that our competition does not?

is responsible for quoting price and offering discounts. As a representative of the selling firm, these quotes legally bind a company to their completion.

Salespeople need complete understanding of their companies' pricing policies. Does the company sell its products for a set price or can the salesperson negotiate? Can the salesperson give additional discounts to get a potential client who the company has been after for years? Does the company allow trade-ins?

Market and Customer Knowledge

Market and customer knowledge is critical to the success of today's salesperson. Some companies today, because of their size, send their salesforce out to call on all customer types. Larger companies typically break their customers into distinct markets. Computer manufacturers may break out their customer types by markets (i.e., salespeople sell to a particular line of business). For instance, the salesperson may only sell to manufacturers, wholesalers, financial institutions, government, education, or medical companies. This allows the salesperson to become an expert in a line of business. For a salesperson to be effective, the salesperson must learn what the client needs, what benefits the client is seeking, and how the salesperson's products satisfy the buyers' specific needs. Buyers are not interested in factual knowledge unless it relates to fulfilling their specific needs. Having the salesforce learn one line of business well allows the salesperson to concentrate on the needs of a specific market. The salesperson can become an expert in one line of business more quickly than if he or she had to know how the entire marketplace used the salesperson's products.

Information about customers is gathered over time and from very different sources. A salesperson can use trade associations, credit agencies, trade magazines, trade directories, newspapers, and the World Wide Web as valuable resources. The AT&T Toll-free Internet Directory has directories on people, business, and Web sites. Using the Web to do an initial search on a company can tell a salesperson about what products a company makes, what markets they serve, and so on. A salesperson must use his or her time wisely when gathering information. John Haack, senior vice president of sales and marketing for Ball-Foster Glass Container Corporation, discusses the importance of team selling and getting to know the customer in "Professional Selling in the 21st Century: The Importance of Team Selling."

Competitor Knowledge

Salespeople will probably be asked how their product stands up against the competition. The buyer may ask, Who are your competitors in our marketplace? How big are you compared with your competitors? How does your company's prices compare with others in your industry? How does your product quality compare with the industry norm? These are important questions that every salesperson must be prepared to answer. Salespeople must have knowledge of their competitor's strengths and weaknesses to better understand their own products' position when comparing. A good salesperson must adjust his or her selling strategy depending on whom he or she is selling against.

Salespeople must be able to deliver complete comparative product information in a sales presentation. Comparisons of competitors' products for a customer's decision are critical especially when your features and benefits are superior to the competitors'.

It is important that salespeople distinguish their products from the competition. The ultimate question a buyer asks is, Why should I use your product over the one I am presently using? A salesperson must have competitive knowledge to answer this question. What are the competitor's relative strengths and weaknesses?

PROFESSIONAL SELLING IN THE 21ST CENTURY

The Importance of Team Selling

John Haack, vice president of sales and marketing, Ball-Foster Glass Container Corporation, states his views on the importance of team selling.

A very large portion of our business is composed of significant, long-term contracts with other large companies. As our customers have narrowed their supplier base, the choice of a glass packaging supplier has taken on increasing importance both for the customer and for Ball-Foster. As this has happened, we have clearly moved from relationships between individuals to relationships between whole organizations. Ideally, we prefer to have cross-functional groups from a potential customer visit and meet their counterparts in our organization, including its character, capabilities, and commitment. The most basic requirement for selling is to have an attractive product. Because we feel we are very effective in our business, we prefer to have customers visit us extensively. We know that this is the best way for them to appreciate the value we could have for them as their supplier. At the same time, by allowing a number of our managers diverse contacts with the organization of a potential customer, we are able to develop a much better appreciation for the customer's specific needs. In our own assessment of what it takes to satisfy the customer, we are less likely to miss important elements that might be ignored by the sales organization alone. During this phase, we develop our commitment to a potential customer. In many cases, personal relationships grow, and this is a natural and satisfying part of our business. Often taking on certain new business creates significant technical challenges and may even necessitate capital investments. It is vital for our people to appreciate fully the commitments that a potential customer represents. In many cases, the sales department has as much selling to do within the organization as with customers. Obtaining a new account is a momentary satisfaction; however, our most critical mission is to successfully and consistently deliver the intended value to the customer. A smooth transition begins well in advance of the business award and hinges on the commitment of the key members of our organization. In building a competitive offer, the true commitment and capability of the organization is key. The team selling process provides a good balance of realism and challenge in our business opportunities. It is also an uncompromising honest approach that establishes trust for what we always hope will be a long-term customer supplier relationship.

What weaknesses make this competitor vulnerable? Once the salesperson can determine the competitor's limitations, the salesperson can demonstrate the superiority of his or her product. A salesperson must answer the questions, How are you different from the competition? How are you better than the competition? A salesperson must be able to determine his or her differential competitive advantage.

Technology Knowledge

Salespeople must use technology to their advantage. Twenty years ago, salespeople had to know where a reliable pay phone was located in each of the cities they visited. Many opportunities were missed because salespeople could not reach prospects while they were in the field. Today's salesperson has the luxury of cell phones, facsimile technology, the World Wide Web, pagers, voice-mail, and e-mail. Salespeople should communicate in the manner preferred by their prospects and clients. Some clients use e-mail extensively and want to use e-mail over phone conversations. Some buyers like to fax orders in and would rather not meet the salesperson face to face. A good salesperson must recognize these preferences and act accordingly. Each of these can either be a bridge to the customer or an obstacle. Salespeople should be building bridges to all their prospects and customers by using technology appropriately (see Exhibit 3.4). If a pager number is on a salesperson's business card, then the salesperson must return pages within a reasonable period of time. Likewise, if a facsimile number is given to prospects, then the fax machine must be turned on at all times and working properly.

Probably the most oversold form of technology is voice-mail. Many companies have gone to this method of communication hoping to free secretaries and making it easier to leave messages for the salesperson. The difficulty arises when a customer wants to talk to a salesperson and can only get a recording. Sometimes, the voice-mail is full and it is impossible to leave a message. It is also possible to use voice-mail to screen calls, and many buyers and salespeople complain that it is virtually impossible to make contact when their counterpart refuses to return their call.

Technology can be a friend or a foe of a salesperson. If used properly, technology can build bridges to prospects and clients and develop relationships. If technology is not used properly, then a salesperson can find him- or herself alienating the customers and turn a potential resource into a reason for a prospect not to do business with the salesperson.

| EXHIBIT 3.4 | Using Technology to Build Bridges to Customers |

Technology	Bridge
World Wide Web	Price updates can be placed on the Web for customers to access. New product information can be made available to customers and prospects.
E-mail	Buyer and salesperson can virtually communicate 24 hours a day. Mass communications can be sent out to all customers and prospects.
Pagers	Buyers with an emergency have immediate access to their salesperson by having them paged.
Facsimile	Nonelectronic documents can be transmitted 24 hours a day. Fax on demand.
Cell Phones	Buyer and seller have immediate access to each other.
Voice-Mail	Salesperson and buyer can leave messages for each other and save time and effort.

Sales Ethics

Ethics refers to right and wrong conduct of individuals and institutions of which they are a part. Personal ethics and formal codes of conduct provide a basis for deciding what is right or wrong in a given situation. Ethical standards for a profession are based on society's standards, and most industries have developed a code of behaviors that are compatible with society's standards. Professions in this country owe much of their public regard to standards of conduct established by professional organizations. Reflecting this, the American Marketing Association has adopted a code of ethics, which appears in Exhibit 3.5.

Salespeople are constantly involved with ethical issues. A sales manager encourages his or her salesforce to pad their expense account in lieu of a raise. A salesperson sells a product or service to a customer that the buyer does not need. A salesperson exaggerates the benefits of a product to get a sale. The list can go on and on.

Recall that sales professionalism requires a truthful, customer-oriented approach. Customers are increasingly intolerant of nonprofessional, unethical practices. Sales ethics is closely related to trust. Deceptive practices, illegal activities, and non-customer–oriented behavior only have to be attempted once for a buyer to lose trust in his or her salesperson. Research has identified some of the sales practices deemed unethical as shown in Exhibit 3.6.

Image of Salespeople

Sales and Marketing Executives International (SMEI) has been concerned with the image of salespeople and has developed a code of ethics as a set of principles that outline the minimum requirements for professional conduct. SMEI has developed a 20–30-hour certification process that declares that a salesperson shall support and preserve the highest standards of professional conduct in all areas of sales and in all relationships in the sales process. Exhibit 3.7 is the SMEI Code of Ethics that pledges a salesperson will adhere to these standards.

A sales professional deserves and receives a high level of respect on the job. Buyers that do not interact with professional salespeople on a regular basis may believe in the negative stereotype of the salesperson as a pushy, shifty, not-to-be-trusted sort. Where does this stereotype come from? Some salespeople are not professional in their approach, and this contributes to the negative stereotype. In the past, television programs, movies, and even Broadway productions have fostered the negative image of salespeople. During the '60s and '70s, the popular press also contributed to the negative image of salespeople. A study of how salespeople are portrayed in the popular press found that salespeople are often associated with deceptive, illegal, and non-customer–oriented behavior.[11] Three of the more important areas of unethical behavior, deceptive practices, illegal activities, and non-customer–oriented behavior, are discussed.

DECEPTIVE PRACTICES   Buyers have been known to be turned off by all salespeople because a few are unscrupulous and are even scam artists. This is unfortunate because all salespeople (good and bad) pay the price for this behavior. Unfortunately, some salespeople do use quota pressure as an excuse to be deceptive. The salesperson has the choice to either ignore the trust-building approach and persuade the customer to buy or go to the next sales meeting and catch the wrath of his or her sales manager for being under quota. Salespeople giving answers when they do not know, exaggerating product benefits, and withholding information may appear to only shade the truth, but when it causes harm to the buyer, the salesperson has jeopardized future dealings with the buyer.

EXHIBIT 3.5   The American Marketing Association's Code of Ethics

Code of Ethics

Members of the American Marketing Association (AMA) are committed to ethical professional conduct. They have joined together in subscribing to this Code of Ethics embracing the following topics.

Responsibilities of the Marketer

Marketers must accept responsibility for the consequences of their activities and make every effort to ensure that their decisions, recommendations, and actions function to identify, serve, and satisfy all relevant publics: customers, organizations, and society.

Marketers' professional conduct must be guided by:

1. The basic rule of professional ethics: not knowingly to do harm.
2. The adherence to all applicable laws and regulations.
3. The accurate representation of their education, training, and experience.
4. The active support, practice, and promotion of this Code of Ethics.

Honesty and Fairness

Marketers shall uphold and advance the integrity, honor, and dignity of the marketing profession by:

1. Being honest in serving consumers, clients, employees, suppliers, distributors, and the public.
2. Not knowingly participating in a conflict of interest without prior notice to all parties involved.
3. Establishing equitable fee schedules, including the payment or receipt of usual, customary and/or legal compensation for marketing exchanges.

Rights and Duties of Parties in the Marketing Exchange Process

Participants in the marketing exchange process should be able to expect that:

1. Products and services offered are safe and fit for their intended uses.
2. Communication about offered products and services are not deceptive.
3. All parties intend to discharge their obligations, financial and otherwise, in good faith.
4. Appropriate internal methods exist for equitable adjustment and/or redress of grievances concerning purchases.

It is understood that the above would include, *but is not limited to,* the following responsibilities of the marketer.

In the area of product development and management:

- Disclosure of all substantial risks associated with product or service usage.

- Identification of any product component substitution that might materially change the product or impact on the buyer's purchase decision.
- Identification of extra-cost added features.

In the area of promotions:

- Avoidance of false and misleading advertising.
- Rejection of high-pressure, manipulations or misleading sales tactics.
- Avoidance of sales promotions that use deception or manipulation

In the area of distribution:

- Not manipulating the availability of a product for purpose of exploitation.
- Not using coercion in the marketing channel.
- Not exerting undue influence over the reseller's choice to handle a product.

In the area of pricing:

- Not engaging in price fixing.
- Not practicing predatory pricing.
- Disclosing the full price associated with any purchase.

In the area of marketing research:

- Prohibiting selling or fund-raising under the guise of conducting research.
- Maintaining research integrity by avoiding misrepresentation and omission of pertinent research data.
- Treating outside clients and suppliers fairly.

Organizational Relationships

Marketers should be aware of how their behavior may influence or impact on the behavior of others in organizational relationships. They should not demand, encourage, or apply coercion to obtain unethical behavior in their relationships with others, such as employees, suppliers, or customers.

1. Apply confidentiality and anonymity in professional relationships with regard to privileged information.
2. Meet their obligations and responsibilities in contracts and mutual agreements in a timely manner.
3. Avoid taking the work of others, in whole, or in part, and representing this work as their own or directly benefiting from it without compensation or consent of the originator or owner.
4. Avoid manipulation to take advantage of situations to maximize personal welfare in a way that unfairly deprives or damages the organization of others.

Any AMA members found to be in violation of any provision of this Code of Ethics may have his or her Association membership suspended or revoked.

EXHIBIT 3.6   **What Types of Sales Behaviors Are Unethical?**

According to a survey of 327 customers, salespeople are acting unethically if they:

1. Show concern for own interest, not clients'
2. Pass the blame for something they did wrong
3. Take advantage of the poor or uneducated
4. Accept favors from customers so the seller feels obliged to bend policies
5. Sell products/services that people don't need
6. Give answers when they don't really know answers
7. Pose as market researcher when doing phone sales
8. Sell dangerous or hazardous products
9. Withhold information
10. Exaggerate benefits of product
11. Lie about availability to make sale
12. Lie to competitors
13. Falsify product testimonials

ILLEGAL ACTIVITIES   Misusing company assets has been a long-standing problem for many sales organizations. Using the company car for personal use, charging expenses that did not occur, and selling samples for income are examples of misusing company assets. Some of these violations of company property also constitutes violations of the Internal Revenue Service (IRS) law and are offenses that could lead to jail or heavy fines.

Bribes are another area that causes some salespeople to run afoul of the law. A competitor may be offering bribes; this, in turn, puts pressure on the salesperson's company to respond with bribes of its own. It is difficult for a salesperson to see potential sales going to the competition. Salespeople offering bribes on their own can be punished. Companies that engage in bribery may find themselves being prosecuted and fined. Rockwell International and Lockheed made illegal payments to foreign customers and had to suffer the humiliation of the bad publicity and the fines.

Another area of legal concern that involves the salesforce is product liability. Salespeople can create product liabilities for a company in three ways: **express warranty, misrepresentation,** and **negligence.** A salesperson can create a product warranty or guarantee that obligates the selling organization even if they do not intend to give the warranty. Express warranties are created by any affirmation of fact or promise, any description, or any sample or model that a salesperson uses, which is made part of the basis of the bargain.

Basis of the bargain is taken to mean that the buyer relied on the seller's statements in making the purchase decision. If a salesperson tells a prospect that a machine will turn out 50 units per hour, a legal obligation has been created for the firm to supply a machine that will accomplish this. Misrepresentation by a salesperson can also lead to product liability even if the salesperson makes a false claim thinking it is true. The burden of accuracy is on the seller. Salespeople are required by law to exercise "reasonable care" in formulating claims. If a salesperson asserts that a given drug is safe without exercising reasonable care to see that this claim is accurate, the salesperson has been negligent. Negligence is a basis for product liability on the part of the seller.

EXHIBIT 3.7   **Certified Professional Salesperson Code of Ethics**

The SMEI Certified Professional Salesperson (SCPS) Code of Ethics is a set of principles that outline minimum requirements for professional conduct. Those who attain SCPS status should consider these principles as more than just rules to follow. They are guiding standards above which the salesperson should rise.

A SCPS shall support and preserve the highest standards of professional conduct in all areas of sales and in all relationships in the sales process. Toward this end a SCPS pledges and commits to these standards in all activities under this code.

As a SCPS I pledge to the following individuals and parties:

I.   With respect to **The Customer,** I will:

Maintain honesty and integrity in my relationship with all customers and prospective customers.

Accurately represent my product or service in order to place the customer or prospective customer in a position to make a decision consistent with the principle of mutuality of benefit and profit to the buyer and seller.

Continually keep abreast and increase the knowledge of my product(s), service(s), and industry in which I work. This is necessary to better serve those who place their trust in me.

II.   With respect to **The Company** and other parties whom I represent, I will:

Use their resources that are at my disposal and will be utilized only for legitimate business purposes.

Respect and protect proprietary and confidential information entrusted to me by my company.

Not engage in any activities that will either jeopardize or conflict with the interests of my company. Activities that may be or which may appear to be illegal or unethical will be strictly avoided. To this effect I will not participate in activities that are illegal or unethical.

III. With respect to **The Competition,** regarding those organizations and individuals that I compete with in the marketplace, I will:

Only obtain competitive information through legal and ethical methods.

Only portray my competitors, and their products and services in a manner which is honest, truthful, and based on accurate information that can or has been substantiated.

IV.   With respect to **The Community** and society which provide me with my livelihood, I will:

Engage in business and selling practices which contribute to a positive relationship with the communities in which I and my company have presence.

Support public policy objectives consistent with maintaining and protecting the environment and community.

Participate in community activities and associations which provide for the betterment of the community and society.

I AM COMMITTED to the letter and spirit of this code. The reputation of salespeople depends upon me as well as others who engage in the profession of selling. My adherence to these standards will strengthen the reputation and integrity for which we strive as professional salespeople.

I understand that failure to consistently act according to the above standards and principles could result in the forfeiture of the privilege of using the SCPS designation.

Candidate's Signature

_____
Signature   Date

Although these tactics may increase sales in the short run, salespeople ruin their trust relationship with their customer and company. Given the legal restrictions that relate to selling practices, a salesperson, as well as the selling organization, should exercise care in developing sales presentations. Some basic guidelines for legal selling include the following:

NON-CUSTOMER–ORIENTED BEHAVIOR   Most of today's sales organizations emphasize trust-building behaviors and are customer oriented. Unfortunately, there are a few salespeople and companies today that concentrate on short-term goals and allow outmoded sales tactics to be practiced. Most buyers will not buy from salespeople who are pushy and practice the hard sell. Too much is at stake to fall for the fast-talking, high-pressure salesperson. Buyers have been through their own training, and they understand the importance of developing a long-term relationship with their suppliers. Exhibit 3.8 summarizes these practices.

How Are Companies Dealing with Sales Ethics?

Many companies spend time covering ethics in their training programs. These programs should cover topics such as the appropriateness of gift giving, the use of expense accounts, and dealing with a prospect's unethical demands. Each company will have its own policies on gift giving. Jenny Osborne of Eli Lilly states, "We are only allowed to spend up to $100 on one of our physicians. Last week I took one of my physicians and three of his children to an Indiana Pacers game. The tickets came to $200. The physician had to write me a check for $100.00!!"[12] Receiving Christmas gifts is another area that must be explained during training. Some buyers are not allowed to accept gifts from salespeople.

Another important training area is the use of expense accounts. Salespeople should be trained in how to fill out the expense account form and what is acceptable for submission. Some companies allow personal mileage to be included; others do not. If guidelines are established, then there is less of a chance for a misunderstanding by the salesperson.

EXHIBIT 3.8   **Areas of Unethical Behavior**

Deceptive Practices	Illegal Activities
Deceptive	Defraud
Deceive	Con
Hustle	Misuse company assets
Scam	
Exaggerate	
Withhold bluff	

Non-Customer–Oriented Behavior

Pushy
Hard Sell
Fast Talking
High Pressure

EXHIBIT 3.9 **Legal Reminders**

For salespeople
1. Use factual data rather than general statements of praise during the sales presentation. Avoid misrepresentation.
2. Thoroughly educate customers before the sale on the product's specifications, capabilities, and limitations.
3. Do not overstep authority, as the salesperson's actions can be binding to the selling firm.
4. Avoid discussing these topics with competitors: prices, profit margins, discounts, terms of sale, bids or intent to bid, sales territories or markets to be served, rejection or termination of customers.
5. Do not use one product as bait for selling another product.
6. Do not try to force the customer to buy only from your organization.
7. Offer the same price and support to buyers who purchase under the same set of circumstances.
8. Do not tamper with a competitor's product.
9. Do not disparage a competitor's product without specific evidence of your contentions.
10. Avoid promises that will be difficult or impossible to honor.

For the sales organization
1. Review sales presentations and claims for possible legal problems.
2. Make the salesforce aware of potential conflicts with the law.
3. Carefully screen any independent sales agents used by the organization.
4. With technical products and services make sure the sales presentation fully explains the capabilities and dangers of products and service.

Sometimes unethical behavior is not initiated by the salesperson but by the buyer. Salespeople must be trained in dealing with prospects who make unethical demands. Buyers can be under pressure from their company to stay within budget or to move up the timetable on an order. A buyer may ask a salesperson to move him or her up on the order list in exchange for more business down the road. One pharmacist set up a deal with one of their salespeople to buy samples illegally. The trust-based salesperson has to shut down any short-term gain for their long-term success. A salesperson's career is over if the word circulates that he or she cannot be trusted.

A salesperson must also be concerned with our legal system and that of other countries. It cannot be an excuse for today's well-trained salesperson to say he or she did not know that a law was being broken. When in doubt the salesperson must check out all state and local laws. In addition, there are industry-specific rules and regulations to be considered. Exhibit 3.9 covers a number of legal reminders.

A salesperson has his or her reputation to tarnish only once. In this day and age of mass communication (phone, e-mail, Web sites), it is easy for a buyer to get the word out that a salesperson is acting unethically and end that salesperson's career.

Summary

1. **Discuss the distinguishing characteristics of trust-based selling.** Trust means different things to different buyers. It can be defined as confidentiality, openness, dependability, candor, honesty, confidence, security, reliability, fairness, and predictability. It is the salespersons' job to determine what trust means to each of their buyers. Salespeople must question their buyers as to what trust attributes are their greatest concerns.

2. **Explain the importance of trust.** In today's increasingly competitive marketplace, buyers typically find themselves inundated with choices regarding both products and suppliers. Buyers are demanding unique solutions to their problems, which are customized on the basis of their specific needs. This shift toward relationship selling has altered both the roles played by salespeople and the activities and skills they exercise in carrying out

these roles—the selling process itself. Today's more contemporary selling process is embedded within the relationship marketing paradigm. As such, it emphasizes the initiation and nurturing of long-term buyer-seller relationships based on mutual trust and value-added benefits. The level of problem-solving activity common to relationship selling requires deliberate and purposeful collaboration between both parities. These joint efforts are directed at creating unique solutions based on an enhanced knowledge and understanding of the customer's needs and the supplier's capabilities so that both parties derive mutual benefits.

3. **Discuss how to earn trust.** Buyers are constantly asking themselves whether the salesperson truly cares about them. Salespeople can answer this question for the buyer by demonstrating trust-building activities. Trust can be earned by demonstrating expertise, customer orientation, competence, dependability, candor, and representation.

4. **Discuss how knowledge bases help build trust and relationships.** Salespeople do not have much time to make a first impression. If a salesperson can demonstrate expertise in the buyer's industry, company, marketplace, competitive knowledge, and so on, then the buyer will more likely be willing to listen to the salesperson if he or she brings valued experience to the buyer.

5. **Understand the importance of sales ethics.** Salespeople are constantly involved with ethical issues. A sales manager encourages his or her salesforce to pad their expense account in lieu of a raise. A salesperson sells a product or service to a customer that the buyer does not need. A salesperson exaggerates the benefits of a product to get a sale. The list can go on and on. How a salesperson handles these situations will go a long way in determining the salesperson's credibility. One wrong decision can end a salesperson's career.

6. **Discuss three important areas of unethical behavior.** Three of the more popular areas of unethical behavior are deceptive practices, illegal activities, and non-customer–oriented behavior.

   Deceptive practices: Salespeople giving answers when they do not know, exaggerating product benefits, and withholding information may appear to only shade the truth, but when it causes harm to the buyer, the salesperson has jeopardized future dealings with the buyer.

   Illegal activities: Misusing company assets has been a long-standing problem for many sales organizations. Using the company car for personal use, charging expenses that did not occur, and selling samples for income are examples of misusing company assets. Some of these violations discovered by company probing also constitutes violations of the Internal Revenue Service (IRS) law and are offenses that could lead to jail or heavy fines.

   Non-customer–oriented behavior: Most buyers will not buy from salespeople who are pushy and practice the hard sell. Too much is at stake to fall for the fast-talking, high-pressure salesperson.

Understanding Professional Selling Terms

- Trust
- Openness
- Dependability
- Candor
- Honesty
- Confidentiality
- Security
- Reliability
- Fairness
- Predictability
- Expertise
- Contribution
- Customer orientation
- Compatibility/likeability
- Competitor knowledge
- Industry knowledge
- Company knowledge
- Service knowledge
- Product knowledge
- Technology knowledge
- Promotion knowledge
- Price knowledge
- Market knowledge
- Customer knowledge
- Ethics
- Express warranty
- Misrepresentation
- Negligence
- Basis of the bargain

Developing Professional Selling Knowledge

1. What is the essence of trust for a salesperson?
2. If trust means different things to different buyers, how is a salesperson to determine what trust means for each buyer?
3. Why is trust important to a salesperson?
4. How might a salesperson go about earning trust?
5. What does it mean for a salesperson to have a customer orientation?
6. How would you rank the five trust-builders in order of importance?
7. Explain why expertise is such an important relationship builder.
8. How do knowledge bases help build trust and relationships?
9. Do you think certain knowledge bases are more important than others? Why?
10. What are the three areas of unethical behavior? Discuss each.

Building Professional Selling Skills

1. Relationship selling is directed toward achieving mutually satisfying results between buyer and seller that sustain and enhance future interactions. In the past several years, there has been a growing recognition that adversarial, "me-against-you" buyer-seller relationships are often nonproductive for both parties. The director of Xerox's training university in Leesburg, Virginia, says the biggest change in its sales training in the past decade is that "we spend a lot more time on what the customer thinks is important."

   Competition has intensified, technology has advanced, and pressure to improve productivity has soared. Given these changes in the marketplace, many firms are cutting down on the number of approved vendors. People are busier than ever, and there is no time for the misinformation and posturing often associated with the old style of selling. In a nutshell, it is increasingly productive to work closely with customers.

   Relationship selling requires a different set of skills and attitudes than is true for transaction-oriented selling. Questioning and listening become more important than talking. High-pressure sales approaches and gimmicky closing methods are taboo in relationship selling. Personality matters but not as much as appealing to the buyer's rational side in an interesting, well-illustrated, concise manner.

   To initiate, develop, and enhance customer relationships, salespeople must demonstrate their trustworthiness. As detailed in the introduction to this module, research has identified at least five characteristics of trust-building salespeople:

   1. **Customer orientation**—Placing as much emphasis on the customer's interest as your own.
   2. **Expertise**—The ability, knowledge, and resources to meet customer expectations.
   3. **Dependability**—The predictability of your actions.
   4. **Candor**—Honesty of the spoken word.
   5. **Compatibility**—Rooted in each party's perception of "having something in common" with the other. Admittedly, an emotional factor, difficult to pin down, yet a powerful force in some buyer-seller relationships.

   What are your ideas about how you can improve your trust-building behavior as you interact with customers? Use the following worksheet as a guide to how you might use each of the trust builders.

   ### IDEAS FOR ACTION (TRUST-BUILDING WORKSHEET)

   1. Customer Orientation

   _____

   _____

   _____

   _____

   _____

   _____

2. Expertise

_____
_____
_____
_____
_____
_____
_____

3. Dependability

_____
_____
_____
_____
_____
_____
_____

4. Candor

_____
_____
_____
_____
_____
_____
_____

5. Compatibility

_____
_____
_____
_____
_____
_____
_____

6. Others

_____
_____
_____
_____
_____
_____
_____

2. Sales professionalism requires a truthful, customer-oriented approach. Customers are increasingly intolerant of nonprofessional, unethical sales practices. Assess the following actions a salesperson might take with regards to their legality, ethicality, and professionalism.

Please circle your response for each category.

1. Shows concern for his or her own interests, not that of the client.

   legal/illegal   **ethical/unethical**   **professional/unprofessional**

2. Passes the blame for something he or she did wrong.

   legal/illegal   **ethical/unethical**   **professional/unprofessional**

3. Takes advantage of the poor and uneducated.

   legal/illegal   **ethical/unethical**   **professional/unprofessional**

4. Accepts favors from customers so that the seller feels obliged to bend policies.

   legal/illegal   **ethical/unethical**   **professional/unprofessional**

5. Sells products or services that people do not need.

   legal/illegal   **ethical/unethical**   **professional/unprofessional**

6. Gives answers when he or she does not really know answers.

   legal/illegal   **ethical/unethical**   **professional/unprofessional**

7. Poses as market researcher when doing phone sales.

   legal/illegal   **ethical/unethical**   **professional/unprofessional**

8. Sells dangerous or hazardous products.

   legal/illegal   **ethical/unethical**   **professional/unprofessional**

9. Withholds information.

   legal/illegal   **ethical/unethical**   **professional/unprofessional**

10. Exaggerates benefits of product.

   legal/illegal   **ethical/unethical**   **professional/unprofessional**

11. Lies about availability of product to make the sale.

   legal/illegal   **ethical/unethical**   **professional/unprofessional**

12. Lies to competitors.

   legal/illegal   **ethical/unethical**   **professional/unprofessional**

13. Falsifies product testimonials.

   legal/illegal   **ethical/unethical**   **professional/unprofessional**

Making Professional Selling Decisions

CASE 3.1   *Schmidt Business Forms*

Background

Congratulations! As a new salesperson for Schmidt Business Forms, you have just completed training and have been assigned the southwest territory. Schmidt Business Forms designs and manufactures a full line of both stock and customized forms for use in all types of business. Operating throughout the United States and Canada, Schmidt is recognized as one of the three leaders in the industry.

Current Situation

Doctors' General Hospital was once a major account in your territory. Over this past year, virtually all the hospital's forms business has been switched from Schmidt to one of your main competitors. Due to the large volume and many types of forms used, Doctors' has placed the purchasing responsibility for all forms in the hands of Jim Adams in the purchasing department. An experienced professional purchasing agent, Jim has been in this position for several years and has purchased significant volumes of forms from Schmidt in the past. In the course of calling on Jim at his office in the hospital, you have learned that Doctors' dropping Schmidt as a forms source did not happen overnight. Although the loss of this account was not related to any single problem, you have learned that the switch to your competitor was basically due to a combination of events that resulted in a loss of trust in Schmidt. Several shipments did not arrive as promised, causing major problems for both billing and admissions. Even though the final proof copies were correct, a newly designed, multipart computer form was found to be short one of its pages. This required emergency room staff to take time and use a copier (located one floor up) until the forms could be rerun and delivered two weeks later. The final straw concerned an admissions form that Schmidt had been supplying the hospital for more than three years. For some reason, a new shipment of the admissions forms was the wrong size and would not fit into patient files without being folded. In each event, the prior salesperson worked with Jim Adams to get the problems resolved and the correct forms delivered. Discounts were also given to help offset the inconvenience incurred. Nevertheless, Schmidt has lost the account, the previous salesperson has quit the company, and you have inherited the challenge of winning back Jim Adams and Doctors' Hospital.

Questions:

1. Put yourself in the role of the salesperson for Schmidt Business Forms in the selling situation just described and review the *trust-building behaviors* presented in this module. Using the following worksheet as a guide, discuss and give examples of how you might use each of the *trust builders* to re-establish a relationship with Jim Adams and win back the Doctors' Hospital account.

Trust-Building Worksheet

1. Customer Orientation:

_____
_____
_____
_____
_____
_____
_____
_____
_____

2. Expertise:

_____
_____
_____
_____
_____
_____
_____
_____
_____

3. Dependability:

_____
_____
_____
_____
_____
_____
_____
_____
_____
_____
_____

4. Candor:

_____

_____

_____

_____

_____

_____

_____

_____

_____

5. Compatibility:

_____

_____

_____

_____

_____

_____

_____

_____

_____

_____

_____

CASE 3.2   *Sales Ethics: A Case Study*

Background

Packaging Systems, Incorporated (PSI), a wholly owned subsidiary of an international oil company, is a major supplier of polyethylene film to various industrial and agricultural markets. In the past, a primary product has been a shredded film that is used for soil erosion control by farmers and commercial landscapers.

In recent years, PSI has become a major supplier in the pallet overwrap market. In this application, film is used to secure a product or products to a pallet for shipping. Compared with PSI's other markets, growth and profits in the pallet overwrap market have been outstanding. The bright prospects for the pallet overwrap market coupled with the stagnation of the shredded film market has led PSI management to make the following decisions: (1) limit production output and marketing activities of shredded film, and (2) expand production output and marketing emphasis of pallet overwrap film.

The PSI salesforce was informed of the shift in emphasis in a memo from Bill Chandler, the sales manager for industrial and agricultural products (see Exhibit 3A.1).

Current Situation

Jeff Braxton is the PSI sales representative in the Chicago area. He had given Chandler's memo a lot of thought before he reluctantly began to implement his sales manager's suggestions. During his weekly phone call to Chandler, Jeff had voiced some of his objections.

Chandler: So, Jeff, how is the shredded film cutback and pallet overwrap expansion coming along in Chicago?

Braxton: O.K., I guess, but personally, I have some problems with it.

Chandler: For example?

Braxton: Some of the shredded film accounts are refusing to roll over and play dead. They are saying that we can't cut them off, and a couple have been pretty hostile. They're talking lawsuit, Bill.

Chandler: That's out of your area of concern, Jeff. Let attorneys worry about that. Besides, I doubt many will sue when they consider the legal and financial resources of our parent company.

Braxton: Whatever you say, Bill. The other thing that bothers me is the written guarantee to provide pallet overwrap film. Seems to me that there could be shortages, strikes, or fires that could prevent us from following through on the promise to supply film.

Chandler: Highly unlikely, Jeff. You are worrying too much. You're new to the game. Do yourself a favor and follow my suggestions.

Braxton: Well, you're the boss . . .

EXHIBIT 3A.1	Memorandum

To: Industrial/Agricultural SalesForce
From: Bill Chandler
Subject: Shredded Film Cutback/Pallet Overwrap Expansion

Effective immediately, we will be putting more emphasis on pallet overwrap film production and marketing. To allow this expansion, we will be cutting back our sales of shredded film by approximately 30 percent. I suggest you terminate your relationship with your marginal customers to accomplish the 30 percent reduction in shredded film. Now is the time to weed out customers who are

1.   Bad credit risks or slow to pay their bills;
2.   Located more than 500 miles from any of our five manufacturing plants;
3.   Low-volume buyers;
4.   Low-loyalty customers, that is, they also buy from competitors.

To help the push in pallet overwrap film, we plan to approach high-potential target accounts with these tactics:
1.   We will guarantee source of supply in writing: This should be attractive because most buyers are nervous about the availability made from petroleum-based raw materials.
2.   We will designate target accounts as national accounts; this is basically to stroke their corporate ego; we do not plan a real national accounts program.
3.   We will designate selling teams to close the target accounts; the team will be made up of one sales representative, a member of management, and technical support personnel; once the accounts are closed, the sales representative will have responsibility for maintaining the account.

I will be talking with each of you in the near future to finalize plans for your respective territory.

Regards,

Bill

In the past 30 days, several events had complicated the PSI strategy. An explosion and resulting fire had destroyed all the pallet overwrap production equipment and inventory in one of the PSI plants. A terrorist group had declared its responsibility for the explosion. PSI sales representatives were instructed to tell their accounts that the damage was minimal and that supply and service levels would not be affected. PSI management hoped to use production from the other four plants to cover the loss until rebuilding could be completed.

Fifteen days after the crippling fire, PSI received another severe blow. A trade dispute with several oil-producing nations erupted. This caused almost immediate raw material shortages for all PSI products. The matter was now becoming unpleasant for PSI. Jeff Braxton's phone call earlier in the day was the first of many bearing bad news for Bill Chandler.

Braxton: Everybody out here is either hostile or not speaking at all. The grapevine is buzzing and practically all of our accounts know about the cover-up on the fire. Maybe that's what is making them take such a hard line on their guaranteed source of supply deal. The consensus is that we guaranteed the source of supply in writ-

ing and did not cite exceptions such as fires and trade disputes. Their message to me is, "You get the product, or we sue. We don't care where you get it, even if you have to buy from one of your competitors and resell it to us, and remember we want the competitive price you promised. Anything short of this, and we'll never buy from you again."

Questions:

1.   An ethical issue exists when there is a question of whether an action is right or wrong. List below the issues that, in your opinion, are ethical issues in this case.
2.   In terms of the SCPS Code of Ethics (Exhibit 3.7), how would you evaluate Jeff Braxton's actions?
3.   In terms of the SCPS Code of Ethics (Exhibit 3.7), how would you evaluate Bill Chandler's actions?
4.   How should the affected customers now be treated to minimize the damage to both PSI and to the customers?

Source: SMEI Accreditation Institute, The University of Memphis.

Communication Skills

Capturing the Power of Relational Communication in Personal Selling

Jamie Benefield, regional sales director for one of the three leading suppliers of hospital furniture and equipment, along with an account representative, had been working for eight months to obtain the furniture and equipment contract for a new hospital being built in Chicago. It appeared that Jamie's relational sales strategy was working as the director of purchasing had indicated that she would get at least 75 percent of the final purchase and even held out the possibility of a sole-source contract for the entire deal.

Approximately seven weeks prior to the final purchase decision, Jamie was sent overseas to assist in opening the company's new European region and left the hospital account in the hands of the account representative who had been working with her. After two weeks, Jamie came back to learn that the hospital account was now being split among three different suppliers. In the short time she had been absent, Jamie's company had seen its share of the business cut to approximately 40 percent of the total purchase.

Over lunch with the lead buyer, Jamie discussed the changes and learned that alterations in the building layout had necessitated changes in the furniture and equipment plan. Jamie's rep had participated in several meetings in which the equipment change orders were developed. However, a more aggressive competitor was able to get many of the changes written in their favor and to Jamie's disadvantage. The buyer further explained that final decisions had not been made, but if Jamie intended to salvage her position, she would need to act quickly.

Jamie pulled out all the stops to get her company back into the driver's seat. Her strategy included interacting and communicating closely with a number of individuals inside and outside of her company. *Internally,* Jamie worked with members of the company's design and manufacturing units to incorporate product features that would provide customer benefits beyond those offered by the competition. She also worked with the account rep to help him learn how to flex his communication style to the changing demands of different situations and people. To maximize interorganization communication and enhance the current relationship, Jamie also assembled an expanded sales team composed of several design and production engineers, the account rep, and herself. *Externally,* Jamie and the members of her sales team worked with multiple hospital departments and personnel: the purchasing department, the architects and designers, key hospital staff members who were high-frequency users of the proposed equipment, and several engineers from the hospital's maintenance and engineering section. Although these individuals were not directly involved in the purchase decision, Jamie knew they could influence the ultimate outcome, and she wanted them on her side.

Learning Objectives

After completing this module, you should be able to

1 Explain the importance of collaborative, two-way communication in personal selling.

2 Explain the primary types of questions and how they are applied in selling.

3 Illustrate the diverse roles and uses of strategic questioning in personal selling.

4 Identify and describe the five steps of the ADAPT questioning sequence.

5 Discuss the four sequential steps for effective active listening.

6 Discuss the superiority of pictures over words for explaining concepts and enhancing comprehension.

7 Describe the different forms of nonverbal communication.

8 List and illustrate the content sections fundamental to effective sales proposals.

The outcome of this product enhancement endeavor and increased level of interaction and communication between key individuals across the two organizations was a sole-source contract for 100 percent of the furniture and equipment. The changes in features did result in a product that outperformed the competition and offered unique benefits to the hospital. However, that alone did not account for the realization of a sole-source contract. As Jamie later learned, the primary reasoning behind the sole-source decision was the increased personal interaction and communication at multiple levels and functions within the hospital. This demonstrated the importance of the hospital to Jamie's company and the level of commitment the supplier was willing to make. The increased collaboration and communication required considerable time and effort, but it made the difference in obtaining a $1.2 million sale.

Source: Personal interview with Jamie Benefield, April 14, 1999.

Jamie Benefield's experience with the potency of relational sales communication presented in this module's opening vignette is not uncommon. On the one hand, communication is selling. The skill and effectiveness of a salesperson's interpersonal communication are fundamental determinants of selling performance. At the same time, however, communication continues to be one of the least understood and studied skills for successful selling.

This module addresses the need to better understand and master the art of collaborative, two-way communication by first examining the basic nature of **relational sales communication.** Building on this understanding, the text breaks relational sales communication down into its component and subcomponent parts to facilitate the study and application of relational communication. The verbal dimension of communication is examined first with an emphasis on three communication subcomponents: (1) developing effective questioning methods for use in uncovering buyers' needs and expectations; (2) using active listening skills to facilitate the interchange of ideas and information; and (3) maximizing the responsive dissemination of information to buyers to explain and bring alive the benefits of proposed solutions. The nonverbal dimension of communication is also examined, with an emphasis on its application and meaningful interpretation in selling. Finally, the written dimension of communication is explored, with an emphasis on how to develop quality sales proposals.

Sales Communication as a Collaborative Process

Neither people nor organizations buy products. Rather, they seek out the satisfaction and benefits that are provided by certain product features. Although traditional selling has been described as "talking *at* the customer," relational selling has been referred to as "talking *with* the customer." Relational sales communication is a two-way and naturally collaborative interaction that allows buyers and sellers alike to develop a better understanding of the need situation and work together to generate the best response for solving the customer's needs. Although trust-based, relational selling has become the preeminent model for contemporary personal selling, the situation described in "An Ethical Dilemma" should serve as a reminder that some salespeople and sales organizations continue to practice more traditional and manipulative forms of selling.

An Ethical Dilemma

Jane Simmons, a junior marketing major, accepted a summer-long internship selling kitchen utensils and supplies to residential customers in the Atlanta area. Jane's first two weeks were spent in a training class with 11 other university student interns. Although selling skills were discussed, the primary emphasis of the training was product knowledge. On the final day of training, each student was assigned a territory and given a pocket card to review periodically as they prepared to call on prospective customers. Along with several motivational slogans, the pocket cards contained the following "keys" to successful selling:

- *The salesperson must take control. Product knowledge is the key. Have a great opening line. Know how to handle objections. Work on your sales pitch. Lead the customer where you want them to go.*
- *It is the seller's job to convince the prospect to buy. Do what it takes to educate the customer and persuade him or her to make the purchase.*
- *Everyone needs the product. It is the salesperson's job to convince prospects that they need it.*
- *Success in selling is just a numbers game. Contact enough individuals, and you will make your sales quota. If you need to sell more—you simply have to make more contacts.*
- *The salesperson has all the answers and must drive the sale. Your knowledge of the product places you in a position of knowing more than the prospect; therefore, you should drive each sale toward a successful close.*
- *Prospects do not know what they need. Prospects do not have your knowledge of the product, its use and many applications, or its high level of quality. Consequently, you must be sure to follow the standard selling message with all customers and ask for the sale.*

If you were Jane Simmons, how would you go about calling on prospective customers for this company in light of these suggestions?

Relational sales communication is the sharing of meaning between buying and selling parties that results from the interactive process of exchanging information and ideas. It is important to note that the purpose of sales communication is not agreement but rather the maximization of common understanding among participants. With this emphasis on establishing understanding, communication is fundamental throughout each stage of the personal selling process. Effective communication skills are needed to identify buying needs and to demonstrate to buyers how a salesperson's proposed solution can satisfy those needs better than competitors. The critical capabilities for effective selling include questioning, listening, giving information, non-verbal communication, and written communication skills. Although each of these skills is pervasive in everyday life, they are literally the heart and soul of the interpersonal exchange that characterizes relational selling.

Verbal Communication: Questioning

There are two ways to dominate or control a selling conversation. A salesperson can talk all the time, or the salesperson can maintain a more subtle level of control by asking good thoughtful questions that guide the discussion. As highlighted in "Professional Selling in the 21st Century: Importance of Asking Questions," successful

---

Importance of Asking Questions

John Jenkins, technical sales executive for STL Technology Partners, talks about the critical importance of carefully planning and purposefully crafting questions to successfully gain the specific information you need from the customer.

As e-business continues to evolve, more and more companies are beginning to establish their business Web and Internet presence, and strong interpersonal communication skills have become critically important in working with clients. The typical business client has limited knowledge about the different functions that can be performed through dynamic Web site designs and is often unaware of the benefits that can result from a well-designed Web site. As a result, we find that two-way and highly collaborative communication between our sales teams and their clients is vital to maximize the client value delivered through our Web site designs. "If the client value is not there, we might make the immediate sale, but long-term we will lose the customer."

Although excellent listening skills are certainly crucial for selling success, questioning skills are even more important. If the salesperson doesn't ask the right questions, they won't have anything of value to listen to! Salespeople must first consider what they need to know to make the sale and compare that with what they already know from prior experience with the account. The difference represents what the salesperson must learn from the buyer to generate and present a customer-centered solution to the client's needs. This difference between what the sales team knows and what they need to know represents the information they must purposefully craft their questions to discover. The day of shooting from the hip is past—salespeople must understand what information is needed and carefully generate the right questions in the right order to elicit the needed information from a client or prospect.

---

salespeople must be masters at effectively creating and using questions. They know exactly what information they need and which type of question is best suited for eliciting that information from a prospective buyer.

Purposeful, carefully crafted questions can encourage thoughtful responses from buyers and provide richly detailed information about the buyers' current situation, needs, and expectations. This additional detail and understanding is often as meaningful for the buyer as it is for the salesperson. That is, proper questioning can facilitate both the buyer's and seller's understanding of a problem and its possible solutions.[1] For example, questions can encourage meaningful feedback regarding the buyer's attitude and the logical progression through the purchase decision process. Questioning also shows interest in the buyer and his or her needs and actively involves the buyer in the selling process. Questions can also be used to tactically redirect, regain, or hold the buyer's attention should it begin to wander during the conversation. In a similar fashion, questions can provide a convenient and subtle transition to a different topic of discussion and provide a logical guide promoting sequential thought and decision making.

Questions are typed by the results they are designed to accomplish. Does the salesperson wish to receive a free flow of thoughts and ideas or a simple yes/no confirmation? Is the salesperson seeking a general description of the overall situation or specific details regarding emergent needs or problematic experiences with current suppliers? To be effective, salespeople must understand which type of question will best accomplish their desired outcome. In this manner, questions can be typed into two basic categories: (1) amount of information and level of specificity desired, and (2) strategic purpose or intent.

Types of Questions Classified by Amount and Specificity of Information Desired

OPEN-END QUESTIONS   **Open-end questions,** also called nondirective questions, are designed to let the customer respond freely. That is, the customer is not limited to one- or two-word answers but is encouraged to disclose personal and/or business information. Open-end questions encourage buyers' thought processes and deliver richer and more expansive information than closed-end questions. Consequently, these questions are typically used to probe for descriptive information that allows the salesperson to better understand the specific needs and expectations of the customer. The secret to successfully using open-end questions lies in the first word used to form the question. Words often used to begin open-end questions include *what, how, where, when, tell, describe,* and *why.*[2] "What happens when . . . ," "How do you feel . . . ," and "Describe the . . . " are examples of open-end questions.

CLOSED-END QUESTIONS   **Closed-end questions** are designed to limit the customers' response to one or two words. This type of question is typically used to confirm or clarify information gleaned from previous responses to open-end questions. Although the most common form is the yes/no question, closed-end questions come in many forms—provided the response is limited to one or two words. For instance, "Do you . . . ," "Are you . . . ," "How many . . . ," and "How often . . ." are common closed-end questions.

DICHOTOMOUS/MULTIPLE-CHOICE QUESTIONS   **Dichotomous questions** and multiple-choice questions are directive forms of questioning. This type of question asks a customer to choose from two or more options and is used in selling to discover customer preferences and move the purchase decision process forward. An example of this form of question would be, "Which do you prefer, the _____ or the _____?"

Types of Questions Classified by Strategic Purpose

PROBING QUESTIONS   **Probing questions** are designed to penetrate below generalized or superficial information to elicit more articulate and precise details for use in needs discovery and solution identification. Rather than interrogating a buyer, probing questions are best used in a conversational style: (1) requesting clarification ("Can you share with me an example of that?" "How long has this been a problem?"); (2) encouraging elaboration ("How are you dealing with that situation now?" "What is your experience with _____?"); and (3) verifying information and responses ("That is interesting, could you tell me more?" "So, if I understand correctly, _____. Is that right?").

EVALUATIVE QUESTIONS   **Evaluative questions** use open- and closed-end question formats to gain confirmation and to uncover attitudes, opinions, and preferences held by the prospect. These questions are designed to go beyond generalized fact finding and uncover prospects' perceptions and feelings regarding existing and desired circumstances as well as potential solutions. Exemplary evaluative questions include "How do you feel about _____?" "Do you see the merits of _____?" and "What do you think _____?"

TACTICAL QUESTIONS   **Tactical questions** are used to shift or redirect the topic of discussion when the discussion gets off course or when a line of questioning proves to be of little interest or value. For example, the salesperson might be exploring the chances of plant expansion only to find that the prospect cannot provide that type of proprietary information at this early stage of the buyer-seller relationship. To avoid either embarrassing the prospect or him- or herself by proceeding on a forbidden or nonproductive line of questioning, the seller uses a strategic question designed to change topics. An example of such a tactical question might be expressed as "Earlier you mentioned that _____. Could you tell me more about how that might affect _____?"

REACTIVE QUESTIONS   **Reactive questions** are questions that refer to or directly result from information previously provided by the other party. Reactive questions are used to elicit additional information, explore for further detail, and keep the flow of information going. Illustrative reactive questions are "You mentioned that _____. Can you give me an example of what you mean?" and "That is interesting. Can you tell me how it happened?"

These different groupings of question types are not mutually exclusive. As depicted in the guidelines for combining question types in Exhibit 4.1, effective questions integrate elements from different question types. For example, "How do you feel about the current trend of sales in the industry?" is open end (classified by format) and evaluative (classified by purpose) in nature.

Regardless of the types of questions combined, Robert Jolles, senior sales training consultant for Xerox Corporation, cautions against the natural tendency to use closed-end questions rather than open-end questions. His experience and research indicate that for every open-end question the average salesperson asks, there will be 10 closed-end questions.[3] This overuse of closed-end questions is dangerous in selling. The discovery and exploration of customer needs are fundamental to relational selling, and discovery and exploration are best done with open-end questions. As discussed above, closed-end questions certainly have their place in selling, but they are best used for clarification and confirmation, not discovery and explo-

---

EXHIBIT 4.1   **Guidelines for Combining Types of Questions for Maximal Effectiveness**

		Strategic Objective or Purpose of Questioning			
		Explore and Dig for Details	**Gain Confirmation & Discover Attitudes/Opinions**	**Change Topics or Direct Attention**	**Follow Up Previously Elicited Statements**
Amount and Specificity of Information Desired	*Discussion and Interpretation*	*Open-end* Questions Designed to be *Probing* in Nature	*Open-end* Questions Designed to be *Evaluative* in Nature	*Open-end* Questions Designed to be *Tactical* in Nature	*Open-end* Questions Designed to be *Reactive* in Nature
	Confirmation and Agreement	*Closed-end* Questions Designed to be *Probing* in Nature	*Closed-end* Questions Designed to be *Evaluative* in Nature	*Closed-end* Questions Designed to be *Tactical* in Nature	*Closed-end* Questions Designed to be *Reactive* in Nature
	Choice from Alternatives	*Dichotomous or Multiple-choice* Questions Designed to be *Probing* in Nature	*Dichotomous or Multiple-choice* Questions Designed to be *Evaluative* in Nature	*Dichotomous or Multiple-choice* Questions Designed to be *Tactical* in Nature	*Dichotomous or Multiple-choice* Questions Designed to be *Reactive* in Nature

ration. An additional issue in overusing closed-end questions is that when they are used in a sequence, the resulting communication takes on the demeanor of interrogation rather than conversation.

Strategic Application of Questioning in Personal Selling

Effective questioning skills are indispensable in selling and are used to address critical issues throughout all stages of the selling process. In practice, salespeople combine the different types of questions discussed earlier to accomplish multiple and closely related sales objectives:

- *Generate Buyer Involvement.* Rather than the salesperson dominating the conversation and interaction, purposeful and planned questions are used to encourage prospective buyers to actively participate in a two-way collaborative discussion.

- *Provoke Thinking.* Innovative and effective solutions require cognitive efforts and contributions from each participant. Strategic questions stimulate buyers and salespeople to thoroughly and pragmatically think about and consider all aspects of a given situation.

- *Gather Information.* Good questions result from advance planning and should be directed toward gathering the information required to fill in the gap between "What do we need to know?" and "What do we already know?"

- *Clarification and Emphasis.* Rather than assuming that the salesperson understands what a buyer has said, questions can be used to further clarify meaning and to further emphasize the important points within a buyer-seller exchange.

- *Show Interest.* In response to statements from buyers, salespeople ask related questions and paraphrase what the buyer has said to demonstrate their interest in and understanding of what the buyer is saying.

- *Gain Confirmation.* The use of simple and direct questions allow salespeople to check back with the prospective buyer to confirm the buyer's understanding or agreement and gain his or her commitment to move forward.

- *Advance the Sale.* Effective questions are applied in a fashion that guides and moves the selling process forward in a logical progression from initiation through needs development and on through needs resolution and follow-up.

With the aim of simultaneously targeting and achieving each of these objectives, several systems have been developed to guide salespeople in properly developing and using effective questions. Two of the more prominent questioning systems are SPIN and ADAPT. Both of these systems use a logical sequencing—a sort of funneling effect—that begins with broad-based, nonthreatening, general questions. Questioning progressively proceeds through more narrowly focused questions designed to clarify the buyer's needs and to logically propel the selling process toward the presentation and demonstration of solution features, advantages, and benefits.

SPIN Questioning System

The **SPIN** system sequences four types of questions designed to uncover a buyer's current situation and inherent problems, enhance the buyer's understanding of the consequences and implications of those problems, and lead to the proposed solution.[4] SPIN is actually an acronym for the four types of questions making up the multiple question sequence: situation questions, problem questions, implication questions, and need-payoff questions.

- **Situation Questions.** This type of question solicits data and facts in the form of general background information and descriptions of the buyer's existing situation. **Situation questions** are used early in the sales call and provide salespeople with leads to further probe to fully develop the buyer's needs and expectations. Situation questions might include "Who are your current suppliers?" "Do you typically purchase or lease?" and "Who is involved in purchasing decisions?" Situation questions are essential, but they should be used in moderation as too many general fact-finding questions can bore the buyer. Further, their interrogating nature can result in irritated buyers.

- **Problem Questions. Problem questions** follow the more general situation questions to further probe for specific difficulties, developing problems and areas of dissatisfaction that might be positively addressed by the salesperson's proposed sales offering. Some examples of problem questions include "How critical is this component for your production?" "What kinds of problems have you encountered with your current suppliers?" and "What types of reliability problems do you experience with your current system?" Problem questions actively involve the buyer and can assist him or her in better understanding his or her own problems and needs. Nevertheless, inexperienced and unsuccessful salespeople generally do not ask enough problem questions.

- **Implication Questions. Implication questions** follow and relate to the information flowing from problem questions. Their purpose is to assist the buyer in thinking about the potential consequences of the problem and understand the urgency of resolving the problem in a way that motivates him or her to seek a solution. Typical implication questions might include "How does this affect profitability?" "What impact does the slow response of your current supplier have on the productivity of your operation?" "How would a faster piece of equipment improve productivity and profits?" and "What happens when the supplier is late with a shipment?" Although implication questions are closely linked to success in selling, even experienced salespeople rarely use them effectively.

- **Need-payoff Questions.** Based on the implications of a problem, salespeople use **need-payoff questions** to propose a solution and develop commitment from the buyer. These questions refocus the buyer's attention to solutions rather than problems and get the buyer to think about the positive benefits derived from solving the problems. Examples of need-payoff questions are "Would more frequent deliveries allow you to increase productivity?" "If we could provide you increased reliability, would you be interested?" "If we could improve the quality of your purchased components, how would that help you?" and "Would you be interested in increasing productivity by 15 percent?" Top salespeople effectively incorporate a higher number of need-payoff questions into sales calls than do less successful salespeople.

ADAPT Questioning System

As illustrated by Figure 4.1, the **ADAPT** questioning system uses a logic-based funneling sequence of questions, beginning with broad and generalized inquiries designed to identify and assess the buyer's situation. Based on information gained in this first phase, further questions are generated to probe and discover more details regarding the needs and expectations of the buyer. In turn, the resulting information is incorporated in further collaborative discussion in a way that activates the

---

| FIGURE 4.1 | Funneling Sequence of ADAPT Technique for Needs Discovery |

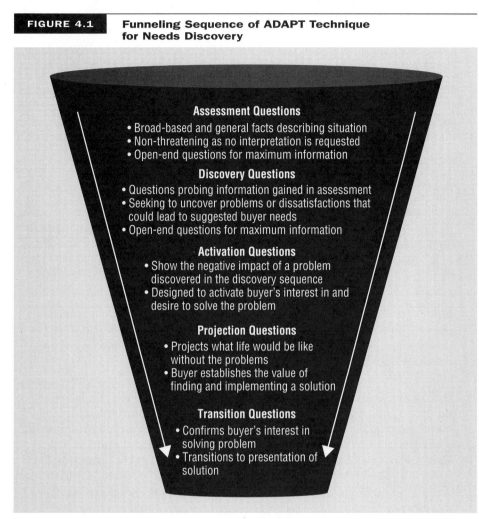

Assessment Questions
- Broad-based and general facts describing situation
- Non-threatening as no interpretation is requested
- Open-end questions for maximum information

Discovery Questions
- Questions probing information gained in assessment
- Seeking to uncover problems or dissatisfactions that could lead to suggested buyer needs
- Open-end questions for maximum information

Activation Questions
- Show the negative impact of a problem discovered in the discovery sequence
- Designed to activate buyer's interest in and desire to solve the problem

Projection Questions
- Projects what life would be like without the problems
- Buyer establishes the value of finding and implementing a solution

Transition Questions
- Confirms buyer's interest in solving problem
- Transitions to presentation of solution

The ADAPT questioning technique logically sequences questions from broad and general inquiries through increasingly detailed questions for effective needs discovery.

buyer's motivation to implement a solution and further establishes the buyer's perceived value of a possible solution. The last phase of ADAPT questioning transitions to the buyer's commitment to learn about the proposed solution and grants the salesperson permission to move forward into the presentation and demonstration of the sales offering. ADAPT is an acronym for the five stages of strategic questioning and represents what the salesperson should be doing at each stage: assessment questions, discovery questions, activation questions, projection questions, and transition questions.[5]

- **Assessment Questions.** This initial phase of questioning is designed to be nonthreatening and to spark conversation that elicits factual information about the customer's current situation that can provide a basis for further exploration and probing. As illustrated in Exhibit 4.2, **assessment questions** do not seek conclusions—rather, at a macro or 40,000-foot level of focus, these questions should address the buyer's company and operation, goals and objectives, market trends and customers, current suppliers, and even the buyer as an individual. The information sought should augment or confirm precall research. Examples would include "What is the current

---

EXHIBIT 4.2 **Assessment Questions**

These questions are designed to elicit factual information about the customer's current situation. These questions do not seek conclusions; rather they seek information that describes the customer and his or her business environment. The information sought should augment or confirm precall research.

Examples:
1. "What types of operating arrangements do you have with your suppliers?"
2. "Who is involved in the purchase decision-making process?"

Assessment questions are generally open end; however, closed-end questions are used when seeking confirmation or basic descriptive information. For example, "So, you currently work with 10 different suppliers?" or "How many years have you been in business?" Assessment questions are necessary for drawing out information early in the sales cycle.

> We use a JIT system with our main suppliers . . .
>
> I make the decisions regarding suppliers . . .

---

level of your production?" "How long has the current equipment been in place?" "How many suppliers are currently being used?" "What are the growth objectives of the company?" and "What individuals have input into purchase decisions?"

- **Discovery Questions.** As portrayed in Exhibit 4.3, these questions follow up on the responses gained from the preceding assessment questions. At a more micro and ground-level focus, **discovery questions** should drill down and probe for further details needed to fully develop, clarify, and understand the nature of the buyer's problems. Facts as well as the buyer's interpretations, perceptions, feelings, and opinions are sought in regard to the buyer's needs, wants, dissatisfactions, and expectations relevant to product, delivery requirements, budget and financing issues, and desired service levels. The goal is to discover needs and dissatisfactions that the salesperson's sales offering can resolve. Examples of discovery questions might include "How often do these equipment failures occur?" "How well are your current suppliers performing?" "What disadvantages do you see in the current process?" "How satisfied are you with the quality of components you are currently purchasing?" and "How difficult are these for your operators to use?"

- **Activation Questions.** The implied or suggested needs gained from discovery questions are not usually sufficient to gain the sale. Often, a buyer will believe that a particular problem does not cause any significant negative consequences, hence the motivation to solve the problem will carry a low priority. Successful salespeople help the customer realistically evaluate the full impact of the implied need through the use of **activation questions.** As detailed in Exhibit 4.4, the objective is to "activate" the customer's interest in solving discovered problems by helping him or her to gain insight into the true ramifications of the problem and to realize that what may initially seem to be of little consequence is, in fact, of significant consequence. Examples include "What effects do these equipment breakdowns have on your business operations?" "To what extent are these increases in overtime expenses affecting profitability?" "How will the supplier's inability to deliver on time affect your planned expansion?" and "When components fail in the field, how does that influence customer satisfaction and repurchase?"

EXHIBIT 4.3   **Discovery Questions**

Discovery questions are used to uncover problems or dissatisfactions the customer is experiencing that the salesperson's product or company may be able to solve. Basically, these questions are used to "distill" or "boil down" the information gained from the preceding assessment questions and from precall research into suggested needs.

Examples:
1. "I understand you prefer a Just-in-Time (JIT) relationship with your suppliers—how have they been performing?"
2. "So, your current suppliers are occasionally late with deliveries?"

> Pretty well . . . an occasional late delivery . . . but pretty well
>
> Yes . . . sometimes

The *suggested* needs gained from discovery questions are used as a foundation for the rest of the sales call. Yet, a *suggested* need is usually not sufficient to close the sale. Often, a customer will believe that a particular problem does not cause any significant negative consequences. If this is the case, finding a solution to the problem will be a very low priority. The professional salesperson must then help the customer to reevaluate the impact of the *suggested* need by asking activation questions.

EXHIBIT 4.4   **Activation Questions**

Activation questions are used to show the impact of a problem, uncovered through Discovery questions, on the customer's entire operation. The objective is to "activate" the customer's interest in solving the problem by helping him or her to gain insight into the true ramifications of the problem and realize that what may seem to be of little consequence is, in fact, of significant consequence.

Examples:
1. "What effect does your supplier's late delivery have on your operation?"
2. "If production drops off, how are your operating costs affected, and how does that affect your customers?"

> It slows production . . . Operating costs go up . . .
>
> Customer orders delayed . . . Potential to lose customers . . .

Activation questions show the negative impact of a problem so that finding a solution to that problem is desirable. Now, the salesperson can help the customer to discover the positive impact of solving the problems by using Projection questions.

- **Projection Questions.** As a natural extension of the activation questions, **projection questions** encourage and facilitate the buyer in "projecting" what it would be like without the problems that have been previously "discovered" and "activated." The use of good projection questions accomplishes several positive outcomes. First, the focus is switched from problems and their associated consequences to the upside—the benefits to be derived from solving the problems. What were initially perceived as costs and expenses are now logically structured as benefits to the buyer and his or her organization—the payoff for taking action and investing in a solution. Second—and equally important—the benefit payoff allows the buyer to establish the realistic value of implementing a solution. In this manner, the benefit payoff is perceived as a positive value received and serves as the foundation for demonstrating what the solution is worth—what the buyer would be willing to pay. As illustrated in Exhibit 4.5, projection questions encourage the buyer to think about how and why he or she should go about resolving a problem. In essence, projective questions assist the buyer in selling himself or herself by establishing the worth of the proposed solution. The customer, rather than the salesperson, establishes the benefits of solving the problem. This reinforces the importance of solving the problem and reduces the number of objections that might be raised. Examples of projection questions include "If a supplier was never late with a delivery, what effects would that have on your overall operation?" "What would be the impact on profitability if you did not have problems with limited plant capacity and the resulting overtime expenses?" "How would a system that your operators found easier to use affect your business operations?" and "If component failures were minimized, what impact would the resulting improvement in customer satisfaction have on financial performance?"

- **Transition Questions. Transition questions** are used to smooth the transition from needs discovery into the presentation and demonstration of the proposed solution's features, advantages, and benefits. As exemplified in Exhibit 4.6, transition questions are typically closed end and evaluative in format. These questions confirm the buyer's desire to seek a solution and give their consent to the salesperson to move forward with the selling process. Examples include "So, having suppliers that are consistently on time is important to you—if I could show you how our company assures

---

EXHIBIT 4.5   **Projection Questions**

Projection questions help the customer to "project" what life would be like without the problems or dissatisfactions uncovered through activation questions. This helps the customer to see value in finding solutions to the problems developed earlier in the sales call.

Examples:
1. **"If a supplier was never late with a delivery, what effects would that have on your JIT operating structure?"**
2. **"If a supplier helped you meet the expectations of your customers, what impact would that have on your business?"**

These questions are used to let the customer tell the salesperson the benefits of solving the problem. By doing so, the customer is reinforcing in his or her mind the importance of solving the problem and reducing the number of objections that might be raised.

> It would run smoother and at lower cost . . .
>
> Increased customer satisfaction would mean more business . . .

EXHIBIT 4.6   **Transition Questions**

Transition questions are simple closed-end questions that confirm the customer's desire to solve the problem(s) uncovered through the previous questions.

Examples:
1. **"So, having a supplier who is never late with deliveries is important to you?"**
2. **"If I can show you how our company ensures on-time delivery, would you be interested in pursuing a formal business arrangement with our company?"**

The primary function of these questions is to make the transition from need confirmation into the sales presentation. In addition, these questions can lead to a customer commitment, provided the salesperson adequately presents how his or her company can solve the customer's problems.

> Yes, it is.
>
> Yes, if I'm convinced your company can guarantee on-time delivery . . .

you of on-time delivery, would you be interested?" "It seems that increasing capacity is a key to reducing overtime and increasing profitability—would you be interested in a way to increase capacity by 20 percent through a simple addition to your production process?" and "Would you be interested in a system that is easier for your operators to use?"

Verbal Communication: Listening

Listening is the other half of effective questioning. After all, asking the customer for information is of little value if the salesperson does not listen. As illustrated by "Professional Selling in the 21st Century: Success in Selling Equates to Effectively Listening," effective listening is rated among the most critical skills for successful selling. Yet, most of us share the common problem of being a lot better at sending messages than receiving them, and effective listening is often considered to be the number one weakness of salespeople.[6]

Poor listening skills have been identified as one of the primary causes of salesperson failure.[7] In order to get the information needed to best serve, identify and respond to needs, and nurture a collaborative buyer-seller relationship, salespeople must be able to listen and understand what was said *and* what was meant. Nevertheless, situations similar to the one depicted in "An Ethical Dilemma" are all too common. As illustrated by Figure 4.2, effective listening can be broken down into six primary facets:

1. Pay attention—Listen to understand, not to reply. Resist the urge to interupt and receive the full message the buyer is communicating.

2. Monitor nonverbals—Make effective eye contact and check to see if the buyer's body language and speech patterns match what is being said.

3. Paraphrase and repeat—Confirm your correct understanding of what the buyer is saying by paraphrasing and repeating what you have heard.

4. Make no assumptions—Ask questions to clarify the meaning of what the buyer is communicating.

PROFESSIONAL SELLING IN THE 21ST CENTURY

Success in Selling Equates to Effectively Listening

Jennifer Blessin, marketing representative for Caterpillar, emphasizes the importance of active listening in today's trust-based selling environment.

The research and information you gather prior to calling on a prospect might tell you exactly what he or she needs—but do not count on it. The ultimate source for information about what the buyer needs is the buyer, and how well the salesperson listens will determine how well he or she sells. Trust-based selling is listening to the customer—finding out what his or her concerns are, discovering what he or she needs, and trying to provide the buyer a unique, value-added solution. The only way to do this is to listen, and listen well.

We emphasize that as long as buyers are providing information, the salesperson should give them undivided attention. Focus on what buyers are saying. Rather than interrupting, let them finish their thoughts and provide them with positive feedback such as nodding the head, paraphrasing what they have said, or saying "I understand" to encourage them to continue. As much as a salesperson might want to jump in and respond to a buyer's comments, he or she must resist the temptation. The words that might be cut off and missed could be the key to making a sale.

An Ethical Dilemma

Traci Sutton is a Regional Account Manager for a large, Chicago-based manufacturer of printing equipment and supplies. Traci feels that her 11 years of experience in the field provide her with a level of expertise and knowledge greater than most prospective buyers. This, combined with her unbridled impatience, often results in Traci interrupting buyers' statements, finishing their thoughts for them, and assuming she understands the buyer's situation and needs. Rather than allowing the buyer to fully describe what is going on and the nature of the buying organization's problems and needs, oftentimes Traci seems to be telling the buyer what his or her organization needs and should expect. Traci continues to sell products; however, her customer retention level is below average and her sales revenues seem to have peaked out. If you were Traci Sutton, how would you go about improving your listening skills in order to set your sales performance back on track?

FIGURE 4.2   Six Facets of Effective Listening

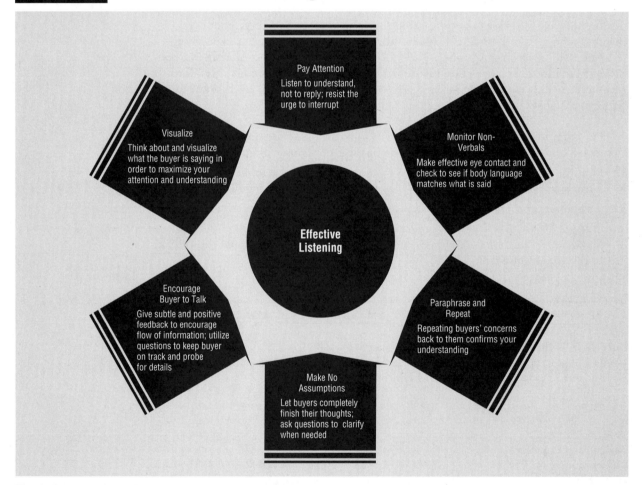

The six facets of effective listening enable salespeople to better pickup, sort out, and interpret buyers' verbal and nonverbal messages.

5. Encourage the buyer to talk—Encourage the flow of information by giving positive feedback and help the buyer stay on track by asking purposeful, related questions.

6. Visualize—Maximize your attention and comprehension by thinking about and visualizing what the buyer is saying.

The practiced listening skills of high performance salespeople enable them to pickup, sort out, and interpret a higher number of buyers' verbal and nonverbal messages than lower-performing salespeople. In addition to gaining information and understanding critical to the relational selling process, a salesperson's good listening behaviors provide the added benefits of positively influencing the formation and continuation of buyer-seller relationships. The effective use and demonstration of good listening skills by a salesperson are positively associated with the customer's trust in the salesperson and the anticipation of having future interactions with the salesperson.[8] Clearly, effective listening is a critical component in trust-based, relational selling, and success requires continuous practice and improvement of our listening skills.

Using Different Types of Listening

Communications research identifies two primary categories of listening: *social* and *serious*.[9] **Social listening** is an informal mode of listening that can be associated with day-to-day conversation and entertainment. Social listening is characterized by low levels of cognitive activity and concentration and is typically used in conversation with a friend or a store clerk or listening to music, a concert, a TV program, or even a play. The received messages are taken at face value and do not require a high degree of concentration or thinking to sort through, interpret, and understand. However, **serious listening** is associated with events or topics in which it is important to sort through, interpret, understand, and respond to received messages. The serious form of listening is often referred to as *active listening*, as it requires high levels of concentration and cognition about the messages being received. *Concentration* is required to break through the distractions and other interference to facilitate receiving and remembering specific messages. *Cognition* is used to sort through and select the meaningful relevant messages and interpret them for meaning, information, and response.

ACTIVE LISTENING   **Active listening** in a selling context is defined as "the cognitive process of actively sensing, interpreting, evaluating, and responding to the verbal and nonverbal messages of present or potential customers."[10] This definition is very useful to those wishing to master active listening skills. First, it underscores the importance of receiving and interpreting both verbal and nonverbal cues and messages to better determine the full and correct meaning of the message. Second, it

| FIGURE 4.3 | SIER Hierarchy of Active Listening |

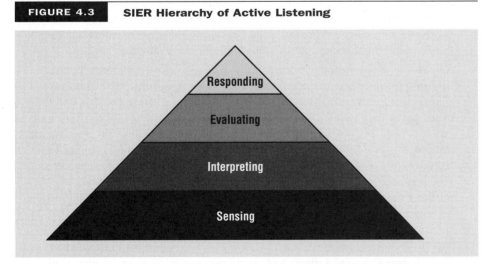

Active listening is a cognitive process of actively sensing, interpreting, evaluating, and responding to verbal and nonverbal messages from buyers and prospects.

incorporates a well-accepted model of listening. As illustrated in Figure 4.3, the **SIER** model depicts active listening as a hierarchical, four-step sequence of sensing, interpreting, evaluating, and responding.[11] Effective active listening requires each of these four hierarchical process activities to be carried out successfully and in proper succession.

- *Sensing.* Listening is much more than simply hearing. Nevertheless, the first activities in active listening are **sensing** (i.e., hear and see) and receiving (i.e., pay attention to) the verbal and nonverbal components of the message being sent. Sensing does not occur without practice and should not be taken for granted. In fact, research indicates that most of us listen at only 25 percent of our capacity. Think about yourself. How often have you had to ask someone to repeat what he or she said or perhaps assumed you knew what the sender was going to say before they could say it? Increased concentration and attention can improve sensing effectiveness. Taking notes, making eye contact with the sender, and not interrupting can improve sensing skills. Let the sender finish and provide the full content of the message. This not only improves the concentration of the receiver but also encourages the sender to provide more information and detail.

- *Interpreting.* After the message is received, it must be correctly interpreted. **Interpreting** addresses the question of "What meaning does the sender intend?" Both content and context are important. That is, in addition to the semantic meaning of the words and symbols, we must consider the experiences, knowledge, and attitudes of the sender to fully understand what was meant. Hold back the temptation to evaluate the message until the sender is through. Note the nonverbal and verbal cues along with possible consistencies and inconsistencies between them. Incorporate knowledge of the sender's background and previous relevant statements and positions into the message interpretation.

- *Evaluating.* Active listening requires the receiver to decide whether he or she agrees with the sender's message. The results from the interpretation stage are evaluated to sort fact from opinion and emotion. Too often, receivers complete this activity prior to receiving the full message, and on hearing something with which they disagree, the sender is effectively tuned out. As a result, communication is stifled. **Evaluating** can be improved through improved concentration and thoughtful consideration of the full message. Summarizing the key points as if they were going to be reported to others can further enhance evaluation skills. Searching for areas of interest rather than prejudging the message can also facilitate the evaluation process.

- *Responding.* **Responding** is both an expectation and requirement for active listening to be effective. Collaborative, two-way communication requires that the listener respond to the sender. Responses provide feedback to the other party, emphasize understanding, encourage further elaboration, and can serve as a beginning point for the receiver to transition into the role of sender for the next message set. Responses can take many forms. Nonverbal cues such as nodding and smiling can indicate that the receiver's message was received. Responses in the form of restating and paraphrasing the sender's message can provide strong signals of interest and understanding. Asking questions can elicit additional details and clarification.

The SIER model provides a useful framework for evaluating communication accuracy and pinpointing the sources of problems. Similarly, it can be effectively used

---

EXHIBIT 4.7	Ten Keys to Effective Listening

	The Key Practice	The Weak Listener	The Strong Listener
1	Find areas of interest	Tunes out dry subjects	Actively looks for opportunities of common interest
2	Judge content, not delivery	Tunes out if the delivery is poor	Skips over delivery errors and focuses on content
3	Hold your fire until full consideration	Evaluates & enters argument prior to completion of message	Does not judge or evaluate until message is complete
4	Listen for ideas	Listens for facts	Listens for central themes
5	Be flexible	Takes intensive and detailed notes	Takes fewer notes and limits theme to central theme and key ideas presented
6	Work at listening	Shows no energy output Attention is faked	Works hard at attending the message and exhibits active body state
7	Resist distractions	Distracted easily	Resists distractions and knows how to concentrate
8	Exercise your mind	Resists difficult expository material in favor of light recreational materials	Uses complex and heavy material as exercise for the mind
9	Keep an open mind	Reacts to emotional words	Interprets color words but does not get hung up on them
10	Capitalize on fact that thought is faster than speech	Tends to daydream with slow speakers	Challenges, anticipates, mentally summarizes, weighs evidence, & listens between the lines

for planning activities and behaviors designed to improve communication effectiveness. As depicted by the SIER model, active listening is a hierarchical and sequential process. One must sense the message before it can be interpreted. In turn, the message must be interpreted before it can be evaluated. Finally, it must be effectively evaluated prior to generating a proper response. When diagnosing a listening breakdown, one should look for the lowest level in the hierarchy where the breakdown could have originated and take proper action to remedy the problem. Exhibit 4.7 describes 10 specific keys to effective listening that can be used in conjunction with the SIER model to pinpoint and improve listening problems.

Verbal Communication: Giving Information

Verbal information refers to statements of fact, opinion, and attitude that are encoded in the form of words, pictures, and numbers in such a way that they convey meaning to a receiver. However, many words and symbols mean different things to different people. Different industries, different cultures, and different types of training or work experience can result in the same word or phrase having multiple interpretations. For instance, to a design or production engineer, the word *quality* might mean "manufactured within design tolerance." However, to a customer it might be translated as "meeting or exceeding expectations." To maximize clarity and minimize misunderstandings, understand and use the vocabulary and terminology that corresponds with the perspective of the customer.

Understanding the Superiority of Pictures over Words

Studies in cognitive psychology have found that pictures tend to be more memorable than their verbal counterparts.[12] The fact that pictures enhance understanding and are more easily recalled than abstract words and symbols has several implications for effective selling.

- The verbal message should be constructed in a manner that generates a mental picture in the receiver's mind. For example, the phrase "Tropicana juices are bursting with flavor" is more visual than the more abstract version "Tropicana juices have more flavor." This can also be accomplished by providing a short and illustrative analogy or illustrative story to emphasize a key point and bring it alive in the buyer's mind.

- Rather than abstract words that convey only a broad general understanding, use words and phrases that convey concrete and detailed meaning. Concrete expressions provide the receiver with greater information and are less likely to be misunderstood than their abstract counterparts. For example, "This web transfer system will increase weekly production by 2,100 units" provides more detail than "This web transfer system will increase production by 10 percent." Similarly, "This conveyor is faster than your existing system" does not deliver the same impact as "This conveyor system will move your product from production to shipping at 50 feet per second as compared with your current system's 20 feet per second."

- Integrate relevant visual sales aids into verbal communication. Sales support materials that explain and reinforce the verbal message will aid the receiver's understanding and enhance recall of the message. As an additional benefit, sales aids such as samples, brochures, graphs, and comparative charts can be left with the buyer to continue selling until the salesperson's next call on the buyer.

Impact of Grammar and Logical Sequencing

Grammar and logical sequencing are also important in the process of giving information to others. The use of proper grammar is a given in business and social communication. In its absence, the receiver of the message tends to exhibit three closely related behaviors. First, the meaning and credibility of the message are significantly downgraded. Second, the receiver begins to focus on the sender rather than the message, which materially reduces the probability of effective communication. Last, the receiver dismisses the sender and the sender's organization as being unqualified to perform the role of an effective supplier and partner. The importance of proper grammar should not be overlooked.

Similarly, whether one is engaged in simply explaining details or making a formal proposal, logical sequencing of the material is critical. The facts and details must be organized and connected in a logical order. This is essential to clarity and assists the receiver in following the facts. A discussion or presentation that jumps around risks being inefficient and ineffective. At best, the receiver will have to ask a high number of clarification questions. At worst, the receiver will dismiss the salesperson as incompetent and close off the sales negotiation. Advance planning and preparation can improve organization. Outline what needs to be covered and organize it into a logical flow. The outline becomes the agenda to be covered and can serve as an aid for staying on track.

Nonverbal Communication

Nonverbal behaviors have been recognized as an important dimension of communication since medieval times. As early as 1605, Francis Bacon focused on the messages conveyed by *manual language*. Verbal communication deals with the semantic meaning of the message itself while the nonverbal dimension consists of the more abstract message conveyed by how the message is delivered. **Nonverbal communication** is the conscious and unconscious reactions, movements, and utterances that people use in addition to the words and symbols associated with language. This dimension of communication includes eyes and facial expressions, placement and movements of hands, arms, head, and legs as well as body orientation, the amount of space maintained between individuals, and variations in voice characteristics. Collectively, the various forms of nonverbal communication carry subtle as well as explicit meanings and feelings along with the language message and are frequently more informative than the verbal content of a message.[13]

Research indicates that highly successful salespeople are capable of picking out and comprehending a higher number of behavioral cues from buyers than less successful salespeople are able to sense and interpret. In addition, evidence shows that 50 percent or more of the meaning conveyed within the communication process stems from nonverbal behavior.[14] As the nonverbal components of a message carry as much or more meaning than the language portions, it is critical for salespeople to effectively sense, accurately interpret, and fully evaluate the nonverbal elements of a message in addition to the verbal components. In addition to sensing verbal messages, learn to sense between the words for the thoughts and feelings not being conveyed verbally.

Facial Expressions

Possibly reflecting its central point of focus in interpersonal communication, the various elements of the face play a key role in giving off nonverbal messages. Frowning, pursed lips, and squinted eyes are common in moments of uncertainty, disagreement, and even outright skepticism. Suspicion and anger are typically accompanied by tightness along the jaw line. Smiles are indicative of agreement and interest while biting of one's lip can signal uncertainty. Raised eyebrows can signify surprise and are often found in moments of consideration and evaluation.

Eye Movements

In North America and western Europe, avoidance of eye contact results in a negative message and is often associated with deceit and dishonesty. However, increased eye contact by the sender infers honesty and self-confidence. Increased eye contact by the receiver of the message signals increasing levels of interest and concentration. However, when eye contact becomes a stare and continues unbroken by glances away or blinking, it is typically interpreted as a threat or inference of power. A blank stare or eye contact directed away from the conversation can show disinterest and boredom. Repeated glances made toward one's watch or possibly an exit door often indicate that the conversation is about to end.

Placement and Movements of Hands, Arms, Head, and Legs

Smooth and gradual movements denote calm and confidence, whereas jerky and hurried movements are associated with nervousness and stress. Uncrossed arms and legs signal openness, confidence, and cooperation. However, crossed arms and legs psychologically close out the other party and express disagreement and defensiveness. Increased movement of the head and limbs hints at increasing tension, as does the tight clasping of hands or fists. The placement of a hand on the chin or a tilted head suggests increased levels of evaluation, whereas nodding of the head expresses agreement. Growing impatience is associated with drumming of the fingers or patting of a foot. The fingering of one's hair and rubbing the back of the neck signifies increasing nervousness and apprehension.

Body Posture and Orientation

Fidgeting and shifting from side to side is generally considered to be a negative message associated with nervousness and apprehension. Leaning forward or sitting forward on the edge of a chair is a general sign of increasing interest and a positive disposition in regard to what is being discussed. Similarly, leaning away can indicate disinterest, boredom, or even distrust. Leaning back with both hands placed behind one's head signifies a perceived sense of smugness and superiority. A rigid erect posture can convey inflexibility or even defensiveness whereas sloppy posture suggests disinterest in the topic. Similar to sitting backward in a chair, sitting on the edge of the table or the arm of a chair is an expression of power and superiority.

Proxemics

Proxemics refers to the personal distance that individuals prefer to keep between themselves and other individuals and is an important element of nonverbal communication. The distance that one places between oneself and others implies a meaningful message and affects the outcome of the selling process. If a salesperson pushes too close to a prospect who requires more distance, the prospect may perceive the salesperson to be manipulative, intimidating, and possibly threatening. However, salespeople who put too much distance between themselves and the customer risk being perceived as rigidly formal, aloof, or even apprehensive.

Proxemics differs across cultures and regions of the world. For example, in North Africa and Latin America business is conducted at a much closer distance than in North America. As depicted in Figure 4.4, North Americans generally recognize four distinct proxemic zones. The *intimate zone* is reserved for intimate relationships with immediate family and loved ones. The *personal zone* is for personal relationships with close friends and associates. The *social zone* is for business client relationships and is the zone in which most business is conducted. The *public zone* is for the general public and group settings such as classrooms and presentations.

It is critical that salespeople understand proxemics and monitor the progression of their buyer-seller relationships so as to properly position themselves with different customers. Typically, salespeople begin working with a prospect at the far end of the *social zone*. As the salesperson-buyer relationship develops, the salesper-

---

FIGURE 4.4   **Personal Space and Interpersonal Communication**

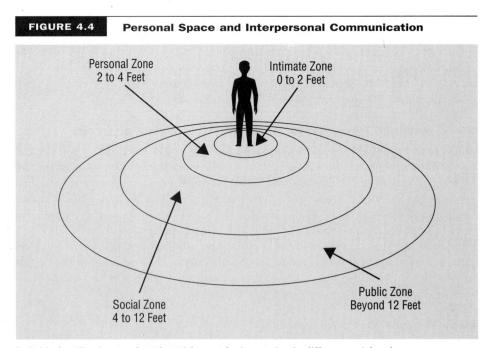

Individuals utilize four preferred spatial zones for interaction in different social and business situations.

son is in a position to move closer without violating the customer's space and causing him or her to become defensive.

Variations in Voice Characteristics

Nonverbal voice characteristics such as speaking rates, pause duration, pitch or frequency, and intensity have been linked to communication effectiveness and selling performance. These voice characteristics convey direct as well as subtle and implied meanings and feelings that can complement or accent the corresponding verbal message.[15]

SPEAKING RATES AND PAUSE DURATION   Within normal speaking rates, faster speakers are generally evaluated more favorably than slower speakers. Contrary to the often-cited fast-talking salesperson being perceived as high pressure; faster rates of speech and shorter pause duration are actually associated with higher levels of intelligence, credibility, and knowledge.[16] Slower speakers are perceived as being less competent as well as less benevolent. However, speech rates that are jerky and beyond normal rates of speech can present problems in sensing and interpreting the complete message. Varying the rate of speech has also been found to be conducive to maintaining interest.

PITCH OR FREQUENCY   Voice pitch carries a great deal of information to the receiver. Varying pitch and frequency during the course of a message is used to encourage attentiveness of the listener and to accent certain forms of statements. A rising pitch during the message is associated with questions and can often be perceived as reflecting uncertainty. Just the opposite, a falling pitch is associated with declarative statements and completion of the message. Overall, high-pitched voices are judged as less truthful, less emphatic, less potent, and more nervous. Lower-pitched voices have been found to be more persuasive and truthful and have a positive impact on selling performance.

INTENSITY AND LOUDNESS   Dominance, superiority, intensity, and aggression are commonly associated with loud voices, whereas soft voices characterize submission and uncertainty. However, it is the variability of intensity that has been found to be most effective in communication. Varying levels of loudness allow the sender to adapt to different situations and environments. Variation also increases the receiver's attention and can provide additional information inputs by accenting key points of a message.

Using Nonverbal Clusters

Nonverbal clusters are groups of related expressions, gestures, and movements. Similar to a one-word expression, a single isolated gesture or movement should not be taken as a reliable indication of the true intent or meaning of a message. Sensing and interpreting groups or clusters of nonverbal cues provide a more reliable indicator of the message and intent. When the individual behaviors and gestures begin to fit together, they form a common and unified message that should be considered by the salesperson. Common nonverbal clusters applicable to selling communication are described in Exhibit 4.8.

Just as nonverbal messages can be interpreted by salespeople to better interpret and understand communication with prospects and buyers, those same prospects and buyers can also sense and interpret the nonverbal messages being sent by the salesperson. Consequently, it is important that salespersons monitor the nonverbal cues they are sending to ensure consistency with and reinforcement of the intended message.

| EXHIBIT 4.8 | Common Nonverbal Clusters |

Cluster Name	Cluster Meaning	Body Posture and Orientation	Movement of Hands, Arms & Legs	Eyes & Facial Expressions
Openness	Openness, flexibility and sincerity	• Moving closer • Leaning forward	• Open hands • Removing coat • Unbutton collar • Uncrossed arms and legs	• Slight smile • Good eye contact
Defensiveness	Defensiveness, skepticism, and apprehension	• Rigid body	• Crossed arms & legs • Clenched fists	• Minimal eye contact • Glancing sideways • Pursed lips
Evaluation	Evaluation and consideration of message	• Leaning forward	• Hand on cheek • Stroking chin • Chin in palm of hand	• Tilted head • Dropping glasses to lower nose
Deception	Dishonesty and secretiveness	• Patterns of rocking	• Fidgeting with objects • Increased leg movements	• Increased eye movement • Frequent gazes elsewhere • Forced smile
Readiness	Dedication or commitment	• Sitting forward	• Hands on hips • Legs uncrossed • Feet flat on floor	• Increased eye contact
Boredom	Lack of interest and impatience	• Head in palm of hands • Slouching	• Drumming fingers • Swinging a foot • Brushing & picking at items • Tapping feet	• Poor eye contact • Glancing at watch • Blank stares

Written Communication: Sales Proposals

Those who lack experience in selling view it primarily as a verbal process rather than as a comprehensive communication process. In reality, professional selling requires that salespeople be well-rounded communicators, skilled in questioning, listening, and presenting information. Verbal communication is extremely important to most salespeople, but written communication is also vitally important.

With multimedia sales presentations becoming more routine, it is natural to think that written sales communication would be declining in importance. Actually, the opposite is true. With the widespread use of multimedia, the standards for all sales communication continue to rise. Buyers expect clear informative sales messages, and they are less tolerant of sloppy communication. Because everyone knows that word-processing programs have subroutines to check spelling and grammar, for example, mistakes are less acceptable than ever.

There are several situations in which written sales communication is especially important. In sales of major magnitude effective written communication becomes critical. Contracts, written sales proposals, and letters often document the entire process and agreement between parties. Many purchasing decisions involve multiple influences. In such situations, written communication can keep all parties informed simultaneously. Further, multipart sales messages, such as detailed sales proposals, can be dissected and evaluated by the appropriate members of the buying team. Written communication is often essential in sales to customers across national boundaries. Another situation in which written communication can be crucial is when legal issues are relevant, including the granting of promises or implied warranties. And, on an everyday basis, salespeople rely on written communication as another means of staying in touch with customers and members of their own organization. Written communication of this type has become even more prevalent due to the widespread acceptance and use of the Internet.

Because written communication provides a permanent record of claims and intentions, salespeople should be careful not to over promise, while still maintaining a positive and supportive tone. No buyer wants to read a proposal full of legal disclaimers and warnings, yet such information may be a necessary ingredient in certain written communication. As with all communication, salespeople should try to give buyers the information they need to make informed decisions.

Written communication offers salespeople a significant opportunity to differentiate themselves from their competitors. Recent college graduates are similar to businesspeople in general in that their verbal communication skills often exceed their written communication skills. Those who work to develop their written communication skills usually stand out from the crowd, and they do not spend as much time laboring to achieve effectiveness in their written communication.

Writing Effective Proposals

Written sales proposals are increasing in both frequency and importance. The total packages of product and service offerings being sold in today's marketplace have continued to grow in complexity. These complex sales require multiple sales calls and, more often than not, some form of a written proposal that becomes an integral part of the sales presentation. In other instances, written proposals are mailed or delivered by express courier rather than in person. In either case, an effective and well-written proposal is capable of continued selling in the absence of the salesperson.

Whether the proposal is in response to a buyer's request for proposals (RFP) or generated to complement and strengthen a sales presentation, it is essential that the proposal be correctly written and convey the required information in an attractive manner. Reflecting back on their research and years of experience as business consultants, Robert Kantin and Mark Hardwick have reduced the most commonly found shortcomings of written proposals to the following list, which they title "The Seven Deadly Mistakes" of proposal writing.[17]

1. Not writing a proposal—substituting a brochure and cover letter for a full proposal.
2. Not fully understanding the customer's business.
3. Missing the buyer's submission deadline.
4. Producing a proposal with little "drive-up" appeal.
5. Not saying anything that really makes a difference.
6. Using a standardized boilerplate approach.
7. No one owning the responsibility or having the authority to create quality and effective proposals.

Clearly, developing a quality proposal takes time and effort. However, the process of writing an effective proposal can be simplified by breaking the proposal down into its primary and distinct parts. The five parts common to most proposals are an executive summary, a needs and benefits analysis, a company description, the pricing and sales agreement, and the suggested action and timeline.[18]

EXECUTIVE SUMMARY   This summary precedes the full proposal and serves two critical functions. First, it should succinctly and clearly demonstrate the salesperson's understanding of the customer's needs and the relevance of the proposed solution. An effective summary will spell out the customer's problems, the nature of the proposed solution, and the resulting benefits to the customer. A second function of the summary is to build a desire to read the full proposal. This is important as many key members of the organization often read little more than the information provided in the summary. A question commonly asked by new salespeople refers to the length of the executive summary. A good rule of thumb is that an executive summary should be limited to two typewritten pages—especially if the main body of the report is fewer than 50 pages in length.

NEEDS AND BENEFITS ANALYSIS   This section is typically composed of two primary parts. First, the situation analysis should concisely explain the salesperson's understanding of the customer's situation, problems, and needs. Second, the recommended solution is presented and supported with illustrations and evidence on how the proposed solution uniquely addresses the buyer's problems and needs. The emphasis in this section should be on the benefits resulting from the solution and not on the product or service being sold. It is important that these benefits be described from the perspective of the customer. Proprietary information required in the proposal can be protected in a number of ways. The most common method is to place a notice on the cover (i.e., "Confidential" or "For Review Purposes Only"). Many technology companies ask the prospect to sign a nondisclosure agreement that is part of the overall document, and in some instances, the selling organization will even copyright the proposal.

COMPANY DESCRIPTION   Information about the supplier company offering the proposal is included to demonstrate why the company is the best vendor for this solution. This section offers a succinct overview and background of the firm, but the emphasis should be on the company's capabilities. Case histories of customers for whom the company solved similar problems with similar solutions have proved to be an effective method to document and illustrate organizational capabilities and past successes.

PRICING AND SALES AGREEMENT   The previous sections are designed to build the customer-value of the proposed solution. Once this value has been established, the proposal should "ask for the order" by presenting pricing information and delivery options. This information is often presented in the form of a sales agreement for the buyer to sign off on and complete.

SUGGESTED ACTION AND TIMETABLE   The purpose of this section is to make it as easy as possible for the buyer to make a positive purchase decision. In effect, this section should say ". . . if you like the proposal and want to act on it, this is what you do." There may be a contract to sign, an order form to fill out, or instructions regarding who to call to place an order or request further information. A timetable that details a schedule of key implementation events should also be included.

The specific content of a written proposal will vary from situation to situation. Nevertheless, there are certain content expectations and contextual issues that are universal. Salespeople desiring to enhance their proposal writing skills should evaluate the completeness and accuracy of each proposal they write. Exhibit 4.9 presents a *Proposal Writing Scorecard* that can provide an effective checklist for evaluating and improving writing skills.

The expectation for *perfect* spelling and grammar is universal. Misspelling a customer's name or misstating the title of the recipient or the exact name of the organization risks turning off a prospect. After all, the quality of a salesperson's written documents is a surrogate for that salesperson's competence and ability as well as the capabilities and overall quality of the organization. For this reason, salespeople are well advised to follow the *Eight Simple Rules for Writing* set out in Exhibit 4.10. Although a well-written proposal is no guarantee of making the sale, a poorly written proposal will certainly reduce the probability of success.

EXHIBIT 4.9   The Proposal Writing Scorecard

The following scorecard evaluates five dimensions that should be contained in effective written proposals: Reliability, Assurance, Tangibles, Empathy, and Responsiveness. Scoring each of the items in the five sections can assist you in detecting strengths as well as weaknesses. Score each item using this scale: 5 = *Excellent;* 4 = *Good;* 3 = *Average;* 2 = *Poor;* and 1 = *Inadequate.*

Reliability: reflects your [the seller's] ability to identify creative, dependable, and realistic solutions and strategies and match them to the buyer's needs and wants.
Does the Proposal:
_____ 1. Clearly articulate proposed solutions & strategies?
_____ 2. Provide creative & innovative solutions and strategies for the buyer?
_____ 3. Present solutions and strategies appropriate for buyer's business operation & organization?
_____ 4. Provide financial justifications that support the proposed solutions and strategies?
_____ 5. Provide references that support and reflect dependability?
_____ TOTAL FOR RELIABILITY

Assurance: builds the buyer's trust & confidence in your ability to deliver, implement, produce, and/or provide the benefits.
Does the Proposal:
_____ 1. Assure the buyer that proposing organization has qualified, experienced, and competent leadership & staff?
_____ 2. Provide adequate specifications and/or benefits that substantiate ability and capability statements?
_____ 3. Present techniques, methodologies, or processes for assuring quality performance?
_____ 4. Concisely and adequately define project or implementation roles and responsiblities?
_____ 5. Clearly identify and define all fees, prices, and expenses for completing the project?
_____ TOTAL FOR ASSURANCE

Tangibles: enhance and support the communication of your message and invite readership by its overall appearance, content, and organization.
Does the Proposal:
_____ 1. Provide a logical flow of information ideas & sense of continuity for solving buyer's business problems?
_____ 2. Convert the intangible elements of the solutions or strategies into tangibles?
_____ 3. Demonstrate high standards for excellence in format, structure, grammar, spelling, and appearance?
_____ 4. Provide positive indicators to differentiate the proposing organization from their competition?
_____ 5. Contain a Letter of Transmittal, Executive Summary, Needs and Benefits Analysis; Company Description; and the Pricing and Sales Agreement?
_____ TOTAL FOR TANGIBLES

Empathy: confirms your thorough understanding of the buyer's business and their specific needs and wants.
Does the Proposal:
_____ 1. Clearly identify the buyer's specific needs and wants?
_____ 2. Demonstrate a thorough understanding of the buyer's business operation and organization?
_____ 3. Provide solutions and strategies that fit within the buyer's business goals?
_____ 4. Fulfill the buyer's original expectations?
_____ 5. Identify and discuss financial and nonfinancial benefits in terms of their impact on the buyer's unique operation and organization?
_____ TOTAL FOR EMPATHY

Responsiveness: developed in a timely manner and demonstrates a willingness to provide solutions for the buyer's needs and wants and to help measure results.
Does the Proposal:
_____ 1. Meet or beat the completion deadline?
_____ 2. Reflect a genuine willingness to understand the buyer's business operation and organization and to provide viable and flexible solutions and strategies?
_____ 3. Reflect the proposing organization's willingness to work closely with the buyer by enthusiastically asking questions, gathering information, presenting options, and reviewing draft proposals?
_____ 4. Did the proposing organization thoroughly review the final proposal with the buyer and respond to their questions or clarify any outstanding issues and concerns?
_____ 5. Are the proposed solutions or strategies within the buyer's budget and implementation timeframes?
_____ TOTAL FOR RESPONSIVENESS

EXHIBIT 4.10	Eight Simple Rules for Writing

- Double check company names, titles, and individuals' names.
- The spelling of words you are not sure of should always be looked up. Do not rely on your word processor's spelling checker.
- Write the proposal and get away from it before proofreading. Give your mind some time away from the document so that it will be fresh when it is time to begin the editing process.
- Proofread and edit for improvements rather than to simply catch mistakes. How can the message be improved in clarity and crispness?
- Repeat the proofreading process and, when possible, have a third party read for meaning, clarity, grammar, and spelling. A third set of eyes can find problems that the writer often overlooks. Don't submit your first draft, as it won't be your best.
- Use hyphens to avoid confusion, but do not place a hyphen after an adverb that ends with *ly*.
- Separate things in a series with a comma, and set off nonessential clauses with a comma.
- Use *that* in restrictive clauses; use *which* in nonrestrictive clauses. (e.g., The sales quota that he announced is too low. He announced the new sales quota, which is too low.)
- Avoid starting sentences with the words *and* or *but*.
- Use *like* for direct comparisons; use *such as* for examples.
- Use a dash to set off and end a thought in a sentence that differs from the preceding concept or thought.
- Periods, commas, and question marks go within quotation marks; semi-colons go outside quotation marks.

Summary

1. **Explain the importance of collaborative, two-way communication in personal selling.** The two-way exchange process inherent in collaborative communication facilitates accurate and mutual understanding of the objectives, problems, needs, and capabilities of each of the parties. As a result of this heightened level of understanding, solutions and responses can be generated that provide mutual benefits to all participants. Without mutual sharing, this would not be possible, and one party or the other would benefit at the expense of the other. Although this might be good for the "winning" party, the disadvantaged party would be less inclined to continue doing business and would seek out other business partners.

2. **Explain the primary types of questions and how they are applied in selling.** Questions can be typed into two basic categories according to (1) the amount of information and level of specificity desired and (2) the strategic purpose of the question.
   - *Typed by the Amount of Information and Level of Specificity Desired.* This category includes open-end questions, closed-end questions, and dichotomous questions. *Open-end questions* are designed to let the customer respond freely and deliver richer and more expansive information than more directed forms of questioning. They are typically used to probe for descriptive information that allows the salesperson to better understand the specific needs and expectations of the customer. *Closed-end questions* are designed to limit the customer's response to one or two words. This type of question is typically used to confirm or clarify information gleaned from previous responses to open-end questions. *Dichotomous questions* are directive forms of questioning in which the buyer is requested to make a choice between two or more alternatives. These questions are used to discover buyer preferences and move the selling process forward.
   - *Types of Questions Classified by Strategic Purpose.* This category of questions includes questions designed for (1) probing, (2) evaluative, (3) tactical, and (4) reactive purposes. *Probing questions* are designed to penetrate beneath surface information to provide more useful details. *Evaluative questions* use an open-end format to uncover how the buyer feels about things (e.g., attitudes, opinions, and preferences held by the prospect). *Tactical questions* are used to shift the topic of discussion when a line of questioning proves to be of little interest or value. *Reactive questions* respond to previous information provided by the other party and ask for additional details

about the previous information. Salespeople *use reactive questions to elicit additional details regarding facts, attitudes, or feelings the customer has mentioned.*

3. **Illustrate the diverse roles and uses of strategic questioning in personal selling.** The most obvious use of questioning is to elicit detailed information about the buyer's current situation, needs, and expectations. Properly applied, questioning facilitates both the buyer's and seller's understanding of a problem and proposed solutions. Questioning can also test the buyers' interest in a problem or solution and increase their cognitive involvement and participation in the selling process. Questions can also be used to subtly and strategically redirect, regain, or hold the buyer's attention should it begin to wander during the conversation. Similarly, questions can provide a convenient and subtle transition to a different topic of discussion and provide a logical guide promoting sequential thought and decision making while advancing the selling process in moving forward.

4. **Identify and describe the five steps of the ADAPT questioning sequence.** Corresponding to the ADAPT acronym, the five steps making up this sequence of effective questioning are assessment questions, discovery questions, activation questions, projection questions, and transition questions.

   - *Assessment Questions.* These are broad and general questions designed to be non-threatening and to spark conversation. Rather than asking for feelings or conclusions, assessment questions elicit factual information about the customer's current situation that can provide a basis for further exploration and probing. These questions should address the buyer's company and operation, goals and objectives, market trends and customers, current suppliers, and even the buyer as an individual.

   - *Discovery Questions.* Following up responses from assessment questions, discovery questions drill down and probe for further details needed to further clarify and understand the buyer's problems. In addition to facts, the buyer's interpretations, perceptions, feelings, and opinions are sought in regard to their needs, wants, dissatisfactions, and expectations relevant to product, delivery requirements, budget and financing issues, and desired service levels. The goal is to discover needs and dissatisfactions that the salesperson's sales offering can resolve.

   - *Activation Questions.* The implied or suggested needs that might be gained from discovery questions are not usually sufficient to gain the sale. Often a buyer will believe that a particular problem does not cause any significant negative consequences, hence the motivation to solve the problem will carry a low priority. Activation questions help the customer realistically evaluate the full impact of the implied need. The objective is to "activate" the customer's interest in solving discovered problems by helping him or her to gain insight into the true ramifications of the problem and realize that what may initially seem to be of little consequence may, in fact, carry significant consequence to the buyer's organization.

   - *Projection Questions.* A natural extension of the activation questions, projection questions encourage and facilitate the buyer in "projecting" what it would be like if the problems or needs did not exist. Projection questions switch the focus from problems to the benefits to be derived from solving the problems—the payoff for taking action and investing in a solution. Focusing on the benefit payoff allows the buyer to establish his or her perceived value of implementing a solution. In this manner, the benefit payoff is perceived as what the solution is worth—what the buyer would be willing to pay. Projection questions assist the buyer in selling himself or herself by establishing the worth of the solution. More important, the customer, rather than the salesperson, establishes the value of solving the problem.

   - *Transition Questions.* Transition questions smooth the transition from needs discovery and activation into the presentation and demonstration of the proposed solution's features, advantages, and benefits. Typically, closed end and evaluative in format, these questions confirm the buyer's desire to seek a solution and give his or her consent to the salesperson to move forward with the selling process.

5. **Discuss the four sequential steps for effective active listening.** Active listening consists of the sequential communication behaviors of (1) sensing, (2) interpreting, (3) evaluating, and (4) responding.

- *Sensing.* The first activity in active listening is to sense and receive the verbal and nonverbal components of the message. Sensing is much more than just hearing the message and requires practice and concentration. Poor or weak sensing can create significant problems in the latter stages of interpreting and evaluating.
- *Interpreting.* After sensing and receiving the message, it must be correctly interpreted in terms of what the sender actually meant. In addition to the meaning of the words and symbols, the experiences, knowledge, and attitudes of the sender should be considered to fully understand what was meant.
- *Evaluating.* Effective communication requires the receiver to decide whether or not he or she agrees with the sender's message. This requires evaluating the results from the interpretation stage to sort fact from opinion and emotion.
- *Responding.* Collaborative communication requires listeners to provide feedback to the other party. Responses can take the form of restating and paraphrasing the sender's message, answering questions, or asking questions to gain additional details and clarification.

6. **Discuss the superiority of pictures over words for explaining concepts and enhancing comprehension**. Evidence is provided by studies in cognitive psychology supporting pictures as being more memorable than words. Using descriptive words to "draw" mental pictures in the buyer's mind can enhance understanding and are more easily recalled than abstract words and symbols. This carries several implications for successful selling:
   - Understanding and recall can be aided by providing a short and illustrative analogy or illustrative story to emphasize a key point and bring it alive in the buyer's mind.
   - Rather than abstract words that convey only a broad general understanding, utilize words and phrases that convey concrete and detailed meaning. Concrete expressions provide the receiver with greater information and are less likely to be misunderstood than their abstract counterparts.
   - Integrate relevant visual sales aids into verbal communication. Sales support materials that explain and reinforce the verbal message will aid the buyer's understanding and enhance recall of the message.

7. **Describe the different forms of nonverbal communication.** Nonverbal behaviors are made up from the various movements and utterances that people use in addition to the words and symbols associated with language. These can be conscious or unconscious and include eye movement and facial expressions, placement and movements of hands, arms, head, and legs as well as body orientation, the amount of space maintained between individuals, and variations in voice characteristics. Sensing and interpreting groups or clusters of nonverbal cues can provide a reliable indicator of the underlying message and intent. When the individual behaviors and gestures begin to fit together, they form a common and unified message that should be considered by the salesperson. Evidence shows that 50 percent or more of the meaning conveyed in the process of interpersonal communication is carried by nonverbal behaviors. Consequently, it is critical that salespeople learn to effectively sense, accurately interpret, and fully evaluate the nonverbal elements of a message.

8. **List and illustrate the content sections fundamental to effective sales proposals.** Written reports will vary in content from situation to situation. Yet, there are five parts common to most proposals: (1) executive summary; (2) needs and benefits analysis; (3) company description; (4) the pricing and sales agreement; and (5) the suggested action and timeline. The *executive summary* is typically limited to a two-page summary of the proposal. It should serve two critical functions. First, the summary should clearly demonstrate the salesperson's understanding of the customer's needs and the relevance of the proposed solution. Just as important, and often overlooked, the summary should generate the user's desire to read the full proposal. *The needs and benefits analysis* summarizes the customer's needs while emphasizing the solution and the benefits to be derived by implementing the solution. It is important that the benefits are stated in terms of the customer. The *company description* section offers relevant highlights about the supplier organization to demonstrate why it is the best vendor for the solution. The *pricing and sales agreement* is designed to ask for the order by presenting pricing information and delivery options. The *suggested action and timeline* portion of the proposal should make it as easy as possible for the buyer to make a positive purchase decision. In effect, this section should say "... if you like the proposal

and want to act on it, this is what you do." There may be a contract to sign, an order form to fill out, or instructions regarding who to call to place an order or request further information. The timetable details mutual expectations regarding the schedule of key implementation events. These sections should integrate in a sequential way that first sensitizes the reader by framing the nature of the proposal. Then the solution is developed and value developed in terms of customer benefits. Based on having established the value of the proposed solution, the last section is designed to build commitment.

Understanding Professional Selling Terms

- Relational sales communication
- Open-end questions
- Closed-end questions
- Dichotomous questions
- Probing questions
- Evaluative questions
- Tactical questions
- Reactive questions
- SPIN
- Situation questions
- Problem questions
- Implication questions
- Need-payoff questions
- ADAPT
- Assessment questions
- Discovery questions
- Activation questions
- Projection questions
- Transition questions
- Social listening
- Serious listening
- Active listening
- SIER
- Sensing
- Interpreting
- Evaluating
- Responding
- Nonverbal communication
- Proxemics
- Nonverbal clusters

Developing Professional Selling Knowledge

1. Explain why talking *with* buyers rather than talking *at* buyers is critical to success in selling.
2. Discuss how salespeople use effective questioning to maintain subtle control over the buyer-seller communication dialogue.
3. Distinguish between open-end and closed-end questions and describe how each of these question formats might best be used in the personal selling process.
4. Explain the difference in the uses of probing, evaluative, tactical, and reactive questions in personal selling.
5. Discuss how effective questioning skills help accomplish the seven closely related sales objectives identified in this module.
6. Identify and explain each of the individual steps involved in the SPIN sequence of questioning. Develop two example questions for each step.
7. Identify and explain each of the individual steps involved in the ADAPT sequence of questioning. Develop two example questions for each step.
8. Discuss how the four sequential elements of sensing, interpreting, evaluating, and responding (SIER) combine to create what is referred to as active listening.
9. Explain what is meant by nonverbal clusters and why they are important to salespeople.
10. What is meant by proxemics? Why is it important for salespeople to understand the concept of proxemics?

Building Professional Selling Skills

1. Listening skill development is an ongoing process. Good listening is a key to success in any business environment. Discovering your attitude about listening and assessing your listening behaviors are important for self-development and improvement. Complete the following exercise and score your listening habits. If the statement describes your listening habits, check "Yes," if not, check "No." After completing the assessment, score your listening habits according to the scale following the checklist.

		YES	NO
a.	I am interested in many subjects and do not knowingly tune out dry-sounding information.	❏	❏
b.	I listen carefully for a speaker's main ideas and supporting points.	❏	❏
c.	I take notes during meetings to record key points.	❏	❏
d.	I am not easily distracted.	❏	❏
e.	I keep my emotions under control.	❏	❏
f.	I concentrate carefully and do not fake attention.	❏	❏
g.	I wait for the speaker to finish before finally evaluating the message.	❏	❏
h.	I respond appropriately with a smile, a nod, or a word of acknowledgment, as a speaker is talking.	❏	❏
i.	I am aware of mannerisms that may distract a speaker and keep mine under control.	❏	❏
j.	I understand my biases and control them when I am listening.	❏	❏
k.	I refrain from constantly interrupting.	❏	❏
l.	I value eye contact and maintain it most of the time.	❏	❏
m.	I often restate or paraphrase what the speaker said to make sure I have the correct meaning.	❏	❏
n.	I listen for the speaker's emotional meaning as well as subject matter content.	❏	❏
o.	I ask questions for clarification.	❏	❏
p.	I do not finish other people's sentences unless asked to do so.	❏	❏
q.	When listening on the phone, one hand is kept free to take notes.	❏	❏
r.	I attempt to set aside my ego and focus on the speaker rather than myself.	❏	❏
s.	I am careful to judge the message rather than the speaker.	❏	❏
t.	I am a patient listener most of the time.	❏	❏

The following scale will help you interpret your present listening skill level based on your current attitudes and habits.

1 to 5 "NO" answers	You are an excellent listener. Keep it up!
6 to 10 "NO" answers	You are a good listener but can improve.
11 to 15 "NO" answers	Through practice you can become a much more effective listener in your business and personal relationships.
16 to 20 "NO" answers	Listen up!!

How do your listening skills compare to those of your class peers? What steps might you take to strengthen your listening skills?

2. Developing ADAPT question sequences takes thought and practice. Using the ADAPT questioning process discussed in this module as a guide, develop a scripted series of salesperson questions and possible buyer responses that might be typical in the following selling situation. For your convenience, a sample ADAPT Questioning Script Template is included following the description of the selling scenario.

The Selling Scenario:

This scenario involves a salesperson representing the Direct Sales Department of American Seating Company (ASC) and a buyer representing the Seattle Music Arts Association (SMAA). Although there are some 12 major manufacturers of auditorium seating, ASC's market share of 21 percent makes the company a leader in this industry. ASC's selling efforts are organized on a basis of market types: one department sells direct to end-users and a second department sells to distributors who in turn sell to retailers of business furniture. Direct sales to end-users are restricted to minimum orders of $200,000.

As an integral part of a major remodeling project, SMAA wants to replace the seats in the Seattle Metropolitan Auditorium. ASC estimates a potential sale of between $350,000 and $500,000. This range represents differences in both quantity and types of seating desired. According to the Request for Proposals, funding for this project is being provided through a bond issue. From this very basic level of knowledge of the buyer's situation, the salesperson is working through the ADAPT questioning sequence with the buyer to better identify and confirm the actual needs and expectations regarding seating.

Use the following ADAPT Script Template to develop a series of salesperson questions and anticipated buyer responses that might apply to this selling situation.

Assessment Questions:

Seller: _____
Buyer: _____

Seller: _____
Buyer: _____

Seller: _____
Buyer: _____

Seller: _____
Buyer: _____

Discovery Questions:

Seller: _____
Buyer: _____

Seller: _____
Buyer: _____

Seller: _____
Buyer: _____

Seller: _____
Buyer: _____

Activation Questions:

Seller: _____
Buyer: _____

Seller: _____
Buyer: _____

Seller: _____
Buyer: _____

Seller: _____
Buyer: _____

Projection Questions:

Seller: _____
Buyer: _____

Seller: _____
Buyer: _____

Seller: _____
Buyer: _____

Seller: _____
Buyer: _____

Transition Questions:

Seller: _____
Buyer: _____

Seller: _____
Buyer: _____

Seller: _____
Buyer: _____

Seller: _____
Buyer: _____

3. Used in combination, open- and closed-end questions help salespeople uncover and confirm customer needs, dissatisfactions, and opportunities. Observe a salesperson calling on a new prospect and notice the different types of questions used and the information that is received in exchange.
   - What open-end questions did the salesperson use?
   - What types of information were gathered by using these open-end questions?
   - What closed-end questions did the salesperson use?
   - What types of information were gathered by using these closed-end questions?

Making Professional Selling Decisions

CASE 4.1   *Pre-Select, Inc.*

Background

You are a salesperson for PRE-SELECT, Inc. (PSI), the Chicago-based industry leader in preinterview assessment and testing for the insurance industry. Focusing primarily on sales-related recruiting and selection, PSI's Interactive Employee Assessment System (IEAS) has been successful in lowering overall payroll costs by reducing sales agent turnover rates. Because of its highly recognized rate of success, PSI's customers include 13 of the top 20 insurance companies in the United States.

Although the system is continuously revised and updated, the basic program has been operating for six years. Using a personal computer in the field—usually at the branch office or general agency location—the IEAS consists of three computer-based components:
1. Preinterview attitude and aptitude testing
2. Interactive simulations of critical work situations for use as part of the interview process
3. Periodic posthiring assessment for input into future training needs

Current Situation

Ron Lovell, national agency director for Secure Future Insurance Company (SFIC), is interested in improving his company's recruiting and selection process for sales agents. SFIC is a national company with 150 agents across the United States. Although not ranked among the top 20 insurers, SFIC is a large and successful firm listed in the *Fortune 1000*. You have met with Ron on four previous occasions exploring problems, opportunities, and needs. During these meetings, you discovered that SFIC's turnover rate among its sales agents approaches 42 percent. Compared with industry averages, that is not all that bad, but it does require hiring 375 new salespeople every year. SFIC's own estimate of hiring, training, and licensing costs is $7,500 per new salesperson hired, for a total annual cost exceeding $2.8 million. Well-documented field experience indicates that, using PSI's computer-based system, turnover would drop to an average turnover rate ranging from 15 to 20 percent, which offers considerable savings to SFIC.

You have been working up the figures for implementing the system at SFIC's headquarters and in each of the company's 150 general agency offices. One-time hardware costs total $610,000. Although minimal training is required, installation and training would be priced out at $75,000 plus another $5,500 for chargeable travel expenses. Software licensing fees would total $135,000 per year. Sales tax on the hardware and software would be computed at 6.5 percent. Finally, software maintenance fees run 15 percent of the annual licensing cost. According to the technical support department, this installation could be completed, with the full system operating and all staff training completed, in just four months from the date of the order.

During your last call, you detailed the basics of the IEAS scaled to meet the needs of SFIC. Ron, along with the other officers attending the presentation, liked what he saw and requested that you put together a formal proposal. On your way out of the building, Ron mentioned that the proposal would have to be detailed enough to allow him to pass it through the capital budgeting department. This means detailing costs, projected savings, the payback period, and the installation-implementation schedule. As another positive indicator, Ron also asked that you arrange a follow-up meeting approximately two weeks after the written proposal is received.

The Learning Assignment

Your task is to develop a follow-up letter and a written sales proposal for his immediate attention and use. These should be developed and written as if they were to be actually sent to the customer.

CASE 4.2   *STAGA Financial Services*

Background

Bart Waits arrived just a few minutes early for his 9:00 a.m. meeting with Kerri Williams, director of purchasing for STAGA Financial Services. This was his first in-person call at STAGA, and he had flown in explicitly for this meeting to present his proposal for a data-mining software package that would be used by the client's IT department. On arrival, Bart did the obligatory check-in with the receptionist in the main lobby. After contacting the purchasing office, the receptionist informed him that they would be right down to escort him to Ms. Williams' office. About 12 minutes later, Ms. Williams' executive assistant entered the lobby and advised Bart that she would escort him to the office where they would be meeting. The executive assistant was friendly and open and provided Bart with a fresh cup of coffee just before taking him into Ms. Williams' office.

Current Situation

On entering the large and well-furnished office, Bart noticed that the layout was a bit different than he had expected. Kerri was sitting behind a large walnut executive desk that was located at an angle in one corner and faced toward the opposite wall of windows. No guest chairs were located adjacent to the desk. Rather, the chairs were set some 10–12 feet from the desk, adjacent to a small table, and facing the desk. In another area of the room, there was a worktable with several chairs pulled up to it.

Kerri was on the phone as he entered and signaled for him to go ahead and be seated. It was obvious that the conversation was drawing to a close, and she made eye contact and smiled at him once or twice to acknowledge his presence. When the phone call was over, she popped up from the desk and walked over to meet him. While shaking hands, each of them introduced themselves, and she mentioned that he should address her as Kerri. She apologized for being on the phone and inquired about his flight. After some small talk, Bart transitioned into his presentation by first outlining the needs as specified in STAGA's original Request for Proposals (RFP). As Bart provided many additional details beyond those in the RFP, Kerri smiled and looked him in the eye as she shifted her chair closer to the table and commented that it was apparent that he had done his homework on the company.

Several times during his presentation, she placed her hand on her cheek and shifted forward to ask numerous questions. Although sparingly, she also took notes at several points of his presentation. Bart's appointment was for one and one-half hours, and he figured that he would need every minute of it. However, about 50 minutes into the meeting he noticed that Kerri would glance at her watch occasionally. After making a major point and demonstrating several significant benefits to STAGA, he noticed that Kerri uncrossed her legs and leaned forward with her glasses on the tip of her nose as she began asking him a series of questions about his software package.

1. Identify the different nonverbal cues that the buyer was providing to Bart.
2. If you were in Bart's place, how would you have interpreted and responded to these different nonverbal cues?

Self-Leadership and Teamwork Skills

Success in the Automotive Supply Business Requires a Different Type of Selling

Despite what is described as the most intense competition in the world, Johnson Controls' Automotive Systems Group (ASG) division is thriving with superior profits and double-digit growth. Competition is fierce in the automotive supply business, and the major manufacturers want to keep it that way, as it serves as a downward force on prices. For decades, auto manufacturers have followed the traditional purchasing format of awarding business on the basis of bids submitted for prespecified parts. To ensure competitive pricing, multiple sources are used—some would even say suppliers are played against one another. The nature of this price-oriented purchasing environment has commoditized the automotive supply industry. Sales tend to be made on the basis of price, suppliers are changed frequently, and salespeople are basically order takers.

ASG has chosen to differentiate itself from the price-oriented order takers by emphasizing a relational strategy based on innovative product offerings that provide added value to the auto manufacturers. Unlike the competition, ASG's salespeople serve as consultants to the buying organizations, helping them to create products that consumers want. This consultative strategy emphasizes trust and collaboration within ASG and between ASG and its customers. Working as a cohesive unit, salespeople team up with other individuals in marketing, design, and production to better determine needs and trends in the marketplace. Through the combined capabilities of the teams, information and understanding of consumer needs are translated into innovative products for the company's automotive manufacturing customers. The mission of ASG's sales team is to walk into car manufacturers' offices, demonstrate innovative products they need in their new cars, translate the products into customer opportunities and benefits, and back it all up with solid research and knowledge. Producing 20 percent annual gains in profitable growth, the strategy seems to be working.

"Our business depends on people sharing ideas and working together to fulfill customers' needs," states Michael Suman, vice president of marketing and advanced sales. Suman credits customer focus and teamwork as the sustaining drivers of the organization's superior performance. ASG has a core set of repeat customers. Consequently, salespeople do not make cold calls. Rather, they are charged with building relationships, discovering customer needs, creating innovative solutions, and presenting new, value-added ideas and products. The selling role is almost purely consultative, and salespeople have to be knowledgeable, customer centered,

Learning Objectives

After completing this module, you should be able to

1 Explain the five sequential steps of self-leadership.

2 Discuss the importance of thorough and effective planning.

3 Identify the four levels of sales goals and explain their interrelationships.

4 Describe two techniques for account classification.

5 Explain the application of different territory routing techniques.

6 Interpret the usefulness of different types of selling technology and automation.

7 Delineate six skills for building internal relationships and teams.

and able to collaborate with other ASG employees, customers, and customers' customers. The focus is on one thing—making sure customers get what they want.

Source: Andy Cohen, "In Control," *Sales and Marketing Management* (June 1999): 32–38.

When observing the actions of a person who has truly mastered the skills of their profession, the manner of their actions seems to come naturally. However, closer consideration will most often reveal that these seemingly innate and natural abilities are actually the result of fervent and purposeful planning combined with many hours of practice over a period of years. This is true for world-class surgeons, sports stars, leading educators, top attorneys—and yes, even high-performance salespeople. Good salespeople are consciously developed, not born. Toward the objective of *developing* strong salespeople, this module builds on the process of self-leadership to generate a framework for developing and enhancing selling skills and abilities. First, setting effective selling goals and objectives is discussed and integrated with methods for territory analysis and account classification. This is followed by a discussion of how the objectives and information from the territory and account analysis become inputs for generating and implementing effective multilevel sales planning. The importance of assessing performance results and level of goal attainment is also reviewed. Wrapping up the module is an examination of teamwork as a vehicle for expanding the capabilities of an individual salesperson, increasing customer value, and creating sustainable competitive advantage for salespeople.

Effective Self-Leadership

How often have you said or thought to yourself, "I just don't have enough time to get everything done"? In reality, most people do not need more time. Rather, they need to reprioritize the time they have. There are only so many hours in a day, and highly effective salespeople know that they can never have enough quality selling time. To maximize their selling time, these high performers have developed strong self-leadership skills and treat time as a valuable, nonreplaceable resource and invest it wisely where it will accomplish the most good.

Self-leadership—a critical requirement for success in any career—has been described as doing the right things and doing them well. It is not simply the amount of effort that determines an achievement, but rather how well that effort is honed and aligned with one's goals. In selling, this is often restated as selling smarter rather than selling harder. That is, before expending valuable time and resources, salespeople must establish priorities in the form of objectives. Then, and only then, do they implement the strategic plan that has been specifically developed to achieve their objectives in the light of the available resources and market potential that exist within the territory. Self-leadership translates to a process of first deciding what is to be accomplished and then placing into motion the proper plan designed to achieve those objectives.

The process of self-leadership is composed of five sequential stages. First, goals and objectives must be set that properly reflect what is important and what is to be accomplished. This is followed by an analysis of the territory and classification of accounts. Next, with goals in place and accounts classified, strategic plans designed to achieve the objectives through proper allocation of resources and effort are implemented. The next stage maximizes the effectiveness of allocated resources through the process of tapping technology and automation to expand resource capabilities. Finally, assessment activities are conducted to evaluate performance and goal at-

| FIGURE 5.1 | Five Sequential Stages of Self-Leadership |

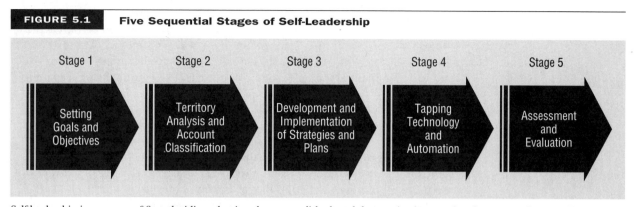

Stage 1	Stage 2	Stage 3	Stage 4	Stage 5
Setting Goals and Objectives	Territory Analysis and Account Classification	Development and Implementation of Strategies and Plans	Tapping Technology and Automation	Assessment and Evaluation

Self-leadership is a process of first, deciding what is to be accomplished, and then setting into motion the proper plan to achieve the desired objectives.

tainment and to assess possible changes in plans and strategies. The nature of the sequential interrelationships between these five stages is illustrated in Figure 5.1.

Stage One: Setting Goals and Objectives

Establishing priorities by setting **goals** and **objectives** is the key to effective self-leadership. This first stage of self-leadership has been appropriately referred to as "beginning with the end in mind."[1] First of all, if a salesperson does not understand what is important, how does that salesperson know what to focus on? Further, if a salesperson does not understand what he or she is setting out to accomplish, how could that salesperson know where to begin, how to proceed, or even which plan is best for getting there? Finally, without clear goals, how could salespeople know when the objective has been achieved? Without clear goals and objectives, it is very natural to drift from task to task and typically focus on minor and less-productive tasks, as they are the easiest to complete. The end result of this natural drift is poor sales performance and frustration. The positive impact of planning ahead and establishing priorities is further evidenced by the experiences of Aaron Simmons, agent for State Farm Insurance, Co., in "Professional Selling in the 21st Century: Planning Ahead."

WHAT MAKES A GOOD GOAL?   Although goals and objectives might best be described as desired outcomes, these two words carry specific meaning. *Desired* implies

---

PROFESSIONAL SELLING IN THE 21ST CENTURY

Planning Ahead
Aaron Simmons, Agent for State Farm Insurance Co., emphasizes the significant and positive effects that planning ahead and establishing priorities has on selling success.

Listing daily goals and activities in their order of importance allows salespeople to maximize the use of time. For example, on any given day there are typically 25 people or more that we would like to meet with, but within that list of 25 are 10 to 15 highly qualified prospects and current clients with whom we absolutely must meet. In addressing this "want-to-do" vs. "must do" paradox, we prioritize our prospects and plan calls and contacts accordingly. For example, the "A" list consists of the 6 to 8 people we absolutely must contact, and the "B" list accounts for those 8 to 10 prospects we'd like to talk to if possible. Our "C" list includes the balance—prospects we would like to call, but who do not have to be contacted that day. Planning ahead is critical to success in selling. Many salespeople do not like to plan, but it has been proven many times that establishing goals and setting priorities out in the form of a plan results in higher sales and brings in more revenue.

that it is something worthy of working toward and expending resources to reach. *Outcome* connotes that it is a specific result or effect resulting from certain activities or behaviors—something that can be described and pointed out. As illustrated in the Exhibit 5.1 checklist, properly developed goals share three key characteristics: (1) realistic, yet challenging, (2) specific and quantifiable, and (3) time specific.

- *Realistic, Yet Challenging*—Goals should be realistic and reachable. When set beyond what is possible, goals cease to motivate and often become a disincentive to performance. At the same time, goals should be challenging. If goals are continually set at a level that is too easy to reach, performance tends to regress to the lower standard. Goals that are challenging tend to be more motivating than goals that are easily achieved.

- *Specific and Quantifiable*—Without specificity, goals become ambiguous and have no clear meaning. For instance, the goal of having the top territory in the district could be interpreted in many ways. Does top territory translate to having the largest increase in sales; having the fewest number of customer defections; having the highest customer satisfaction scores; having the smallest number of price discounts; or possibly having the largest reduction in travel expenses? Without specificity, the goal becomes a moving target, and it is difficult to know where to apply one's effort. In a similar fashion, goals should be quantifiable—that is, they should be measurable. The goal of increasing sales is certainly commendable, but how might it be judged as having been accomplished? Is a 1 percent increase sufficient or is 12 percent more in line with expectations? If a 12 percent increase is the expectation, then the goal should be a 12 percent increase in sales—a quantifiable and measurable outcome that can be objectively measured and assessed.

- *Time Specific*—Stating a specific timeline is the third requirement of goals and objectives. A goal of achieving a 12 percent increase in sales by December 31 is much more appealing than simply stating that one's goal is to increase sales by 12 percent. Associating timelines with goals establishes a deadline for planning purposes and provides motivation by instilling a sense of urgency for taking action.

WORKING WITH DIFFERENT LEVELS AND TYPES OF GOALS   For maximum effectiveness, salespeople establish goals at four different levels: personal goals, sales call goals, account goals, and territory goals. Although each level requires different types of effort and produces different outcomes, each of the levels is interrelated and interdependent on the others. These interrelationships and dependencies are illustrated in Exhibit 5.2. A salesperson's **personal goals** might include achieving a

---

EXHIBIT 5.1   **Required Characteristics of Goals and Objectives**

Effective Goals and Objectives Must Possess Three Fundamental Characteristics

X	Goals should be realistic, yet challenging
X	Goals should be specific and quantifiable
X	Goals should be time specific

| EXHIBIT 5.2 | Four Interdependent Levels of Salesperson Objectives |

Personal Goal Desired Annual Income	$ 70,000
Is dependent on Annual Territory Sales Goal (11% Commission on Sales)	$636,364
Is dependent on Annual Account Sales Goal (19 equally sized accounts)	$ 33,493
Is dependent on Sales Call Goal (each account is called on twice a month)	$ 1,396

$70,000 annual income during the current year ending December 31. If the salesperson receives a commission of 11 percent on sales, this personal goal is directly related to and dependent on achieving the **territory goal** of selling $636,364 in products across the territory in the same time period. Assuming 19 equally sized accounts comprise the territory, the territory goal is dependent on achieving the **account goal** of an average of $33,493 in products sold to each account over the course of the year. Considering that each account is called on twice every month, a **sales call goal** of $1,396 in sales per call is required to achieve the account goal. As illustrated in this example, each higher-level goal is ultimately dependent on the salesperson setting and achieving lower level, specific goals for each and every sales call.

Although illustrative of the interdependence between different levels of goals, the above example is admittedly simplistic in its exclusive use of goals based on sales volume. In reality, there are many different types of goals that a salesperson might effectively use. Exhibit 5.3 illustrates examples of common sales goals.

Stage Two: Territory Analysis and Account Classification

Territory analysis and classification of accounts, the second stage of self-leadership, is all about finding the customers and prospects who are most likely to buy. Who are they, and where are they located? What and why do they buy? How much and how often do they purchase? Who has the authority to buy, and who can influence the purchase decision? What is the probability of selling this account? What is the potential share of account that might be gained?

Many sources offer intelligence that will assist the salesperson in answering these questions, and the information boom on the Internet makes accessing this information easier than ever before. In addition to numerous yellow page suppliers available on the Web, commercial business information suppliers such as *OneSource Information Services, Hoovers, Standard and Poor's, Dun and Bradstreet,* and *The Thomas Register* offer easy-to-use databases that are fully searchable by company, industry, and geographic location. Salespeople can also access individual company Web sites, trade directories, professional association membership listings, and commercial mailing list providers. Personal observation, discussions with other selling professionals, and company sales records are also excellent sources for gaining valuable information.

Much of this information can be plotted to develop detailed territory maps that will begin to pinpoint pockets of existing and potential business. In addition, understanding the territory at the individual account level provides the input required for account classification.

ACCOUNT CLASSIFICATION   **Account classification** places existing customers and prospects into categories based on their sales potential and assists salespeople in

EXHIBIT 5.3	Common Types of Sales Goals
• Financial Goals	Income, Financial Security
• Career Advancement Goals	Work in Chosen Field, Advancement,
• Personal Development Goals	Education, Training, Relationships Outside Work
• Sales Volume Goals	Dollar Sales, Unit Sales, Number of Orders, Aggregates or By Groups
• Sales Call Activity Goals	Calls Made, Calls/Day, Calls/Account, Presentations Made
• Sales Expense Goals	Total Expenses, By Category, Percent of Sales
• Profitability Goals	Gross Profits, Contribution Margin, Returns and Discounts
• Market Share	Total Share of Potential Market, Peer Group Comparisons
• Share of Account	Share of Customer's Purchases
• Ancillary Activity Goals	Required Reports Turned In, Training Conducted, Service Calls Made
• Customer Retention Goals	Number of Accounts Lost, Complaints Received, Lost Account Ratios
• New Account Goals	Number of New Accounts
• Customer Service Goals	Customer Goodwill Generation, Level of Satisfaction, Receivables Collected
• Conversion Goals	Ratio of Number of Sales to Number of Calls Made

prioritizing accounts for call planning and time allocation purposes. During the process of account classification, it is common for salespeople to find that 80 percent of their sales potential is generated by 20 percent of the total accounts. Consequently, the results of account classification can guide salespeople in more efficient allocation of time, effort, and resources while simultaneously enabling them to be more effective in achieving sales goals. Two commonly used methods for classifying accounts are single-factor analysis and portfolio analysis.

Single-Factor Analysis   **Single-factor analysis,** also referred to as **ABC analysis,** is the simplest and most often used method for classifying accounts. As the name suggests, accounts are analyzed on the basis of one single factor—typically the level of sales potential. On the basis of sales potential, the accounts are placed into three or four categories denoted by letters of the alphabet, "A," "B," "C," "D." Accounts with the highest potential are traditionally sorted into category "A," whereas those with medium potential go into "B," and so on. All accounts in the same category receive equal selling effort. For example, "A" accounts may be called on every two weeks, "B" accounts every four to six weeks, and "C" accounts might receive a personal sales call once a year and be serviced by the seller's telemarketing team during the interim. Single-factor classification schemas used by three different sales organizations are summarized in Exhibit 5.4.

The simplicity of single-factor analysis is a prime contributor to its popularity for use by field salespeople. It is straightforward and requires no statistical analysis or data manipulation. Although this lack of complexity is appealing, its ability to only use one factor for analyzing and classifying accounts is also a significant limitation. Sales potential is certainly an important input in allocating selling effort, but other factors should also be considered. Possible other factors of interest are the selling company's competitive strength in each account, the account's need for additional attention and effort, profitability of the account, and amount of competitive pressure on the account.

Portfolio Analysis   Also referred to as two-factor analysis, the **portfolio analysis** method attempts to overcome the weakness of single-factor analysis by allowing two factors to be considered simultaneously. Each account is examined on the basis of the two specified factors and sorted into the proper segment of a matrix. This matrix is typically divided into four cells, and accounts are placed into the proper classification cell on the basis of their individual ratings ("high" and "low" or "strong"

| EXHIBIT 5.4 | Different Single-Factor Account Analysis Schema Used by Different Companies |

Class of Account	Schema One: InquisLogic Inc.	Schema Two: Web Resource Associates, LLC	Schema Three: Federal Metal Products
"A" Accounts	Accounts with highest potential (the 20% that do or could account for 80% of sales)	Accounts with highest potential (the 20% that do or could account for 80% of sales)	High volume current customers (the 20% that currently account for 80% of sales volume)
	Annual number of calls = 24	Annual number of calls = 52	Annual number of calls = 48
"B" Accounts	Medium potential accounts. (the 80% that account for 20% of sales volume)	Accounts with moderate sales potential, but who are regular and reliable customers	Accounts with high potential, but who are not current customers
	Annual number of calls = 12	Annual number of calls = 24	Annual number of calls = 12
"C" Accounts	Accounts with the least sales potential	Lower sales potential accounts	Medium potential accounts that are current customers
	Annual number of calls = 4	Annual number of calls = 8	Annual number of calls = 12
"D" Accounts	None. This Schema only uses 3 classes of accounts	Accounts that cost more in time and energy than they produce in sales or profits	Accounts with medium potential, but who are not current customers
		Annual number of calls = 0	Annual number of calls = 6

and "weak") on each factor of interest. Cell location denotes the overall attractiveness of the different accounts and serves as a guide for the salesperson's allocation of resources and effort. Typically, each account in the same cell will receive the same amount of selling effort.

Exhibit 5.5 details the account characteristics and suggested selling effort allocations for a typical portfolio analysis incorporating the factors of (1) account opportunity and (2) seller's competitive position. Account opportunity takes into consideration the buyer's level of need for and ability to purchase the seller's products, along with financial stability and growth prospects. Competitive position denotes the relationship between the account and the seller and would include variables such as seller's share of account, competitive pressure, and key decision maker's attitude toward the seller. Accounts sorted into Segment One are high on opportunity, exhibit strong competitive positions, and should receive the highest level of selling effort. Accounts falling into Segment Two are high on opportunity but weak on competitive position. These accounts should receive a high level of attention to strengthen the seller's competitive position. Segment Three contains the 80 percent of accounts doing 20 percent of the seller's volume. These accounts are loyal and regular customers (high on competitive position) but offer weak opportunity.

Strategically, these accounts should receive a lower investment of selling effort designed to maintain the seller's current competitive position. Accounts sorted into Segment Four are considered as unattractive and allocated minimal selling effort as they are characterized by low opportunity and weak competitive position. Within the past several years, many sellers have been successful in servicing Segment Three and Four accounts outside the personal selling channel by using alternatives such as telemarketing, direct mail, and the Internet.

Portfolio analysis offers the advantages of enhanced flexibility and ability to incorporate multiple variables for analyzing and sorting accounts. Reflecting these strong points, the use of portfolio analysis is gaining in popularity.

EXHIBIT 5.5   **Portfolio/Two-Factor Account Analysis and Selling Strategies**

Competitive Position

	Strong	**Weak**
High (Account Opportunity)	**Segment One** **Level of Attractiveness:** Accounts are very attractive because they offer high opportunity, and the seller has a strong competitive position. **Selling Effort Strategy:** Accounts should receive a heavy investment of effort and resources in order to take advantage of high opportunity and maintain/improve competitive position. **Exemplary Sales Call Strategy = 36 calls/yr.**	**Segment Two** **Level of Attractiveness:** Accounts are potentially attractive due to high opportunity, but seller currently has weak competitive position. **Selling Effort Strategy:** Where it is possible to strengthen seller's competitive position, a heavy investment of selling effort should be applied. **Exemplary Sales Call Strategy = 24 calls/yr.**
Low (Account Opportunity)	**Segment Three** **Level of Attractiveness:** Accounts are moderately attractive due to seller having a strong competitive position. However, future opportunity is low. **Selling Effort Strategy:** Accounts should receive a moderate level of selling effort that is sufficient to maintain current competitive position. **Exemplary Sales Call Strategy = 12 calls/yr.**	**Segment Four** **Level of Attractiveness:** Accounts are very unattractive. They offer low opportunity and seller has weak competitive position. **Selling Effort Strategy:** Accounts should receive minimal personal selling effort. Alternatives such as telemarketing, direct mail, and Internet should be explored. **Exemplary Sales Call Strategy = 6 calls/yr.**

Stage Three: Development and Implementation of Strategies and Plans

Stage one provides the salesperson with the guidelines of what is important and the goals to be accomplished at the levels of individual sales calls, accounts, and the overall territory. Stage two identifies and establishes the priority and potential of each account in the territory along with the relative location of each account. Top salespeople do not stop there! They use this information to develop strategies and plans that will guide them toward achieving their goals by applying their available resources in a deliberate and organized fashion that effectively cultivates and harvests the potential sales available in the territory.

ESTABLISHING AND IMPLEMENTING SELLING TASK AND ACTIVITY PLANS   When properly executed, **sales planning** results in a schedule of activities that can be used as a map for achieving objectives. First, start with the big picture—a long-term plan spanning the next 6 to 12 months. This big picture highlights commitments and deadlines and facilitates setting up the activities required to meet those commitments and deadlines. In turn, the longer-range plans provide the basis for shorter time-frame plans and selling activities. The salesperson planning program at Federal Metal Products (FMP) offers a good overview and prototype of effective salesperson planning.

> FMP, a middle market supplier of metal production components, trains its salespeople to prepare and submit annual territory plans and budgets by November 15 each year. With that recurring deadline marked on their schedules, FMP salespeople work backward on their calendars to establish key checkpoints for their planning activities. This establishes a timeline to guide and assist salespeople in making the submission deadline.

If the salesperson projects that it will take four weeks to assemble and draft their territory sales plan, they work back four weeks from the November 15 date and establish October 15 as the date to begin assembling their data and building their plans, how long will it take to properly collect the needed data? Six weeks? If so, their schedule should reflect beginning that activity by September 1.

Sales plans should take into consideration scheduled meetings and training sessions, holidays, trade shows, and vacation time. Plans should also contain periodic checkpoints for assessing progress toward goals. A salesperson's objective of $750,000 in sales for the year equates to a goal averaging $62,500 in sales every month. Accordingly, the long-term master plan should include monthly checkpoints to compare the schedule versus actual performance data. Is performance on course, ahead, or lagging behind? If not on schedule, the corresponding and more detailed weekly plans should be revised to reflect the salesperson's strategies for getting back on course.

Salespeople at FMP develop weekly plans from their longer-term annual plan. These shorter-term plans detail the selling-related activities to be accomplished that week. To create a weekly plan, first identify the priorities that must be accomplished to stay on schedule. Then, for each of these priorities, detail the associated activities and schedule the time it will take for completion. What areas of the territory will be focused on? What accounts will be called on, and what is the objective for each call? What are the best times to call for appointments? Are there account preferences as to what days and times they work with salespeople? How much time must be allowed for travel, waiting, and working with each account? What products will be featured? What information and materials will be needed?

In turn, the priorities and activities identified in the weekly plan should become the points of focus for the daily plan. Days that end on a successful note begin with a thorough and written schedule detailing tasks and priorities for that day and the activities that must be carried out to achieve them. The optimum schedule emphasizes tasks and activities that will make the greatest sales impact—working with customers. As illustrated by the FMPs' *Daily Sales Plan Worksheet* shown in Exhibit 5.6, daily plans should detail the amount of time projected for each scheduled task and activity. To maximize the effectiveness of daily sales plans, salespeople should adhere to two guiding principles.[2]

- *Do them, and do them in writing.* Written plans are better developed and provide more motivation and commitment for salespeople to carry them through to completion. Furthermore, written plans help to ensure that priority items do not fall through the cracks because something was forgotten.
- *Keep it current and flexible.* Make a new daily plan every day. Try as we might, things do not always go as planned. Consequently, changes may be needed, and uncompleted priorities or activities from one day may have to be carried over to the next.

ESTABLISHING TERRITORY ROUTING PLANS   Territory routing plans incorporate information developed in the territory analysis and account classification stage to minimize the encroachment of unproductive travel time on time that could be better spent working with customers. Good routing plans minimize the backtracking and crisscrossing that would otherwise occur and allow the salesperson to use time more efficiently.

Knowing how many calls can be made each day, the required call frequency for each account classification, and the relative geographic location of and distance between accounts, a salesperson can plot different routing strategies and decide the optimal plan. Many sales professionals continue to use the traditional colored map

EXHIBIT 5.6　Example of a Typical Daily Plan

Federal Metal Products
Daily Sales Plan Worksheet

Salesperson: _Earnie Cravits_　　Day: _Friday_　　Date: _8/29_

Time	Task or Priority	Activity	People Involved	Time Needed	Goal/Anticipated Results	Notes & Comments
8:30 am	Set appointments	Phone calls	Jill Attaway, Digital Systems	10 min	Appointment for next week	Requested that I come by
	"	"	Bart Waits, EnterpriseOne	10 min	"	
	"	"	Kerri Williams, Flo-Forms	10 min	"	Will be placing order in 3 weeks
9:00 am	"	"	Marilyn Henry, InQusLogic	10 min	Clarify service problem	Send info to engineering
10:30 am	Demonstrate new bearing line	Sales Call	Mike Humphreys, ICOM	60 MIN	Info. gathering	Currently buying from Gem Rollers
12 noon	Get order commitment	Sales call-Lunch	Rodney Moore, MDQG	120 min	$12,000 order	Gem submitted proposal 8/20
3:00 pm	Take sample of proposed line	Sales call	Aimee Williams, MOCO, Inc	60 min	$15,200 order	Ready to buy, wants to see pdct. sample
4:30 pm	Check on delivery	Service call	Ron Meier, Web Resources	50min	Delight the customer	First time to buy from us!!
6:00 pm	Complete paperwork	Submit call reports		45 min		
7:00 pm	Prepare daily schedule	Planning		45 min		

pins and felt-tip markers on a wall map. However, a variety of easy-to-use and affordable computer applications that plot optimal routing plans are available and are growing in popularity.[3] Optimized routing plans correspond to one of five common patterns: straight line, cloverleaf, circular, leapfrog, and major city.

Straight Line   With a **straight line plan,** salespeople start from their offices and make calls in one direction until they reach the end of the territory. As illustrated in Figure 5.2, at that point they change direction and continue to make calls on a straight line following the new vector. This continues until the salesperson returns to the office location. The straight-line pattern works best when accounts are located in clusters that are some distance from one another.

Cloverleaf   The **cloverleaf plan** pattern is best used when accounts are concentrated in different parts of the territory. On each trip, the salesperson works a different part of the territory and travels in a circular loop back to the starting point. An example of the cloverleaf routing plan is depicted in Figure 5.3. Each loop could take a day, a week, or longer to complete. A new loop is covered on each trip until the entire territory has been covered.

FIGURE 5.2   **Straight Line Route Pattern**

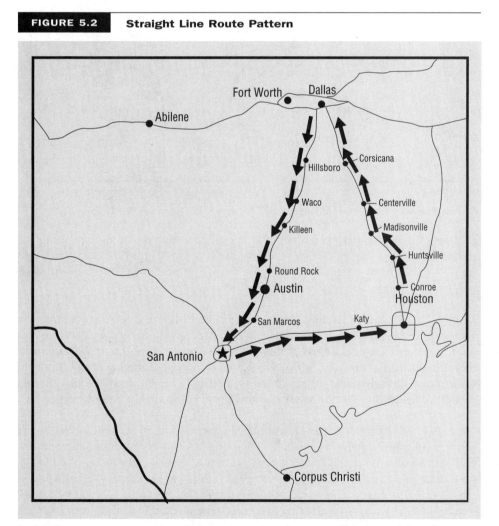

Straight line territory routes make calls across the territory, first in one direction, and then change directions to work back to the starting point.

FIGURE 5.3	**Cloverleaf Route Pattern**

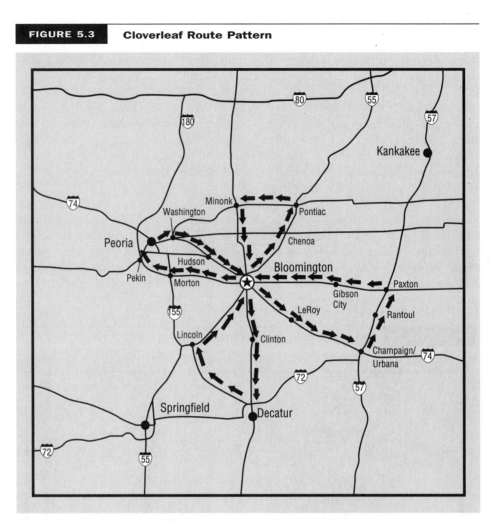

Cloverleaf territory routes work different parts of the territory in a series of circular loops.

Circular   **Circular routing plans** begin at the office and move in an expanding pattern of concentric circles that spiral across the territory. Figure 5.4 traces an exemplary circular routing plan working from an office in Dallas. This method works best when accounts are evenly dispersed throughout the territory.

Leapfrog   The **leapfrog routing plan** is best applied when the territory is large and accounts are clustered into several widely dispersed groups. Beginning in one cluster, the salesperson works each of the accounts at that location and then jumps to the next cluster. As shown in Figure 5.5, this continues until the last cluster has been worked and the salesperson jumps back to the office or home. When the distance between clusters is great, the salesperson will typically make the jumps by flying.

Major City   When the territory is composed of a major metropolitan area, the territory is split into a series of geometric shapes reflecting each one's concentration and pattern of accounts. Figure 5.6 depicts a typical **major city routing plan.** Downtown areas are typically highly concentrated with locations controlled by a grid of city blocks and streets. Consequently, the downtown segment is typically a small square or rectangular area allowing accounts to be worked in a straight-line fashion street by street. Outlying areas are placed in evenly balanced triangles or pie-shaped quadrants, with one quadrant being covered at a time in either a straight line or cloverleaf pattern.

| FIGURE 5.4 | **Circular Route Pattern** |

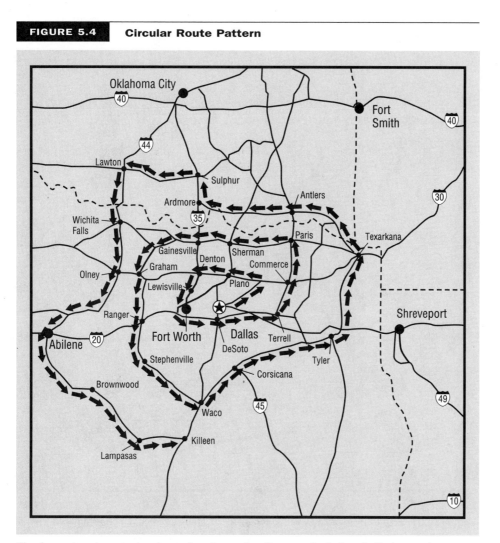

Circular territory routes cover the territory in a series of concentric circles spiraling across the territory.

Stage Four: Tapping Technology and Automation

Selling technology and automation tools are here to stay and are being transformed from neat toys to necessary tools. Properly applied, selling technology spurs and creates creativity and innovation, streamlines all aspects of the selling process, generates new and improved selling opportunities, facilitates cross-functional teaming and intraorganizational communication, and enhances communication and follow-up with customers.[4] In summary, tapping the proper selling technologies and sales force automation tools allow salespeople to expand their available resources for enhanced selling performance and outcomes. Experiences with improved selling efficiency and customer satisfaction are further detailed in "Professional Selling in the 21st Century: Technology Impacts Sales Efficiency and Effectiveness."

Salespeople, sales managers, and customers are unanimous in their agreement that the best salespeople are those who stay up with changes in and developments of technologies with selling applications. With a multitude of rapidly changing and evolving technology choices, salespeople must not only master the technology itself, but they also must understand when and where it can be applied most effectively. Exemplary selling technologies being used by today's salespeople include the following tools.[5]

FIGURE 5.5   **Leapfrog Route Pattern**

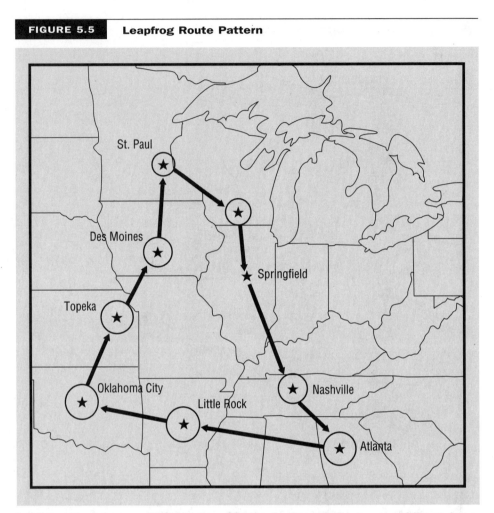

Leapfrog territory routes work accounts clustered in one location and then jump to a different cluster of accounts.

COMPUTERS   At the center of virtually every selling technology is the computer. Choices include desktops, notebooks, laptops, and palmtops. For immediate immersion into the high-tech side of selling, simply walk through the waiting areas of any major airport. Salespeople can be seen generating reports and proposals by using standard word-processing packages and even customized online electronic forms. Others are analyzing customer accounts by using spreadsheet applications and query-based database programs that access and analyze a database according to the questions the user wishes to have answered. Several will be observed reviewing and updating customer files by using one of the many affordable and highly capable contact management software applications such as *Siebel Systems, ACT!, Maximizer, ActiveSales,* and *Sales Logix.* These user-friendly programs provide salespeople with a convenient option to catalogue, search, and access comprehensive information regarding individual customers. Looking closer, numerous salespeople will be revising and polishing graphics and presentations with software such as *Power Point* and *Astound.* Still others will be checking and responding to e-mail, submitting electronic reports, accessing online territory route maps, and using scheduling programs to set up the next day's call plans.

FIGURE 5.6   Major City Route Pattern

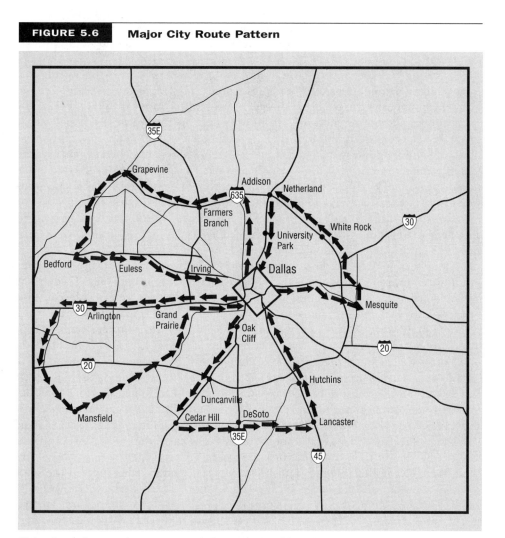

Major city territory routing patterns work downtown on a basis of street grids and work outlying areas using a cloverleaf or straight line pattern.

PROFESSIONAL SELLING IN THE 21ST CENTURY

Technology Impacts Sales Efficiency and Effectiveness

Todd Reffett, Director of Sales and Marketing for the Market-Driven Quality Group (MDQG), explains how the use of technology and automation has impacted selling activities.

Regardless of industry or location, advances in selling technology have brought about major changes in the jobs of selling and the lives of salespeople. We make extensive use of desktop PCs and laptop computers interlinked by a local area network (LAN), Internet, Intranet, and Extranets. Combined with specialized software packages, the convenience and extensive availability of e-mail has virtually replaced our use of regular mail for customer contact and communication. Cell phones have practically replaced conventional wired phones and give us immediate contact with staff members, customers, and strategic partners regardless of their location. The resulting extensive communication capabilities allow us to be more professional and do a better job in service and follow-up—plus the customers really like the increased accessibility. However, this dependence on technology can have a downside, in that you get to the point of having to have it in order to function. When there is a problem with the network or a computer, we panic. It can virtually shut us down.

INTERNET AND WORLD WIDE WEB   Company networks have been used for many years; however, the advent of the Internet has made them much more affordable and easier to maintain.

Accessing the **Internet** instantly networks a salesperson with the world: customers, information sources, other salespeople, sales management, and others. More important, the Internet puts the salesperson into contact with their customer-community and support networks from anywhere in the world, 24 hours a day, seven days a week. Going beyond the convenience of e-mail, many sales organizations are setting up **Intranets** and **Extranets**—secure and proprietary organizational Web sites that are protected by passwords and security authorizations. Intranets are networks within the organization using the Internet or commercial channels to provide direct linkages between company units and individuals. Extranets are a special form of Intranet that is still for proprietary and restricted use but links to specific suppliers and customers to allow them controlled and secure access to the organization's network to facilitate communication and exchange.

These secure Web sites become instant organizational Intranets used for communication, training, videoconferencing, and secure data interchange. Using such Web-enabled Intranets, Diamond Equipment Corporation's salespeople can link to the latest product information and spec sheets, obtain updated inventory and production numbers, download company information, and print customized proposals for customer presentations from anywhere in the world. CDW Computer Systems provides each of their major accounts with a customized Extranet that provides the customer with access to CDW on a 24-hour, seven-day-a-week basis. Buyers can track orders online, download product and technical specifications, access customer support technicians, check prices and availability of products, and even place orders for next-day delivery throughout the United States. Rather than spending time traveling to customers' offices, Digital Equipment Corporation's salespeople deliver their presentations by combining teleconferences and Web presentations. The use of Internet- and Intranet-based technologies shorten the sales cycle by allowing sales meetings and presentations to be created and delivered in less time than traditional face-to-face processes would take. If a salesperson can save just 10 minutes a day by using Web-based presentation libraries and online product and pricing information, he or she will gain an additional week's worth of productivity over the course of a year. However, as illustrated by the situation described in "An Ethical Dilemma," the acceptance and adoption of advanced technologies is not always an easy thing to accomplish.

PAGERS AND CELL PHONES   Innovations in portable communication such as pagers and cell phones allow salespeople to stay in touch with customers, the home office, and even the family while traveling cross-country or just walking across the parking lot to make a customer call. Today's pagers allow customers and others to access the carrier anywhere and anytime. Much more than the simple beeper of yesterday, today's pagers are capable of receiving full-text messages and e-mail. Several paging companies, such as SkyTel, have introduced pagers capable of responding to messages as well as e-mail. Cell phones have also experienced a tremendous increase in technological advances. In addition to increased coverage and smaller sizes, newer phones offer wireless faxing, e-mail, scheduling, and contact management database capabilities. The ability to use two-way communication during time that would otherwise be nonproductive can significantly increase selling time, customer satisfaction, and sales productivity.

VOICE MAIL   Ever played the frustrating game of telephone tag? The demands on people's time are continuing to increase, and the projected result will be even more difficulty in completing a telephone call on the first try. Rather than simply using

An Ethical Dilemma

Commercial Risk Associates (CRA) is a major property and casualty insurance company with sales agents across the United States and Canada. CRA sells through its own field salesforce of registered agents who work out of franchised agency offices and exclusively sell CRA products.

As part of its recent information systems expansion, CRA has replaced many of its systems and added a Web-enabled corporate Intranet. As part of this program, new equipment was also installed in the agency offices linking each of them into the corporate-wide system. Sales agents were impressed with the many advantages that they would gain with the system. The new electronic forms and communication network would greatly expedite the filing of paperwork and significantly reduce the multitude of forms required under the previous system.

The transformation to the new system was going smoothly until the Annual Agent Meeting last week. During a special Q & A session regarding the new computer information system, the agents discovered that several departments at corporate headquarters, including marketing and customer service, would have full access to the agents' customer account databases. As the discussion continued, a great deal of dissension began to develop.

The sales agents are suspicious of Corporate's ability to access their customer files. They think that these files are their property, and no others (especially Corporate) should have access to them. In fact, many agents were commenting that they were not going to allow their files to be put on the system. Corporate, however, thinks that they need access to the files to properly service customers and develop new products for the agents to sell.

The question as to who owns customer account files—the salespeople or the selling organization—has been a point of contention for sometime. It is nothing new. However, the advent of new information technologies and increased salesforce automation has brought this question back under the spotlight.

How do you feel about this issue? If you were one of the corporate decision makers associated with this program at CRA, how would you address and resolve this potentially divisive issue?

voice mail to notify the other party that they called—top salespeople have become adept at using voice mail to convey and receive information to and from customers as well as sales management and support centers at the home office. Mastering the ability to use voice mail as an extension of oneself generates a significant savings in time and effort that can be redirected to provide additional time for selling.

HIGH-TECH SALES SUPPORT OFFICES   Organizations having salesforces widely dispersed geographically or traveling across multiple regions of the nation or world have found it advantageous to establish **high-tech sales support offices** at multiple locations. Both resident and nonresident salespeople use these offices to access the wider range of selling technology than could be easily carried on a notebook or laptop computer. These offices also provide points of access to the various networks, Intranets, and Extranets maintained by the organization. IBM maintains high-tech offices such as these at its installations around the world. An IBM representative in Dallas might find himself working as part of a team on a project in Chicago. While in Chicago, the representative has access to the same technology and support as was available in Dallas. Full access is available to company networks, customer accounts, communication links, and software applications. Consequently, convenience and productive time are maximized for the benefit of all parties.

Stage Five: Assessment of Performance and Goal Attainment

A critical, and often overlooked, stage in the process of self-leadership is the periodic assessment of progress. Although certainly important, this stage should involve more than a simple check at the end of the period to determine whether goals were achieved or not. Assessment checkpoints should be built into plans at progressive points in time to encourage and facilitate the evaluation of one's progress. These frequent comparisons of actual performance with periodic checkpoints allow time to consider revisions or modifications before it is too late to make a difference. In addition to assessing progress, evaluation should also consider what is working well and what could be improved. This knowledge and understanding can be used to guide modifications in the various plans, tasks, and activities that populate the different stages of self-leadership to further enhance future success and performance.

Increasing Customer Value Through Teamwork

Quality customer service is taking on a key role in competitive business strategy, and as customer expectations and needs continue to grow in complexity, selling organizations are finding they can no longer depend solely on salespeople as the exclusive arbiter of customer satisfaction. Teamwork, both inside the organization and with customers, is being emphasized as the key to customer focus and sales performance.

Internal Partnerships and Teams

The practices and experiences of sales organizations such as ASG in this module's opening vignette, as well as considerable sales research studies, support the emphasis on teamwork as a key to long-term selling success. The results from three studies of more than 200 companies that employ some 25,000 salespeople supported the belief that cooperating as a team player was critical for success in selling.[6] Similar results have been found in other studies that examine what business-to-business buyers expect from suppliers. In two studies incorporating 6,708 customer evaluations of vendor performance and customer satisfaction in the financial services industry, the suppliers' performance in building internal and external partnerships was found to be the key driver of customer satisfaction.[7]

Building **external relationships** is the focal point of contemporary selling techniques and reflects the ongoing paradigm shift in today's salesforces. This emphasis on building *external* customer relationships could overshadow the critical role of building *internal*, close working relationships with other individuals in their own company. The importance of these **internal relationships** would seem to be logical, as a salesperson's success depends on the degree of support he or she receives from others in the various functional areas of the organization. Ultimately, the salesperson owns the responsibility for customer relationships, but the strength of those customer relationships depends on the joint efforts and resources contributed by multiple individuals across the selling organization.

Account managers at Contour Plastics Corporation have full responsibility for bringing together individuals from functional departments across the organization to work as a sales team dedicated to selling and providing pre- and post-sale services to a specific account. As needed, team members will incorporate research chemists, application specialists, production engineers, and logistics specialists. Coordinated by the salesperson, each team member contributes his or her special expertise toward maximizing the understanding of the customer's situation and needs, and then working together to create a unique, value-added solution that few, if any, competitors can equal.

Teamwork results in a synergy that produces greater outcomes and results for all parties than would be possible with multiple individuals acting independently of one another. Consequently, it is important that salespeople also develop the ability to sell internally as they represent their customers to the selling organization and give recognition to the important role others play in winning, keeping, and growing customer accounts.

James Champy, chairman of consulting for Perot Systems, notes that customers are expecting and receiving better service and product options than ever and characterizes the role of the salesperson as having been transformed to that of a trusted advisor.[8]

In this advisor role, the salesperson works with customers to develop a mutual understanding of the customer's situation, needs, possibilities, and expectations. On the basis of this information, the salesperson assembles a team of individuals, experts from across the selling organization, who work together creating a product response that will deliver more unique customer value than the competitors' offerings. In delivering this unique and added value for customers, salespeople often find themselves working with other individuals in sales, marketing, design and manufacturing, administrative support, shipping, and customer service.

SALES PARTNERSHIPS   Within the sales department, salespeople often team with other salespeople to gain the strengths and expertise required for a specific selling situation or customer. Partnerships with sales managers and other sales executives are also important in winning support for developing innovative responses to customer needs. XL Capital is a global leader in alternative risk transfer products, financial risk management, and surplus lines of commercial property and casualty insurance. Selling to Fortune 500 and Fortune 1000 customers, XL Capital's salespeople (customer business unit managers) specialize along customer and industry lines. It is common for XL's salespeople to work together in teams to bring together the experience and expertise required to work with customers whose businesses span a large number of different industries.

MARKETING PARTNERSHIPS   Teaming with individuals in the marketing department is critical for salespeople in generating integrated solutions for customers over the long term. Marketing is responsible for developing organizational marketing strategies that serve as guidelines for the salesforce. Using information gathered in the field by the salesforce, marketing also assists in the generation of new market offerings in response to changing customer needs and requests. Marketing can also be a valuable partner for salespeople in accessing information and developing sales proposals.

At Pocahontas Foods, a top-10 institutional food broker with nationwide operations, account managers regularly work with members of the marketing department to communicate changes in customer needs and activities of competitors. This collaborative partnership allows Pocahontas to continue bringing innovative product offerings to the marketplace that are designed around the inputs from their salespeople.

Design and Manufacturing Partnerships Salespeople often find themselves selling ideas for product designs and changes in manufacturing schedules to meet the needs of customers. When individuals from design, manufacturing, and sales work as a team, performance and delivery commitments are more likely to be met and customer satisfaction further enhanced. Wallace works to maintain its industry leadership in business forms and systems by aggressively nurturing a company-wide culture emphasizing customer orientation and support. As part of their training, salespeople actually work in production facilities to understand what has to be done to meet product design and delivery requirements that the salespeople might commit to in the field. By-products of this cross-training come about in the form of one-to-one personal relationships between salespeople and production staff. In the case of complex customer needs or special delivery needs, these relationships become invaluable.

ADMINISTRATIVE SUPPORT PARTNERSHIPS   Salespeople work with others from administrative support functions such as management, finance and credit, billing, and information systems. Like sales, each of these functional units has certain goals and objectives that translate to policies and procedures that govern their own activities and affect operations throughout the organization—including sales. Customer needs are served best when salespeople have worked to establish effective relationships within these units and all parties work together for the mutual good of the organization and customer. Jim Gavic, account manager for Great Lakes Trucking, manages a territory stretching from the industrial sector of south Chicago east to Gary, Indiana, and south to Indianapolis. Jim credits his close relationships with individuals in the company's finance and credit department for making 20 percent of his annual sales. By working together, they were able to establish special billing terms for several of his larger accounts. If Finance and Credit had simply enforced Great Lake's standard terms, these customers would have been lost to a competitor with more flexible credit policies.

SHIPPING AND TRANSPORTATION PARTNERSHIPS   Salespeople periodically find themselves facing an urgent customer need that requires special handling of an order. Perhaps it is an expedited shipment for immediate delivery or the processing and shipping of an interim order of less than economical size. Whatever the need, it will affect other shipments getting out on time and could even increase the department's operating costs. Curtis James, territory manager for General Electric Appliances, found sales going better than usual at a new store opening in Oklahoma City. To keep the customer from being caught short, he hand-carried a fill-in order to the GE district office, walked it through credit approval, hand-delivered the shipping order to the warehouse, and helped load the truck. Teamwork enabled Curtis to accomplish in less than a day what normally would have taken 8 to 10 days. It takes a team effort to work through exceptions such as these, and it is common to find the salesperson actually helping to make it happen by pulling orders, packing boxes, and even helping to load the truck.

CUSTOMER SERVICE PARTNERSHIPS   Teamwork between sales and customer service can create a synergy that has a broad-based impact that can translate to higher customer satisfaction, higher rates of customer retention, and increased sales performance. On the one hand, customer service personnel, such as call center operators and service technicians, often have more extensive contact with customers than the account representatives. As such, they can serve as an early warning system for salespeople and provide valuable information regarding customer complaints, problems, developing needs, and changes that they encounter through customer contacts. As a salesperson for Thompson School Supply, Cap Williams regularly checks in and visits with the company's customer service personnel to keep abreast of contacts that they might have with any of his customers. The information he receives allows him to get ahead of any possible customer problems, provide an uncanny level of after-sale support that continues to mystify upper management, and helps to secure his consistent receipt of Top Salesperson of the Year Award year after year. When salespeople such as Cap Williams act on the information provided by customer service to further customer relationships and increase sales, customer service personnel will also be further inclined to work together to benefit the team. On the other hand, salespeople often assist customer service personnel by working directly with customers to address problems before they become complaints and provide instruction and training to assist customers in using products sold.

Building Teamwork Skills

As illustrated in "An Ethical Dilemma," effective teams do not form by default. Nor can a team be effective in producing synergistic benefits solely because it is called a team. Like customer relationships, internal relationships are built on reciprocal trust. The salesperson that arbitrarily and repeatedly asks for special production runs, extensions to customers' lines of credit, expedited shipments, or special attention from customer service is simply asking for quick fixes. These quick fixes serve the objectives of the customer and salesperson but often work against the objectives of the functional unit and the organization as a whole.

An Ethical Dilemma

Ron James has been selling business services for Phoenix-based EQUISOURCE for just over three years. During his first two years with EQUISOURCE, Ron's sales led the Western U.S. region. However, his performance over the last two quarters has been below projections. During his last assessment meeting with his sales manager, Ron attributed his flat sales to the finance department's new customer credit requirements. He explained that the finance department had developed and introduced higher financial standards for granting customer credit that seemed to have an extraordinary negative impact in his territory. Many of his existing customers had experienced reduced lines of credit, which had translated to lost sales in his territory. Even though these were long-term customers who had never been late on a payment, the finance department was intent on enforcing the new standards across all accounts and in all territories. Not only was Ron losing established business in existing accounts, the higher credit requirements were also making it difficult to win new business that might help to close his performance gap. As a result of the credit policy changes, EQUISOURCE has seen many of its competitive advantages neutralized, and the competition has begun making significant inroads. If you were Ron, who would you go about teaming with the finance department to solve this problem?

Synergistic teamwork requires a commitment on the part of all parties to look for and work for win/win solutions. However, in the rush to take care of a customer, it is all too easy for salespeople to fall into a win/lose orientation. It is not that they want anyone to lose, but rather that they get what they want. This win orientation is most common in everyday negotiation—in which people think and act in terms of accomplishing their own goals and leave it to others to attain theirs. As illustrated in Figure 5.7, optimum solutions develop from a team orientation based on the philosophy of win/win alternatives. In turn, this can only happen when there are high levels of mutual trust and communication: "Not your way, not my way, but a better way."

In his bestseller book for personal development, Steven Covey offers six keys to developing synergistic relationships and teams.[9] These are the six **teamwork skills** that salespeople must learn and sincerely apply in their process of building internal partnerships that translate to increased sales and organizational performance.

- *Understanding the Other Individuals*—Fully understanding and considering the other individuals in the partnership is necessary to know what is important to them. What is important to them must also be important to the salesperson if the partnership is to grow and be effective. This means that salespeople must take time to learn the objectives of other functional areas and consider how those needs and requests might affect the salesperson's goals and objectives.

- *Attending to the Little Things*—The little kindnesses and courtesies are often small in size and great in importance. In building relationships, the little things are the big things. Properly attended to and nurtured, they enhance

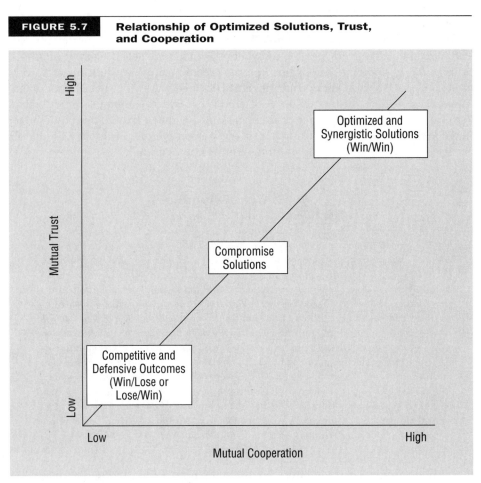

FIGURE 5.7   Relationship of Optimized Solutions, Trust, and Cooperation

Optimum buyer-seller solutions result from a team orientation and require high levels of mutual trust and mutual cooperation.

the interrelationships. At the same time, if they are neglected or misused, they can destroy the relationship very quickly.

- *Keeping Commitments*—We all build our hopes and plans around the promises and commitments of others. When a commitment is not kept, disappointment and problems result. As a result, credibility and trust suffer major damage that is always difficult and often impossible to repair. However, consistency in keeping commitments builds and solidifies trust-based relationships.

- *Clarifying Expectations*—The root cause of most relational difficulties can be found in ambiguous expectations regarding roles and goals—exactly where are we going and who is responsible for what? Investing the time up front to clarify expectations regarding goals and roles can save even more time on down the road when misunderstandings become compounded and turn into goal conflicts and breakdowns in communication.

- *Showing Personal Integrity*—Demonstrating personal integrity generates trust, whereas a lack of integrity can quickly undermine the best of teamwork orientations. People can seek to understand others, carry through on the little things, keep commitments, and clarify expectations but still fail to build trust by being inwardly duplicitous and pursuing a personal agenda. Be honest, open, and treat everyone by the same set of principles.

- *Apologizing Sincerely When a Mistake Is Made*—It is one thing to make a mistake. It is another thing to not admit it. People forgive mistakes. What is harder to forgive are the ill intentions and motives justifying any attempt to cover up. "If you are going to bow, bow low." The apology must be perceived as sincere and not simply an automated lip-service response.

Summary

1. **Explain the five sequential steps of self-leadership.** As a process, self-leadership is composed of five sequential stages. First, goals and objectives must be set that properly reflect what is important and what is to be accomplished. In turn, an analysis of the territory and classification of accounts is conducted to better understand the territory potential and prioritize accounts according to revenue producing possibilities. With goals in place and accounts prioritized, the third step develops corresponding strategic plans designed to achieve sales goals through proper allocation of resources and effort. The next stage maximizes the effectiveness of allocated resources by incorporating technology and salesforce automation to expand salesperson resource capabilities. Finally, assessment activities are conducted to evaluate performance and goal attainment and to assess possible changes in plans and strategies.

2. **Discuss the importance of thorough and effective planning.** Success in any career has been described as doing the right things and doing them well. It is not simply the amount of effort that determines an achievement, but rather how well that effort is honed and aligned with one's goals. In selling, this is often restated as selling smarter rather than selling harder. That is, before we expend our valuable time and resources, we must establish our priorities in the form of objectives. Then, and only then, do we implement the strategic plan that has been specifically developed to achieve our goals in the light of the available resources and market potential that exist within our territory. Self-leadership translates to a process of first deciding what is to be accomplished and then placing into motion the proper plan designed to achieve those objectives.

3. **Identify the four levels of sales goals and explain their interrelationships.** There are four different levels of goals that salespeople must establish to maximize sales effectiveness:
   (a) personal goals—what one wants to accomplish relative to oneself;
   (b) sales call goals—the priorities that are set out to be accomplished during a specific call;
   (c) account goals—the objectives relative to each individual account; and
   (d) territory goals—what is to be accomplished for the overall territory.

   Each level requires different types of effort and produces different outcomes, and each of the levels is interrelated and interdependent on the others. Ultimately, each higher-level goal is dependent on the salesperson setting and achieving the specific goals for each lower level.

4. **Describe two techniques for account classification.** There are two basic methods of classifying accounts. In ascending order of complexity, these methods are: single-factor analysis and portfolio analysis (also referred to as two-factor analysis).
   - *Single-Factor Analysis*—Single-factor analysis, also referred to as ABC analysis, is the simplest and most often used method for classifying accounts. Accounts are analyzed on the basis of one single factor—typically the level of sales potential—and placed into either three or four categories denoted by letters of the alphabet, "A," "B," "C," "D." All accounts in the same category receive equal selling effort.
   - *Portfolio Analysis (Two-Factor Analysis)*—This classification method allows two factors to be considered simultaneously. Each account is examined on the basis of the two factors selected for analysis and sorted into the proper segment of a matrix. This matrix is typically divided into four cells, with accounts placed into the proper classification cell on the basis of their individual ratings ("high" and "low" or "strong" and "weak") on each of the two factors. Accounts in the same cell share a common level of attractiveness as a customer and will receive the same amount of selling effort.

5. **Explain the application of different territory routing techniques.** Territory routing plans incorporate information developed in the territory analysis and account classification to minimize unproductive travel time that could be better spent working with customers. Good routing plans minimize the backtracking and crisscrossing that would otherwise occur. Routing plans correspond to one of five common patterns.

    Straight line—With a straight line plan, salespeople start from their offices and make calls in one direction until they reach the end of the territory. At that point, they change direction and continue to make calls on a straight line on the new vector.

    Cloverleaf—Using the cloverleaf pattern, a salesperson works a different part of the territory and travels in a circular loop back to the starting point. Each loop could take a day, a week, or longer to complete. A new loop is covered on each trip until the entire territory has been covered.

    Circular—Circular patterns begin at the office and move in an expanding pattern of concentric circles that spiral across the territory. This method works best when accounts are evenly dispersed throughout the territory.

    Leapfrog—When the territory is exceptionally large and accounts are clustered into several widely dispersed groups, the leapfrog routing methodology is most efficient. Beginning in one cluster, the salesperson works each of the accounts at that location and then jumps (typically by flying) to the next cluster. This continues until the last cluster has been worked and the salesperson jumps back to the office or home.

    Major City—Downtown areas are typically highly concentrated with locations controlled by a grid of city blocks and streets. Consequently, the downtown segment is typically a small square or rectangular area allowing accounts to be worked in a straight-line fashion street by street. Outlying areas are placed in evenly balanced triangles or pie-shaped quadrants, with one quadrant being covered at a time in either a straight-line or cloverleaf pattern.

6. **Interpret the usefulness of different types of selling technology and automation.** Properly applied, selling technology spurs creativity and innovation, streamlines the selling process, generates new selling opportunities, facilitates communication, and enhances customer follow-up. Salespeople must not only master the technology itself, but they must also understand when and where it can be applied most effectively. A wide selection of different-sized computers is at the center of most selling technologies. They provide the production tools for generating reports, proposals, and graphic-enhanced presentations. Spreadsheet applications and database applications facilitate the analysis of customer accounts and searching for information needed by customers. Contact management software enables the salesperson to gather and organize account information and schedule calls. Access to the Internet and World Wide Web provide salespeople access to an assortment of public and corporate networks that enable one to communicate, research, and access company information and training from anywhere in the world. Using pagers and cell phones puts salespeople in touch with customers, the home office, and even the family while traveling cross-country or just walking across the parking lot to make a customer call. Voice mail voids the previous restrictions of time and place that accompanied the requirement to make personal contact. Messages can now be left and received 24 hours a day and seven days a week. High-tech sales support offices provide geographically dispersed salespeople with a common standard of computing technology, access to software applications, and portals to organizational networks at offices around the world. Wherever they may be working, they have the tools and capabilities identical to those available to them in their home offices.

7. **Delineate six skills for building internal relationships and teams.**
    (a) *Understanding the Other Individuals*—Fully understanding and considering the other individuals in the partnership is necessary to know what is important to them. What is important to them must also be important to the salesperson if the partnership is to grow and be effective.
    (b) *Attending to the Little Things*—The little kindnesses and courtesies are small in size, but great in importance. Properly attended to and nurtured, they enhance the interrelationships. However, when neglected or misused, they can destroy the relationship very quickly.

(c) *Keeping Commitments*—We build hopes and plans around the promises and commitments made to us by others. When a commitment is not kept, disappointment and problems result and credibility and trust suffer major damage that will be difficult or impossible to repair.

(d) *Clarifying Expectations*—The root cause of most relational difficulties can be found in ambiguous expectations regarding roles and goals. By clarifying goals and priorities as well as who is responsible for different activities up front, the hurt feelings, disappointments, and lost time resulting from misunderstandings and conflict can be prevented.

(e) *Showing Personal Integrity*—Demonstrating personal integrity generates trust. Be honest, open, and treat everyone by the same set of principles.

(f) *Apologizing Sincerely When a Mistake Is Made*—It is one thing to make a mistake. It is another thing to not admit it. People forgive mistakes, but ill intentions and cover-ups can destroy trust.

Understanding Professional Selling Terms

- Self-leadership
- Goals and objectives
- Personal goals
- Territory goal
- Account goal
- Sales call goal
- Territory analysis
- Account classification
- Single-factor analysis
- ABC analysis
- Portfolio analysis
- Sales planning
- Straight line routing plan
- Cloverleaf routing plan
- Circular routing plan
- Leapfrog routing plan
- Major city routing plan
- Selling technology and automation
- Internet
- Intranet
- Extranets
- High-tech sales support offices
- External relationships
- Internal relationships
- Teamwork skills

Developing Professional Selling Knowledge

1. Explain why setting goals and developing formalized selling plans are represented as key requirements for success in selling.
2. Identify and discuss the three required characteristics of a goal or objective.
3. Explain the five sequential stages of self-leadership and how they affect selling success.
4. Develop an example of the four different levels of goals and how they are interrelated.
5. Using a map of your state or region, use city and town locations to establish routing plans by using the straight line, cloverleaf, circular, leapfrog, and major city methods.
6. Explain how a salesperson might use Internet-based, online product catalogues and presentation libraries to enhance their sales productivity.
7. Explain the weaknesses and strengths of the two methods for account classification.
8. Why is a teamwork orientation important in selling?
9. Who are the individuals within the organization that salespeople are likely to team with, and how could such a team be advantageous to the salesperson?
10. What are the six teamwork skills? Explain why they are important for success in developing interpersonal relationships.

Building Professional Selling Skills

1. What are your strengths and weaknesses when it comes to managing time? Complete the following worksheet by checking off the answer that best reflects your situation and score your answers according to the instructions at the end of the worksheet.

Time Management Skills Worksheet			
Always	**Sometimes**	**Never**	
			Do you plan your day according to the daily "emergencies" of others?
			At the end of the day do you have a lot of tasks undone?
			Do you repeatedly run out of household necessities such as milk, juice, or ingredients for the next meal?
			Are you frequently late to appointments?
			Do you find that you are a procrastinator?
			Do you freqiently have to work late or start early to meet deadlines?
			If you needed to find a specific piece of paper (bill, invitation, or note), would it take more than five minutes?
			Do you forget friends' and relatives' birthdays more often than you would like to admit?
			Is your desk frequently piled with papers?
			Are you up to date on your filing?
			Do you let mail pile up?
			Do you do tasks yourself because it is easier than teaching it to someone else?
			Do you interrupt yourself by jumping up to do something else when you are working on a project?
			Do you let other people waste your time with overly long phone calls or drop-by visits that never end?
			Do you find that you are always losing things (e.g., your keys, assignment book, or library books)?
			Add up the number of checks in each column and enter the number in the corresponding square.

Scoring the Time Management Skills Worksheet:

If you have fewer than three checks in the Always column—You are doing well.

If you have four to five checks in the Always column—You are well on your way to becoming overwhelmed, but not yet over the edge. Make a few changes in your habits, and you will quickly be back in control of your time.

If you have more than five checks in the Always column—Life's fast track has gotten the better of you, and you are significantly overwhelmed. It will take a significant commitment, but you can regain control. Examine your scoring pattern on the worksheet. Look for the checks in the Always column where you can begin taking control. Start there and work up through the rest over time.

2. As a territory manager for Chicago Plastics, you have total sales responsibility for the state of Missouri. Chicago Plastics has just introduced a new line of plasitisol-based products targeted for use by accounts that mold raw plastic materials into consumer and industrial products. You are in the process of identifying prospects in your Missouri territory and establishing a route that will allow you to call on each of them.

Having become a regular user of the Internet and World Wide Web in digging out business-related information on prospects and accounts, you are aware that the *Big Yellow Pages* site has the capability to search specific geographic areas by SIC-related industry types and provide (1) a total count of the number of firms active in a specific industry and located within a specified area and (2) a complete listing of firms, including name, location, and telephone numbers.

A.   Access the *Big Yellow Pages* Web site at the URL http://www.bigyellow.com and generate a listing of firms active in the business/industry described as "molded plastics" within the state of Missouri. Print the listing in a form suitable to hand in to your instructor.

B.   Go to the Map Quest Web site at the URL http://mapquest.com and complete the short registration information sheet to become a free user of this informative site. Use Map Quest to access a map of Missouri. Print the map, and locate the prospects provided from your search of *Big Yellow Pages* by placing a locator mark on the map. Considering that you live in and work out of an office located in Springfield, Missouri, examine the pattern of locator marks to determine which territory routing method would be most efficient for you to use. Using a colored marker, trace the routing onto the map.

C.   Discuss and explain why you selected the method that you selected over the other methods available to you.

3.   When was the last time you said something like, "I just do not understand where all my time goes"? This exercise is designed to help you find out by actually tracking your time for one full day. Tear out or make a copy of the following time chart. Carry it with you and record what activities you are involved in throughout the day. The chart is set up to be easy to use—you just need to get in the habit of using it. You will probably be surprised at how much time is really lost during a single day. Imagine what it would look like if you charted your time for a full week!

   After you complete your time chart, study it to get an idea of where your time goes.

A.   How much time is actually spent in activities that are high priorities for you?

B.   How much time do others take from you?

C.   How much time is lost running errands?

D.   How much time is lost to interruptions?

E.   What changes could you make to reclaim some of your time?

Time Activity Chart

5:00 A.M.	5:00
5:15	5:15
5:30	5:30
5:45	5:45
6:00	6:00
6:15	6:15
6:30	6:30
6:45	6:45
7:00	7:00
7:15	7:15
7:30	7:30
7:45	7:45
8:00	8:00
8:15	8:15
8:30	8:30
8:45	8:45
9:00	9:00
9:15	9:15
9:30	9:30
9:45	9:45
10:00	10:00
10:15	10:15
10:30	10:30
10:45	10:45
11:00	11:00
11:15	11:15
11:30	11:45
11:45	12:00 Midnight
12:00 Noon	12:15
12:15	12:30
12:30	12:45
12:45	1:00
1:00	1:15
1:15	1:30
1:30	1:45
1:45	2:00
2:00	2:15
2:15	2:30
2:30	2:45
2:45	3:00
3:00	3:15
3:15	3:30
3:30	3:45
3:45	4:00
4:00	4:15
4:15	4:30
4:30	4:45
4:45	5:00

Making Professional Selling Decisions

CASE 5.1   *Emron Control Corp.*

Emron Control Corp. is a leading supplier for process control systems and equipment used in a wide variety of production and distribution applications. You have taken a sales representative job with Emron, and having just completed training, you have been given a territory of your own. Your district manager has provided you with a list of accounts as well as several boxes of notes and files that had been assembled and used by your predecessor. These are the accounts currently buying your products. You are expected to build these accounts and add new accounts to the list as you increase your territory's sales performance. You have summarized the account information into the following summary set of account profiles.

Questions

1. Develop a portfolio classification of accounts and assess the allocation of sales calls made by your predecessor over the past year.
2. What problems do you find with the previous allocation of calls on these accounts?
3. Based on your account classification analysis, suggest a new sales call allocation strategy that would make better use of your time in the territory.

Account Name	Account Opportunity	Competitive Position	Annual Number of Sales Calls Last Year
Mueller Distribution	High	Low	30
Tri-State Specialties	Low	High	20
Birkey Paper Co.	Low	High	26
Normal Supply	Low	Low	12
Darnell Aggregate Products	Low	High	21
Reinhart Chemicals	High	High	26
ACCO Manufacturing	Low	High	23
Tri-State Manufacturing	High	Low	28
Ideal Engineering	Low	Low	11
Terracon	High	High	25
Lowry Foods	High	Low	26
SCS Industrial	High	High	27
Lowell Services	Low	High	18
Bowles and Sons	Low	High	21
American Foundry	High	Low	22
Hewitt & Associates	Low	Low	16
Bright Metals Inc.	High	High	22
Decatur Extrusions	Low	Low	14
King Chemicals	Low	High	22
Bear's Steel Corp.	Low	High	20
Hoffman Pharmaceuticals	High	Low	20
Barlow & Clark Systems	Low	High	18

Making Professional Selling Decisions

CASE 5.2   *Mark Cassidy and Milligan Adhesives Corporation*

Mark Cassidy has just graduated and taken a job as a sales representative for the Milligan Adhesives Corporation, a supplier of adhesives used in the construction and manufacturing industries. Mark's west Dallas territory is full of opportunity, and like many new salespeople, Mark is finding it difficult to get everything done that needs his attention. The following Daily Time and Activity Log is an actual day copied from Mark's records that he thinks is typical. Analyze Mark's Time and Activity Log.

Questions

1. What problems do you find?
2. What suggestions could you make to help Mark make better use of his selling time?

DAILY TIME & ACTIVITY LOG

Salesperson Name: | *Mark Cassidy* | Date: | *Monday 8/7*

Territory: | *West Dallas*

Time	Activity	Company/People	Notes & Comments
9:15–10:00	*Sales call*	*Mike Humphreys Mid West Construction Supply*	*Called on buyer to demo our 810 line of adhesives. Wrote 2 orders: $11,300 for this quarter; $12,450 following quarter*
10:00–10:25	*Travel time*	*Jill Attaway Horner Construction job site@ 310 Maple*	*Service problem with $600 worth of wallboard adhesive. Was supposed to meet project manager this morning, but she was not at the job site yet.*
10:25–10:45	*Travel & phone call*	*"*	*Used pay phone at Walgreens to call Attaway on her cellphone. She is on way to job site to meet me*
10:45–11:00	*Travel back to job site*	*"*	
11:00–11:35	*Service call*	*"*	*Met with Jill Attaway re: product problem. FedExing replacement for arrival tomorrow morning. Customer is OK with everything.*
11:35–12:05	*Travel time*	*Terrell Manufacturing Kerri Williams*	*Have appointment for 12:00 lunch*
12:05–1:15	*Sales call and lunch*	*"*	*Follow-up call from 2 weeks ago. Closed a sale for our 2000 wood/laminate production adhesive. We will supply 50% of their needs. Should produce $12,000 per month over the year.*
1:15–1:20	*Travel time*	*TriState Cabinets Bart Waits*	*Cold call on high-potential prospect located 2 blocks down from Terrell Mfg. Already nearby—thought I would make a personal contact*
1:20–1:45	*Waited in lobby*	*"*	*Bart Waits, head buyer, was busy but wanted to see me. Ask that I wait in lobby until he got free.*
1:45–2:10	*Sales call*	*"*	*Met with head buyer & gathered information—he wants a proposal on our 2000 line and ask that I drop back in sometime this next week to present a proposal. No definite time—just drop in.*
2:10–2:55	*Travel time*	*Comanche Table Mfg. Aimee Williams*	*Drove across town to keep a 3:30 appointment with Aimee. Comanche has regularly purchased $8,000 monthly and is getting ready to open a plant expansion that will double production*
2:55–4:00	*Sales call*	*"*	*Clarified delivery dates for added product needs. Our orders will increase to $10,000 monthly in 2 months.*
4:00–4:05	*Travel time*	*Dalco Laminates Rodney Moore*	*Cold call. Dalco is located down the street from Comanche Table. Already on this side of town and have been meaning to make a prospecting call.*
4:05–4:30	*Sales call*	*"*	*Worked with buyer to explore their needs, plans, and current suppliers. Their parent company is National Chemical, and they currently buy all adhesives from National. Low potential to sell!!*
4:30–5:55	*Return to office*	*Need to complete paperwork & orders*	*Crossing town in peak traffic. Took forever. Late getting home— family had already left for son's ball game.*

MODULE *6*

Strategic Selling Process

Bryan Hollingsworth:
Trustworthy Sales Professional

George F. Cram Company, a globe and map supplier, is fortunate to have Bryan Hollingsworth on its sales team. Hollingsworth knows that earning the customer's trust is the key to successful selling. Asked to define trust, he says, "To me, trust is an unwritten agreement between two parties for one party to perform a set of agreed-on activities and the other party to perform an agreed-on set of activities, and here's the key part of it—without fear of change from the other party. You trust me to do what I said I would, and I trust you to do the same. That's my definition."

According to Hollingsworth, salespeople must make an extra effort to show their trustworthiness. He believes that honest salespeople have nothing to hide and that they will be forthright with the buyer on all matters. For Hollingsworth, this begins when he first contacts a prospective customer. Rather than being evasive about why he wishes to see the prospect, Hollingsworth gets right to the point and refuses to be pushy if the prospect is not interested in buying globes or maps. Hollingsworth notes, "I'm not here to waste my time or theirs."

To gain the respect of the prospect, Hollingsworth does his homework and customizes his presentations to the buyer's situation and personal style: "Based on the response to the benefit, I can usually tell what kind of personality I'm dealing with. Some individuals want the bottom line right away, and if they say they need to know their potential gross profit margin when they sell my products in their stores, I'll tell them. That builds trust because they see that I get right up to speed and play the game the way they play it."

Seemingly minor details can make a difference in building trust with customers. Hollingsworth cautions salespeople not to use the phrase *to be honest with you,* because it implies that up to that point perhaps the salesperson has been less than honest. He also advises salespeople never to fake a response to a buyer question. He would answer a tough question about delivery by saying, "Okay, you want to buy this many globes to ship on this date. I don't know. It depends on these factors. If I find out by this time tomorrow and get back to you, is that soon enough?"

Finally, Hollingsworth knows that consistently doing what you say you will do over time is essential for gaining customer trust: "I'll do what you ask, and I'll do it in a timely fashion, so you can expect that from me when and if the day comes that we can conduct business together."

Source: Dana Ray, "Bank on Trust," *Selling Power* (March, 1999): 23–25.

Learning Objectives

After completing this module, you should be able to

1 Distinguish between transaction-focused traditional selling and trust-based relationship selling.

2 Discuss five alternative approaches to personal selling.

3 Describe the three primary roles fulfilled by consultative salespeople.

4 Identify five salesperson attributes that are essential for building customer trust.

5 Discuss the sales process as a series of interrelated steps.

149

Bryan Hollingsworth is a fine example of successful salespeople in today's demanding business world. He views sales as a long-term process of gaining buyer trust and generating beneficial results for both buyer and seller. In this module, we take a closer look at alternative approaches to personal selling that professionals such as Hollingsworth may choose from to best interact with their customers. Some of these approaches are simple. Other approaches are more sophisticated and require that the salesperson play a strategic role to use them successfully. We also devote considerable discussion to the sales process, whereby salespeople initiate, develop, and enhance customer relationships.

Classification of Personal Selling Approaches

More than three decades ago, four basic approaches to personal selling were identified: stimulus response, mental states, need satisfaction, and problem solving.[1] Since that time, another approach to personal selling, termed *consultative selling,* has gained popularity. All five approaches to selling are practiced today. Furthermore, many salespeople use elements of more than one approach in their own hybrids of personal selling.

As a prelude to our discussion of different approaches to personal selling, an expansion of two key points is in order. Recall that personal selling differs from other forms of marketing communications because it is a personal communication delivered by employees or agents of the sales organization. Because the personal element is present, salespeople have the opportunity to alter their sales messages and behaviors during a sales presentation or as they encounter different sales situations and different customers. This is referred to as **adaptive selling.** Because salespeople often deal with multicultural buyers in domestic and international markets, adaptive selling is an important concept.

A second point is that personal selling is moving from transaction-based methods to relationship-based methods. Rather than trying to maximize sales in the short run, relationship-based selling approaches focus on solving customer problems, providing opportunities, and adding value to the customer's business over an extended period. Exhibit 6.1 illustrates how transaction-based selling differs from relationship-based selling. We now explore one element of Exhibit 6.1 in detail—personal selling approaches.

Stimulus Response Selling

Of the five views of personal selling, **stimulus response selling** is the simplest. The theoretical background for this approach originated in early experiments with animal behavior. The key idea is that various stimuli can elicit predictable responses. Salespeople furnish the stimuli from a repertoire of words and actions designed to produce the desired response. This approach to selling is illustrated in Figure 6.1 on page 152.

An example of the stimulus response view of selling would be **continued affirmation,** a method in which a series of questions or statements furnished by the salesperson is designed to condition the prospective buyer to answering "yes" time after time, until, it is hoped, he or she will be inclined to say "yes" to the entire sales proposition. This method is often used by telemarketing personnel, who rely on comprehensive sales scripts read or delivered from memory.

Stimulus response sales strategies, particularly when implemented with a canned sales presentation, have some advantages for the seller. The sales message can be structured in a logical order. Questions and objections from the buyer can usually be anticipated and addressed before they are magnified during buyer–seller

	Transaction-Focused Traditional Selling	Trust-Based Relationship Selling
EXHIBIT 6.1	**Comparison of Transaction-Focused Traditional Selling with Trust-Based Relationship Selling**	
Primary perspective	The salesperson and the selling firm	The customer and the customer's customers
Personal selling approaches	Stimulus response, mental states	Need satisfaction, problem solving, consultative
Desired outcome	Closed sales, order volume	Trust, joint planning, mutual benefits, enhance profits
Role of salesperson	Make calls and close sales	Business consultant and long-term ally Key player in the customer's business
Nature of communication	One-way, from salesperson to customer	Two-way and collaborative
Degree of salesperson's involvement in customer's decision-making process	Isolated from customer's decision-making process	Actively involved in customer's decision-making process
Knowledge required	Own company's products Competition Applications Account strategies Costs Opportunities	Own company's products and resources Competition Applications Account strategies Costs Opportunities General business and industry knowledge and insight Customer's products, competition, and customers
Typical skills required	Selling skills	Selling skills Information gathering Listening and questioning Strategic problem solving Creating and demonstrating unique, value-added solutions Teambuilding and teamwork
Postsale follow-up	Little or none: move on to conquer next customer	Continued follow-through to Ensure customer satisfaction Keep customer informed Add customer value Manage opportunities

interaction. Inexperienced salespeople can rely on stimulus response sales methods in some settings, and this may eventually contribute to sales expertise.

The limitations of stimulus response methods, however, can be severe, especially if the salesperson is dealing with a professional buyer. Most buyers like to take an active role in sales dialogue, and the stimulus response approach calls for the salesperson to dominate the flow of conversation. The lack of flexibility in this approach is also a disadvantage, as buyer responses and unforeseen interruptions may neutralize or damage the effectiveness of the stimuli.

Considering the net effects of this method's advantages and disadvantages, it appears most suitable for relatively unimportant purchase decisions, when time is severely constrained and when professional buyers are not the prospects. As consumers in general become more sophisticated, this approach will become more problematic.

Mental States Selling

Mental states selling, or the *formula approach* to personal selling, assumes that the buying process for most buyers is essentially identical and that buyers can be led through certain mental states, or steps, in the buying process. These mental states

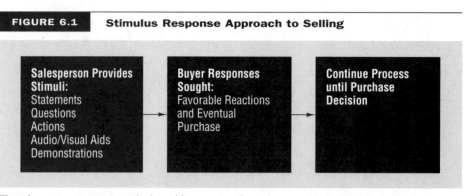

FIGURE 6.1   **Stimulus Response Approach to Selling**

| Salesperson Provides Stimuli: Statements Questions Actions Audio/Visual Aids Demonstrations | Buyer Responses Sought: Favorable Reactions and Eventual Purchase | Continue Process until Purchase Decision |

The salesperson attempts to gain favorable responses from the customer by providing stimuli, or cues, to influence the buyer. After the customer has been properly conditioned, the salesperson tries to secure a positive purchase decision.

are typically referred to as **AIDA,** (attention, interest, desire, and action). Appropriate sales messages provide a transition from one mental state to the next.

Like stimulus response selling, the mental states approach relies on a highly structured sales presentation. The salesperson does most of the talking, as feedback from the prospect could be disruptive to the flow of the presentation.

A positive feature of this method is that it forces the salesperson to plan the sales presentation prior to calling on the customer. It also helps the salesperson recognize that timing is an important element in the purchase decision process and that careful listening is necessary to determine which stage the buyer is in at any given point.

A problem with the mental states method is that it is difficult to determine which state a prospect is in. Sometimes a prospect is spanning two mental states or moving back and forth between two states during the sales presentation. Consequently, the heavy guidance structure the salesperson implements may be inappropriate, confusing, and even counterproductive to sales effectiveness. We should also note that this method is not customer oriented. Although the salesperson tailors the presentation to each customer somewhat, this is done by noting customer mental states rather than needs. See "An Ethical Dilemma" for a situation in which the salesperson is contemplating the movement of the prospect into the "action" stage.

The mental states method is illustrated in Exhibit 6.2. Note that this version includes "conviction" as an intermediate stage between interest and desire. Such minor variations are commonplace in different renditions of this approach to selling.

An Ethical Dilemma

Rachel Duke sells advertising for her college newspaper. One of her potential clients is contemplating buying an ad for an upcoming special issue featuring bars and restaurants. Over the past two weeks, Rachel has tried unsuccessfully to get a commitment from the restaurant owner to place an ad. Her sales manager has suggested that Rachel call the prospect and tell him that there is only one remaining ad space in the special issue, and that she must have an immediate answer to ensure that the prospect's ad will appear in the special issue. The sales manager said, "Rachel, this guy is stalling. You've got to move him to action, and this technique will do the trick." Rachel was troubled by her manager's advice, since the special issue had plenty of ad space remaining. If you were Rachel, would you follow her sales manager's advice? Why or why not?

EXHIBIT 6.2	Mental States View of Selling	
Mental State	*Sales Step*	*Critical Sales Task*
Curiosity	Attention	Get prospects excited, then get them to like you
Interest	Interest	Interview: needs and wants
Conviction	Conviction	"What's in it for me?"
		Product—"Will it do what I want it to do?"
		Price—"Is it worth it?" "The hassle of change?"
		"Cheaper elsewhere?"
		Peers—"What will others think of it?"
Desire		Priority—"Do I need it now?" (sense of urgency)
Action	Desire	Overcome their stall
	Close	Alternate choice close: which, not if!

Need Satisfaction Selling

Need satisfaction selling is based on the notion that the customer is buying to satisfy a particular need or set of needs. This approach is shown in Figure 6.2. It is the salesperson's task to identify the need to be met, then to help the buyer meet the need. Unlike the mental states and stimulus response methods, this method focuses on the customer rather than on the salesperson. The salesperson uses a questioning, probing tactic to uncover important buyer needs. Customer responses dominate the early portion of the sales interaction, and only after relevant needs have been established does the salesperson begin to relate how his or her offering can satisfy these needs.

Customers seem to appreciate this selling method and are often willing to spend considerable time in preliminary meetings to define needs prior to a sales presentation or written sales proposal. Also, this method avoids the defensiveness that arises in some prospects when a salesperson rushes to the persuasive part of the sales message without adequate attention to the buyer's needs.

Problem-Solving Selling

Problem-solving selling is an extension of need satisfaction selling. It goes beyond identifying needs to developing alternative solutions for satisfying these needs. The problem-solving approach to selling is depicted in Figure 6.3. Sometimes even competitors' offerings are included as alternatives in the purchase decision.

FIGURE 6.2	Need Satisfaction Approach to Selling

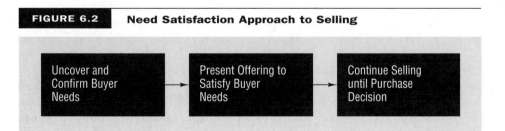

The salesperson attempts to uncover customer needs that are related to the salesperson's product or service offering. This may require extensive questioning in the early stages of the sales process. After confirming the buyer's needs, the salesperson proceeds with a presentation based on how the offering can meet those needs.

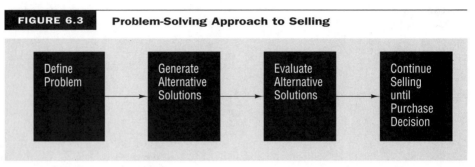

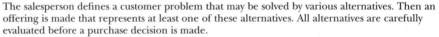

The salesperson defines a customer problem that may be solved by various alternatives. Then an offering is made that represents at least one of these alternatives. All alternatives are carefully evaluated before a purchase decision is made.

The problem-solving approach to selling is practiced by Square D sales representative Randy Scott in Altamonte Springs, Florida. Scott sells electronic products to industrial distributors. According to Scott,

> Certainly the product has to solve a problem for the customer. With our customers, that means either reducing or removing costs. Distributors want to keep their inventory at a low cost. When we come out with something new, they're hesitant to put it out without any proven wins for them. So first, it has to be a problem solver—it has to address a concern they have about the existing product. Second, we demo it for them, show them how it will work. Third, we have to leave samples with them. Fourth, and this actually takes place before the other three, we have to plant the seed of enthusiasm for the product in the customer's mind ahead of time.[2]

As the Square D example points out, the problem-solving approach to selling can take a lot of time. In some cases, the selling company cannot afford this much time with each prospective customer. In other cases, the customers may be unwilling to spend the time. Insurance salespeople, for example, report this to be so in their field. The problem-solving approach appears to be most successful in technical industrial sales situations, in which the parties involved are usually oriented toward scientific reasoning and processes and thus find this approach to sales amenable.

Consultative Selling

Consultative selling is the process of helping customers reach their strategic goals by using the products, services, and expertise of the sales organization.[3] Notice that this method focuses on achieving strategic goals of customers, not just meeting needs or solving problems. Salespeople confirm their customers' strategic goals, then work collaboratively with customers to achieve those goals.

In consultative selling, salespeople fulfill three primary roles: strategic orchestrator, business consultant, and long-term ally. As a **strategic orchestrator,** the salesperson arranges the use of the sales organization's resources in an effort to satisfy the customer. This usually calls for involving other individuals in the sales organization. For example, the salesperson may need expert advice from production or logistics personnel to fully address a customer problem or opportunity. In the **business consultant** role, the salesperson uses internal and external (outside the sales organization) sources to become an expert on the customer's business. This role also includes an educational element—that is, salespeople educate their customers on products they offer and how these products compare with competitive offerings. As a **long-term ally,** the salesperson supports the customer, even when an immediate sale is not expected.

Among the successful consultative selling organizations is Airgas, a large industrial gas company with 950 salespeople in North America. In selling oxygen, nitrogen, and argon for various applications, Airgas becomes the long-term ally of its customers by fulfilling the two additional roles of the consultative seller. According to Pat Visintainer, Airgas sales and marketing vice president, sales personnel serve as strategic orchestrators in that they recognize that they "can no longer do it all alone. Good salespeople recognize the resources at their disposal and tap into those resources." According to Mr. Visintainer, Airgas salespeople fulfill the business consultant role by focusing on vendor reduction and process cost reduction for their customers rather than simply selling at a lower price. By identifying customer cost savings, Airgas salespeople become value-added long-term consultants rather than one-shot low-price sellers.[4] For more on consultative selling, see "Professional Selling in the 21st Century: Consultative Selling."

Sales Process

The nonselling activities on which most salespeople spend a majority of their time are essential for the successful execution of the most important part of the salesperson's job, the **sales process.** The sales process has traditionally been described as a series of interrelated steps beginning with locating qualified prospective customers. From there, the salesperson plans the sales presentation, makes an appointment to see the customer, completes the sale, and performs postsale activities.

As you should recall from the discussion of the continued evolution of personal selling in Module 1 (refer to Exhibit 1.1), the sales process is increasingly being viewed as a relationship management process, as depicted in Figure 6.4. In this conceptualization of the sales process, salespeople strive to attain lasting relationships with their customers. The basis for such relationships may vary, but the element of trust between the customer and the salesperson is an essential part of enduring relationships. To earn the trust of customers, salespeople should be customer oriented, honest, dependable, competent, and likable.[5] These attributes are reflected by Blake Conrad, who sells medical supplies for Centurion Specialty Care. Conrad, based in Denver, says:

PROFESSIONAL SELLING IN THE 21ST CENTURY

Consultative Selling
L.A. Mitchell, sales planner for Lucent Technologies, comments on the increasing use of consultative selling.

Professional selling is becoming much more of a consultative process than in years past. The pace of business has accelerated, and it is hard for individual buyers to be experts on everything they buy. That's where consultative selling comes in. When buyers know they have a problem, but don't know how to solve it, our salespeople can offer a tailored solution. The solution must fit within the buyer's allotted budget, and it must be consistent with the goals and strategies within the buying organization. Consultative salespeople must also be on the scene after the sale to be sure that any necessary training and service issues are handled to the client's satisfaction. With consultative selling, making the sale is important, but the real focus is on providing expertise which enables clients to improve company operations and productivity.

FIGURE 6.4   **Sales Process**

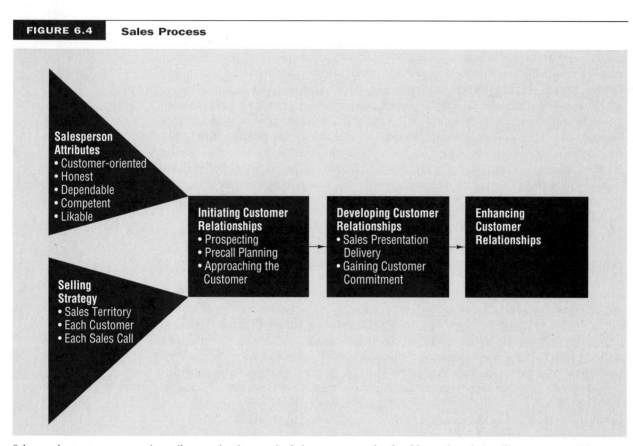

Salespeople must possess certain attributes to inspire trust in their customers and to be able to adapt their selling strategy to different situations. One or more selling approaches are used in the sales process. The three major phases of the sales process are initiating, developing, and enhancing customer relationships.

You simply cannot have productive relationships with your customers unless they trust you. I work really hard to show customers that I care about their bottom line, and I would never sell them something they don't really need. If I don't have an answer for them on the spot, I make every effort to get the answer and get back to them the same day. Customers appreciate the fact that I do what I say and follow up on all the details. To me, being customer oriented and dependable is just part of my job. It makes selling a lot more fun when your customers trust you, and—guess what—I sell more to customers who trust me.[6]

Another important element of achieving sound relationships with customers is to recognize that individual customers and their particular needs must be addressed with appropriate selling strategies and tactics. In selling, we discuss strategy at four levels: corporate, business unit, marketing department, and the overall sales function. An individual salesperson is strongly guided by strategy at these higher levels in the organization but must also develop selling strategies and tactics to fit the sales territory, each customer, and ultimately, each sales call.

When studying the sales process, we should note that there are countless versions of the process in terms of number of steps and the names of the steps. If, however, you were to examine popular trade books on selling and training manuals used by different corporations, you would find that the various depictions of the sales process are actually more alike than truly unique. The sales process shown in Figure 6.4 is comparable with most versions of the sales process, with the exception of those versions that advocate high-pressure methods centering on how to get the customer to "say yes" rather than focusing on meeting the customer's true needs. This version of the sales process suggests that salespeople must have certain attributes to inspire trust in their customers and that salespeople should adapt their selling strategy to fit the situation. The three phases of the sales process are initiating, developing, and enhancing customer relationships. For discussion purposes, the first two phases have been subdivided into a total of five steps. The sixth and final step in the sales process is that of enhancing customer relationships, which, in many cases, extends over a prolonged time period.

Another point that should be stressed is that the sales process is broken into steps to facilitate discussion and sales training, not to suggest discrete lines between the steps. The steps are actually highly interrelated and, in some instances, may overlap. Further, the stepwise flow of Figure 6.4 does not imply a strict sequence of events. Salespeople may move back and forth in the process with a given customer, sometimes shifting from step to step several times in the same sales encounter. Finally, completion of the sales process typically will require multiple sales calls.

As we proceed to discuss the steps in the sales process, we present an overview of each step. The overviews describe the objectives of each step and identify key issues to be dealt with in each step. Selected techniques and activities that are usually associated with each step are presented as well.

Initiating Customer Relationships

PROSPECTING   The term *prospecting* as used in the sales context is analogous to the prospecting process for gold as practiced in the 1800s. The prospector for gold would work a stream, separating the sludge and mud in a search for strains of the precious metal. The contemporary salesperson locates a pool of potential customers and then screens them to determine which ones are qualified prospects. In some situations, such as in most retail operations, salespeople are only slightly involved in prospecting; usually, however, they play an important role.

Locating Prospects   The initial part of the prospecting process is the generation of a pool, or list, of potential customers. Various methods are used to locate potential prospects. As Exhibit 6.3 indicates, a salesperson may use sources outside the organization along with internal company sources. Exhibit 6.3 includes some methods in which the salesperson plays a fairly passive role in this part of prospecting and others in which the salesperson is directly responsible for locating the potential customer.

Screening Prospects   After potential prospects are located, they must be evaluated in terms of **screening criteria** to determine whether they merit further sales attention. These criteria vary from one sales organization to the next, but some that are commonly used follow:

- compatibility—between the seller's product and the needs or wants of the prospect
- accessibility—to the prospect
- eligibility—in terms of geographic location and type of business the prospect is engaged in
- authority—to make the purchase decision
- profitability—as estimated based on the prospect's willingness and ability to pay and on predicted sales expenses

EXHIBIT 6.3	Prospecting Methods

Category	*Prospecting Techniques*
1. External sources	Referral approach: Ask each prospect for the name of another potential prospect. Community contact: Ask friends and acquaintances for the names of potential prospects. Introduction approach: Obtain introduction by one prospect to others via phone, by letter, or in person. Contact organizations: Seek sales leads from service clubs and chambers of commerce. Noncompeting salespeople: Seek leads from noncompeting salespeople. Cultivate visible accounts: Cultivate visible and influential accounts that will influence other buyers.
2. Internal sources	Examine records: Examine company databases, directories, telephone books, membership lists, and other written documents. Inquiries to advertising: Respond to customer inquiries generated from company advertising. Phone/mail inquiries: Respond to phone or mail inquiries from potential prospects.
3. Personal contact	Personal observation: Look and listen for evidence of good prospects. Cold canvassing: Make cold calls on potential prospects (by phone or in person).
4. Miscellaneous	Surf the Web: Identify prospects by name and location. Hold/attend trade shows: Organize or participate in a trade show directed toward potential prospects. Bird dogs: Have junior salespeople locate prospects that senior salespersons will contact. Sales seminar: Prospects attend as a group to learn about a topic in which the salesperson's product is involved.

Questions involving these criteria may be hard to answer fully in the prospecting stage. As a case in point, consider the profitability element. A salesperson may not be able to estimate whether a prospect will prove profitable at some future point in time. It is certainly possible for a prospect to become an unprofitable customer in the future and subsequently lose customer and prospect status with the selling firm. However, the prospecting stage does not require irrevocable decisions regarding the suitability of a prospect, only sufficient indications that the prospect is worthy of sales pursuit.

Prospecting Issues Three managerial issues of extreme interest occur in the prospecting stage. One is the persistent question of which method or methods work best for locating qualified prospects. The second is the problem of **cold-call reluctance** in many salespeople. The third is the issue of using technology to complete the basic tasks of prospecting.

Which method or methods work best? There is no answer to this question without some experimentation by the selling firm. For one firm, a trade show may be a bonanza, whereas another will find it more profitable to rely exclusively on cold canvassing. With the costs of personal sales calls continuing to rise, sales managers and salespeople must experiment with new prospecting methods in an effort to reduce selling expenses and optimize personal contact activities.

The subject of cold-call reluctance is especially important, because this method of locating prospects is crucial in many sales situations. Call reluctance experienced later in the sales process is generally not as acute as in the prospecting stage, in which the salespeople are encountering strangers on their (the strangers') turf and may feel as if they are intruding. Many have a hard time dealing with the face-to-face rejection that often accompanies this prospecting method.

Salespeople may also be reluctant to make cold calls because they know that many customers do not particularly like the tactic. Buyers are busy individuals, and a cold call can be an unwelcome interruption. Recognizing that many customers are annoyed by cold calls, American Express Financial Advisors (Amex) have banned the practice for its 8,000 Amex financial advisors.[7] Amex financial planners now rely more heavily on referrals from satisfied clients to find additional prospects.

Noting that the origins of call reluctance are multiple and complex, experts in this phenomenon have reported that approximately 40 percent of all salespeople will experience at least one serious encounter with cold-call reluctance during their careers.[8] The problem is of sufficient magnitude that sales managers and sales trainers frequently address it in training and development programs. For advice on how to deal with cold-call reluctance, see "Professional Selling in the 21st Century: Overcoming Call Reluctance."

Another prospecting topic that is generating considerable discussion among sales managers is the use of technology to perform some or all prospecting. In recent years, automated systems combining computers with communications equipment have become widely available. Some systems extend beyond prospecting to include other sales functions such as account tracking and postsale follow-up. An example of such a system is shown in Exhibit 6.4. The system uses the computer to screen prospects against initial qualifying criteria. Potential prospects are further qualified by phone, with some receiving sales contact and eventually becoming customers. As the quest for improving sales productivity continues, the use of the latest technology to perform certain prospecting activities has become commonplace.

Precall Planning

PREAPPROACH   In the **preapproach,** the salesperson gathers information about the prospect that will be used to formulate the sales presentation. During this step, the salesperson may determine buyer needs, buyer motives, and details of the buyer's situation that are relevant to the upcoming sales presentation.

Various information sources may be consulted in this undertaking. Published materials such as industry newsletters, magazine articles, and newspaper accounts may be useful. The Internet is a valuable source of information, as are online services, such as DIALOG, Dow Jones News/Retrieval, and LEXIS-NEXIS. Another alternative is to call on the prospect for information-gathering purposes.

In addition to gathering information to be used in the sales presentation, the preapproach offers other benefits. Because of the information it provides, the

---

PROFESSIONAL SELLING IN THE 21ST CENTURY

Overcoming Call Reluctance

L.A. Mitchell, sales planner for Lucent Technologies, offers this advice on overcoming call reluctance:

Most salespeople will tell you that there are times when they just don't feel like making cold calls. But cold calls can be an important step in building future sales, and there are some things salespeople can do to overcome call reluctance. Most importantly, salespeople have to be absolutely convinced that their product or service delivers value to the customer. When you know you have a great product, you feel good about telling any and all potential customers about it. Putting yourself in the buyer's shoes can be helpful in overcoming call reluctance. Just ask yourself, "If I were the customer, would I want to know about this opportunity?" Salespeople should also de-personalize rejection if it occurs. Just because a buyer is too busy to see you at the moment doesn't mean he or she dislikes you or that you won't eventually do business together.

EXHIBIT 6.4   **Prospect Screening and Tracking System**

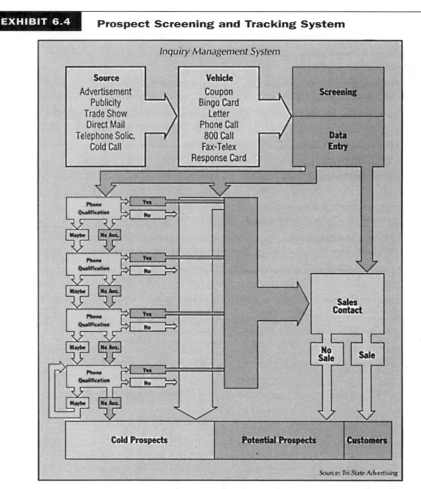

This exhibit illustrates a system for screening prospects by computer and telephone. Appropriate follow-up is conducted by the salesforce, with some of the prospects becoming active customers.

salesperson may avoid serious blunders based on false assumptions. Also, the self-confidence of the salesperson is increased by the acquisition of knowledge, and the salesperson's credibility with the prospect is enhanced.

The preapproach raises two issues worthy of management attention. First is the question of how extensive the preapproach should be. Second is the issue of invasion of privacy.

The extensiveness of the preapproach depends on the nature of the sales situation. For example, if the salesperson is in the consultative selling mode, the preapproach will be extensive to clarify the customer's strategic goals and how the sales organization can help the customer achieve those goals. The preapproach will be more extensive in high-stakes situations—those that are very important to the salesperson and the sales organization. The preapproach also tends to be more extensive when the solution to the buyer's problem is not obvious. In other situations, such as when selling a simple, low-cost product with obvious benefits, the preapproach may be less extensive.

Sales managers and salespeople should also be sensitive to the issue of invasion of privacy when conducting the preapproach. There have been instances in which surreptitious methods were used to learn personal details about prospects. Such tactics are unethical, and they often backfire if the prospect becomes aware of the practice. A related tactic is the use of so-called market research that purports to be "selling nothing" when, in reality, selling is precisely the purpose. As was indicated in the previous module, straightforward sales techniques have proved more effective over the long run.

SALES PRESENTATION PLANNING   This step has become more important in recent years, as evidenced by increased coverage on the topic in sales training programs. The requirements of professional selling today make **sales presentation planning** imperative, and it is often extensive, because it is increasingly viewed as a critical link in the sales process.

As with other planning processes, the salesperson must begin with a specifically stated objective, or perhaps multiple objectives, for each sales presentation. Typical objectives might be stated as order quantities or dollar values, or even in communications terms, such as reaching an agreement in principle with the prospect. Once a clearly stated objective has been formulated, the salesperson can focus on how the benefits of his or her offering can best serve the needs of the prospect.

Taken to the ultimate, sales presentation planning might actually result in a script to guide sales encounters. Not to be confused with a scripted sales message to be delivered over the telephone, this script would be a guide to expected sales activities given a particular buying situation. Research has been conducted that suggests that scripts could help salespeople learn how to adapt to the customer and the selling situation, while developing their own personal style and sales tactics.[9]

Sales Presentation Format   To plan the sales presentation, salespeople must decide on a basic **presentation format.** Alternatives include a canned sales presentation, an organized presentation, and the written sales proposal. A salesperson might use one or more of these formats with a particular customer. Each format has unique advantages and disadvantages.

The highly structured, inflexible, **canned sales presentation** does not vary from customer to customer. When properly formulated, it is logical and complete and minimizes sales resistance by anticipating the prospect's objections. It can be used by relatively inexperienced salespeople and perhaps is a confidence builder for some salespeople.

The major limitation of the canned sales presentation is that it fails to capitalize on the strength of personal selling—the ability to tailor the message to the prospect. Further, it does not handle interruptions well, may be awkward to use with a broad product line, and may alienate buyers who want to participate in the interaction.

Despite its limitations, the canned sales presentation can be effective in some situations. If the product line is narrow and the salesforce is relatively inexperienced, the canned presentation may be suitable. Also, many salespeople may find it effective to use canned portions in a sales presentation to introduce their company, to demonstrate the product, or for some other limited purpose.

Sales presentations that are tailored to each prospect are far more popular with salespeople than are canned sales presentations. In the **organized sales presentation,** the salesperson organizes the key points into a planned sequence that allows for adaptive behavior by the salesperson as the presentation progresses. Feedback from the prospect is encouraged, and therefore this format is less likely to offend a participation-prone buyer.

One reality of this presentation format is that it requires a knowledgeable salesperson who can react to questions and objections from the prospect. Further, this format may extend the time horizon before a purchase decision is reached, and it is vulnerable to diversionary delay tactics by the prospect. Presumably, those who make these arguments think that a canned presentation forces a purchase decision in a more expedient fashion.

Overall, however, most agree that the organized presentation is ideal for most sales situations. Its flexibility allows a full exploration of customer needs and appropriate adaptive behavior by the salesperson.

A written sales presentation, the **sales proposal,** may be developed after careful investigation of the prospect's needs; or, alternatively, a generic proposal may be presented. With the increasing prevalence of word processing, computer graphics, and desktop publishing, the written sales proposal is being used in a growing number of situations. These technologies have minimized the traditional disadvantage of the written proposal—the time it takes to prepare it.

The sales proposal has long been associated with important, high-dollar-volume sales transactions. It is frequently used in competitive bidding situations and in situations involving the selection of a new supplier by the prospect. One advantage of the proposal is that the written word is usually viewed as being more credible than the spoken word. Written proposals are subject to careful scrutiny with few time constraints, and specialists in the buying firm often analyze various sections of the proposal.

Sales proposals are often combined with face-to-face presentations and question-and-answer periods. Their content is similar to other sales presentations, focusing on customer needs and related benefits offered by the seller. In addition, technical information, pricing data, and perhaps a timetable are included. Most proposals provide a triggering mechanism such as a proposed contract to confirm the sale, and some specify follow-up action to be taken if the proposal is satisfactory.

Sales Mix Model   To this point, our discussion of the sales presentation planning process should have clearly suggested a need for a specific objective for each presentation and a need to determine the basic format of the presentation. In general terms, we have spoken of blending information into a palatable sales message. This is best done within the context of the **sales mix model** shown in Figure 6.5. The model includes five variables that require planning effort: presentation pace, presentation scope, depth of inquiry, degree of two-way communication, and use of visual aids.

FIGURE 6.5   **Sales Mix Model**

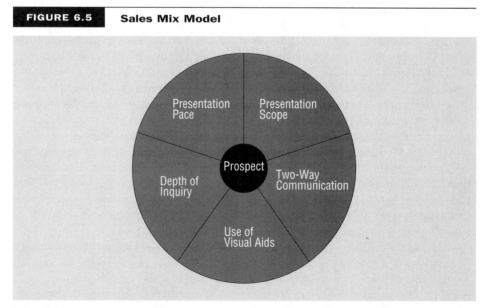

Five variables require planning effort after the salesperson has set objectives for the presentation and selected a basic presentation format.

Presentation pace refers to the speed with which the salesperson intends to move through the presentation. The appropriate pace will be determined largely by the preference of the prospect and may be affected by such variables as complexity of the product or the number of products to be presented. Another determinant of pace would be past experiences with a particular customer, as a quicker pace may be possible with a familiar customer.

Presentation scope involves the selection of benefits and terms of sale to be included in the presentation. This narrowing-down process can be a challenge for the knowledge-laden salesperson, who may know more about the product than will be of interest to the prospect. Time and again, we see reports of jargon-spouting salespeople who have talked themselves out of a sale through indiscriminate use of their extensive product knowledge. An illustration of this problem comes from Charles O'Meara, an expert who advises customers on how to buy stereo equipment. O'Meara says that if a salesperson "tries to, say, inundate your aural sensibility with a plethora of polysyllabic terminology—watch out! Either the salesperson is trying to confuse you or he is a techie who can't relate to other human beings. The salesperson should talk technical only if the customer wants to talk technical."[10]

Depth of inquiry refers to the extent to which the salesperson goes to ascertain the prospect's needs and decision process. Some of this information may have been gained in the preapproach, and some probing is usually necessary during the presentation. The planning task is simply to identify gaps in needed information and plan the presentation accordingly.

The issue of **two-way communication** is partially addressed when the salesperson selects a basic format for the presentation. By definition, the canned presentation does not allow for significant two-way communication. The organized presentation allows for, and usually encourages, a two-way flow. The degree of interactive flow is often dictated by buyer expertise, with more allowance for two-way flow planned with expert buyers.

Visual aids to supplement the spoken word have become an important element in sales presentations, and their use must be carefully planned. Unless sales aids are used with caution, they may actually detract from rather than enhance the sales presentation. When properly orchestrated, visual aids ranging from flip charts to video demonstrations can be valuable tools during the sales presentation. The computer is increasingly being used as the basic tool for enhancing presentations. Multimedia packages are plentiful and inexpensive, and packages such as Power Point are routinely used to construct and integrate photographs, graphics, statistical data, sound effects, and video into a complete presentation.

After the sales presentation is planned, the salesperson is ready to shift to an active selling mode. Although the customer may have been contacted earlier in the sales process, the emphasis has been on information gathering and planning. Now, the actual selling begins as the salesperson seeks an interview with the prospect.

Approaching the Customer

Approaching the customer involves two phases. The first phase is securing an appointment for the sales interview. The second phase covers the first few minutes of the sales call. Each step in the sales process is critical, and the approach is no exception. In today's competitive environment, a good first impression is essential to lay the groundwork for subsequent steps in the sales process. A bad first impression on the customer can be difficult or impossible to overcome.

GETTING AN APPOINTMENT   Most initial sales calls on new prospects require an appointment. Requesting an appointment accomplishes several desirable outcomes.

First, the salesperson is letting the prospect know that the salesperson thinks the prospect's time is important. Second, there is a better chance that the salesperson will receive the undivided attention of the prospect during the sales call. Third, setting appointments is a good tool to assist the salesperson in effective time and territory management. The importance of setting appointments is clearly proclaimed in a survey of secretaries, administrative assistants, and other "gatekeepers" responsible for scheduling appointments. A majority of respondents thought that arriving unannounced to make a sales call is a violation of business etiquette.[11] Given this rather strong feeling of those who represent buyers, it is a good idea to request an appointment if there is any doubt about whether one is required.

Appointments may be requested by phone, mail, or personal contact. By far, setting appointments by telephone is the most popular method. Combining mail and telephone communications to seek appointments is also commonplace. Regardless of the communications vehicle used, salespeople can improve their chances of getting an appointment by following three simple directives: give the prospect a reason why an appointment should be granted; request a specific amount of time; suggest a specific time for the appointment. These tactics recognize that prospects are busy individuals who do not spend time idly.

In giving a reason why the appointment should be granted, a well-informed salesperson can appeal to the prospect's primary buying motive as related to one of the benefits of the salesperson's offering. Being specific is recommended. For example, it is better to say that "you can realize gross margins averaging 35 percent on our product line" than "our margins are really quite attractive."

Specifying the amount of time needed to make the sales presentation alleviates some of the anxiety felt by a busy prospect at the idea of spending some of his or her already scarce time. It also helps the prospect if the salesperson suggests a time and date for the sales call. It is very difficult for busy individuals to respond to a question such as, "What would be a good time for you next week?" In effect, the prospect is being asked to scan his or her entire calendar for an opening. If a suggested time and date are not convenient, the interested prospect will typically suggest another.

STARTING THE SALES CALL   Having secured an appointment with a qualified, presumably interested prospect, the salesperson should plan to accomplish some important tasks during the first few minutes of the call. First in importance is to establish a harmonious atmosphere for discussion. Common rules of etiquette and courtesy apply here. Some preliminary small talk is usually part of the ritual, then the discussion should turn to business. Adaptive salespeople can learn how to interpret the prospect's signals and move into the sales message reasonably soon.

Another important aspect in starting a sales call is to ascertain the customer's needs as related to the benefits of the salesperson's offering. In many cases, salespeople will ask questions pertaining to the prospect's situation and then, at the appropriate time, show the prospect how the salesperson's product or service can benefit the customer. It is well known that successful salespeople ask more questions that do those who are less successful. Further, successful salespeople focus on the benefits of their offering, rather than the features of the offering. For example, Frito-Lay salespeople can offer their customers next-day delivery, a feature of their offering. The benefits of next-day delivery include reduction of inventory cost, avoidance of out-of-stock situations, and fresher product for the consumer.

Developing Customer Relationships

SALES PRESENTATION DELIVERY   During the **sales presentation,** the salesperson expands on the basic theme established in the first few minutes of the sales call or during previous sales calls. Specifically, more details are furnished regarding how offered benefits will meet customer needs. If the prior steps in the sales process have been properly implemented, the salesperson is now interacting with a qualified interested prospect at a convenient time. Given these circumstances, three major goals remain: building credibility, achieving clarity, and coping with questions and objections raised by the prospect.

BUILDING CREDIBILITY   With any major purchase, prospects perceive a considerable amount of risk. To be able to reduce that perception of risk in the prospect, the salesperson must appear a credible source of information. In a classic study, Harvard professor Theodore Levitt found *source credibility* for salespeople to be a function of three factors: the individual salesperson, the company image, and the product being sold.[12] In our discussion of source credibility, we concentrate on factors that can, to a significant degree, be controlled by the salesperson. These factors can be divided into two categories—personal behavior and sales techniques.

Personal Behavior   The basics of personal behavior that build credibility are dressing appropriately, showing common courtesy for all personnel in the prospect's organization, and being customer oriented. As previously mentioned, all words and actions should be consistent with the traits of honesty and integrity. These findings confirm that building credibility is a worthwhile activity for salespeople.

One approach to building credibility through personal behavior is to become a good listener. Obviously, there is a strong correlation between listening and being able to answer customer questions. Both skills are essential for **building credibility** with the customer. As the benefits of listening become more apparent, popular sales training programs have increased their coverage of this subject. Good listening skills enable the salesperson to learn more about the prospect and also keep the prospect interested in the sales proposition, because individuals are usually more interested in listening to someone else when they, too, are given the chance to talk. Moreover, by listening, the salesperson is, in effect, complimenting the prospect and showing respect for the prospect's point of view. The result is a reciprocation process in which the prospect repays the salesperson by listening to the sales presentation more attentively. The platform for credibility is built by the salesperson's willingness and ability to be an effective listener.

We discussed listening as a personal behavior because most effective listeners practice the art all the time, not just during sales presentations. We would not argue, however, with those who propose that listening is a sales technique rather than a personal behavior.

Sales Techniques   One sales technique used to build credibility with prospects is that of **conservative claims** regarding the benefits of the offering. The idea is that prospects may expect claims to be exaggerated, so on discovering that the salesperson has conservatively stated the claims, they tend to rate the credibility of the salesperson higher.

Another technique is to use **third-party evidence** to support a contention. **Testimonials** from satisfied customers are sometimes used for this purpose, as are research reports and product reviews from trade magazines. In the early stages of establishing credibility, salespeople often find that third-party information, particularly if it is written, may be more acceptable than the salesperson's spoken word.

Guarantees and warranties are other sales tools that can improve a salesperson's credibility. A strong warranty without a plethora of fine-print exceptions can go a long way toward eliminating the prospect's perceived risk and elevating the salesperson's credibility. Gregory Brennan of Brennan Communications in California used a strong guarantee to secure a contract with Mervyn's department stores to produce employee-training videos. Mervyn's was reluctant to give Brennan an opportunity to produce the videos because he had not done any work for retailers and thus lacked a desirable level of credibility. Brennan took a cue from Mervyn's liberal return policy, which offers customers refunds with few questions asked. He wrote to the Mervyn's buyer, saying, "Hire me, and if you are not satisfied with my work, I won't bill you." This credibility-building tactic worked, and Brennan earned his first contract with Mervyn's, a $40,000 deal.[13]

Another method is to let the prospect try the product or service under actual usage conditions. This can be as simple as a test-drive in a new automobile or as extensive as installing a computer system on a trial basis. This method permits the prospect to raise and answer questions without immediate persuasive pressure from the salesperson.

Even salespeople who work for companies with good reputations cannot assume that source credibility is a given. Further, they cannot assume that it will be easy to establish. They must recognize the skepticism and perceived risk in many sales situations and then combine appropriate personal behavior and sales techniques to overcome it. For a situation in which the salesperson's credibility might be damaged, see "An Ethical Dilemma."

ACHIEVING CLARITY   Salespeople begin the task of **achieving clarity** during sales presentation planning. Recall the sales mix model in which the salesperson plans such presentation elements as depth of inquiry, pace, and visual aids. The sales mix model also includes the presentation scope and the degree of two-way communication to be accomplished. At this point in the sales presentation, we are ready to implement those plans made with the assistance of the sales mix model.

To supplement the forethought given to achieving clarity as implied in the sales mix model, salespeople must adapt to the dynamics of the sales presentation. That is, as changes in the sales situation occur, salespeople must be adept at soliciting, intercepting, and reacting to feedback from the prospect. Again, listening and questioning skills emerge as important.

Sales aids, such as charts, graphs, printed literature, photographs, films, slides, and portable computers, are excellent tools for achieving clarity. Such sales aids should be used only where they can make the presentation more effective, not merely to "put on a show." After all, the medium should not overpower the message.

ADDRESSING CUSTOMER CONCERNS   The solicitation of feedback from the prospect will usually raise concerns in the form of questions and objections related to the salesperson's offering. Addressing these concerns is a routine part of the salesperson–customer relationship. In some cases, these concerns represent an unwillingness to buy unless the problem is resolved. In other cases, the buyer is asking for clarification of a point, or seeking information, perhaps reassurance on a particular point. In still other cases, prospects raise objections and ask questions as a bargaining tactic in an attempt to negotiate a more favorable deal.

Regardless of the reasons for raising objections and asking questions, the salesperson must be ready to respond effectively. Veteran salespeople generally look forward to dealing with questions and objections, viewing them as indicators of interest and therefore of an imminent purchase decision. Accordingly, they treat objections and questions with respect, even when they must tell the prospect that he or she is in error on a point.

Gaining Customer Commitment

A successful relationship requires that all parties in the relationship make firm commitments to each other. Assuming that the earlier steps in the sales process have been properly conducted, a joint commitment is the next logical step. In a sales context, this means that both the customer and the salesperson agree to a course of action. This may involve a purchase agreement or other courses of action, such as agreements to continue sales negotiations, to conduct a product usage test, or perhaps to sign a long-term distribution contract.

The reality of a competitive marketplace dictates that salespeople actively seek a commitment, because more than one firm can usually meet the customer's needs adequately. Customers expect salespeople to seek commitments, but they do not appreciate being pressured into premature decisions, nor do they appreciate high-pressure gimmicks designed to force a positive decision.

The question of when to seek commitment remains open. The stock answer in days gone by was "early and often," meaning that salespeople should try to conclude the sale quickly by using repeated closing attempts. This approach is, however, risky; if the closing attempt is inappropriately early, a negative response is more likely; and once a negative response has been voiced by the prospect, principles of *cognitive consistency* dictate that the prospect will tend to reinforce the decision. The question of timing, therefore, is important in seeking commitment.

Although there are no unimpeachable guidelines to timing, if the presentation has been completed without questions or objections from the prospect, it is logical that commitment should be sought without delay. Likewise, if all questions and objections have been satisfactorily handled, seeking commitment is in order. In many instances, salespeople can interpret cues, or signals, from the prospect that indicate that gaining commitment is the next logical step. For example, the prospect might ask, "Can you deliver by next Tuesday?" Such a question would not be asked by an indifferent or unreceptive prospect. In the final analysis, the question of when to seek commitment is a judgment call to be made by the salesperson, sometimes with the assistance of the prospect.

An Ethical Dilemma

Ron Jackson, sales representative for GEONAV, was wrapping up his fourth sales call on JBL Transport, a prospect for GEONAV's satellite-based tracking systems. Ron felt that he would get a commitment for a large purchase order from JBL. But first, he wanted to be sure that he had answered all of Mr. McKenzie's questions: "Frank, I appreciate the time you have spent with me over the past month helping me understand your requirements. Before I recommend our next step, I was wondering if you have any questions." Frank thought for a minute, then replied, "I guess not, Ron. You have been very thorough in explaining how your systems work. On second thought, I do have one question: if you were me, would you ask any more questions before making a purchase decision?" Ron was surprised at Frank's question, but replied, "Can't think of a thing, Frank," then proceeded to secure a major purchase order from JBL Transport. As he drove to his next sales call, Ron wondered whether he should have told Frank the system he ordered had been experiencing periodic downtime due to a programming glitch in the satellite. Frank had not specifically asked about reliability of the system, and Ron hoped the problem would soon be solved. Should Ron have disclosed the potential reliability problem to Mr. McKenzie? Justify your answer.

Enhancing Customer Relationships

The importance of a diligent effort to maintain and enhance customer relationships is well understood by Franco DiCarlo, director of sales for Calvin Klein. With such customers as Saks Fifth Avenue, Barneys in New York, and Ultimo in Chicago, DiCarlo says, "Making the sale is only the beginning. After that you have to keep track of the goods every step of the way. You have to make sure they get delivered on time and that the selling staff knows how they should be displayed." DiCarlo continues, "Anybody can move product. I can go out and sell a ton of something, but if it's not right for that particular store, it's just going to end up back on my doorstep at the end of the season."[14]

Clearly, professional salespeople such as Franco DiCarlo view their customer base as far too valuable an asset to risk losing through neglect. In maintaining and enhancing customer relationships, salespeople are involved in performing routine postsale follow-up activities and in enhancing the relationship as it evolves by anticipating and adapting to changes in the customer's situation, competitive forces, and other changes in the market environment.

One objective in this step is to create a strong bond with the customer that will diminish the probability of the customer's terminating the relationship. In effect, the salesperson's firm earns the business through a number of successive trials and strengthens its position as time passes.

RELATIONSHIP ENHANCEMENT ACTIVITIES Specific **relationship enhancement** activities vary substantially from company to company, but some of the more common ones are entering and expediting purchase orders, assisting in product installations, training customer personnel, and resolving problems with shipping and billing. Salespeople should continually add to the value received by customers through an ongoing diagnosis of customer needs and opportunities. Salespeople can then recommend new solutions, products, and services when appropriate. Salespersons could hold formal status-of-the-business reviews with the customer on a regular basis, reinforcing the importance of the customer to the selling firm. During review sessions, regular sales calls or through surveys, salespeople can solicit feedback on how to improve the product and provide better service.

Salespeople can also enhance the relationship by providing the customer with information relating to how expectations have been met. For example, salespeople can identify and quantify contributions to cost savings and quality improvement programs. They should seek acknowledgment from the customer that the benefits and satisfaction that were sought have been delivered.

As mentioned at the beginning of this module, **building trust** is an important element in a buyer–seller relationship. Throughout the sales process, the salesperson works to earn the trust of the customer. Sales technique is part of the trust-earning process, but the central truth of the matter is

> While it is important to consciously work to convince the buyer that you can be trusted, in the long run nothing is likely to work better than doing what you say you will do, keeping all your promises, and always telling the truth. In the short run, certain behaviors have been shown to speed this attribute of trustworthiness. But over the long run, nothing will earn the buyer's trust like being a trustworthy individual.[15]

Summary

1. **Distinguish between transaction-focused traditional selling and trust-based relationship selling.** Summarized in Exhibit 6.1, trust-based selling focuses more on the customer than does transaction-focused selling. The salesperson will act as a consultant to the customer in trust-based selling, whereas transaction-based selling concentrates more on making sales calls and closing sales. There is far more emphasis on post-sales follow-up with relationship selling than with transaction selling, and salespeople must have a broader range of skills to practice relationship selling.

2. **Discuss five alternative approaches to personal selling.** Alternative approaches to personal selling include stimulus response, mental states, need satisfaction, problem solving, and the consultative approach. Stimulus response selling often uses the same

sales presentation for all customers. The mental states approach prescribes that the salesperson lead the buyer through stages in the buying process. Need satisfaction selling focuses on relating benefits of the seller's products or services to the buyer's particular situation. Problem-solving selling extends need satisfaction by concentrating on various alternatives available to the buyer. Consultative selling focuses on helping customers achieve strategic goals, not just meeting needs or solving problems. In consultative selling, salespersons fulfill three primary roles: strategic orchestrator, business consultant, and long-term ally to the customer.

3. **Describe the three primary roles fulfilled by consultative salespeople.** The three roles are strategic orchestrator, business consultant, and long-term ally. As a strategic orchestrator, salespeople coordinate the use of the sales organization's resources to satisfy the customer. As a business consultant, the salesperson becomes an expert on the customer's business and educates the customer on how his or her products can benefit the customer. The consultative salesperson acts as a long-term ally to the customer, acting in the customer's best interest even when an immediate sale is not expected.

4. **Identify five salesperson attributes that are essential for building customer trust.** As indicated in Figure 6.4, to build trust with customers, salespeople must be customer oriented, honest, dependable, competent, and likable. By consistently displaying these attributes over time, salespeople can build mutually beneficial long-term relationships with customers.

5. **Discuss the sales process as a series of interrelated steps.** As presented in Figure 6.4, the sales process has six steps. The first three steps—prospecting, precall planning, and approaching the customer—are concerned with initiating a relationship wit the customer. The next two steps—sales presentation delivery and gaining customer commitment—are related to developing the salesperson–customer relationship. The final step in the sales process, and in many cases the most important one, is enhancing the relationship with the customer. It is important to note that one step builds on the previous step and that it usually takes several sales calls to confirm an initial sale to a prospect.

Understanding Professional Selling Terms

- Adaptive selling
- Stimulus response selling
- Continued affirmation
- Mental states selling
- AIDA
- Need satisfaction selling
- Problem-solving selling
- Consultative selling
- Strategic orchestrator
- Business consultant
- Long-term ally
- Sales process
- Prospecting
- Screening criteria
- Cold-call reluctance
- Preapproach
- Sales presentation planning
- Sales presentation format
- Canned sales presentation
- Organized sales presentation
- Sales proposal
- Sales mix model
- Presentation pace
- Presentation scope
- Depth of inquiry
- Two-way communication
- Visual aids
- Approaching the customer
- Sales presentation
- Building credibility
- Conservative claims
- Third-party evidence
- Testimonials
- Guarantees and warranties
- Achieving clarity
- Relationship enhancement
- Building trust

Developing Professional Selling Knowledge

1. How are need satisfaction and problem-solving selling related? How do they differ?
2. How does the consultative selling approach differ from problem-solving and need satisfaction selling? Explain the three key roles of consultative salespersons.
3. When do you think stimulus response selling would be most effective?

4. How important is teamwork between the customer and the sales organization in practicing consultative selling? How does teamwork within the sales organization factor into consultative selling?
5. Is adaptive selling as important in domestic markets as it is in international markets?
6. What is the purpose of each step in the sales process?
7. Discuss the final step of the sales process as related to the evolution of personal selling, which was covered in Module 1.
8. Discuss the elements of the sales mix model shown in Figure 6.5.
9. Describe the three different sales presentation formats in terms of their advantages and disadvantages.
10. Which do you feel is the most important—planning the sales presentation or delivering it?

Building Professional Selling Skills

1. Skillful questioning is an integral part of the sales process. A good way to think about different types of questions is to use the ADAPT model.[16] According to this model, there are five categories of questions:

   Assessment questions to elicit factual information about the customer's current situation.

   Discovery questions to uncover problems or opportunities that can be addressed by the salesperson's company.

   Activation questions to activate the customer's interest in solving the problem or realizing an opportunity.

   Projection questions to assist the customer in "projecting" what life would be like if the problem is solved or opportunity realized.

   Transition questions confirm the customer's desire to move toward problem resolution or opportunity realization.

   A. Where would the following questions fit into the ADAPT model?
      1. To better meet your needs, I need to ask a few questions. First, could you tell me who else in your company will be involved in developing the specifications for your new computer system?
      2. If we installed a new loading system for you, we could cut your damaged goods expenses to practically zero. Even though the initial investment is substantial, you might want to consider a new system. What do you think?
      3. It sounds like you can really benefit from our in-store merchandising program. It will take about 30 minutes to get the information I need to complete your customized proposal. Do you have time now, or would you prefer to book another appointment?
      4. You mentioned that your current supplier is a bit erratic. Could you tell me what you mean?
      5. A lot of companies are focusing on what they do best and outsourcing the rest. If we take over your cafeteria operation, you no longer have to worry about menu development, staffing, or health inspections. You can concentrate on running your manufacturing business. Is that something you would like to pursue?
   B. Assume you are making your first sales call on the general manager of a small hotel chain that is a target customer for your institutional furniture company. The chain has 15 hotels, 50 rooms per hotel. Existing furniture is several years old. An exterior renovation is underway in most of the hotels to be followed by interior renovation (paint and carpet) and updating of furniture, List several assessment and discovery questions for your first sales call that would serve as the basis for future sales calls during which you could use activation, projection, and transition questions to move toward earning a commitment from the general manager.
2. Salespeople routinely use the Internet to learn more about industries, customers, and competitors to develop sales strategy and plan sales presentations. A useful Internet site for information about manufacturers is found at http://mfginfo.com. Go to this site and select Internet Industry Resources. Then select Thomas Register. Now select

Helpful Buying Hints for one of the product/service categories listed. Write a brief analysis of how this information could be used by a salesperson in the selected category.

3. Assume you are selling PACSEAL, an automatic package-sealing device. One of your current prospects is a manufacturer of windshield wiper blades that ships approximately 5,000 boxes of blades per day to its customers. The cost of PACSEAL is $20,000. The customer can expect to save a penny per box shipped if PACSEAL is installed. The PACSEAL system has a guaranteed life of 5 years. How could you use this information in a sales proposal? How would you illustrate the key selling points derived from this information?

Making Professional Selling Decisions

CASE 6.1   *Biomod, Inc.*

Background

Biomod, Inc., a California-based manufacturer of educational models of the human body, has been in business since the mid-1960s. The company's products, sold primarily to middle schools in the United States, are available in plastic or as computer images. Accompanying products include lesson plans for teachers and workbooks and computer programs for students. Biomod has enjoyed healthy sales increases in recent years, as schools increasingly integrated computer-assisted instruction into their curricula. Five years ago, Biomod began selling consumer versions of its models through selected specialty educational toy stores and recently began selling on its own Web site. In addition, Biomod is also selling on the Web through Hypermart.com and Ed-Toys. Further, Biomod has had discussions with Toys-R-Us, and the giant retailer seems eager to stock Biomod products.

Current Situation

Biomod has employed Zack Wilson, a recent graduate of San Diego State University, for the past 6 months. He has become familiar with all aspects of marketing the Biomod product line and is now the sales representative for electronic retailing accounts. Zack is truly excited about his job, as he sees the explosive growth potential for selling Biomod products on the Internet. His first big success came when he convinced Hypermart.com to sell Biomod products. After all, Hypermart has the reputation in most circles as the premier electronic retailer. Thirty days after his initial sales to Hypermart, Zack was thrilled to land Ed-Toys as his second electronic retailer.

No doubt about it, Zack Wilson was on a roll. Securing commitments from Hypermart and Ed-Toys within a month was almost too good to be true. In fact, there was only one problem facing Zack Wilson. Hypermart had begun discounting the Biomod product line as much as 20 percent off suggested retail, and Ed-Toys was unhappy with the intense price competition. The following conversation had just taken place between Zack and Ed-Toys buyer Andrea Haughton:

Andrea: Zack, your line looked really promising to us at suggested retail prices, but meeting Hypermart's pricing sucks the profit right out of the equation. Are you selling Hypermart at a lower price than us?

Zack: Absolutely not! Hypermart just decided to promote our line with the discounts.

Andrea: So the discounts are just a temporary promotion? When will Hypermart stop discounting?

Zack: Well, I don't really know. What I mean by that is that Hypermart often discounts, but in the case of the Biomod line, I've got to believe it's just a temporary thing.

Andrea: Why do you think so?

Zack: Because they haven't asked me for a lower price. Like you, they can't be making much of a profit after the discounts.

Andrea: Well, Zack, we need to stop the bleeding! I can't go on meeting their prices. If they're not making money either, maybe it's time you get them to stop the discounting. Can you talk with them about getting up to suggested retail?

Zack: Andrea, you know I can't dictate retail selling prices to them any more than I could to you.

Andrea: Nor am I suggesting you try to dictate prices. I am simply suggesting that you let them know that if they choose to go back to suggested retail, we will surely follow. If we can't sell at suggested retail, we will have little choice but to stop selling the Biomod line. I'm sure you can appreciate the fact that we have profit expectations for every line we sell. At 20 percent off, Zack, the Biomod line just doesn't cut it for us.

Zack: O.K., I will see what I can do.

Later in the day, Zack checked his e-mail and found a disturbing message from Barbara Moore, a Biomod sales representative for the retail store division. Barbara's message informed Zack that one of her key retailers had visited the Hypermart Web site and was extremely upset to see the heavy discounting on the Biomod line. Barbara claimed that she was in danger of losing her account and that she feared a widespread outcry from other specialty stores as word of the Hypermart discounting would quickly spread. Barbara strongly urged Zack to do what he could to get Hypermart back to suggested retail. Zack noted that Barbara had copied both her sales manager and Rebecca Stanley, Zack's sales manager, with her e-mail message.

The following day, Zack called on Warren Bryant, Hypermart's buyer for the Biomod line. He conveyed to Bryant that Ed-Toys and some of the store retailers were upset with the discounting. Bryant shrugged off the news, commenting only that "it's a dog-eat-dog" world and that price competition was part of the game. Zack asked Bryant if he was happy with the profit margins on the Biomod line, and Bryant responded that he was more concerned with growing Hypermart's market share than with profit margins. He told Zack, "Our game plan is grab a dominant share, then worry about margins." At this point, Warren Bryant gave Zack something else to think about:

Warren: Hey, Zack, I noticed you guys are selling the same products on your own Web site as the ones we're selling on ours.

Zack: True, what's the problem?

Warren: Well, I just read in the trade press where Home Depot told their vendors that they don't buy from their (Home Depot's) competitors and that they view vendor Web sites as competitors to their retail business. Maybe we feel the same way. We sell on the Web, and if you do too, then you're really a competitor for us.

Zack: Warren, you know that we only do a little volume on the Web. Our site is really more of an information site.

Warren: But you do offer an alternative to other electronic retailers and us by selling on your own site. And by the way, don't your store retailers oppose your selling on the Web?

Zack: At this point, most of them are small retailers, and frankly speaking, they view you as more of a threat than us selling on our own site. Besides, our store division salesforce is working on a software package that will enable our store retailers to easily set up their own Web sites over the next 6 months or so.

Warren: Unbelievable! What you're saying is that another division in your company is creating even more Web-based competition for me! I thought we had a real future together, but I've got to do some heavy-duty thinking on that. Thanks, Zack, but I'm really busy and need to move on to some other priorities this afternoon. Call me if you have any new thoughts on where we go from here.

Zack left Hypermart and began the hour-long drive back to the office. "Good thing I've a little time to think about this situation," he thought as he drove along. "I need to talk with Rebecca Stanley just as soon as I get to the office."

Questions

1. How do you think Zack got into this dilemma?
2. If you were Rebecca Stanley, Zack's sales manager, what would you advise Zack to do?

CASE 6.2   *Plastico, Inc.*

Background

Plastico, Inc., located in New York, is a manufacturer of plastic components. The company is noted for producing high-quality products. Its salesforce calls on large accounts, such as refrigerator manufacturers who might need large quantities of custom-made products, such as door liners. Recent increases in new-home sales over the past several years have fueled refrigerator sales and, subsequently, sales at Plastico. Moreover, federal regulations requiring that dishwasher liners be made of plastic, rather than porcelain, have enhanced Plastico's sales.

Current Situation

Sharon Stone had recently been assigned to the central Michigan territory. Although this was her first sales job, she felt confident and was eager to begin. She had taken a sales course in college and had just completed the company's training program. The company stressed the use of an organized sales presentation in which the salesperson organizes the key points into a planned sequence that allows for adaptive behavior by the salesperson as the presentation progresses. She was familiar with this approach because she had studied it in her college sales course.

Sharon's first call was on a small refrigerator manufacturer in Ann Arbor. She had called the day before to set up an appointment with materials purchasing manager David Kline at 9:00 a.m. On the morning of her meeting, Sharon was running behind schedule because of an alarm clock malfunction. As a result, she ended up in traffic she did not anticipate and did not arrive for her appointment until 9:10 a.m. When she informed the receptionist she had an appointment with David Kline, she was told he was in another meeting. He did agree, however, to see Sharon when his meeting was finished, which would be about 9:45 a.m. Sharon was upset Kline would not wait 10 minutes for her and let the receptionist know it.

AT 9:50 a.m. Sharon was introducing herself to Kline. She noticed his office was filled with University of Michigan memorabilia. She remembered from her training that the first thing to do was build rapport with the prospect. Thus she asked Kline if he went to the University of Michigan. This got the ball rolling quickly. Kline had graduated from Michigan and was a big fan of the basketball and football teams. He was more than happy to talk about them. Sharon was excited; she knew this would help her build rapport. After about 25 minutes of football and basketball chitchat, Sharon figured it was time to get down to business.

After finally getting Kline off the subject of sports, Sharon began to discuss the benefits of her product. She figured if she did not control the conversation Kline would revert to discussing sports. She went on and on about the material compounds comprising Plastico plastics, as well as the processes used to develop plastic liners. She explained the customizing process, the product's durability, Plastico's ability to provide door liners in any color, and her company's return and credit policies. After nearly 25 minutes, she finally asked Kline if he had any questions.

Kline asked her if she had any product samples with her. Sharon had to apologize—in all the confusion this morning she ran off and left the samples at home. Then Kline asked her about the company's turnaround time from order to delivery. Knowing quick turnaround was important to Kline, and feeling this prospect may be slipping away, she told him it was about 4 weeks, although she knew it was really closer to five. However, she thought, if Kline ordered from them and it took a little longer, she could always blame it on production. When the issue of price emerged, Sharon was not able to clearly justify in Kline's mind why Plastico was slightly higher than the competition. She thought that she had clearly explained the benefits of the product and that it should be obvious that Plastico is a better choice.

Finally, Kline told Sharon he would have to excuse himself. He had a meeting to attend on the other side of town. He thanked her for coming by and told her he would consider her offer. Sharon thanked Kline for his time and departed. As she reflected on her first call she wondered where she went wrong. She thought she would jot down some notes about her call to discuss with her sales manager later.

Questions

1. What problems do you see with Sharon's first sales call?
2. If you were Sharon's sales manager, what would you recommend she do to improve her chances of succeeding?

Initiating the Relationship

Making Prospecting a Priority

Kim Lucas, district sales manager for IKON Office Solutions, firmly believes prospecting is more important to sales success than any other single sales activity. She emphasizes to her sales staff that if they make contact with enough qualified prospects they are practically guaranteed increased sales. Her final words of advice to her salesforce are that they must make time in their schedule each day to prospect. Her approach to prospecting begins with goal setting; each rep must turn into her that week's prospect list to contact. Each rep can turn in any number he or she wants as long as it is at least one! Over the past two years, the weekly average turned in by her salesforce has been 6.8. She allows her salesforce to turn in a number that they will be comfortable with because she knows they will be more likely to accomplish it.

The second thing that she recommends is for each of her sales reps to use prospecting methods that they are comfortable using. Her more experienced reps are best at referrals and networking. One of her more productive reps has been very successful using mailings. Kim thinks that customized letters are a must, and her company uses unique promotional items with each mailing. One of her new hotshot college graduates has an understanding of databases and regularly identifies good prospects by using number of employees, SIC codes, and credit rating scores. Kim remembers her days in sales when everyone had to use the same prospecting methods. She once tried to get her sales manager to purchase some lists and directories and was told that "we don't use that method around here." It has been her experience that each rep is different and has different things going on each week. She remembers her boss sending out a blanket goal for prospecting. It actually was a demotivator for those salespeople who had a major presentation that week that would require a lot of time writing a proposal and practicing the presentation.

Kim has seen her district improve dramatically over the past two years. She is convinced that the major reason for this is the emphasis she is placing on prospecting. Kim often is asked how she motivates her salespeople to do such a good job prospecting. Her explanation is simple: "Prospecting must be a part of each of my sales reps' daily routine. I know they spend an average of 15 minutes to two hours per day prospecting. Each week at our sales meetings I make prospecting my number one agenda item. I let my reps know how important I think prospecting is. Finally, I let each rep use the prospecting method that best suits his or her personality and style." She shrugs her shoulders and finishes by saying, "This is all pretty straightforward to me. We all think prospecting is the lifeline of our organization, and we treat it accordingly."

Source: Personal interview with Kim Lucas, IKON Office Solutions, October 22, 1999.

After completing this module, you should be able to

1 Explain strategic prospecting.

2 Discuss why prospecting can be a challenging task for a salesperson.

3 Explain where salespeople find prospects.

4 Understand the importance of gathering and studying precall information.

5 Discuss the importance of planning the initial sales call.

6 Explain how to approach and initiate contact with each prospect.

7 Explain the importance of questioning skills and discovering needs.

Kim Lucas states, "If the lifeline of an organization is repeat business, then a close second is prospecting." She goes on to say,

> During any given year, customers die, go out of business, move out of your territory, or they might decide to buy from another supplier because of a merger or any other number of reasons. These customers must be replaced. A good salesperson must balance keeping existing customers satisfied and finding new ones. Every day competitors are calling on not only their own, but also on their competitor's customers, trying to get them to change suppliers. A salesperson must recognize the importance of this activity and work to keep his or her existing accounts and pry a few away from the competitors.[1]

Kim clearly understands the importance of prospecting. She understands that any number of prospecting methods can work and each salesperson should use those prospecting methods that work for him or her. In this module, we will examine strategic prospecting and take a closer look at prospecting reluctance. Sources of prospecting methods are examined, as well as how to qualify a prospect. Gathering precall information is covered. Finally, the importance of planning the initial sales call and initiating contact with a prospect is discussed.

The Challenges of Prospecting

The glamour in sales is bringing in the big order. It is much more exciting for a salesperson to make an immediate sale than to spend countless hours prospecting for new customers. Unfortunately, many salespeople are focused on the immediate sale instead of doing the tedious task of gathering information about their prospects.

The sales process starts off with the salesperson seeking out prospective customers (sometimes called suspects). These "suspects" may be individuals or companies who might turn out to be prospects, and who in turn might become customers.

The only way to determine the value of the "suspect" is by proper qualification. Two things happen during this stage. First, the salesperson must spend many hours collecting information to determine if the suspect is a good prospect. Second, the salesperson will hear the word *no* many times. The act of prospecting can be very discouraging, especially if few prospects turn into customers. Prospecting can be defined as the act of locating and separating prospects from "suspects."

If salespeople are asked to name the toughest part of their job, they will usually respond with comments such as "It is difficult to find time to prospect," "I do not like doing paper work," and "I find it difficult to ask for the order." Why do salespeople find prospecting challenging? The obvious reason most salespeople find prospecting challenging is their fear of rejection. Today's buyers are busy, and many are reluctant to see salespeople with whom they are not currently doing business. Experienced salespeople know that preplanning their sales calls greatly increases their chances of getting a commitment from the buyer. However, cold calls rarely result in a sale. This can be discouraging. Conventional wisdom indicates that less than 5 percent of unplanned cold calls result in a sale, whereas roughly 25–30 percent of preplanned calls produce a sale. Here are some of the reasons buyers will not take the time to see a salesperson:

1. They may have never heard of the salesperson's firm.
2. They may have just bought the salesperson's product category, and there is presently no need.
3. Buyers may have their own deadlines on other issues, and they are not in a receptive mood to see any salespeople.

4. Buyers are constantly getting calls from salespeople and do not have time to see them all.

5. Gatekeepers in any organization screen their bosses' calls and are often curt and even rude.

A novice salesperson who is not used to rejection can find this experience unsettling. Training programs and experienced sales reps must help their new hires learn the prospecting process. Time and experience help salespeople learn what techniques work in their product category and territory.

Strategic Prospecting

The objective of **prospecting** lies not only in accumulating sales leads, but also in turning a lead into a qualified prospect. As shown in Figure 7.1, a salesperson's job is to do his or her homework and determine whether a potential customer will be a profitable account. The salesperson must also determine whether the buyer has an interest in doing business with his or her company.

Strategic prospecting involves the identification of qualified potential customers, usually called prospects. When we say a prospect is qualified, it means that the prospect meets or exceeds screening criteria that have been established by the salesperson or the sales organization. For example, qualified prospects must be compatible with sales strategy. A low-price buyer is inconsistent with a selling strategy that commands a premium price for a high-quality product, and thus would be eliminated as a prospect. Although Kmart would be compatible with the selling strategy of many clothing companies, it would not be compatible with the selling strategies Tommy Hilfiger or Liz Claiborne, two companies that seek a limited number of upscale retail distribution outlets rather than a low-price mass distribution system such as Kmart.

Prospecting is extremely important to most salespeople. Salespeople who do not regularly prospect are operating under the assumption that the current customer base will be sufficient to generate the desired level of future revenue. This is a shaky assumption in that market conditions may change, causing existing customers to buy less. Another possibility is that customers may go out of business or be bought by another firm, with the buying decisions now being made outside the salesperson's territory. The salesperson may simply lose customers due to competitive activity or dissatisfaction with the product, the salesperson, or the selling firm. Because there is typically a considerable time lag between the commencement of prospecting and the conversion of prospects to customer status, salespeople should

| FIGURE 7.1 | **Salespeople Must Develop Leads into Qualified Prospects** |

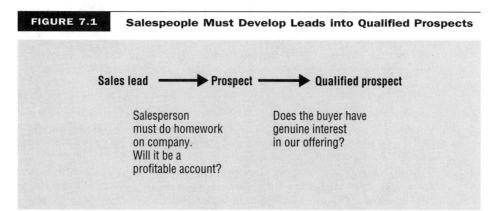

The objective of prospecting lies not only in accumulating sales leads, but also in turning a lead into a qualified prospect. Salespeople must determine whether the buyer has an interest in doing business with this company.

spend some time prospecting on a regular basis. Otherwise, lost sales volume cannot be regained quickly enough to satisfy the large majority of sales organizations—those that are growth oriented.

In the midst of the current knowledge and technology explosion, information about prospective customers is readily available. For example, cumbersome printed directories have been replaced by computer disks or online services. These computerized directories can be easily searched for specific keyword criteria, and prospects can be categorized by size, location, and many other variables. The *Harris Directory* data, for instance, can be searched for headquarter locations or whether companies export or not. Some computerized directories can be linked with mapping software so that it is possible to identify the number of prospects in different geographic locations. This is only one example of how salespeople learn about prospects. "Professional Selling in the 21st Century: Getting Appointments over the Phone," describes the importance of using the telephone to prospect and the difficulty in securing appointments. Taking time to prospect and having a plan are critical to prospecting success. With all the different prospecting methods available (you will learn about these in this module), it is important that salespeople have a prospecting plan or system.

A prospecting plan should fit the individual needs of the salesperson and include specific objectives for numbers of new prospects in a specified time period. The plan should also allocate an adequate amount of time on a daily or weekly basis for prospecting activities. Within the plan, allowances should be made for experimentation with different prospecting methods to find the most productive means of finding prospects. A tracking system should be part of the plan to assist in planning and execution of sales activities. This tracking then allows for the modifications to be made when present methods become less effective. Many tracking forms exist. An example can be found in Exhibit 7.1.

As with all phases of the sales process, salespeople must exercise judgment and set priorities in prospecting. There is a limited amount of time for prospecting, and a better understanding of the concepts and practices illustrated in the module can help a salesperson be more productive. An added bonus is that the sales process is more enjoyable for salespeople calling on bona fide prospects who can benefit from the salesperson's offering. Salespeople must be able to determine the sources that produce their best leads. By using a tracking system, a salesperson can evaluate which leads are turning into customers. Figure 7.2 illustrates prospecting pools from which leads originate.

PROFESSIONAL SELLING IN THE 21ST CENTURY

Getting Appointments over the Phone

Phil Clark, a district manager and agent for Northwestern Mutual Life in Indianapolis, understands the importance of gaining new business. Here are a few of his thoughts on how he uses the telephone to prospect:

I need to make two appointments per day to be successful; some days it takes 15–30 calls to make those appointments. I understand this is my lifeline. If I don't get a commitment in a matter of seconds, the prospect is lost. My points have to be direct, compelling, and brief, very brief. I have to be well organized. I don't use a script, but I do have my points outlined.

My philosophy is to keep my opening short and sweet. I briefly introduce myself, I mention referrals right away when I can, and I resist the temptation to make a full-blown sales presentation over the phone. I try to sell the appointment. It may sound obvious but always be extremely polite. One last thought, if someone already has a good relationship with an agent, thank them for their time, and let them know you are available if anything changes.

EXHIBIT 7.1   **Personal Prospecting Log**

Personal Prospecting Log

Name _Todd Jenkins_

Team _Indianapolis Commercial_   Date _4/16_

1st Contact	Organization	Contact Person	Source of Lead	Phone	Date of Appointment	Outcome of Call	Follow-up Activity
6/96	Cummins Engine	Tyler Huston	Personal contact	765-444-1234	4/11 8:30 AM	Need info on printer	Send in mail
9/97	Cosco	Fred Banks	Referral Tom Oats John Deere	219-888-4111	will call with dates/times	liked our numbers decision next week	send info on satisfied customers
9/99	Ball-Foster	MaryLou Hinkle	called in on 800#	765-365-4242	4/13 Lunch	Great lunch need proposal	will work up proposal set date & present
4/19/00	Ontario Systems	Darrell Beaty	referral	765-223-4117	4/19 4 PM		
4/17/00	Cincinnati Reds	Sharon Bristow	Referral Stacey Jones Indianapolis, Indiana	513-452-REDS	4/17 8 AM		
2/98	BANK ONE	Alice Arnold	Direct mail sent back 6/99	317-663-2214	4/16 Lunch	Didn't seem impressed need more work	Need more contact with Alice PACERGAME?
2/99	Davis & Davis	Frank Chapman	800 call in	317-211-8811	Bob Evans 4/15 Breakfast 7 AM	will include their DP department at next call	schedule DP
3/95	ABB	Jerome Parker	Personal contact	317-927-4321	4/14 2 PM	Liked our proposal	call Monday for answer
3/99	Thomson Consumer Electronics	Doug Lyon	phone	317-212-4111	4/15 3 PM	Had bad experience with us several years ago	This one will take time.

FIGURE 7.2   **Prospect Pools**

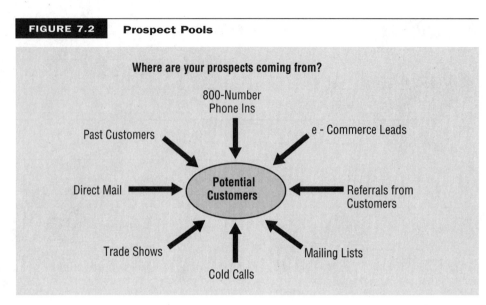

Where are your prospects coming from?

Locating Prospects

A good sales organization and salesperson will have a number of ongoing prospecting methods in place at any given time. The salesperson must continually evaluate prospecting methods to determine which methods are bringing in the best results. New methods (e.g., World Wide Web) must also be evaluated and tested for their effectiveness. "An Ethical Dilemma" illustrates the difficulty in getting sales reps to locate potential new business.

An Ethical Dilemma

Tom Linker has sold office furniture for the past 10 years. The second year he was with the company he won a district contest and placed eighth in the national contest during his third year. The past seven years have been very disappointing. Tom has had some success at getting his current clients to upgrade and make repeat purchases. His downfall has been his inability to locate new business. Tom's boss, Larry Davis, started a new prospecting program in which each salesperson had to contact five new leads per month and discuss them at their monthly sales meetings. After several months, Tom still seems to be having problems generating new business from the leads that he has been turning in to his boss. After six months of no new business, Larry decided to investigate to find out what Tom's problem might be. Larry had to make only three phone calls to determine that Tom has been turning in names that he has never called on! What should Larry do?

EXTERNAL SOURCES

Referrals   A referral is a name of a company or person given to the salesperson as a lead by a customer or even a prospect who did not buy at this time. Many training programs teach their salesforce to ask each prospect for the name(s) of other potential prospects. A salesperson who practices relationship selling should wait until a customer has been able to judge a salesperson and his or her ability to meet and exceed the customer's expectations prior to asking for a referral. Logic should tell a salesperson that if a prospect is not willing to buy at this time, the prospect probably will be reluctant to pass on the names of business associates. A good referral program can be started after the salesperson has cultivated strong relationships by keeping promises and providing outstanding service.

Introductions   The **introduction approach** is a variation of the referral technique. In addition to requesting the names of prospects, the salesperson asks the prospect or customer to prepare a note or letter of introduction that can be sent to the potential customer. The best letter is actually a testimonial prepared by a satisfied customer. This technique can also be done on the phone or in person. The buyer must hold the person doing the referring in high esteem for the technique to be effective.

Community Contacts (**Center of Influence**)   In most communities, well-known, influential people exist that can help the salesperson prospect and gain leads. A good relationship-building salesperson will first gain this person as a satisfied client and then ask him or her to help locate new prospects. Accountants, bankers, lawyers, business owners, teachers, and politicians or city officials can be good center-of-influence individuals. Salespeople can join civic organizations or social groups such as country clubs and fraternal organizations to meet key community people.

Organizations   Some salespeople will seek memberships in various civic groups that give them the opportunity to meet individuals who can become prospects for their product or service. These groups generally meet on a regular basis, and this gives the salesperson time to build relationships. A salesperson must set contact goals for each meeting to make this approach beneficial. Salespeople must let the group know what they do and that they are interested in helping others. If a salesperson joins only to get something from the group (e.g., names, leads), other members will soon see that agenda as self-serving, and this technique will not be beneficial.

Noncompeting Salespeople   Salespeople for noncompeting products can be a good source for getting prospects' names. Reciprocity is the key for agreeing to be another set of eyes for a noncompeting salesperson. This approach was demonstrated when a Hershey Chocolate, U.S.A., salesperson went out of his way to tell a Hormel sales rep about a new food mart going into their territory. The Hormel rep was the first of his competitors to meet with the new food mart management team and was given valuable shelf space that his competitors could not get. A few months later, the Hormel sales rep returned the favor when he found that an independent grocer was changing hands. The Hershey salesperson was able to get into the new owner's store early and added valuable shelf space for his products. The operating principle of "you scratch my back, and I scratch yours" works when information flows in both directions.

It is important for salespeople to strike up conversations with other sales reps while waiting to see buyers. Noncompeting salespeople can be found everywhere and can help in getting valuable information about prospects.[2]

Visible Accounts   In addition to making community contacts or working with key center-of-influence types, salespeople can also cultivate visible and influential accounts that will influence other buyers. In smaller communities, buyers may be impressed if a salesperson is selling to one of the communities' larger companies (e.g., GM, Ford, Westinghouse). Doing business with this customer may give the salesperson credibility with other prospects, and these customers could become key accounts, especially if the larger company is well respected for choosing good suppliers. Testimonials from a key account may influence other companies in the salesperson's territories.

INTERNAL SOURCES

Company Records   Any company that is looking for more business should examine their company records and make a list of former customers that stopped ordering during the past five or 10 years. There may be a number of reasons (not all bad) why customers stop ordering. Often, the company stopped calling on them, or perhaps a new buyer took over the account and is buying from his or her previous supplier. Whatever the reason, a call asking about their status may determine that the buyer is ready to resume purchasing from the salesperson and company again. Although it sounds difficult, the salesperson should ask why the company lost the business and not be afraid to ask what it will take to win it back. A good relationship-building salesperson realizes that it is going to take a number of calls to regain the buyer's confidence.

Lists and Telephone Directories   Telephone books today contain a business section that lists all the community's businesses. This list is usually broken down further by business type. Manufacturers, medical facilities, pharmacies, and grocery stores, to name a few, can be easily identified by using the business pages of the phone book. Many **lists and directories** exist, such as chamber of commerce directories, trade association lists, *Moody's Industrial Directory, Standard & Poor's Register of Corporations, Directors and Executives,* to name a few.

Directories are a gold mine of information if they are used correctly. A salesperson must remember that the day these lists are published they start to become obsolete. Sending a letter to a buyer who is no longer with the company makes the salesperson look bad. Companies change their names, merge with others, and even change their addresses. Salespeople must verify information before using it. Exhibit 7.2 refers to many of the directories that top salespeople have at their disposal.

Advertising Inquiries   One manufacturer's rep in the natural gas industry speaks highly of his company's advertising plan. They only advertise in trade magazines that they believe their buyers read. The salesperson's territory is Idaho, Utah, Montana, and Wyoming. Their advertising message is simply, "If we can help you with any of your natural gas needs (e.g., flow meters, odorizers), please give us a call." These leads are then turned over to the salesperson who calls on that territory. Territories of this size cannot be covered extensively by one salesperson. The advertising program qualifies the prospect (with the help of the telephone) before the salesperson is sent out on the call.[3]

Telephone Inquiries   Many organizations today use both inbound (prospect calls the company) and outbound (salesperson contacts the prospect) telemarketing. Inbound telemarketing involves a telephone number (usually an 800 number) that prospects or customers can call for information. Companies distribute their 800 number by direct mail pieces (brochures), advertising campaigns, and their outbound telemarketing program. United Insurance Agency in Muncie, Indiana, uses both inbound and outbound telemarketing to serve their market niche of hotels across America.[4] They use outbound telemarketing to generate and then qualify leads for their salesforce. Qualified leads are turned over to experienced salespeople. Usually, interns do all the outbound telemarketing. Inbound telemarketing is used to resolve problems, answer questions of prospects, as well as take orders from existing customers.

EXHIBIT 7.2   **List of Secondary Lead Sources**

1. *Harris Directory,* Harris InfoSource, Indiana, Illinois, Kentucky, Michigan, Ohio, Pennsylvania, Virginia, West Virginia; features company profiles, key contacts with titles, street and mailing addresses, extended zip codes, phone, fax and toll-free numbers, headquarters location and phone, employment figures, import/export, product description, annual sales, facility size, and more.
2. *Sales and Marketing Management* magazine discusses strategies and tactics of marketing and evaluates the market for various products and services. Of more interest to salespeople in the field is its *Annual Survey of Buying Power,* which helps salespeople determine how many individuals in a particular territory can afford their particular product or service. It also provides information about the most promising sales targets and tips on applying statistical data to your particular marketing plans.
3. *Moody's Industrial Directory* is an annual publication with a wide range of statistical information about particular firms that might be prospects for a specific product or service. Names of executives, description of the company business, and a brief financial statement for more than 10,000 publicly held firms.
4. *Standard & Poor's Register of Corporations, Directors, and Executives* is an excellent source of personal information about individuals in companies. Such information can be used for qualifying prospects and for learning enough about them to plan an effective approach and presentation. This annual publication lists names, titles, and addresses for 50,000 firms.
5. *Thomas Register of American Manufacturers,* published annually, provides information about who makes what and where almost anything may be purchased. Information is also provided about the corporate structure of the manufacturer and about its executives. If a company sells supplies, raw materials, or components used by a certain type of manufacturer, a salesperson can find an exhaustive list of all companies that might need that product. If a company markets a service, a salesperson can find companies in his or her area whose business fits the description of the ideal client. An index allows recovery of information by geographic location, by product or service, by company name, and by product trade name.
6. *Polk City Directory* supplies detailed information on individuals living in specific communities. Polk publishes more than 1,100 directories covering 6,500 communities throughout the United States and Canada. The local chamber of commerce should have access to this directory.
7. *Trade Shows & Professional Exhibits* lists more than 3,500 trade shows including their location, when they are held, and attendance expected.
8. *The International Corporate 1000* provides information and profiles of the 1,000 largest companies in the world: 350 are from the United States and Canada; the remaining 650 are from Europe, South America, the Pacific Basin, and the Middle East.
9. *Database America* has 11 million businesses and 97 million households in their databases. They provide prospect lists (perfect for sales lead generation and telemarketing), tape and PC diskettes (enables printing of sales leads and labels), and mailing labels (useful for direct mail campaigns). Visit Web site: http://www.databaseamerica.com.
10. *Middle Market Directory* (Dun & Bradstreet) lists 14,000 firms worth between $500,000 and $1 million.
11. *Million Dollar Directory* (Dun & Bradstreet) lists names, addresses, and business lines of firms worth more than $1 million.
12. *Encyclopedia of Associations* (Gale) lists 21,500 national associations, more than 4,000 international organizations, and more than 50,000 regional, state, and local organizations.
13. *Directory of Corporate Affiliations* (Macmillan Directory Division) lists 4,000 U.S. firms as well as their more than 40,000 divisions, subsidiaries, and so on.
14. *U.S. Industrial Directory* (Time) annually lists sales, employees, and financial statistics for the 500 largest industrial firms and 50 largest diversified service firms.
15. *World Scope: Industrial Company Profiles* (Wright Investor's Service) provides extensive coverage of 5,000 companies from 25 countries, within 27 major industry groupings.
16. *National Trade and Professional Associations* (Columbia Books) lists more than 6,200 trade and professional associations, along with pertinent information about each.

Mail Inquiries   **Direct mail** is heavily dependent on using the right mailing list. Mailing lists must be reviewed carefully. The product under consideration must also be considered when purchasing a mailing list. The salesperson must understand that response rates with direct mail are typically low; however, the cost of direct mail programs are inexpensive compared with other prospecting methods. Typically, only a few leads will be generated for every 100 letters sent.

Internet or World Wide Web   Many firms today have turned to **Web** sites to attract potential customers. A Web site is a collection of information about the company that usually includes company history, products, prices, and how to order or reach a salesperson if there is an interest in the products. Companies today are creatively using text, pictures, sound, and video to attract prospects. Advertising and promotion campaigns focus on Web site addresses and encourage prospects to browse their site.

The disadvantage of using a Web site occurs if companies do not update them periodically. One farm implement dealer learned this the hard way when posting used farm equipment on its Web site. Seventy-five percent of the equipment was sold the first month the Web site was available. Before the site was updated later that year, sales reps had to tell prospective buyers that the equipment had been sold. In fact, almost everything on the site was sold. Some companies find they have to update their sites weekly and even daily.

Personal Contact

OBSERVATION   Careful observation in a salesperson's territory can reveal the names of potential customers. Pharmaceutical salespeople are constantly looking for new offices being built by hospitals, new pharmacies being built in neighborhoods, and even grocery stores adding their own pharmacies. These are new places to call on that competitors may not have noticed.

Salespeople who work for the natural gas industry usually keep a pair of boots in their car. They are looking for heavy moving equipment. Whenever they see ground being moved, they tromp across the field and ask the operators if they know what is going to be built on the land. Sometimes, they hear a strip mall is going in, other times a middle school. The rep then drives to the school system and asks for the plans and whether the heating and cooling decisions have been made yet.[5] Observation can play a big role in beating competitors to the punch when looking for new prospects. As described in "Professional Selling in the 21st Century: What Is Your Prospecting Advantage?," observation plays a big role in how a salesperson's present customers are using his or her product. This information can be used in prioritizing which prospects are the best candidates to purchase those products.

PROFESSIONAL SELLING IN THE 21ST CENTURY

What Is Your Prospecting Advantage?

Greg Burchett, district sales manager from Wallace, spends quite a bit of time with each of his sales reps going over Wallace's prospecting advantage.

I know every Wallace product or service has some advantage over the others on the market. By defining our advantages and then fitting them to the market, we make prospecting a more rewarding activity. I have my salespeople list their present customers and how they use Wallace's products, what they like about it, and what benefits it has brought to them. Next, we have them make a list of prospects they think could use our products. Next, we have them cross-match the lists to show which benefits would fit each prospect. Those who cross-match in many ways will be priority prospects. Those who do not cross-match at all are very low-priority prospects. By assigning a numerical value to each prospect, we automatically eliminate wasted prospecting time and develop a prospecting advantage image of our ideal prospect. When it's time to prospect again, we already know exactly what prospects will be the best for Wallace to call.

COLD CANVASSING   Making unannounced calls on prospects is called **cold canvassing,** or cold calling. This is probably the least successful form of prospecting. Buyers may be annoyed by the salesperson for not having an appointment. Other buyers may have full schedules and no time to see the salesperson. Still others may not be in, and the cold call resulted in a wasted trip. Many salespeople only use cold canvassing as a last resort when other techniques are not producing good leads or if their day is not full of scheduled appointments.

It takes a lot of time and persistence to knock on every door in a prospecting area to uncover potential buyers. Salespeople who do cold calls should set goals as to what they hope to accomplish during a cold call. At a minimum, they should introduce themselves to the receptionist or secretary and start to build rapport with them. At a later date when they phone, the receptionist will now have a face with the name. Ask the receptionist or secretary for information about the company and the buyer. This may make him or her feel important. A second goal may be to get an appointment for a later date. It is easier to turn down an appointment request over the phone than it is in person. Finally, one may get in to see the buyer and actually get to make a sales call. In any case, this time should be used wisely to set the stage for further prospecting.

TRADE SHOWS   Attending conventions and **trade shows** presents salespeople with excellent opportunities to collect leads. Generally, the company purchases booth space and sets up a stand that clearly identifies the company and its offerings. Salespeople are available at the booth to demonstrate their products or answer questions. Potential customers walk by and are asked to fill out information cards indicating an interest in the company or one of its products. The completed information card provides leads for the salesperson. Trade shows can stimulate interest in products and provide leads. For example, bank loan officers attend home improvement trade shows and can offer the homeowner immediate credit to begin a project. Those who sign immediately may be offered a reduction in interest rate.

BIRD DOGS (SPOTTERS)   An introduction to sales for many companies' new salespeople is to start them out locating prospects that senior salespeople will later contact. One large architecture firm in Cincinnati, Ohio, requires all their new hires to act as **spotters** their first 18 months with the company. Quotas are set, and potential clients must be identified for the senior architects to call on.

Agreements can be made to pay spotters for providing leads for salespeople. Sometimes, the salesperson pays the fee for the name of the lead, and others require the lead to turn into a sale before paying the spotter. Noncompeting salespeople can be great spotters.

SALES SEMINARS   Firms can use **seminars** to generate leads and provide information to prospective customers. For example, a financial planner will set up a seminar at a local hotel, inviting prospects by direct mail, word of mouth, or advertising on local television and radio, to give a presentation on retirement planning. The financial consultant discusses a technique or investing opportunities that will prepare the audience for retirement. Those present will be asked to fill out a card expressing their interest for follow-up discussions. The financial consultant hopes this free seminar will reward him or her with a few qualified prospects.

Qualifying Prospects

Prospects must meet criteria such as being financially capable of making the purchase, able to truly benefit from what is being sold, accessible to the salesperson, and in a position to make or support a purchase decision. In addition to these common criteria, it is likely that salespeople or their companies will impose additional criteria for qualifying prospects (e.g., salesperson can only sell to financial institutions or companies with gross sales of $10 million or more). The personal attributes of the buyer will also come into play. Honeywell has had a history of allowing their salespeople to turn prospects over to another salesperson if the personalities of the salesperson and buyer did not mesh.[6]

Initiating customer relationships includes the search for and identification of qualified prospects. At a minimum, qualified prospects are those who:

1. Can benefit from the sales offering.
2. Have the financial wherewithal to make the purchase, whether cash, credit, or barter capacity.
3. Play an important role in the purchase decision process.
4. Are eligible to buy based on a fit within the selling strategy (i.e., they fit the profile of the desired customer).
5. Are reasonably accessible and willing to consider the sales offering.
6. Can be added to the customer base at an acceptable level of profitability to allow a mutually beneficial relationship between buyer and seller. This is hard to judge at this stage in the sales cycle, but a preliminary assessment must be made.

In addition to those listed above, there may be additional criteria required by the seller based on a particular situation. Additional criteria might include: Does the buyer have a sense of urgency? Are the buyers working under a time constraint such as their copier is broken and work is piling up? Is the buyer open minded to the offering? Have the buyers been known to try new technologies or must they see it working somewhere else before they will try it? Does the buyer give feedback or must the salesperson continually probe to get any feedback at all? Some buyers will tell the salesperson everything they know; others will be tight lipped. Is the buyer trusting in nature, or will it take a lot of effort to win this buyer's trust?

A firm may have a need for a new fax machine, but if the buyer is not open minded to the technology, he or she might not be a good prospect at this time. Other buyers have needs but are unwilling to listen for a variety of reasons (e.g., busy on other projects, recently burned by a salesperson and the buyer is taking it out on all salespeople). A good prospect readily gives feedback. A silent buyer makes it difficult to determine the extent of interest by the buyer. Possibly, the best prospect is the one who has a sense of urgency and wants to act now. Regular calls by the salesperson are needed to stay close to each buyer so that when a need arises, the salesperson will be positioned to get the order.

Gathering and Studying Precall Information

Once potential customers are identified, the salesperson must begin the process of collecting information. During this stage, the salesperson gathers information about the prospect that will be used to formulate the sales presentation. Buyers' needs, buyers' motives, and details of the buyer's situation should be determined. Some organizations spend a great amount of time determining the salesperson's and buyer's communication style. Effectively sensing and interpreting customers' communications styles allow salespeople to adapt their own interaction behaviors

| EXHIBIT 7.3 | Information to Gather on a Prospect and Who to Contact |

Information Needed	How to Collect Information
The prospect's name.	Correct spelling and pronunciation can be gathered by asking the receptionist or secretary to verify information.
The prospect's correct title.	This can be determined by asking the gatekeepers to verify.
Is this prospect willing to take risks? Are they confident with decision making?	The salesperson may have to ask the prospect about willingness to take risks.
Is the prospect involved in the community? Does the prospect belong to any clubs or professional organizations?	The salesperson may be able to observe club or organizational honors displayed in the office.
Does the prospect have hobbies or interests he or she is proud of? (coin collector, sports enthusiast)	Observation of the office might give away this information.
What is the prospect's personality type? Easygoing? All business?	Observation and experience with the buyer will give the answer to the salesperson.
Where was the prospect educated? Where did this prospect grow up?	Look for diploma on the wall. The salesperson may have to ask for this information.

in a way that facilitates buyer-seller communication and enhances relationship formation. Appendix 7 at the end of this module covers communication style in great detail.

The more the salesperson knows about his or her buyer, the better chance he or she has to sell. Over time, the salesperson should be able to accumulate knowledge about the prospect. The information that the salesperson needs varies with the kind of product that he or she is selling. As a rule, a salesperson should definitely know a few basic things about his or her customers (e.g., the prospect's name, correct spelling, and correct pronunciation). A salesperson can learn a great deal about a customer over time by collecting bits and pieces of information, sorting them out, and developing a personalized presentation for the customer.

Obtaining Precall Information on the Buyer

A salesperson must do some preliminary homework once a company has been identified as a potential client. The first stage of information gathering is to concentrate on the individual prospect. Several questions need to be answered that will identify how the buyer will behave toward the salesperson. Exhibit 7.3 details some of the questions that a salesperson needs to ask. Not only knowing a prospect's name but the correct spelling and pronunciation show the buyer that the salesperson has done his or her homework.

It is not unusual for gatekeepers to prohibit the salesperson access to the buyer over the phone if the salesperson mispronounces the buyer's name. Mail is thrown away without being opened if the name is misspelled or the title is incorrect.

Precall information should be used to develop rapport with the prospect and to eventually tailor the presentation to fit the buyer's needs. A salesperson can establish a relationship with a prospect by discussing such mutual points of interest as an alumni association with the same college or support for the same athletic team. As illustrated in "An Ethical Dilemma," information gathering must be done thoughtfully. It can take many sales calls and months to gather all the useful information needed by a salesperson.

An Ethical Dilemma

Teresa Wolf had just completed her sales training with Foster Supply (a distributor of component parts for small engines), and she really took to heart the importance of pre-call information gathering. Her company kept a customer profile and planning sheet that gathered information such as

Name _____

Address _____

Type of Business _____

Name of Buyer _____

Buyer's Hobbies _____

Decision Maker _____

Key Influences in the Company _____

Buyer Profile _____

Buyer Personality Type _____

Name of Owner _____

Age of Company _____

Primary Products Produced, etc. _____

She had only been in her territory two weeks when her sales manager, Ted Hart, started receiving complaints from Teresa's prospects and customers. The callers complained that she had been aggressively collecting information on their company and buyers by interviewing everyone that would see her in their companies. One caller even termed one of her sales calls an interrogation. Ted reviewed her profile sheets, and he was amazed at how complete they were. What should Ted Hart do?

Gathering Information on the Prospect's Organization

Gathering information about the prospect's company helps salespeople better understand the environment in which they will be working. Exhibit 7.4 details some of the questions that provide useful information about the prospect's organization. Is the prospect presently buying from a single supplier? How long has the prospect been buying from this supplier? If the answer is 20 years and he or she is extremely satisfied with the current salesperson, products, and services, then the prospect should be thanked for his or her time, and the salesperson should move on to other accounts.

Sources of Information

A good salesperson uses all available information sources to gather valuable information. Lists and directories will have names, addresses, phone numbers, and other key information. The Web can be a valuable tool as companies provide more than enough vital information for a salesperson. Walker Group in Indianapolis has one person dedicated to daily seeking critical Web information about their clients and competitors.[7] Salespeople have access to a large quantity of current information and should use it to gain a competitive edge over their competitors.

Secretaries and receptionists can be a friendly source of information. They can certainly be used to verify name, title, pronunciation, and correct spelling.

EXHIBIT 7.4	Gathering Information about the Organization

Information Needed	How to Collect Information
What type of business are we dealing with: manufacturer, wholesaler, retailer, government, educational, medical, financial institution?	This can be gathered from a directory.
To what market does the company sell? Who are the organization's primary competitors? What does the company make and sell?	Annual reports may be helpful in answering these questions.
Who does the prospect presently buy from? Do they buy from a single vendor? Multiple vendors? How long have they purchased from their suppliers? What problems does the company face? In what volume does the company buy? What is the organization's financial position?	The salesperson may have to ask for this information.

Also, noncompeting salespeople can help a salesperson fill in information on accounts.

Finally, a salesperson should be gathering information about each of its companies and buyers. Some companies provide the salesforce with contact management software like ACT or Goldmine. Salespeople may develop their own system for gathering pertinent information. Exhibit 7.5 illustrates the types of information that can be gathered in a customer profile.

Determining Other Buyers' Influences

As products become more complex, we often see an increase in the number of buying influencers and decision makers involved in the purchase. The salesperson should attempt to determine the various buying influencers. For example, if a salesperson concentrates on the purchasing agent in an organization and ignores other key players (e.g., department head, data processing) in the decision-making process, the salesperson takes the risk that he or she is potentially selling to the wrong person.

The salesperson must use observation and questioning to determine the role of each member of the buying team and the amount of influence each exerts; each member's needs should be determined before or during the presentation. Department heads may be interested in how the product will benefit their department, whereas the CFO may only care about the price. During group presentations, all the members of the buying party must feel involved. The salesperson must be sure to direct questions and comments to all potential decision makers in the group.

If a salesperson has only one contact (e.g., purchasing agent) in an organization, he or she runs the risk that the key contact could die, get fired, change jobs, get transferred, or retire. By having contact with many influencers in an organization, the salesperson will always have a number of people who have had previous experiences to pass on to the new purchasing agent or team member. In the first instance, the salesperson must start the entire relationship process again; in the second, the salesperson will have help keeping the relationship in place.

EXHIBIT 7.5   **Customer Profile**

1. Name of Business _____
2. Address _____
3. Phone _____

4. Name of Buyer(s) _____ Title _____
   Personality, Hobbies, Interests _____
   _____ Title _____
   _____ Title _____
   _____ Title _____

5. Source of prospect (i.e., referral, cold call) _____

6. Other Key People Receptionists _____
   Personality, Hobbies, Interests _____
   Secretaries _____
   Personality, Hobbies, Interests _____
   Department Heads _____
   Personality, Hobbies, Interests _____
   Other Influencers—Who? _____
   Personality, Hobbies, Interests _____

7. What products does the company produce? _____
8. History and current standing in the industry _____
9. How many employees? _____
10. Extent of operations—local, regional, national, international _____
11. Is buying done by individuals or committee? _____
12. Does the company buy from single or multiple sources? _____

Planning the Initial Sales Call

Once the salesperson has sufficient background information, he or she is ready to plan the initial sales call. A well-planned sales call can help reduce stress and give the salesperson needed confidence. Many sales organizations today are making the first call that a salesperson makes a "getting-to-know-you" call that introduces the seller by collecting information on the buyer's background and needs. The first call is not to sell the product but to lay the groundwork for future calls and eventual sales.

Once the salesperson has completed the precall homework (i.e., he or she knows the prospect's full name, address, phone number, and previous history with the firm), he or she has to decide whether a phone call to set an appointment or a drop-in introductory call is appropriate. There are many advantages to appointments, such as the buyer knows the salesperson is coming and has allotted time for the visit. In this instance, having scheduled an appointment, the salesperson is not viewed as an interruption on the day but a part of it. The drop-in call could result in the buyer not being in or having a busy schedule and not having the time to see a salesperson. A professional salesperson should call first to set appointments and save drop-ins for hard-to-see buyers who do not normally take appointments.

A salesperson can improve his or her chances of getting an appointment by doing the following: Give the prospect a reason to grant the appointment (e.g., potential dollar savings); request a specific amount of time (e.g., 10 minutes); and suggest a specific time for the appointment that is convenient for the buyer (e.g., late afternoon). Once a salesperson has an appointment with the prospect and all the objectives have been established, the salesperson should send a fax or e-mail that outlines the agenda for the meeting and reminds the buyer of the appointment.

Finally, the salesperson must establish presentation objectives for each sales call. The salesperson must ask himself or herself what he or she hopes to accomplish on this sales call. Salespeople know that most sales are not closed during the first or even second contact with the customer. Getting the order is the ultimate objective, but most of the time salespeople call on buyers to accomplish other objectives such as:

1. Introduce the salesperson and his or her company
2. Obtain personal and business information
3. Provide company literature for the prospect to review
4. Conduct a needs assessment
5. Demonstrate a new product offering
6. Provide postsale service

Approaching and Initiating Contact

The old adage "you only get one chance to make a first impression" has never been truer than in the sales arena. Proper dress, etiquette, and courtesy will be the first things that a buyer notices about the salesperson. The second thing that the buyer will notice is the first few words that come out of the salesperson's mouth. Although salespeople do not want to sound as if their words and messages are memorized, they should be rehearsed and flow freely. For example,

> Mr. Smith, I want to thank you for taking the time to see me. I'm Betty Brown from Hershey Chocolate, U.S.A. The reason I am here today is to introduce myself and my company and to find out a few things about you and your store (generally done while shaking hands).

An introduction approach by itself falls short of gaining the customer's attention. The introductions are usually followed by a statement that gets the customer to react and start talking. Salespeople have used many different approaches effectively over the years. The salesperson must attempt to use an approach to gain the prospect's attention. Depending on the selling situation, several strategies can be effectively used to approach the prospect. We briefly discuss some of the more popular approaches, and they are summarized in Exhibit 7.6.

INTRODUCTORY APPROACH   The **introductory approach** is the most frequently used technique, but by itself it is one of the weakest. It does not gain the prospect's attention. For example, the salesperson walks into the buyer's office and says: "Hello, I am Jon Jacobs from Hormel." This approach gains minimal attention and probably generates the least interest. Therefore, an introductory approach should be used with other approaches to generate more interest. A possible approach might be: "Hello, I am Joe Jacobs from Hormel; we have introduced a new chili in

EXHIBIT 7.6	Possible Approach Methods
Introductory Approach	Professionally greet prospect with name and company.
Product Approach	Immediately show the prospect the product to see and touch.
Benefit Approach	Offer the prospect a benefit that most buyers think is appropriate.
Question Approach	Get the prospect involved in the sales call by asking an appropriate question.
Referral Approach	Mention the name of a mutual friend that referred you to the prospect.
Compliment Approach	Offer a compliment to the buyer about the buyer or the company.
Survey Approach	Ask the prospect for permission to survey the company's needs in your product category.

our test markets that has outsold all other chili's by 35 percent. I have brought some for you to sample." This statement gathers attention, promotes interest, and provides a transition to the sales presentation.

PRODUCT APPROACH   Some products can be easily carried into the buyer's office to handle, try, feel, taste, or smell. Thus, the **product approach** should maximize the use of a prospect's senses. This can be an excellent way to show the buyer the benefits being offered and gain prospect involvement. Sometimes, a salesperson cannot bring the actual product to the buyer because of its size. The salesperson must use other means to simulate the actual product. Literature, sample output, or any usual tool such as computer-generated graphics, slides, or videotapes can be used.

BENEFIT APPROACH   Many successful approaches begin with a strong statement about a benefit that the product brings to the customer. Benefits might include 30 percent faster, 20 percent less expensive, better value, more efficient, or more market coverage. The **benefit approach** is especially valuable if it is addressed to the buyer's dominant buying motive. The downside to this approach centers on describing benefits that may not be important to the buyer. This approach is better left until after specific needs are determined.

QUESTION APPROACH   The **question approach** is best used by describing an interesting characteristic about the product and then following it up with a question. It is hoped that a good question will trigger the prospects' thinking about a problem they need solved. The salesperson might say: "We've added three new flavors to our product line. Do you have time for me to tell you about them?"

Once the salesperson asks the question, he or she must listen carefully to the response. If the answer is yes, then the salesperson should proceed with an enthusiastic presentation of the three new flavors. If the answer is no, then the salesperson should find out when an appropriate time might be.

REFERRAL APPROACH   Citing the name of a satisfied customer or friend of the prospect (after receiving their approval to use their name) can begin an effective sales call. It is important to remember that the **referral approach** can have a negative effect if the prospect and referral are not as good friends as the referral thinks. It is important not to drop names and act as if buyers are happy customers when they are not. An example of a referral approach might be: "Mr. Todd, I am here at the suggestion of your south side store manager, Mr. Frost. He thought you might be interested in our new product line. We put it in for them last month, and Mr. Frost is very happy with the results."

COMPLIMENT APPROACH   Everyone enjoys a compliment. If the **compliment approach** is sincere, it may be an effective beginning to a sales call. However, insincere flattery is often obvious and offensive to prospects. Compliments must be both specific and sincere and of real interest to the prospect.

A salesperson's use of an inappropriate compliment follows: "Mr. Smith, I really like the open concept of your office building." On the surface, this compliment does not appear to be anything that a salesperson should not say. However, the compliment was not specific and agitated the buyer. The buyer hated the open concept because there was no privacy and it was impossible to shut the door when the office building was noisy.

The salesperson should have said: "Mr. Smith, the open concept of your office building really makes the rooms look bigger." The buyer could now respond that it certainly makes the rooms appear bigger, but he dislikes it because there is no privacy and the rooms are too noisy.

SURVEY APPROACH   The **survey approach** uses gathering information as an attention-getting statement. The salesperson approaches clients and offers to survey their business in a particular functional area. For instance, a computer salesperson might survey all the departments to determine whether all their data processing needs are being met. This approach is time-consuming, and the salesperson runs the risk of doing a lot of work with no guarantee of an order. Some organizations provide the survey approach as a service to promote goodwill and build the relationship with the customer.

Assessing the Situation and Discovering Needs through Questioning Skills

One of the most important communication skills for salespeople is questioning skills. Asking the right questions at the right time helps salespeople identify needed information about the organization's buying process. This ensures that the buyer understands what the salesperson is communicating. Developing and asking effective questions requires planning and practice. Planning a general questioning strategy can be an effective approach to actively engage a buyer during a sales interaction. The ADAPT process, as covered in Module 4, is one approach that can be used in many selling situations. The acronym ADAPT is appropriate for this questioning process because, as the name implies, it is flexible and can be made to apply to almost any situation. The ADAPT process emphasizes specific types of questions to help a buyer identify problems and needs. **Assessment questions** are designed to elicit factual information about the customer's current situation. These questions do not seek conclusions, rather they seek information that describes the customer and his or her business environment. The information sought should augment or confirm precall research.

Discovery questions are used to uncover problems or dissatisfactions the customer is experiencing that the salesperson's product or company may be able to solve. Basically, these questions are used to "discover" or "boil down" the information gained from assessment questions and from precall research into suggested needs.

Understanding Customer Needs

Activation questions and projection questions demonstrate to the buyer the salesperson's ability to understand his or her specific problems or situation. Most salespeople traditionally ask a few questions and attempt to sell a solution based on limited information. A good salesperson takes this step further to show the buyer his or her depth of understanding. Only through activation and projection questions can this be demonstrated. Activation questions are used to show the impact of a problem, uncovered through discovery questions, on the customer's entire operation. The objective is to "activate" the customer's interest in solving the problem by helping him or her to gain insight into the true ramifications of the problem and to realize that what may seem to be of little consequence is, in fact, of significant consequence. **Projection questions** help the customer to "project" what life would be like without the problems or dissatisfactions uncovered through activation questions. This helps the customer to see value in finding solutions to the problems developed earlier in the sales call.

Illustrating the Value of Fulfilling Needs

The last thing left for the salesperson to confirm is the customer's desire to solve the problem(s) discovered through the previous questions. If the buyer does not think that this problem warrants fixing, the salesperson must go back and look for other problems to solve. If the buyer agrees that the problem is worth fixing, the salesperson is now ready to prepare a sales presentation that addresses the issues discovered during the ADAPT process.

Summary

1. *Explain strategic prospecting.* Strategic prospecting involves the identification of qualified potential customers, usually called prospects. When we say a prospect is qualified, it means that the prospect meets or exceeds screening criteria that have been established by the salesperson or the sales organization. Prospects must meet criteria such as being financially capable of making the purchase, able to truly benefit from what is being sold, accessible to the salesperson, and in a position to make or support a purchase decision.

2. *Discuss why prospecting can be a challenging task for a salesperson.* Prospective buyers may be difficult to contact because they have never heard of a salesperson's firm and do not want to take the time with a potential new supplier. Buyers are constantly getting calls from salespeople and do not have time to see them all. Gatekeepers have been trained to screen their bosses' calls and often are not pleasant to the salesperson.

3. *Explain where salespeople find prospects.* A good sales organization and salesperson will have a number of ongoing prospecting methods in place at any given time. Asking present customers for leads (referral), working with noncompeting salespeople, buying directories or lists, advertising for interested companies to call or mail in their interest, telemarketing, the Web, direct mail, and observation are a few of the techniques that salespeople can use to generate leads.

4. *Understand the importance of gathering and studying precall information.* Salespeople must gather information about the prospect that will be used to help formulate the sales presentation. Buyer's needs, buyer's motives, and details about the buyer's situation should be determined. The more a salesperson knows about the buyer, the better chance he or she will have to meet the buyer's needs and eventually earn the commitment.

5. *Discuss the importance of planning the initial sales call.* Once the salesperson has sufficient background information, he or she is ready to plan the initial sales call. A well-planned sales call can help reduce stress and give the salesperson needed confidence.

6. *Explain how to approach and initiate contact with each prospect.* Salespeople only get one chance to make a first impression. Proper dress, etiquette, and courtesy will be the first things that a buyer notices about the salesperson. The first few words that come out of a salesperson's mouth may be critical to his or her success. An introduction approach should be used with other approaches to generate more interest.

7. *Explain the importance of questioning skills and discovering needs.* A salesperson has two choices. He or she can either tell the buyer what is needed or ask effective questions and discover the needs and try to fill them. The ADAPT process is one method that can be used to determine a prospect's needs. The ADAPT process emphasizes specific types of

questions to help a buyer identify problems and needs. If a buyer's needs are properly determined, often the salesperson has a better chance of satisfying the customer's needs and keeping him or her as a lifetime customer.

Understanding Professional Selling Terms

- Prospecting
- Referral approach
- Center of influence
- Noncompeting salespeople
- Telephone directories and lists
- Direct mail
- Cold canvassing
- Trade shows
- Bird dogs/spotters
- Seminars
- Web

- Introduction approach
- Product approach
- Benefit approach
- Question approach
- Referral approach
- Compliment approach
- Survey approach
- Assessment questions
- Discovery questions
- Activation questions
- Projection questions

Developing Professional Selling Knowledge

1. Why should a salesperson be concerned with prospecting—isn't it enough to concentrate on your present customers and grow your new business from them?
2. What should be the objectives of strategic prospecting?
3. Why is prospecting difficult for some salespeople?
4. Why should a salesperson wait until they have a track record with a buyer before they ask for a referral?
5. Why is there the potential for cold canvassing not to be an effective prospecting method?
6. At a minimum, what should a qualified prospect look like?
7. Why is it important to collect precall information on the buyer and the company?
8. What sources of information can a salesperson use to gather information on their prospects?
9. Why is it important to determine other buying influences?
10. What are some typical objectives a salesperson might hope to accomplish when calling on a prospect?

Building Professional Selling Skills

1. You have recently graduated from college and are selling a new line with X-tra Clear Copiers. You have been assigned to a new territory in a city of 100,000 near your campus. You do not have any clients who currently own X-tra Clear Copiers. Your boss asks you to develop a prospect list in 10 days. How might you go about generating this list of prospects?

Provide a list of sources that you might use to generate leads.

1. _____
2. _____
3. _____
4. _____
5. _____
6. _____
7. _____
8. _____

9. _____

10. _____

Provide a list of establishments that would be prospects for X-tra Clear Copiers. Can you identify a person to call on? What information should you try to collect?

1. Company _____

   Who to call on _____

   Info to collect _____

2. Company _____

   Who to call on _____

   Info to collect _____

3. Company _____

   Who to call on _____

   Info to collect _____

4. Company _____

   Who to call on _____

   Info to collect _____

5. Company _____

   Who to call on _____

   Info to collect _____

6. Company _____

   Who to call on _____

   Info to collect _____

7. Company _____

   Who to call on _____

   Info to collect _____

8. Company _____

   Who to call on _____

   Info to collect _____

9. Company _____

   Who to call on _____

   Info to collect _____

10. Company _____

   Who to call on _____

   Info to collect _____

2. The effectiveness of the various methods available for salespeople to make contact with prospects and customers will vary according to what the salesperson hopes to accomplish. This exercise requires that you consider certain outcomes that a salesperson might desire and designate which contact method(s) might be the most effective. To encourage your thoughtful consideration of each method's strengths and weaknesses, the exercise also requires you to explain why you made your selections.

For each of the following desired outcomes, indicate which customer contact method would be the best to use. Indicate your choice by entering the letter(s) corresponding to the chosen contact method(s):

In Person (P)   E-mail (E)
Form Letter (F)   Personalized Letter (L)
Telephone (T)   World Wide Web (W)

After you have made your selection, briefly explain why you believe this to be the optimal choice. This information will be used for class discussion.

Creating awareness of product or company. _____

Why: _____

_____

_____

Introducing yourself. _____

Why: _____

_____

_____

Providing detailed product information. _____

Why: _____

_____

_____

Summarizing a specific proposal. _____

Why: _____

_____

_____

Closing a sale. _____

Why: _____

_____

_____

Getting an initial appointment. _____

Why: _____

_____

_____

Getting a follow-up appointment. _____

Why: _____

_____

_____

Confirming an appointment. _____

Why: _____

_____

_____

Getting acquainted. _____

Why: _____

_____

_____

Building your credibility. _____

Why: _____

_____

_____

Demonstrating products. _____

Why: _____

_____

_____

Discovering customer needs. _____

Why: _____

_____

_____

Confirming a major point. _____

Why: _____

_____

_____

Confirming a minor point. _____

Why: _____

_____

_____

Making Professional Selling Decisions

CASE 7.1   *How to Prospect for New Customers*

Background

Pete Tsuleff has been interested in the food and beverage industry since he was a little boy. His father owned a restaurant/tavern. Pete spent his evenings, weekends, and summers working in the restaurant. At age 21, he began to work as a bartender. He had firsthand experience ordering food, hiring, firing, and running the entire operation by the time he was 25. At age 30, he bought his father out.

During the next 10 years, he opened another restaurant/bar and two package liquor stores. Peter's first love was experimenting with new recipes. He had a chili that won competitions in his hometown. He made a spaghetti sauce that was world class. His garlic bread and garlic cheese bread were legendary. Pete decided to get out of the tavern and liquor business, and he opened a line of spaghetti shops. Sales over the first five years were outstanding, and he opened a new store every six months.

Pete continued to experiment with recipes and developed a line of barbecue sauces. He believes that he is the first to dual franchise spaghetti and barbecue in the same building.

Current Situation

Pete is convinced that a good market exists (e.g., groceries, restaurants, gas stations) for his garlic bread and spaghetti and barbecue sauces. He has seen his sales grow by 18 percent per year over the past five years, and the trend is expected to continue for at least the next three years.

One of his first problems is to obtain a list of prospects.

Questions

1. What prospecting method should Pete use?
2. How can Pete qualify the leads he receives? What qualifying factors will be most important?
3. How can Pete organize his prospecting activities?
4. How should he keep records of his prospects?
5. What precall information is needed by Pete? How will he collect this information?

CASE 7.2   *Approaching Prospects for the First Time*

Background

You work for IKON Solutions selling office equipment and have been through months of training on your products. You feel very confident in your sales ability. You have been given the green light to call on your prospect list. Your first call is to a large employer in your territory.

Current Situation

You walk into the business office and introduce yourself and your company to the receptionist. You hand her your card and ask to see the purchasing agent in charge of buying office equipment.

She immediately asks you if you have an appointment and wants to know what you want.

Questions

1. How do you respond to her questions?
2. Should you give her a presentation to get her attention in hopes she will pass you on to the purchasing department?
3. What if she simply tells you they have no office equipment needs at this time and shows you the door?

Communication Styles

Verbal and nonverbal messages can also provide salespeople with important cues regarding buyers' personalities and communication styles. Experienced salespeople emphasize the importance of reading and responding to customer communication styles. Effectively sensing and interpreting customers' communication styles allows salespeople to adapt their own interaction behaviors in a way that facilitates buyer-seller communication and enhances relationship formation. Most sales training programs use a two-by-two matrix as a basis for categorizing communication styles into four primary types.[8] As illustrated by Figure 7A.1, the four styles are based on two determinant dimensions: assertiveness and responsiveness.

ASSERTIVENESS Assertiveness refers to the degree to which a person holds opinions about issues and attempts to dominate or control situations by directing the thoughts and actions of others. Highly assertive individuals tend to be fast paced, opinionated, and quick to speak out and take confrontational positions. Low-assertive individuals tend to exhibit a slower pace. They typically hold back, let others take charge, and are slow and deliberate in their communication and actions.

RESPONSIVENESS Responsiveness points to the level of feelings and sociability an individual openly displays. Highly responsive individuals are relationship oriented and openly emotional. They readily express their feelings and tend to be personable, friendly, and informal. However, low-responsive individuals tend to be task oriented and very controlled in their display of emotions. They tend to be impersonal in dealing with others, with an emphasis on formality and self-discipline.

The actual levels of assertiveness and responsiveness will vary from one individual to another on a continuum ranging from high to low. An individual may be located anywhere along the particular continuum, and where the individual is located determines the degree to which he or she possesses and demonstrates the particular behaviors associated with that dimension. The following figures illustrate the range of behaviors commonly associated with each dimension.

Overlaying the assertiveness and responsiveness dimensions produces a four-quadrant matrix as illustrated in Figure 7A.2. The four quadrants characterize an individual as exhibiting one of four different communication styles on the basis of his or her demonstrated levels of assertiveness and responsiveness. *Amiables* are high on responsiveness but low on assertiveness. Expressives are defined as high on both responsiveness and assertiveness. *Drivers* are low on responsiveness but high on assertiveness. *Analyticals* are characterized as being low on assertiveness as well as responsiveness. A salesperson's skill in properly classifying customers can provide valuable cues regarding customer attitudes and behaviors. In turn, these cues allow the salesperson to be more effective by adapting his or her communication and responses to better fit the customer's style.

FIGURE 7A.1   **Comparison of the Principal Characteristics of Assertiveness and Responsivenesss**

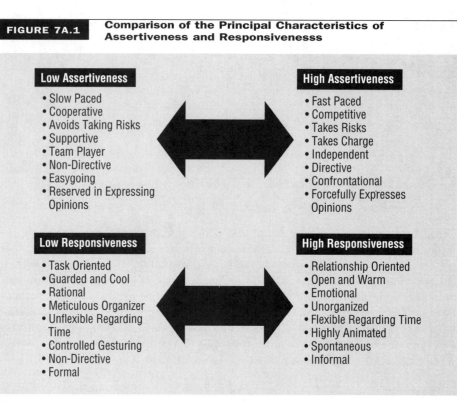

Low Assertiveness
- Slow Paced
- Cooperative
- Avoids Taking Risks
- Supportive
- Team Player
- Non-Directive
- Easygoing
- Reserved in Expressing Opinions

High Assertiveness
- Fast Paced
- Competitive
- Takes Risks
- Takes Charge
- Independent
- Directive
- Confrontational
- Forcefully Expresses Opinions

Low Responsiveness
- Task Oriented
- Guarded and Cool
- Rational
- Meticulous Organizer
- Unflexible Regarding Time
- Controlled Gesturing
- Non-Directive
- Formal

High Responsiveness
- Relationship Oriented
- Open and Warm
- Emotional
- Unorganized
- Flexible Regarding Time
- Highly Animated
- Spontaneous
- Informal

Most sales training programs use a two-by-two matrix as a basis for categorizing communication styles into four primary types. The four styles are based on two dimensions: assertiveness and responsiveness.

FIGURE 7A.2   **Communication Styles Matrix**

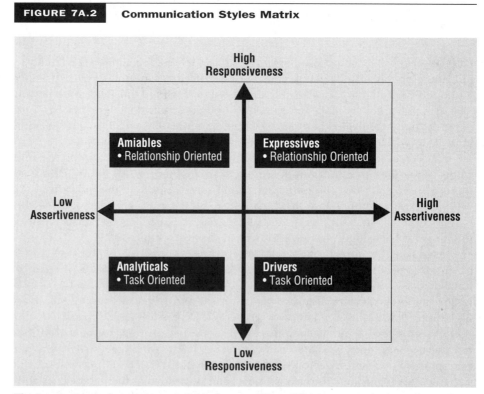

High Responsiveness

Amiables
- Relationship Oriented

Expressives
- Relationship Oriented

Low Assertiveness

High Assertiveness

Analyticals
- Task Oriented

Drivers
- Task Oriented

Low Responsiveness

The four quadrants characterize an individual as one of four different communication styles on the basis of his or her demonstrated levels of assertiveness and responsiveness. A salesperson's skill in properly classifying customers can provide valuable cues regarding customer attitudes and behaviors.

AMIABLES   Developing and maintaining close personal relationships is important to amiables. Easy-going and cooperative, they are often characterized as friendly backslappers due to their preference for belonging to groups and their sincere interest in other people—their hobbies, interests, families, and mutual friends. With a natural propensity for talking and socializing, they have little or no desire to control others but rather prefer building consensus. Amiables are not risk takers and need to feel safe in making a decision. Somewhat undisciplined with regard to time, amiables appear to be slow and deliberate in their actions. They avoid conflict and tend to be more concerned with opinions—what others think—than with details and facts. When confronted or attacked, amiables tend to submit. In working with an amiable customer, salespeople should remember that their priority "must-have" is to be liked and their fundamental "want" is for attention.

EXPRESSIVES   Expressives are animated and highly communicative. Although very competitive by nature, they also exhibit warm personalities and value building close relationships with others. In fact, they dislike being alone and readily seek out others. Expressives are extroverted and are highly uninhibited in their communication. When confronted or crossed, they will attack. Enthusiastic and stimulating, they seem to talk in terms of people rather than things and have a ready opinion on everything. Yet, they remain open-minded and changeable. Expressives are fast paced in their decision making and behavior and prefer the big picture rather than getting bogged down in details. As a result, they are very spontaneous, unconcerned with time schedules, and not especially organized in their daily lives. They are creative, comfortable operating on intuition, and demonstrate a willingness to take risks. The two keys for expressives that salespeople must keep in mind are the "must-have" of never being hurt emotionally and their underlying "want" is attention.

DRIVERS   Sometimes referred to as the director or dictator style, drivers are hard and detached from relationships with others. Described as being cool, tough, and competitive in their relationships, drivers are independent and willing to run over others to get their preferred results. As they seek out and openly demonstrate power and control over people and situations, they are difficult to get close to and appear to treat people as things. Drivers are extremely formal, business-like, and impatient, with a penchant for time and organization. They are highly opinionated, impatient, and quick to share those opinions with those around them. When attacked or confronted, drivers will dictate. Drivers exhibit a low tolerance for taking advice, tend to be risk takers, and favor making their own decisions. Although they are highly task oriented, drivers prefer to ignore facts and figures and instead rely on their own gut feelings in making decisions—after all, they do know it all. When working with drivers, salespeople should remember that this style's "must-have" is winning and their fundamental "want" is results.

ANALYTICALS   The descriptive name for this style is derived from their penchant for gathering and analyzing facts and details before making a decision. Analyticals are meticulous and disciplined in everything they do. Logical and very controlled, they are systemic problem solvers and thus very deliberate and slower in pace. In stressful situations and confrontations, analyticals tend to withdraw. Many times, they appear to be nit-picky about everything around them. They do not readily let their feelings hang out nor are they spontaneous in their behaviors. As a result, they are often seen as being cool and aloof. Analyticals shy away from personal relationships and avoid taking risks. Time and personal schedules are close to being a religious ritual for the analytical. The two fundamentals that salespeople must keep in mind when working with this style are the "must-have " of being right and the underlying "want" for analytical activities.

Mastering Communication Style Flexing

In addition to sensing and interpreting the customer's communication style, salespeople must also be aware of their own personal style. Mismatched and possibly clashing styles can be dysfunctional and present significant barriers to communication and relationship building. To minimize possible negative effects stemming from mismatched styles, salespeople can flex their own style to facilitate effective communication. For example, an expressive salesperson calling on an analytical buyer would find considerable differences in both pace and relationship/task orientation that could hinder the selling process unless adjustments are made. Flexing his or her own style to better match that of the buyer enhances communication. In terms of our example, the salesperson would need to make adjustments by slowing down his or her natural pace, reining in the level of spontaneity and animation, and increasing task orientation by offering more detailed information and analysis.

Adapting to buyers by flexing their own communication style has been found to have a positive impact on salespeople's performance and the quality of buyer-seller relationships. Nevertheless, flexing should not be interpreted as meaning an exact match between a salesperson's style and that of a customer. Not only is it not required, exact matches could even be detrimental. For example, a buyer and seller with matching expressive styles could easily discover that the entire sales call regressed to little more than a personal discussion with nothing of substance being accomplished. However, a buyer and seller matched as drivers could find it difficult, if not impossible, to reach a decision that was mutually beneficial. Rather than matching the buyer's style, flexing infers that the salesperson should adjust to the needs and preferences of the buyer to maximize effectiveness. Growmark, an international agricultural product and service organization, teaches their salespeople to flex throughout their interaction with a buyer by studying different behaviors a salesperson might demonstrate with each style of buyer (see Exhibit 7A.1).

Study and compare the flexing behaviors that Growmark recommends their salespeople demonstrate while working with each different buyer communication style. Note the differences in recommended salesperson behavior and rationalize them in terms of the specific characteristics of each buyer's style. Overlaying and integrating these two sets of information will enhance the understanding of how to flex to different buyers and why that form of flexing is recommended.

It is not always possible to gain much information about a buyer's communication style, especially if the buyer is new. If this is the case, it may be more appropriate to assume the buyer is an analytical-driver and prepare for this style. If the buyer proves to be close to an amiable-expressive, then the salesperson can easily adapt. It is much more difficult to prepare for the amiable-expressive and then switch to an analytical-driver style.

EXHIBIT 7A.1   Recommended Flexing Behaviors for Different Communication Styles

Selling Task or Objective	Selling to the Analytical	Selling to the Driver	Selling to the Amiable	Selling to the Expressive
Setting an Appointment	• Send a business letter specifying details about yourself and the company. Follow the letter with a phone call to confirm expectations and set appointment.	• Drivers may not take time to read your letter. • Contact them by phone first and follow up with a letter. • Keep call businesslike and to the point by identifying yourself, explain the business problem addressed by your product, and ask for appointment. • Letter should simply confirm time and date of appointment and include materials the driver might review prior to the meeting.	• Send a letter with a personal touch stating who you are and why you are contacting the Amiable. • Letter should include your experience working with clients the prospect knows by reputation or experience; your reliability and follow-through; and the quality of your product/service. • Follow letter with a personal phone call. • Take time to be friendly, open, sincere, and to establish trust in the relationship.	• Generally, a phone call is most appropriate. • Make your call open and friendly, stressing quick benefits, personal service, your experience, and your company's experience with its products and services. • If you send a letter, make it short and personal, stressing who your are, how you know of the Expressive, and what you are interested in talking about.
Opening the Call	• Provide background information about you and the company. • Approach in an advisory capacity acknowledging buyer's expertise. • Show evidence that you have done your homework on buyer's situation. • Offer evidence of providing previous solutions. • Be conscious of how you are using buyer's time.	• Listen and focus on drivers' ideas and objectives. • Provide knowledge and insight relevant to driver's specific business problems. • Be personable but reserved and relatively formal. • Present factual evidence that establishes the business problem and resulting outcome. • Maintain a quick pace. Drivers value punctuality and efficient use of time.	• Engage in informal conversation before getting down to business. • Demonstrate that you are personally interested in the Amiable's work and personal goals. • You will have to earn the right to learn more personally about the Amiable. • Demonstrate your product/service knowledge by referencing a common acquaintance with whom you've done business.	• Quickly describe the purpose of your call and establish credibility—you must earn the right to develop a business relationship with the Expressive. • Share stories about people you both know. • Share information the Expressive would perceive as exclusive. • Share your feelings and enthusiasm for the Expressive's ideas and goals. • Once the Expressive has confidence in your competence, take time to develop an open and trusting personal relationship.
Gathering Information	• Ask specific, fact-finding questions in a systematic manner. • Establish comprehensive exchange of information. • Encourage buyer to discuss ideas while focusing on factual information. • Be thorough and unhurried—listen. • Explain that you are in alignment with their thinking and can support their objectives.	• Ask, don't tell. Ask fact-finding questions leading to what the driver values and rewards. • Make line of questioning consistent with your call objective. • Follow up on requests for information immediately. • Support the buyer's beliefs; indicate how you can positively affect goals. • Clarify the driver's expectations.	• Create a cooperative atmosphere with an open exchange of information and feelings. • Amiables tend to understate their objectives, so you may need to probe for details and specifics about their goals. • Listen responsively. Give ample amounts of verbal and nonverbal feedback. • Verify whether there are unresolved budget or cost justification issues. • Find out who else will contribute to the buying decision. • Summarize what you believe to be the Amiable's key ideas and feelings.	• Begin by finding out the Expressive's perception of the situation and vision of the ideal outcome. • Identify other people who should contribute to analysis and planning. • Listen, then respond with plenty of verbal and nonverbal feedback that supports the Expressive's beliefs. • Question carefully the critical data you'll need. • Keep the discussion focused and moving toward a result. • If the Expressive shows limited interest in specifics, summarize what has been discussed and begin to suggest ways to move the vision toward reality.

Source: Growmark Inc., 1998.

EXHIBIT 7A.1   **Recommended Flexing Behaviors for Different Communication Styles—cont'd.**

Selling Task or Objective	Selling to the Analytical	Selling to the Driver	Selling to the Amiable	Selling to the Expressive

Reinforcing the Need to Change
 	
Providing the Sales Story
	• Use their records to supply information.
	• Use a logical approach.
	• Illustrate with dollars and cents.
	• Provide detailed written proposal as part of presentation.
	• Include strongest cost-benefit justifications.
	• Support with third-party data.
	• Be reserved and decisive but not aggressive.
	• Limit emotional or testimonial appeals.
	• Recommend specific course of action.
	• Give buyer chance to review all documents related to purchase and delivery.
		• Be fast-paced and business like. Be sure of your figures. Show the Driver the bottom line.
		• Appeal to rational thinking and avoid appeal to emotions.
		• Present your recommendation so that the Driver can compare alternative solutions and their probable outcomes.
		• Provide documented options.
		• Offer the best quality given the cost limitations.
		• Be specific and factual without overwhelming the driver with details.
		• Appeal to esteem and independence needs.
		• Reinforce the driver's preference for acting in a forthright manner.
		• Summarize content quickly, then let driver choose a course of action.
			• Address emotional needs in line with safety and comfort needs.
			• Use the Amiable's own figures rather than your own.
			• Do not push!
			• Define clearly in writing and make sure the Amiable understands:
			  • What you can do to support the Amiable's personal goals;
			  • What you will contribute and what the Amiable needs to contribute;
			  • The support resources you intend to commit to the project.
			• Provide a clear solution to the Amiable's problem with maximum assurances that this is the best solution and that there is no need to consider others.
			• Ask the Amiable to involve other decision makers.
			• Satisfy needs by showing how your solution is best now and will be best in the future and support it with references and third-party evidence.
			• Use testimonials from perceived experts and others close to the Amiable.
				• Support the Expressive's ideas and goals.
				• Work toward his/her esteem needs.
				• Supply data from people seen as leaders to the Expressive.
				• Provide specific solutions to the Expressive's ideas—in writing.
				• Build confidence that you have the necessary facts, but do not overwhelm the Expressive with details.
				• Do not rush the discussion. Spend time developing ways to implement ideas.
				• Appeal to personal esteem needs.
				• Try to get commitments to action in writing.

EXHIBIT 7A.1   Recommended Flexing Behaviors for Different Communication Styles—cont'd.

Selling Task or Objective	Selling to the Analytical	Selling to the Driver	Selling to the Amiable	Selling to the Expressive

Asking for the Commitment	• Ask for commitment in a low-key but direct manner.
	• Expect to negotiate changes.
	• Pay special attention to pricing issues.
	• Work for commitment now to avoid Analytical's tendency to delay decisions.
	• Cite data supporting company's service records.
	• Respond to objections by emphasizing the Analytical's buying principles and objectivity.
		• Ask for the order directly;
		• Put your offer in clear factual terms.
		• Offer options and alternatives.
		• Be prepared to negotiate changes and concessions.
		• Drivers sometimes attach conditions to a sale.
		• Offer the Driver time to consider the options.
		• Anticipate objections in advance and come prepared with facts.
		• Respond to objections based on Driver's values and priorities.
			• Ask for the order indirectly—do not push.
			• Emphasize the guarantees that offer protection to the Amiable.
			• Do not corner the Amiables, they want a way out if things go wrong.
			• Guard against "buyer's remorse"— get a commitment even if you have to base it on a contingency.
			• Stress your personal involvement after the sale.
			• Encourage the Amiable to involve others in the final purchase decision.
			• Welcome objections and be patient and thorough in responding to them.
			• When responding to objections:
			  • Describe financial justification;
			  • Refer to experts or others the Amiable respects;
			  • Keep in mind how the Amiable feels about and will be affected by the purchase decision.
				• When you have enough information to understand the need and have tested the appropriateness of the recommendation, assume the sale and ask for the order in a casual and informal way.
				• When the opportunity presents itself, offer incentives to encourage the purchase.
				• Do not confuse the issue by presenting too many options or choices.
				• Get a definite commitment. Be sure the Expressive understands the decision to purchase.
				• Save the details until after you have a firm buying decision. The Expressive believes it is the salesperson's job to handle details.
				• In handling objections:
				  • Describe what others have done to get over that hurdle;
				  • Respond to the Expressive's enthusiasm for their goals;
				  • Deal with how the recommendation meets with this buyer's options;
				  • Restate benefits that focus on the satisfaction a buying decision will bring.

Providing Follow-up	• Provide detailed implementation plan.
	• Maintain regular contact.
	• Check to confirm satisfactory and on-schedule delivery.
		• Set up communication process with the Driver that encourages quick exchange of information about checkpoints and milestones.
		• Make sure you have a contingency plan to responsively implement corrections and incorporate changes.
		• Make sure there are no surprises.
			• Immediately after the purchase decision is made, make a follow-up appointment.
			• Initiate and maintain frequent contacts providing services such as:
			  • Periodic progress reports on installation;
			  • Arrangements for service and training;
			  • Introduction of new products and services;
			  • Listening carefully to concerns, even those that seem trivial.
				• As soon as the order is signed, reaffirm the schedule for delivery and your personal relationship with the buyer, and introduce the implementation person or team.
				• A social situation such as a lunch can be a very effective opportunity for following up on business with this buyer.
				• Work toward becoming an ongoing member of the buyer's team.
				• In case of any complaints, handle them yourself. Never refer them to another in your organization without the buyer's assent.

Exercises for Appendix 7

1. Use the following Communication Styles Survey to assess your communication style. First, complete the *Assertiveness Scale* and the *Responsiveness Scale* by circling the number that best represents your self-evaluation regarding each of the paired characteristics. Give your candid reaction—there is no right or wrong answer. After completing each set, complete the scoring as instructed and plot your scores on the grid chart.

Assertiveness Scale

I perceive myself as being:

Cooperative				Competitive
1	2	3	4	5

Submissive				Authoritarian
1	2	3	4	5

Accommodating				Domineering
1	2	3	4	5

Hesitant				Decisive
1	2	3	4	5

Reserved				Outgoing
1	2	3	4	5

Compromising				Insistent
1	2	3	4	5

Cautious				Risk-Taking
1	2	3	4	5

Patient				Hurried
1	2	3	4	5

Complacent				Influential
1	2	3	4	5

Quiet				Talkative
1	2	3	4	5

Shy				Bold
1	2	3	4	5

Supportive				Demanding
1	2	3	4	5

Relaxed				Tense
1	2	3	4	5

Restrained				Assertive
1	2	3	4	5

Scoring for Assertiveness Scale:
Add the circled numbers on this page and enter the sum here _____
Divide this sum by 14 to compute your Assertiveness Score and enter it here _____

Responsiveness Scale

I perceive myself as being:

Disciplined	←			→ Easy-Going
1	2	3	4	5
Controlled				Expressive
1	2	3	4	5
Serious				Light-Hearted
1	2	3	4	5
Methodical				Unstructured
1	2	3	4	5
Calculating				Spontaneous
1	2	3	4	5
Guarded				Open
1	2	3	4	5
Stalwart				Humorous
1	2	3	4	5
Aloof				Friendly
1	2	3	4	5
Formal				Casual
1	2	3	4	5
Reserved				Attention-Seeking
1	2	3	4	5
Cautious				Carefree
1	2	3	4	5
Conforming				Unconventional
1	2	3	4	5
Reticent				Dramatic
1	2	3	4	5
Restrained				Impulsive
1	2	3	4	5

Scoring for Responsiveness Scale:

Add the circled numbers on this page and enter the sum here _____

Divide this sum by 14 to compute your Responsiveness Score and enter it here _____

Use the following grid chart to plot your Assertiveness Score and your Responsiveness Score to determine your individual communication style.

What is your communication style?

Do you feel this is an accurate portrayal of your style? Why or why not?

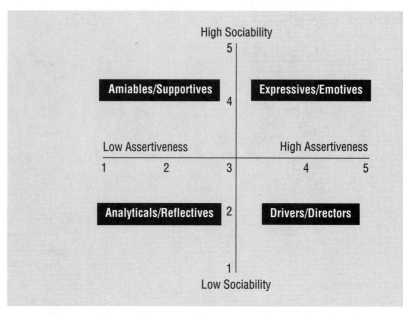

2. Based on your understanding of (a) interpersonal communication styles and (b) your personal communication style, respond to each of the following questions. These questions refer to how and why you would flex your style to better relate to buyers characterized by various communication styles.

A. What preparations and style flexing would you make to better relate to and communicate with customers characterized as *Drivers/Directors?*
B. What preparations and style flexing would you make to better relate to and communicate with customers characterized as *Analyticals/Reflectives?*
C. What preparations and style flexing would you make to better relate to and communicate with customers characterized as *Expressives/Emotives?*
D. What preparations and style flexing would you make to better relate to and communicate with customers characterized as *Amiables/Supportives?*

Developing the Relationship

Customizing the Proposal and Sales Presentation

Sales manager Steve Pidgeon of Mayflower puts a premium on his salesforce's ability to determine customer needs. His salesperson's favorite question during the needs assessment call is to ask what problems or opportunities keep the buyer up at night. Steve thinks that if his salespeople understand the pressing problems of the buyer and the buyer's company, then they have a better chance of recommending the right product to solve the problem.

The next strategy that Steve requires of his salesforce is to provide every prospect with a written sales proposal to go along with each presentation the salesperson gives. The proposals have become elaborate. The situation analysis section of the proposal clearly describes the problem to be solved or the opportunity to be provided. It clearly points out who has the problems and who in the company can benefit from the problem going away. Only those features and benefits that are important to the buyer are covered in the proposal.

The recommendation section of the proposal suggests, specifically, what to buy and when to buy. The proposal uses charts and graphs to support the recommendations in an easy-to-read fashion. Steve is not afraid to bring in financial experts to help explain what the problem is costing at this time and what costs will go away if the problem is solved. The final section of the proposal gives a recommended timetable, which details a schedule of key events that must be implemented. The finishing touches of the proposal include binding the proposal in a hardback cover and customizing the cover with gold lettering.

Steve wants the proposal to be a road map for the buyer to purchase. In effect, Steve states, "If you like the proposal and want to act on it, this is what you need to do." Steve's team understands the importance of linking solutions to needs and planning the proposal and presentation. Steve's records indicate that since they have been customizing their proposals and presentations, they have improved earning commitment by 23 percent.

Source: Interview with Steve Pidgeon, Mayflower, June 11, 1998.

After completing this module, you should be able to

1 Discuss how salespeople select appropriate customer offerings by assessing customer needs.

2 Discuss the different types of sales presentations and what goes into their planning.

3 List and explain the different tools that can be used to customize a sales presentation.

4 Explain how a salesperson can link solutions to needs by using features, potential benefits, and confirmed benefits.

5 Explain why prospects raise objections.

6 Describe the different types of objections.

7 Explain how the LAARC method can be used to overcome buyer resistance.

8 List and explain the earning commitment techniques that enhance relationship-building.

9 Discuss the importance of using a sales presentation checklist.

The emphasis in selling today is on adaptive selling and relationship selling. This current selling focus is a balanced approach in which the buyer and seller are viewed as equals working together to create opportunities and solve problems. Effective communication techniques are critical to today's salesperson as he or she must ask questions, interview the buyer, listen, and respond to the specific needs of each buyer. Steve Pidgeon understands these principles and has his salespeople select only those features and benefits of the product that are relevant to the identified needs of their buyers.

Steve notes, for decades, salespeople have been exhorted to "sell the sizzle, not the steak" and to remember that "when a customer says no, you are just beginning to sell." He knows such advice rings hollow as we move into the new millennium of professional selling. Although dramatic and emotionally charged sales presentations may be effective on certain occasions (e.g., trade shows), they are not likely to consistently produce sales unless the rational motives of the prospect have been given primary consideration.[1] In contrast to the stereotypical heavy-handed, song-and-dance, personality-plus sales relics of the past, the contemporary professional salesperson relies more on printed sales support material, audio-visual aids, and sales technologies such as laptop computers. Research indicates that the visual and vocal elements of a sales message are more memorable than the actual content of the message. Consequently, effective salespeople use every clarity-enhancing tool at their disposal. By being knowledgeable about their products, the competition, and their customers' needs, successful salespeople are able to adapt readily to the situation—without appearing to be self-serving, transparent chameleons who mirror every movement of the prospect.

A brief discussion follows that overviews the steps in developing a relationship with a prospect. Following a discussion of **needs analysis**, this module discusses the importance of selecting the appropriate offering. Different types of sales presentations are explained. This is followed by a description of how to customize presentations and why it is important to link solutions to needs. Next, anticipating and negotiating buyer resistance and earning commitment are reviewed. Finally, a sales presentation checklist is covered.

Steps in Developing the Relationship

Figure 8.1 overviews the steps in developing the relationship. As stated in Module 7, the approach stage is the information-gathering stage. The salesperson works to build rapport and gets acquainted with the prospect. The salesperson should select the appropriate offering only after assessing the prospect's needs. During step 2, the salesperson must ask questions and listen carefully to what the prospect is saying. This step may take a number of calls, depending on the amount of probing and clarifying that must take place to understand the prospect's needs. The salesperson can use the presentation checklist that is discussed later in this module to help ensure all bases are covered. Eventually, the salesperson will have to choose the presentation format and develop a customized presentation for the prospect. The salesperson must determine which features and benefits are important to the prospect and incorporate them into his or her presentation. Ultimately, the sales conversation must turn to the salesperson's solution, and the salesperson must gain agreement that the solution will work and is viable. All this must be done while overcoming the prospect's concerns by answering questions in a manner that eliminates any doubt the prospect might have.

| FIGURE 8.1 | Steps in Developing the Relationship |

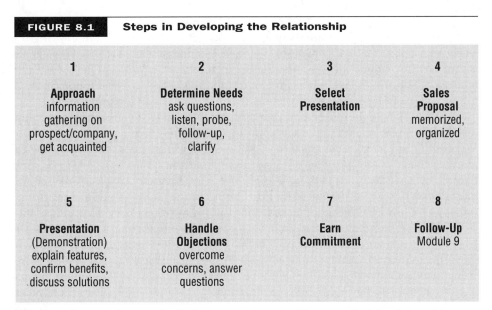

1	2	3	4
Approach information gathering on prospect/company, get acquainted	**Determine Needs** ask questions, listen, probe, follow-up, clarify	**Select Presentation**	**Sales Proposal** memorized, organized

5	6	7	8
Presentation (Demonstration) explain features, confirm benefits, discuss solutions	**Handle Objections** overcome concerns, answer questions	**Earn Commitment**	**Follow-Up** Module 9

This figure illustrates the stages in developing a relationship with a buyer. Early in relationship building it is more important to gather information than to give it.

Selecting Appropriate Customer Offerings by Assessing Needs

The salesperson's primary goal is to uncover the prospect's specific needs or problems and then focus on what products or services will solve the problem or meet the specific needs. The salesperson's primary motivation is to create added value for the customer. To accomplish this, the salesperson must have a thorough understanding of the prospect's needs. Customer needs result from a discrepancy between an actual and desired state of being. Some customer needs are rational, and some are emotional.

Customer needs, whether rational or emotional, may be classified as unrecognized, potential, or confirmed (by the customer). Unrecognized needs are those of which the customer is completely unaware or dismissed by the customer as trivial. Examples of customer statements indicating unrecognized needs include "I don't need a fax machine, I am happy with my overnight mail service."

Potential needs are reflected in customer statements of general problems, difficulties, and dissatisfactions, such as "Our mail-handling system is a bit slow," "We have experienced some lost time due to machine breakdowns," or "Some of the items in our current mix are not moving out of inventory quickly enough."

Confirmed needs are indicated by statements that clearly indicate that the customer wants to take action to solve a problem. Examples of confirmed-need statements include "We are soliciting bids for three new copiers," "We are looking for a system that will be compatible with our existing network," or "It is essential that we improve our accounting system to improve our receivables situation."

It stands to reason that if the customer is ready to take action to satisfy a need, the salesperson has a better chance of making a successful presentation than if the customer's needs are unrecognized or merely suggested. Research supports this contention and further reinforces that just because a customer has a problem does not automatically mean that the customer has a desire to solve the problem.

From information gained in prospecting or from previous sales calls, the salesperson may know the customer's needs. If not, needs must be clarified during the early stages of the sales call. Questioning and listening are the keys to needs analysis and confirmation. "Professional Selling in the 21st Century: A Query for Every Question," illustrates the importance of questioning whether a salesperson is handling sales resistance, probing for customer needs, or earning commitment.

Needs analysis should enable the salesperson to state the customer's problem or opportunity as related to the sales offering. There may be multiple problems and opportunities for each customer, and salespeople must pursue these in a logical manner. First, which problem or opportunity does the customer seem to be most interested in addressing? Is there a good reason to pursue one opportunity before the others? It is entirely possible that the customer may have an opportunity to improve operations but has no idea that such an opportunity exists. This will require a different selling strategy and different sales tactics than when the customer is acutely aware of an opportunity or is seeking the solution to a significant problem.

The emphasis in selling today is on determining customer needs and then creating or selecting customer-fitted solutions to satisfy those needs. Salespeople must take their time and give careful consideration to recommending a solution. Salespeople must also select a product or service that most closely matches their customer's needs and creates maximum satisfaction. Salespeople must not only be aware of their product options but also those of their competitors. Successful salespeople are those who have the ability to accurately diagnose their prospect's needs and select the best product to fill these needs. "An Ethical Dilemma" describes a salesperson that thinks he knows the diagnoses for each of his buyers.

An Ethical Dilemma

Tom Lawrence had a good idea about which of his product's features were hot buttons for most prospects. During each of his sales calls, he hammered home those features and benefits that he thought were important to most of his prospects. His sales manager made calls with him for a few days and made the observation that he should do more listening and only sell those features and benefits that were relevant to each prospect. Tom stated: "I feel that is a waste of time. Most of my buyers are busy. They don't have time to answer questions all day. I'm the expert, I should know what they need." What are the dangers in the way Tom thinks? What can his sales manager do to help Tom change?

Along with needs analysis, a salesperson should attempt to determine the prospect's buying motives. Buying motives can be either functional (i.e., usually dominant) or psychological in nature. Functional motives are driven by the price, quality, and service a salesperson can supply. Psychological motives also have an impact on the buyer's decision and deal with a buyer's habits, emotional stress, and confidence. A salesperson's job is to determine which combination is at play when the buyer is making the decision.

Another important factor to consider is the competitive situation. To find the best solution to a prospect's problem, a salesperson should analyze all the competitors he or she is up against. Understanding a competitor's strengths and weaknesses allows the salesperson to evaluate all possible solutions to the prospect's problem and put the best solution forward.

Once these areas have been covered, the salesperson is now in a position to determine the sales presentation objective (i.e., what does the salesperson hope to accomplish during this sales call).

A Query for Every Occasion

Tom Avila, manufacturer's rep for Davis and Davis, has sold in the natural gas industry for more than 15 years. Tom understands the importance of effective questioning. He states, "The successful salesperson has the ability to ask the right question at the right time. Whether I am handling objections, probing for customer needs, or earning commitment, there's a question that can help a salesperson do it more effectively."

I use questions to open my sales call. Questions that address issues such as dollar savings and time savings can be very effective. For instance, I might ask one of my customers if he or she would like to save $1,000 each month in maintenance costs. If the answer is yes, then I must be able to effectively demonstrate this. I also use questions when I analyze needs. I am always asking my customers what features they would like to see in a product. Questions also help me get at the real issues when I run into sales resistance. I can't be afraid to ask a prospect to explain why he or she feels a certain way. Finally, questions help me test customers and prospects for their readiness to buy. As you can see, effective questioning is the most important tool a salesperson has. Use it wisely, and a salesperson will have great results.

Types of Sales Presentations

In planning a sales presentation, salespeople may choose between three basic types of presentations: memorized or **canned presentations, organized presentations,** and **written sales proposals.** To be successful, these presentations must be credible and clear. In addition, the salesperson must deliver the presentation in the right environment at an appropriate time to maximize the probability of a successful outcome.

For any of the three presentation types, salespeople must plan to be as specific as possible in developing their sales message. For example, it is better to tell a prospect "This electric motor will produce 4800 RPM and requires only one hour of maintenance per week" than to say "This motor will really put out the work with only minimum maintenance."

Canned Presentations

Canned sales presentations include scripted sales calls, memorized presentations, and automated presentations. Automated presentations rely heavily on computer images, movies, tapes, or slides to present the information to the prospect.

Most canned sales presentations have been tested for effectiveness with real customers before dissemination to the salesforce. As discussed in Module 6, canned presentations are usually complete and logically structured. Objections and questions can be anticipated in advance, and appropriate responses can be formulated as part of the presentation.

Canned sales presentations make an implicit assumption that customer needs and buying motives are homogeneous. Therefore, canned presentations fail to capitalize on a key advantage of personal selling—the ability to adapt to different types of customers and various selling situations. Unfortunately, most consumer-based telemarketing sales calls are canned and follow this formula. The canned presentation can be effective but is not appropriate for many situations—simply because customer opportunity to interact is minimized. During a memorized presentation, the salesperson talks 80–90 percent of the time, only occasionally allowing the prospect to express his or her feelings, concerns, or opinions. Figure 8.2 illustrates this process. Unfortunately, the salesperson does not attempt to determine the prospect's needs during the sales interview but gives the same memorized sales talk to all prospects. The salesperson can only assume the buyer's need and must hope that a lively presentation of product benefits will cause the prospect to buy.

Organized Presentations

To best address individual customers and different selling situations, salespeople should consider an organized presentation, which allows the implementation of appropriate sales strategies and tactics. These strategies and tactics should be outlined by the salesperson from information gathered during previous sales calls. Such an approach allows much-needed flexibility to adapt to buyer feedback and changing circumstances during the presentation. Organized presentations may also include some canned portions. For example, a salesperson for Caterpillar may show a videotape to illustrate the earth-moving capabilities of a bulldozer as one segment of an organized presentation. Due to its flexibility during the sales call and its ability to address various sales situations, the organized presentation is the most frequently used format for professional sales presentations.

The trust-based relational selling presentation often referred to as the need-satisfaction/consultative model, is a popular form of an organized presentation. It is different from the canned as it is designed as a flexible interactive sales presentation. The first stage of the process, the need development stage, is devoted to a discussion of the buyer's needs. As seen in Figure 8.3, during this phase the buyer should be talking 60–70 percent of the time. The salesperson accomplishes this by using the first four questioning techniques of the ADAPT process. The second stage of the process (need awareness) is to verify what the buyer thinks his or her needs are and to make the buyer aware of potential needs that may exist. For instance,

FIGURE 8.2	Prepared Approach to a Sales Presentation

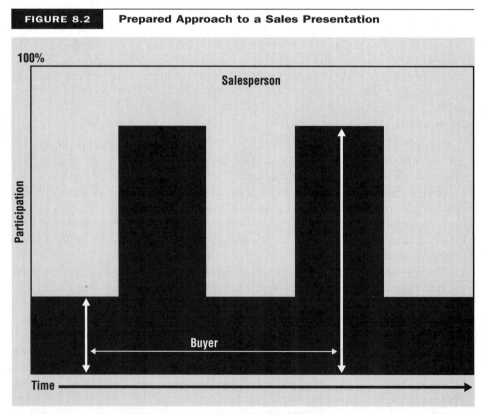

During a memorized presentation, the salesperson talks 80 to 90 percent of the time, only occasionally allowing the prospect to express his or her feelings, concerns or opinions.

FIGURE 8.3	The Trust-Based Selling Process: A Needs-Satisfaction Consultative Model

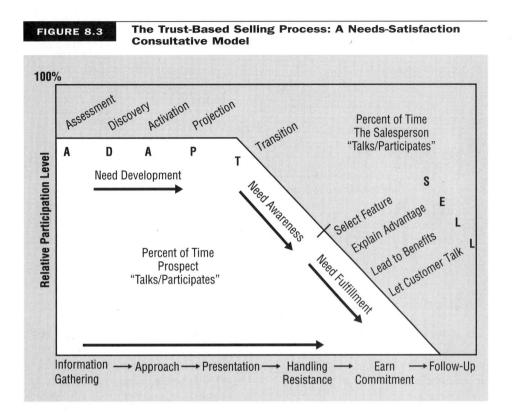

many firms were comfortable sending out overnight mail. Until facsimile technology came along, overnight mail was sufficient. Hewlett-Packard salespeople had to make their prospects aware of the benefits of the new technology. They had to find prospects who could benefit from getting information to their customers faster than overnight mail. The need-awareness stage is a good time to restate the prospect's needs and to clarify exactly what the prospect's needs are. During the last stage of the presentations, (the need-fulfillment stage), the salesperson must show how his or her product and its benefits will meet the needs of the buyer. As seen in Figure 8.3, the salesperson during the need-fulfillment stage will do more of the talking by indicating what specific product will meet the buyer's needs. The salesperson, by being a good listener early in the process, will now have a better chance to gain the buyer's interest and trust by talking about specific benefits the buyer has confirmed as being important.

Written Sales Proposals

The third basic type of sales presentation, as explained in Module 6, is the written sales proposal. The proposal is a complete self-contained sales presentation, but it is often accompanied by other verbal sales presentations before or after the proposal is delivered.

In some cases, the customer may receive a proposal and then request that the salesperson make a sales call to further explain the proposal and provide answers to questions. Alternatively, preliminary sales presentations may lead to a sales proposal. In any event, the sales proposal should be prepared after the salesperson has made a thorough assessment of the buyer's situation as it relates to the seller's offering. This can be accomplished by using a sales presentation checklist that is found at the end of the module. Exhibit 8.1 summarizes the types of sales presentations used by sales professionals.

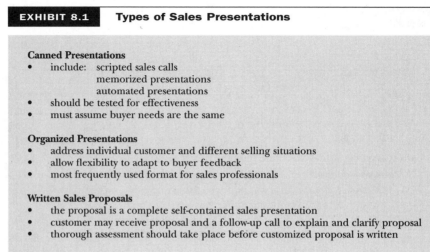

EXHIBIT 8.1   **Types of Sales Presentations**

Canned Presentations
- include: scripted sales calls
             memorized presentations
             automated presentations
- should be tested for effectiveness
- must assume buyer needs are the same

Organized Presentations
- address individual customer and different selling situations
- allow flexibility to adapt to buyer feedback
- most frequently used format for sales professionals

Written Sales Proposals
- the proposal is a complete self-contained sales presentation
- customer may receive proposal and a follow-up call to explain and clarify proposal
- thorough assessment should take place before customized proposal is written

Sequence of the Sales Presentation

The tactical planning of the sales presentation is to determine the basic sequence for the key points in the presentation. With an organized presentation, there should be some flexibility to allow adaptation to prospect questions and interests. Nonetheless, it is a good idea to have the key points arranged in a logical, sequential order.

There are few ironclad rules about how to order a sales presentation. Certainly, the appropriate sequence will be dictated by the situation, including priority to the prospect's preferences. A few general rules can be offered:

- Following an adequate introduction of the salesperson and the salesperson's company, questions, careful listening, and confirmation statements should be used to clarify and define explicit customer needs as related to the salesperson's offering.

- Benefits should be presented in order of importance according to the prospect's needs, and these benefits may be repeated during the presentation and at the conclusion of the presentation.

- If the sales presentation is a continuation of one or more previous sales calls, a quick summary should be made of what has been agreed on in the past, moving quickly into the prospect's primary area of interest.

- As a general rule, pricing issues should not be focused on until the prospect's needs have been defined and the salesperson has shown how those needs can be addressed with the product or service being sold. After prospects fully understand how the product or service meets their needs, they can make informed judgments on price/value issues.

Customizing the Presentation

The task of customizing presentations for individual prospects is made easier with word processing, because most presentations contain some generic information, which is part of all proposals. The important aspect of proposal appearance, or "merchandising" the proposal, is enhanced by the use of graphics, spreadsheet calculations, and professional-looking proposal covers. Because the salesperson has complete control over the content and appearance of the proposal, it should reflect careful preparation and have an attractive appearance that reinforces a professional image.

Using Visual Aids to Customize and Dramatize the Presentation

Visual aids can be used to customize and dramatize a sales presentation. A brief discussion of each aid follows.

CHARTS AND GRAPHS   **Charts** are useful in showing trends and illustrating relationships. Charts can show the prospect what the problem is costing them. Charts often depict relationships in terms of bars, circles, or squares. Charts and **graphs** can show significant changes or benefits by using the salesperson's solution. For example, Chris Crabtree, a salesperson for Ikon, asked one of his customers for his previous three years' cost to take his copying to an outside copy center.[2] He used a bar graph to show him the savings if he had purchased his own copier. The graph made its point to the owner of the company, who immediately purchased a copier. Salespeople can customize charts and graphs by using information pertaining to the prospective client company. Company sales, expenses, number of new product introductions, and so on, can be found in annual reports and used to demonstrate specific knowledge about the prospect.

PHOTOGRAPHS AND ADVERTISEMENTS   Photographs are easy to produce and relatively inexpensive. Using pictures allows the salesperson to present a realistic portrayal of the product or service. Many products cannot be taken into a prospect's office because of their size. A clear photograph can give the prospect an idea of product appearance and size. Many copier salespeople delight their prospects by showing them how small some of their copiers are in size. They can easily fit on a counter or a small table. Many purchasers of older model copiers remember huge machines that required a lot of space in an office. Taking recent advertisements to prospects can appeal to prospects and customers, especially ads that stress product benefits.

CATALOGS AND BROCHURES   **Catalogs** and **brochures** can help salespeople communicate key points of the company and products. Brochures and catalogs often summarize important features and benefits and can be effectively used not only during presentations but left as reminder pieces to the buyer after the salesperson has left. During subsequent phone calls with the buyer, the salesperson can review important topics and point out information to the buyer that is included in the catalog or brochure.

ELECTRONIC MEDIA   Salespeople today can customize graphical presentations with their laptop computers, VCRs, and slide and overhead projectors. Customizing presentations by using electronic media can be done inexpensively and in a fairly short period of time. Microsoft Power Point or Lotus Approach, for example, allows the salesperson to build a complete graphical presentation for individual customers. Using the following technologies gives the salesperson no reason to deliver a "canned presentation."

1. **Computer-based Presentation**
   Presentation software today allows the salesperson to create powerful customized presentations. Pictures of products, video testimonials of satisfied customers, and product comparisons can all be included in a Power Point presentation. Editing with computer-based artwork and different fonts also

enhances the presentation. Once completed, the Power Point software produces notes that can be used as handouts during the presentation.

2. **Videos**

   Many salespeople are using video to help demonstrate their products. Pharmaceutical companies provide lunch for a physician's office and show a video of a new product or how a piece of medical equipment (e.g., open MRI) is better than the equipment presently being used. Video can be a good way to educate customers and prospects.

3. **Slides**

   Many companies produce relatively inexpensive slides for their salespeople to use during presentations. Glaxo-Welcome uses before and after slides to depict the effectiveness of a topical cream it sells. The first slide shows an affected area of the skin, and the next slide shows the cleared skin after three days of treatment. The slide also indicates that 93 percent of the patients on this cream clear up after three days.[3] Slide shows can easily be changed depending on the audience. Slide shows have become more sophisticated as multiple projectors are used, and some companies even add musical sound tracks to their production.

4. **Overhead Transparencies**

   One sales manager says the use of computers and presentation software has just about eliminated his company's need for overhead projectors. Overhead projectors can still be used for a room full of people and when more sophisticated methods are not available. Overhead transparencies are easy to make and inexpensive to produce. Last-minute changes of transparencies are easily made on most copy machines. Color printers can also produce color transparencies, which can draw more attention to the presentation and create greater impact.

SALES PORTFOLIOS   Many companies have developed **sales portfolios** for their salesforces, which are simply collections of visual aids that can be used during a sales call. Portfolios tend to be more generic, and their intended purpose is not for customization but to have information available depending on the prospect's interest. Visual aids that a salesperson might keep in the portfolio include charts and graphs, photographs, sales manuals, catalogs, brochures, and advertisements.

Salespeople must use need-based questions to determine the prospect's problems or opportunities. Once specific needs are uncovered, salespeople must match specific product features and benefits that will solve the problem. Salespeople can create powerful customized presentations by using the communication tools described in the previous sections.

Linking Solutions to Needs (Features, Potential Benefits, and Confirmed Benefits)

After determining the basic needs of the prospect, the salesperson must decide which information to include in the presentation. At this point in the planning process, it is suggested that the salesperson ask, "If I were making this purchase decision, what would I want to know to make an informed decision?" It is unlikely that the customer will be interested in every detail of the salesperson's offering, and certainly some aspects of the offering will be more important to a particular prospect than will others. Essentially, salespeople should strive to communicate these crucial elements: how customer needs will be met, or how an opportunity can

EXHIBIT 8.2   **Features/Potential Benefits/Confirmed Benefits**

Features	Potential Benefits	Confirmed Benefits/Unconfirmed
1. Natural surface cohesiveness of Ultramid, a high-tech plastic golf club	1. Better launch angle More distance on shot	1. Golf pro does not see this as true benefit—*not confirmed* Golf pro has easy time selling longer distance—*confirmed benefit*
2. Bell-shaped nozzle on vacuum cleaner	2. Optimum air flow improves cleaning ability	2. Hard for most consumers to understand how bell-shape improves cleaning—*not confirmed*
3. Daily delivery of Frito-Lay potato chips	3. Retailer can reduce inventory costs Product freshness leads to customer satisfaction	3. Not a serious issue for this retailer—*not confirmed* Store manager puts huge emphasis on product freshness—*confirmed benefit*
4. Technical support personnel for a computer system	4. Assistance in installation, maintenance, and expansion	4. Support is needed—*confirmed benefit*

be realized as a result of a purchase; how product features translate, in a functional sense, to meaningful benefits for the customer; and why the customer should purchase from you as opposed to a competitive salesperson.

To do an adequate job in planning a presentation, salespeople must understand the concepts of features, potential benefits, and confirmed benefits. A **feature** (F) is a factual statement about a characteristic of the product or service being sold. A **potential benefit** (PB) describes how the product or service may meet a customer need that is assumed to be important by the salesperson. When a customer acknowledges the importance of a benefit to his or her buying situation, it is a **confirmed benefit** (CB). Examples of features and corresponding benefits are shown in Exhibit 8.2.

Extensive research by Learning International, a major sales training and consulting firm, concludes that stating features and potential benefits may result in successful sales calls or at least may lead to a continuation of the sales dialogue on the next sales call. This same research, however, concluded that a far more promising way to achieve sales call success is to seek customer confirmation of potential benefits. According to Learning International, successful sales calls have approximately five times as many confirmed benefit statements as unsuccessful sales calls.

The Learning International research strongly suggests that using feature statements and potential benefit statements will help a salesperson avoid failure but will not ensure success. These same conclusions were reached in a study by a British-based consulting firm of 5,000 sales calls involving high-technology products.[4]

In selecting specific benefits to be stressed, salespeople should focus on any unique benefits not offered by the competition, as long as the benefits are of interest to the prospect. These might include product benefits, along with non-product–related benefits such as delivery, extraordinary customer service, or additional sales support available to the customer.

Anticipating and Negotiating Concerns and Resistance

Over the years, many salesforces were taught that **sales resistance** was bad and would likely slow down or stop the selling process. Salespeople were also told that if they received resistance, then they had not done a good job explaining their product.

These notions have changed over the years to where objections now are viewed as opportunities to sell. Salespeople should be grateful for objections and always treat them as questions. The buyer is just asking for more information. It is the salesperson's job to produce the correct information to help buyers understand their concern. Inexperienced salespeople need to learn that sales resistance is a normal, natural part of any sales conversation. The prospect that does not question price, service, warranty, and delivery concerns is probably not interested.

Although many salespeople fear sales resistance from their prospects or customers, it should be viewed as a normal part of the sales process. At a minimum, the salesperson now has the prospect involved. The salesperson can now start to determine customer interest and measure the buyer's understanding of the problem. Finally, if the sales resistance is handled correctly, the outcome can lead to customer acceptance.

Reasons Why Prospects Raise Objections

There are many reasons why prospects will raise objections.

1. The prospect wants to avoid the sales interview. Some prospects do not want to create any more work for themselves than they already have. Granting a sales interview takes time, and buyers already have a busy schedule handling normal day-to-day tasks. Buyers may want to avoid the salesperson because they view his or her call as an interruption in their day. Most buyers do not have the time to see every salesperson that knocks on their door.

2. The salesperson has failed to prospect and qualify properly. Sometimes, poor prospects slip through the screening process. The prospect may have misunderstood the salesperson's intentions when asked for the interview. The salesperson should attempt to qualify the prospect during the sales call. For example, a computer software company used telemarketing to qualify prospects. Leads were turned over to the salesforce for in-person visits. The major product line was an inventory control package that costs $20,000. The salesperson asked the owner of the company if she had a budget for this project. The owner answered $5,000. The salesperson gave the owner the names of a couple of inexpensive software companies, thanked the owner for her time, and moved on. The owner was not about to spend $20,000 and said so early in the sales conversation. This resistance actually helped the salesperson. What if this resistance had stayed hidden for four to six weeks while the salesperson continued to call on the owner? Both the salesperson's and owner's time would have been wasted.

3. Objecting is a matter of custom. Many purchasing agents have a motto never to buy on the first call with a salesperson. Trust has not yet been developed, and a thorough understanding of the salesperson, his or her company, and the products has not been accomplished. The buyer will need most of this information to make a decision. Many buyers may say no during the first few calls to test the salesperson's persistence.

4. The prospect resists change. Many buyers like the way they are presently doing business. Thus, buyers will tell the salesperson that they are satisfied with what they have now. Many prospects simply resist change because they dislike making decisions. Prospects may fear the consequences of deciding and dread disturbing the status quo. A purchase usually involves dismissing the present supplier and handling all the arrangements (price, terms, delivery, and product specifications) to smoothly move the new supplier in.

EXHIBIT 8.3	Why Prospects Raise Objections and Strategies for Dealing with Them

Buyer wants to avoid the sales interview
    Strategy: set appointments to become part of the buyer's daily routine

Salesperson has failed to project and qualify properly
    Strategy: ask questions to verify prospect's interest

Buyer won't buy on the first sales call
    Strategy: regular calls on the prospect lets the prospect know the salesperson is serious about the relationship

Prospect does not want to change the present way of doing business
    Strategy: salesperson must help the prospect understand there is a better solution than the one the prospect is presently using

Prospect has failed to recognize a need
    Strategy: salesperson must show evidence that sparks the prospect's interest

Prospect lacks information on a new product or on the salesperson's company
    Strategy: salesperson must continually work to add value by providing useful information

Once a buyer is comfortable with his or her suppliers, he or she will generally avoid new salespeople until a major need arises.

5. The prospect fails to recognize a need. The prospect may be unaware of a need, uninformed about the product or service, or content with the present situation. In any case, the lack of need creates no motivation to change suppliers. Many purchasing agents were content with their overnight mail service and were slow to recognize the fax machine as a viable solution to getting information to their customers quickly. The poor quality of the reproduced document turned off many buyers. Only when the need for the information outweighed the aesthetics of the document did buyers readily embrace the fax machine.

6. Prospect lacks information. Ultimately, all sales resistance comes back to the fact that the prospect simply lacks the information he or she needs to comfortably make a decision. The salesperson must view this as an opportunity to put the right information in front of the buyer. If the salesperson diagnoses correctly and presents the right information, then the resistance problem can be more easily overcome. Exhibit 8.3 summarizes why prospects raise objections and lists strategies for dealing with them.

Types of Objections

Although there appears to be an infinite number of objections, most fall into five or six categories. Buyers use delay techniques to avoid taking immediate action. Comments such as "Give me a couple of weeks to think it over" can save the buyer the discomfort of saying no at the end of a presentation. "Your price is too high" or "I have no money" are easy ways for purchasing agents not to buy a salesperson's offering. Price is probably the most often cited objection but usually is not the most important issue. It is obvious that buyers do not buy merely on price, if this were true, then the lowest price supplier would get all the business and eventually be the only supplier left selling the product. "No need at this time" is another typical objection. The buyer may not be in the market to purchase at this point in time.

It is not unusual for salespeople to encounter **product objections.** Most buyers have fears associated with buying a product. The buyer may be afraid that the product's reliability will not perform up to the standards the salesperson said it would. Not only do the salespeople have to demonstrate that their product will perform at

EXHIBIT 8.4	Types of Objections
Delaying	Buyer needs time to think it over "Get back with me in a couple of weeks."
Price is too high	Buyer has a limited budget "We have been buying from another supplier who meets our budget constraints."
Product Objection	Buyer may be afraid of product reliability "I'm not sure the quality of your product meets our needs."
Service Objection	Buyer may be afraid of late deliveries, slow repairs, etc. "I'm happy with my present supplier's service."
Company Objection	Buyer is intensely loyal to the present supplier "I am happy with my present supplier."
No Need	Buyer has recently purchased or does not see a need for the product category "I'm not interested at this time."

the level they say it will, they must also show how it stacks up to the competition. A competitor introducing a new technology (e.g., e-commerce) may change the way a salesperson competes on a particular product line (e.g., office products).

Many buyers are constantly assessing their supplier on service (e.g., delivery, follow-up, warranties, guarantees, repairs, installation, and training). If the service is good and department heads are not complaining, the buyer is likely to stay with the status quo. Service is one variable that companies and salespeople can use to differentiate their product. Enterprise Rent-a-Car will deliver cars to the home of the renter and has made this an issue in its advertising. A salesperson for a wholesale distributor may make the point for a prospect that their fresh fruit, fish, and meat can be delivered daily when their competitors only deliver three times per week.

Many buyers will feel intense loyalty to their present suppliers and use this as a reason not to change. Buyers may be equally committed to the salesperson from whom they are presently buying. As a nonsupplier to the company, the salesperson must continue to call on the buyer and look for opportunities to build trust with the prospect. The salesperson may want to investigate whether the buyer has had any previous bad experience with his or her company that is causing the buyer not to do business with that company. Finally, some salespeople and their buyers will not hit it off. The salesperson has to recognize these feelings and move on if several calls do not result in an eventual sale. As stated in Module 7, Honeywell Information Systems (HIS) allowed members of its salesforce to stop calling on any account they were not connecting with and pass it on to another HIS salesperson to try his or her luck creating a relationship with the buyer. Exhibit 8.4 summarizes some of the more common types of objections.

Using LAARC: A Process for Negotiating Buyer Resistance

The term **LAARC** is an acronym for listen, acknowledge, assess, respond, and confirm and describes an effective process for salespeople to follow to overcome sales resistance:

- **Listen:** Salespeople should listen to what their buyers are saying. The ever-present temptation to anticipate what buyers are going to say and cut them off with a premature response should be avoided. Learning to listen is important—it is more than just being polite or professional. Buyers are trying to tell the salesperson something that they consider important.

EXHIBIT 8.5	Questioning (Assess) to Overcome Sales Resistance

Example 1
Buyer: I'm not sure I am ready to act at this time.
Salesperson: Can you tell me what is causing your hesitation?

Example 2
Buyer: Your price seems to be a little high.
Salesperson: Can you tell me what price you had in mind? Have other suppliers quoted you a lower price?

Example 3
Buyer: Your delivery schedule does not work for us.
Salesperson: Who are you comparing me to? Can you please tell me what delivery schedule will work for your company?

- **Acknowledge:** As buyers complete their statements, salespeople should acknowledge that they received the message and that they appreciate and can understand the concern. Salespeople should not jump in with an instantaneous defensive response. Before responding, salespeople need a better understanding about what their buyers are saying. By politely pausing and then simply acknowledging their statement, salespeople set themselves up to be a reasonable person—a professional who appreciates other people's opinions. It also buys salespeople precious moments for composing themself and thinking of questions for the next step.

- **Assess:** This step is similar to assessment in the ADAPT process of questioning. This step in dealing with buyer resistance calls for salespeople to ask assessment questions to gain a better understanding of exactly what their buyers are saying and why they are saying it. Equipped with this information and understanding, salespeople are better able to make a meaningful response to the buyer's resistance. Exhibit 8.5 illustrates the type of assessment questions salespeople should ask when they encounter sales resistance.

- **Respond:** Based on his or her understanding of what and why the buyer is resisting, the salesperson can respond to the buyer's resistance. Structuring a response typically follows the method that is most appropriate for the situation. The more traditional methods for response include putting off the objection until a more logical time in the presentation, switching focus, using offsetting strategies, using denial, building value, and providing proof.

- **Confirm:** After responding, the salesperson should ask confirmatory questions— response checks to make sure that the buyer's concerns have been adequately met. Once this is confirmed, the presentation can proceed. In fact, experience indicates that this form of buyer confirmation is often a sufficient buying signal to warrant the salesperson's attempt to gain a commitment.

Once the salesperson has answered all the buyer's questions and has resolved resistance issues that have come up during the presentation, the salesperson should summarize all the pertinent buying signals.

Summarizing Solutions to Confirm Benefits

The mark of a good salesperson is the ability to listen and exactly determine the customer's needs. It is not unusual for salespeople to incorporate the outstanding benefits of their product into the sales presentation. A salesperson can identify many potential benefits for each product and feature. However, it does not make sense for a salesperson to talk about potential benefits that the buyer may not need. The salesperson must determine the confirmed benefits and make these the focal point of the sales summary before asking for the business. A salesperson must be alert to the one, two, or three benefits that generate the most excitement to the buyer. The confirmed benefits that are of greatest interest to the buyer deserve the greatest emphasis. These benefits should be summarized in such a way that the buyer sees a direct connection in what he or she has been telling the salesperson over the course of the selling cycle and the proposal being offered to meet his or her needs. Once this is done, it is time to ask for the business.

Securing Commitment and Closing

Ultimately, a large part of most salespeople's performance evaluation is based on their ability to gain customer commitment, often called closing sales. Because of this close relationship between compensation and getting orders, traditional selling has tended to overemphasize the importance of gaining commitment. In fact, there are those who think that just about any salesperson can find a new prospect, open a sale, or take an order. These same people infer it takes a trained, motivated, and skilled professional to close a sale. They go on to say that the close is the keystone to a salesperson's success, and a good salesperson will have mastered many new ways to close the sale. This outmoded emphasis on closing skills is typical of transaction selling techniques that stress making the sales call at all cost.

Another popular but outdated suggestion to salespeople is to "close early and often." This is particularly bad advice if the prospect is not prepared to make a decision, responds negatively to a premature attempt to consummate the sale, and then (following the principles of cognitive consistency) proceeds to reinforce the prior negative position as the salesperson plugs away, firing one closing salvo after another at the beleaguered prospect. Research tells us that it will take several sales calls to make an initial sale, so it is somewhat bewildering to still encounter such tired old battle cries as "the ABCs of selling which stand for Always Be Closing."

Manipulative closing gimmicks are less likely to be effective as professional buyers grow weary with the cat-and-mouse approach to selling that is still practiced by a surprising number of salespeople. It is also surprising to find many salespeople who view their customers as combatants over whom victory is sought. Once the sale is made by salespeople who have adversarial, me-against-you attitudes, the customer is likely to be neglected as the salesperson rides off into the sunset in search of yet another battle with yet another lowly customer.

One time-honored thought that does retain contemporary relevance is that "nobody likes to be sold, but everybody likes to buy." In other words, salespeople should facilitate decision making by pointing out a suggested course of action but should allow the prospect plenty of mental space within which a rational decision can be reached. Taken to its logical conclusion, this means that it may be acceptable to make a sales call without asking for the order. Salespeople must be cognizant, however, of their responsibility to advance the relationship toward a profitable sale, lest they become the most dreaded of all types of salespeople—the paid conversationalist.

It has already been mentioned that the salesperson has taken on the expanded roles of business consultant and relationship manager, which is not consistent with pressuring customers until they give in and say yes. Fortunately, things have changed to the point that today's professional salesperson attempts to gain commitment when the buyer is ready to buy. The salesperson should evaluate each presentation and attempt to determine the causes of its success or failure with the customer. The difference between closing and earning commitment is that commitment is more than just securing an order. Commitment insinuates the beginning of a long-term relationship.

Guidelines for Earning Commitment

Earning commitment or gaining commitment is the culmination of the selling process. However, it should not be viewed as a formal stage that only comes at the end of the presentation. Many salespeople fail to recognize early buyer commitment by focusing on their presentation and not the comments being made by the buyer. **Commitment signals** are favorable statements that may be made by the buyer, such as:

> I like that size.
> That will get the job done.
> The price is lower than I thought it would be.
> I didn't realize you delivered every day.

These statements should be considered green lights that allow the salesperson to move the process forward. They also may come in the form of trial commitments.

Throughout the presentation it is appropriate to determine a prospect's reaction to a particular feature or product. At this time, a trial commitment is a question designed to determine a prospect's reaction without forcing the prospect to make a final yes or no buying decision. The trial commitment is an effort to elicit how far along the prospect is in his or her decision making. Confirmation on the prospect's part on key features helps the salesperson determine how ready the prospect is to buy.

Open-ended questions are a good way to test prospect readiness. A salesperson might ask during his or her presentation, "What do you think of our computer's larger memory capacity?" The answer to this will help direct the salesperson to his or her next sales points. However, many statements made by buyers should be considered red lights, a formal objection. The salesperson must consider each of these objections and work to overcome them. Red light statements might include:

> I'm not sure that will work.
> The price is higher than I thought it would be.
> Your delivery schedule does not work for us.
> I don't see the advantage of going with your proposal.

Red light statements are commitment caution signals and must be resolved to the buyer's satisfaction before asking for a commitment. Closing early and often and having a closing quota for each sales call are traditional methods that are not liked by buyers. The salesperson should put himself or herself in the buyer's shoes and think about how he or she would like to be hammered with many closes throughout a sales presentation, particularly if a few red lights are introduced. Many times, the best method for earning commitment is to simply ask for the business. If the prospect has been qualified properly and a number of confirmed benefits have been uncovered, then the natural next step is to ask for the business. When does the salesperson ask for the business? When the buyer is ready to buy. The example in "Professional Selling in the 21st Century: To Close Sales—Ask Questions" describes why questioning is important to earning buyer commitment.

Techniques to Earn Commitment

Some sales trainers will try to teach their salesforces literally hundreds of commitment techniques. One trainer recommended to his salesforce that the salespeople learn two new commitment techniques per week. Then at the end of the year, they

---

To Earn Commitment—Ask Questions

Missy Rust of Glaxo-Welcome uses questions to help her earn commitment with her physicians.

I feel by asking the right questions most physicians will sell themselves with their answers. I believe in using these sales tools to gain the confidence of my physicians. I know these tools work and all salespeople can use them effectively. I use questioning skills in the following areas: Questions help me Qualify Prospects. A few questions can tell me quickly if this physician is a qualified prospect. They also help me Uncover Needs. By asking questions and understanding the physician's needs, I can determine which benefits the prospect will buy. Sometimes I will use a question to help me Clarify Needs. Some physicians don't really understand their own needs. It is my job to help the physician clarify his or her needs and help him or her make an informed choice about my products. Questions also help me To Gain Respect. Sophisticated prospects will want to know that I know what I am talking about. Knowing my market and my product or service and doing my homework about this prospect are important. Questions help me To Build Long-Term Relationships. I may perform fine on the first call, but what do I do for an encore? My goal is to keep my physicians I have for many years, I have to build relationships that endure. To do so, I must acquire a deeper understanding of their needs. Because I may be speaking with physicians many times and over many years, developing a list of questions helps me to return to them with fresh questions and ideas. I must also Involve the Physician. I ask questions that will help get and keep my physician's attention. An involved physician will tell me how to sell him or her. I let the physicians vent their feelings and ideas. I also use questions to establish rapport and a climate of trust and confidence. I always try to Maintain Control. Asking questions is a subtle way of controlling the sale without making your physician feel controlled. Questions lead rather than push. I try to create a positive atmosphere filled with agreement rather than conflict. Asking questions lets me evaluate how much interest a physician has and if the phyician or his or her company is in a position to buy at this time. I ask questions to lead toward the close and to determine if the physician is ready to take action. My physicians will let me know if they aren't ready to buy. Finally, I can't be afraid to ask the physicians for their business. I want my physicians to know I am serious about my proposal and when there is a good match between their patients' needs and my product offering, I expect them to use my offering.

---

would have more than 100 commitment techniques ready to use. Relationship managers today do not need many commitment techniques. A few good ones will suffice. Five techniques that are conducive to relationship building follow:

1. **Ask for the Order/Direct Commitment**

   It is not unusual for inexperienced salespeople to lose an order simply by not asking the customer to buy. Professional buyers report that an amazing number of salespeople fear rejection. When the buyer is ready to buy, the salesperson must be prepared to ask for the buyer's commitment. The direct commitment is a straightforward request for an order. A salesperson ought to be confident if he or she has covered all the necessary features and benefits of the product and matched these with the buyer's needs. At this time, the salesperson cannot be afraid to ask "Tom, can we set up an office visit for next week?" or "Mary, I'd like to have your business, if we can get the order signed today, delivery can take place early next week." Many buyers appreciate the direct approach. There is no confusion as to what the salesperson wants the buyer to do.

2. **Legitimate Choice/Alternative Choice**

   The legitimate choice asks the prospect to select from two or more choices. For example, will the HP 400 or the HP 600 be the one you want? An investment broker might ask his or her prospect, "Do you feel your budget would allow you to invest $1000 a month or would $500 a month be better?

| EXHIBIT 8.6 | T-Account Close |

Reasons to Buy	Reasons Not to Buy
• Daily delivery schedule meets our needs • Warranty agreement is longer than the one I have now (5 years versus 3 years) • You provide a training program • Your service department is located in our city	• Because of extra services Your price *is too high*

The theory behind this technique suggests buyers do not like to be told what to do but do like making a decision over limited choices.

3. **Summary Commitment**

A very effective way to gain agreement is to summarize all the major benefits the buyer has confirmed over the course of the sales calls. Salespeople should keep track of all the important points covered in previous calls so they can emphasize them again in summary form.

In using the **summary commitment** techniques, a computer salesperson might say:

Of course, Tom, this is an important decision, so to make the best possible choice, let's go over the major concepts we've discussed. We have agreed that Thompson Computers will provide some definite advantages. First, our system will lower your computing costs, second, our system will last longer, and has a better warranty, thus saving you money, and finally, your data processing people will be happier because our faster system will reduce their workload. They'll get to go home earlier each evening.

The summary commitment is a valuable technique in that it reminds prospects of all the major benefits that have been mentioned in previous sales calls.

4. **The T-Account or the Balance Sheet Commitment**

The **T-Account commitment** or balance sheet commitment is essentially a summary commitment on paper. With the T-account commitment, the sales representative takes out a sheet of paper and draws a large "T" across it. On the left-hand side, the salesperson and buyer brainstorm the reasons to buy. Here, the salesperson will list with the buyer all the positive selling points (benefits) they discussed throughout the selling process. Once this is completed, the salesperson asks the buyer for any reasons that he or she would not want to purchase. Visually, the left-hand side should help the buyer make his or her decision as seen in Exhibit 8.6. This will not work if the weight of the reason not to buy outweighs the reasons to buy. In the example in Exhibit 8.6, the buyer wants to act, but does not have the money at this time.

5. **Success Story Commitment**

Every company has many satisfied customers. These customers started out having problems, and the sales representative helped solve these problems by recommending the product or products that matched the customer's needs. Buyers are thankful and grateful when the salesperson helps solve problems. When the salesperson relates a story about how one of his or her customers had a similar problem and solved it by using the salesperson's product, a reluctant buyer can be reassured that the salesperson has done this before successfully. If the salesperson decides to use the customer's name and company, then the salesperson must be sure to get permission to do so. A success story commitment may go something like this:

EXHIBIT 8.7	Techniques to Earn Commitment

1. **Direct Commitment**—Simply ask for the order
2. **Legitimate Choice/Alternative Choice**—Give the prospect a limited number of choices
3. **Summary Commitment**—Summarize all the confirmed benefits that have been agreed to
4. **T-Account/Balance Sheet Commitment**—Summary close on paper
5. **Success Story Commitment**—Salesperson tells a story of a business that successfully solved a problem by buying his or her product

Tom, thanks for sharing your copier problems with me. I had another customer you might know, Betty Brown, who had the same problem over at Thompson Electronics. We installed the CP 2000 and eliminated the problem completely. Please feel free to give Betty a call. She is very happy with our solution.

Some companies will use the success-story commitment by actually taking the prospect to a satisfied customer. The salesperson may leave the prospect alone with the satisfied customer so the two can talk confidentially. A satisfied customer can help a salesperson earn commitment by answering questions a reluctant prospect needs answered before they can purchase. A summary of relationship-building earning commitment techniques can be found in Exhibit 8.7.

Probing to Earn Commitment

Every attempt to earn commitment will not be successful. Successful salespeople cannot be afraid to ask a prospect why he or she is hesitating to make a decision. It is the salesperson's job to uncover the reason why the prospect is hesitating by asking a series of questions that get at the key issues. For instance, a buyer may state that he or she is not ready to sign an order. The salesperson must ask, "Mary, there must be a reason why you are reluctant to do business with me and my company. Do you mind if I ask what it is?" The salesperson must then listen and respond accordingly. A salesperson cannot be afraid to ask why a prospect is reluctant to purchase.

Other Traditional Methods

Sales trainers across the nation teach hundreds of techniques to earn commitment. Exhibit 8.8 is a summary of the traditional commitment techniques. The vast majority of these are not conducive to building a strong buyer-seller relationship. As prospects become more sophisticated, most will be turned off by these techniques and they will be ineffective. "An Ethical Dilemma" describes a salesperson who puts too much emphasis on earning commitment in one sales call.

An Ethical Dilemma

Vivian Arnold has been selling now for more than 20 years. Her war cry is to close early and close often. Her college professor taught her to close a minimum of three times during any sales call. Her company's sales trainers have been on record proclaiming that a good call requires up to five closes. She recently bought a book on closing techniques in hopes of learning new methods to improve her closing ratio. What advice do you have for Vivian? How many earning commitment techniques should a good salesperson have ready to use on a sales call?

EXHIBIT 8.8	Traditional Commitment Method

Method	How to Use it
Standing-Room-Only Close	This close puts a time limit on the client in an attempt to hurry the decision to close. "These prices are only good until tomorrow."
Assumptive Close	The salesperson assumes that an agreement has been reached. The salesperson places the order form in front of the buyer and hands him or her a pen.
Fear or Emotional Close	The salesperson tells a story of something bad happening if the purchase is not made. "If you don't purchase this insurance and you die, your wife will have to sell the house and live on the street."
Continuous Yes Close	This close uses the principle that saying yes gets to be a habit. The salesperson asks a number of questions, each formulated so that the prospect answers yes.
Minor-Points Close	Seeks agreement on relatively minor (trivial) issues associated with the full order. "Do you prefer cash or charge?"

Sales Presentation Checklist

Many organizations are requiring their salesforces to use a sales presentation checklist to be sure that all the pertinent content areas are covered with each prospect. Information is needed from the prospect that will be used to customize the proposal presentation. Exhibit 8.9 illustrates the types of information that a salespeople should be collecting throughout the sales process. Section 1 covers specific information on the company name, key contact person, the buyer's job title, and the type of business. Many salespeople, when asked, are not sure from where their business is coming. By keeping track of this information, a salesperson may be able to identify from which industries and types of customers they are earning commitment. It is critically important to determine any others who may influence the purchase decision. What departments are involved? What role do they play? This information should be gathered and documented in part B. It is important that the salesperson make sure all the key players are receiving the appropriate information and getting the proper attention they deserve. A mistake often made by salespeople is not identifying all the buying influences.

Salespeople must take the time to uncover the prospect's needs. This can be done by determining a problem (e.g., not enough computer memory) or opportunity (e.g., plant expansion) (section 2, part A of the checklist). At this time, salespeople's ability to gather information is much more important than their ability to give information. A salesperson must refrain from dominating the sales conversation early on with product information before needs are uncovered. As needs are identified, a salesperson should match his or her product's solutions to the needs of the buyer to determine if they can solve the problem (section 2, part B). Salespeople should determine whether they have a good solution. Sometimes, it is in the salesperson's best interest to pass on the business and recommend a competitor's solution. This is a great way to build trust with a buyer.

Section 3 is a difficult area for salespeople to uncover. Rational buying motives may be easy to uncover when a buyer is simply trying to replace a broken copier. In this situation, there is a sense of urgency and a solution is needed quickly. **Emotional**

EXHIBIT 8.9   **Sales Presentation Checklist**

1. **PROSPECT INFORMATION**
A. **Key Person Information**

Company Name: _____   Type of Business: _____

Contact Person: _____   Job Title: _____

B. **Other Influences on the Purchase Decision**

Name(s)	*Department*	*Role in Purchase Decision*

2. **NEEDS AND/OR OPPORTUNITY ANALYSIS**
A.

Statement of prospect's problem and/or opportunity as related to sales offering

B.

Brief description of product or service that will meet the prospect's problem/opportunity

3. **PROSPECT'S BUYING MOTIVES**

Rational Motives	*Emotional Motives*

EXHIBIT 8.9   **Sales Presentation Checklist—cont'd.**

4. **COMPETITIVE SITUATION**

Competitor	Strengths	Weaknesses

Check whoever is currently supplying the product to the company if applicable

5. **SALES PRESENTATION OBJECTIVES**

Major Objectives	Minor Objectives

6. **SALES PRESENTATION PLANNING**
A. **Specific Features/Benefits**

Benefits to be stressed arranged in priority order (sequence to be followed in presentation)

B. **Information to Support Claims**

Information needed to support claims for each benefit

C. **Reinforcing Verbal Content (e.g., AV, collateral material, illustrations, testimonials)**

EXHIBIT 8.9   Sales Presentation Checklist—cont'd.

D.   First Few Minutes

Plans for the first few minutes of a sales presentation

Introduction _____

Need clarification _____

Statement of Purpose _____

Agenda of the Sales Call _____

E.   The ADAPT Method
Approach (Build rapport, then use ADAPT method)

Use questioning to gather information

Introduction, thanks, then: **Assessment** **Discovery** **Activation** **Projection** **Transition to Presentation**	_____ _____ _____ _____ _____ _____

F.   Questions and Objections

Anticipated Prospect questions and objections, and planned responses:

Questions and Objectives	*Responses*

motives are difficult for the salesperson and may never be uncovered. The buyer for one school corporation bought a copier from his wife's brother at his wife's insistence (e.g., emotional purchase). No one questioned the purchase because the brother had a different last name!

Understanding the competitive situation can make the bid process go more smoothly. Section 4 not only asks the salesperson to determine who the competition is but also asks him or her to identify competitors' strengths and weaknesses. Knowing who the competition is helps a salesperson determine how high or low he or she can go on a bid. The salesperson must also determine who is currently supplying the product to the company. This may tell the salesperson something about the buyer (e.g., buyer looks for high quality).

EXHIBIT 8.9   **Sales Presentation Checklist—cont'd.**

G. **Prospect Commitment**

A preliminary plan for how the prospect will be asked for a commitment related to the sales presentation objective:

H. **Follow-Up Action**

Statement of follow-up action needed to ensure that the buyer/seller relationship moves in a positive direction.

Section 5 asks the salesperson to determine the objective for his or her sales call. Salespeople must have an objective for each sales call. Many salespeople think there is only one objective and that is to get an order. Other sales objectives do exist. For instance, during an introductory call the objective may be simply to introduce the salesperson and his or her company and to gather information on the buyer's needs. Eventually, the major sales presentation objective will be to present the proposal for the buyer's acceptance. After the sale is made, the objective may be to follow up and determine whether the customer is satisfied with the salesperson's efforts. The salesperson can also look for openings to cover additional objectives. Gwen Tranguillo of Hershey's always looks for ways to introduce other products in her presentation if the buyer expresses interest. Gwen made a major sales presentation on a Halloween display of king-size candies and found the buyer very interested in adding more king sizes immediately. She shifted gears and gained commitment on the new king-size display and later in the presentation went back to her Halloween proposal.[4] At the very least, the heart of any presentation should be to advance the process toward an order.

Section 6 covers the sales presentation planning process. After the salesperson has gathered all the information needed (i.e., buyer has need, who are the competitors, and what are the specific sales presentation objectives), he or she must determine what specific feature/benefits are of interest to the buyer (part A). Those features/benefits of high importance to the buyer should be covered first. It may only take one or two benefits to gain commitment. The salesperson should look for buying signals as each feature/benefit is explained. During this stage, the salesperson should be using information (e.g., satisfied clients, success stories) to support the claims for each benefit (part B). The salesperson must be able to support competitive claims for each benefit that he or she discusses with the customer (i.e., how does this benefit compare to your competitors?). The salesperson will not always be asked to provide support for claims he or she makes, but he or she must be prepared to offer support for competitive claims if asked to do so by the customer. Different ways to support competitive claims include testimonials from satisfied customers, third-party information as provided by research studies or trade publications, and any other type of evidence that the salesperson may develop to support his or her claims.

The salesperson should have at his or her disposal visual sales aids that can help sell a point (section 6, part C in the checklist). Salespeople must realize that although what they say is important, it is extremely critical to pay attention to how they say it and how they illustrate it with appropriate sales tools. The salesperson should be cautious with the use of humor, taking care to avoid anything that may be exploitative, tactless, or self-deprecating.

Salespeople should remember that sales tools are to be used only to make the sales message more credible, more clear, and more memorable. They should support the main points in the presentation rather than bombard the prospect with information. Too many illustrations, films, and demonstrations can confuse the prospect and be counterproductive to the sales effort.

Part D of section 6 emphasizes the need to plan very carefully before going in to see a prospect or customer. During the first few minutes of the sales call, the salesperson must establish rapport with the prospect, focus his or her attention on the offering, and make a smooth transition into the presentation. The salesperson must be sure that he or she properly introduces himself or herself when calling on a new prospect. During the first few minutes of the sales call, it is recommended that the salesperson use questions to get the prospect involved in the call and that the salesperson listen very carefully to what the prospect has to say about his or her situation. Salespeople should be positive and friendly here and throughout the sales presentation. The salesperson should tell the customer why he or she is making the call. This helps to establish an agenda and put the customer at ease. The salesperson should be flexible and willing to adjust if the customer has other ideas about the agenda. Salespeople only have a few minutes to make a good first impression with the buyer. Planning the first few minutes can help guarantee things get started well early in the sales call.

Eventually, the salesperson will ask questions to assess the buyer's needs. The ADAPT method should be followed closely to determine the buyer's interest and awareness of the salesperson's offering (section 6, part E). Good salespeople have thought about and practiced responses to common questions and objections that they are typically asked. Salespeople should rarely be caught off guard with questions and objections that they cannot answer (section 6, part F). Once questions have been adequately answered, this is a good time to look for commitment opportunities. As the buyer sees that his or her preliminary concerns are not concerns at all (e.g., salesperson explains deliveries can be made daily), then the salesperson must be ready to ask for the business (section 6, part G).

Finally, the salesperson must always be looking for ways to enhance the relationship and move it in a positive direction (section 6, part H). The salesperson should always make a note of any promises that he or she has made during the sales calls and especially during the proposal presentation. The buyer may ask for information that the salesperson is not prepared to give during the presentation. By taking notes, the salesperson ensures that the appropriate follow-up activities will happen.

This sales presentation checklist is an extremely useful tool for all salespeople and especially to inexperienced salespeople. It guarantees that all the appropriate steps are covered and all the pertinent information needed is collected. Using a sales presentation checklist will make the task of customizing the sales presentation easier.

Summary

1. *Discuss how salespeople select appropriate customer offerings by assessing customer needs.* Questioning and listening are the keys to needs analysis and confirmation. Needs analysis should enable the salesperson to state the customer's problem or opportunity as related to the salesperson's sales offering. The ability to match relevant features and benefits to the needs of the buyer is critical to the salesperson's success.

2. *Discuss the different types of sales presentations and what goes into their planning.* The three types of presentations most organizations use are canned presentations, organized presentations, and written sales proposals. Canned presentations include scripted sales calls, memorized presentations, and automated presentations. Most canned presentations have been tested for effectiveness with real customers before they are used by the entire salesforce. Canned presentations are usually complete and logically structured. Objectives are anticipated in advance, and appropriate responses can be formulated as part of the presentation.

   Organized presentations best address individual customers and different selling situations. A salesperson must be prepared to adapt to each prospect's specific needs. Only those benefits that meet that specific buyer's needs will be addressed.

   A written sales proposal is a complete, self-contained sales presentation. A sales proposal should be prepared after the salesperson has made a thorough assessment of the buyer's situation as it relates to the seller's offering.

3. *List and explain the different tools that can be used to customize a sales presentation.* Salespeople can use a number of different tools. Visual aids help customize and dramatize the presentation. Charts can be used to show trends and illustrate relationships. Catalogs and brochures can help salespeople communicate to the buyer key points of a salesperson's company and products. Finally, electronic media can be used to customize graphical presentations by using laptop computers, videos, slides, and overhead transparencies.

4. *Explain how a salesperson can link solutions to needs by using features, potential benefits, and confirmed benefits.* A feature is a factual statement about a characteristic of a product or service being sold. A potential benefit describes how the product or service may meet a customer need that is assumed to be important by the salesperson. Many traditional salespeople assume all potential benefits are important to the prospect and talk about things that are irrelevant to the buyer. A good salesperson must listen carefully for the prospect or customer to acknowledge the importance of a benefit to his or her buying situation. The salesperson must link his or her product offerings to the confirmed benefits of the buyer.

5. ***Explain why prospects raise objections.*** Some prospects are happy with their present suppliers and want to avoid the sales interview. In other instances, the salesperson has failed to properly qualify the prospect. A prospect who has recently purchased a product is probably not in the market for another. Sometimes, prospects simply lack information on the salesperson's product category and they are uncomfortable making a decision.

6. ***Describe the different types of objections.*** Typically, objections include "The price is too high," "I have no money," "Product quality is poor," "I am concerned about poor service," "I had a bad experience with your company many years ago."

7. ***Explain how the LAARC method can be used to overcome buyer resistance.*** LAARC allows the salesperson to carefully listen to what the buyer is saying. It allows the salesperson to better understand the buyer's objections. After this careful analysis, the salesperson can then respond. The buyer feels the salesperson is responding to his or her specific concern rather than giving a pat answer.

8. ***List and explain the earning commitment techniques that enhance relationship building.*** Many techniques can be used to earn commitment. Most are gimmicky in nature and reinforce the notion of traditional selling. Successful relationship-building techniques include the summary commitment, the success story commitment, and the direct commitment or ask for the order.

9. ***Discuss the importance of using a sales presentation checklist.*** The sales presentation checklist is extremely useful to inexperienced salespeople. It guarantees that all the appropriate steps of the sales process are covered and all pertinent information is collected. Using the checklist will make the task of customizing the sales presentation easier.

Understanding Professional Selling Terms

- Canned presentations
- Organized presentations
- Written sales proposals
- Charts and graphs
- Catalogs
- Brochures
- Computer-based presentation
- Videos
- Slides
- Overhead transparencies
- Sales portfolios
- Feature
- Potential benefits
- Confirmed benefits
- Sales resistance
- Product objections
- LAARC
- Commitment Signals
- Summary commitment
- Emotional motives

Developing Professional Selling Knowledge

1. Why is it important for salespeople to uncover their prospect's or customer's needs?
2. Do you see the need for any salesperson to ever use a canned sales presentation?
3. Shouldn't salespeople make sure they cover all their product features so their buyers do not miss any?
4. Some trainers have been heard to say, "If a salesperson gets sales resistance, then he or she has not done a very good job during the sales presentation explaining things." Do you agree with this?
5. Under what circumstances does a salesperson want sales resistance?
6. What are the advantages to a salesperson to use visual aids during a sales presentation?
7. Some trainers and sales experts think that closing is the most important stage of the sales process. Do you feel this way?
8. Shouldn't a good salesperson have many closing techniques ready to use during a sales call? Explain.
9. Can the LAARC method be used for all types of sales resistance? Explain.
10. What are the advantages to a salesperson to use a sales presentation checklist?

Developing Professional Selling Skills

1. Please respond to the following statements:
   a) What is the main objective of a good presentation?
   b) How long should a good presentation be?
   c) Why are questions an important part of a presentation?
   d) When should you terminate a presentation?
   e) How should you terminate a sales call?

2. The salesperson's appearance and manner must convey a favorable impression. Within the first few minutes that the prospect and the salesperson are together, the prospect makes judgments that will have a direct effect on the interaction to follow. The first few words the salesperson says set the tone of the entire presentation. There are several approaches that can be used to gain the prospect's interest and attention.
   a) Introduction—The sales rep states his or her name and the name of the company.
   What are the strengths and weaknesses of this opening?
   b) Referral—Start out by mentioning that so-and-so suggested the prospect would be interested in your product.
   What are the strengths and weaknesses of this opening?
   c) Question—Asking a meaningful question gets the prospect's attention, encourages a response, and initiates two-way communication.
   What are the strengths and weaknesses of this opening?
   d) Benefit—Focus the prospect's attention on a product benefit.
   What are the strengths and weaknesses of this opening?
   e) Curiosity—Arouse interest by making an unexpected comment to intrigue the prospect.
   What are the strengths and weaknesses of this opening?
   f) Compliment—Offer a sincere and specific compliment.
   What are the strengths and weaknesses of this opening?
   g) Shock—Get attention by using a gimmick or a shocking statement.
   What are the strengths and weaknesses of this opening?
   h) Develop an approach that uses a combination of the preceding methods.
   What are the strengths and weaknesses of this opening?
   Which methods did you select to combine? Why?

3. Explain why each of the following statements would be considered a signal commitment.
   a) The prospect makes a positive statement.
   b) A worried look is replaced by a happy look.
   c) The prospect starts playing with a pen or the order form.
   d) The prospect looks at the product with a favorable expression.
   e) The prospect touches the product.
   f) The prospect is using or trying out the product.
   g) The prospect's tone of voice changes or his or her body relaxes.
   h) The prospect questions price, usage, or delivery.

4. Using the following list, address each of the indicated buyer objections by using the LAARC process. The Listen step is implicit and omitted from the written responses. Take time to write out your answers. Responses will be used in class discussion.
   a.) Your price is too high.
   Acknowledge
   Assess
   Respond
   Confirm
   b.) I like what I see, but I need to talk with my boss before I do anything.
   Acknowledge
   Assess
   Respond
   Confirm

c.) I just don't think we need it; we already use your competitor's products and they work all right.
Acknowledge
Assess
Respond
Confirm

d.) I'm just not sure our employees can adapt to the new technology.
Acknowledge
Assess
Respond
Confirm

e.) The last time we bought from your company we had problems with product reliability.
Acknowledge
Assess
Respond
Confirm

Making Professional Selling Decisions

CASE 8.1   *The Overhead Door Company*

Mary Tyler sells for The Overhead Door Company. She has sold garage doors to contractors and individual home-owners for two years. When Mary first began selling, she used to introduce herself and the name of her company. Next, she made a brief opening remark and then moved quickly into her presentation. Although this resulted in selling many garage doors, Mary thought that there must be a better method.

Questions

1. What can you recommend to Mary to strengthen the introduction of her sales calls?
2. If Mary is successful using her present method, why should she change?

CASE 8.2   *Thompson Engineering*

Tyler Houston sells for Thompson Engineering. He has been calling on Hudson Distributors for close to two years. Over the course of 15 calls, he has sold them nothing to date. He thinks that he is extremely close to getting an order. Tyler knows that Hudson is happy with its present supplier, but he is aware that they have received some late deliveries. Tom Harris, Hudson's senior buyer, has given every indication that he likes Tyler's products and Tyler.

During Tyler's most recent call, Tom told him that he'd have to have a couple of weeks to go over Tyler's proposal. Tom really didn't have any major objections during the presentation. Tyler knows his price, quality, and service are equal to or exceed Hudson's present supplier.

Questions

1. Tom told Tyler that he needed a couple of weeks to think about his proposal. How should Tyler handle this?
2. What should Tyler have done during the sales presentation when Tom told him that he needed to think it over?
3. What techniques should Tyler have used to overcome the forestalling tactic?

Expanding Customer Relationships

Building Goodwill

Mary Grant has been given the top award that her company gives for building goodwill with her customers. She ranks the highest of 600 sales reps for customer satisfaction with her 200 accounts. Mary has been able to blend calls on prospects with calls on existing customers to keep her new business growing and keep her existing accounts as repeat purchasers. Mary has been asked what her secret to success is. She shared her secrets at a recent national sales meeting.

I am flattered that I am here today talking about how I balance my workload of existing customers with bringing in new business each year. First, let me say that there is not a stronger tool that a salesperson has to use than personal visits to see a new customer or call on a hot prospect. I try to make eight calls a day or 40 calls per week and I generally make 20 calls on my existing customers and 20 calls on prospects. This may vary depending on who will see me in any given week. I have made as many as 30 calls on existing customers in a week and as few as 10. You may remember last year when we introduced the software upgrade, I personally called on all 200 of my accounts in one month and didn't make a single call for new business. I felt my existing customers needed assurance from me the upgrade would go smoothly and if they had any trouble I was only a phone call away. I like to use personal follow-up to keep my customers informed of new developments, new products, and our new applications and upgrades. Providing this information has paved the way for additional sales. I want to make a very important point, I have to bring value to each of these calls, I don't stay too long, I make my points, answer questions, and thank my customers for their time. We do some talking about personal things, but I do not allow these sessions to turn into chit-chat sessions. The second thing I try to do each month is touch all of my prospects with another form of communication. Some of my bigger clients get telephone calls once or twice per month. The cell phone is a wonderful tool. I have e-mail addresses on 175 of my customers, and I use the e-mail to provide useful information when I can. I love to send faxes to my customers, especially if I have important information to pass on. I get a sense that any customer feels a fax has a certain urgency to it and it gets read more often.

I try to also write handwritten notes when customers place big orders, thanking them for their business. I write other notes when I notice things about my customers who have accomplished something such as a promotion. They are always glad I noticed and took the time to recognize them. I try to keep all my call report notes up to date so I remember birthdays or special events in my customers' lives.

As you can see, it is not just one thing I do to follow up with my customers. I have to be well organized to orchestrate all of this, but I feel it is well worth it.

I then take all of these ideas and try to do as many as I can with my prospects to build relationships with them. This has worked for me over the past 10 years. If done properly, they can work for you. Follow-up is the key to success for any salesperson.

Thank you for this award.

After completing this module, you should be able to

1 Explain how to follow up to assess customer satisfaction

2 Explain how to harness technology to enhance follow-up and buyer-seller relationships

3 Discuss how to take action to assure customer satisfaction

4 Discuss how to maintain open, two-way communication

5 Explain how to encourage critical encounters

6 Discuss how to expand collaborative involvement

7 Explain how to add value and enhance mutual opportunities

EXHIBIT 9.1	Relationship Enhancers and Detractors

Enhancers	*Detractors*
Focus on Long Term	Focus on Short Term
Deliver more than Salesperson Promises	Over Promise—Underdeliver
Call Regularly	Call Sporadically
Add Value	Show Up for Another Order
Keep Communication Lines Open	Can never Reach Salesperson
Take Responsibility for Problems	Lie, Exaggerate, Blame Someone Else

In traditional selling, salespeople too often thought that their job was over when they closed the sale. Once the order was obtained, they moved on to the next prospect. Any follow-up or customer service was minimal. The lifeline of an organization today is repeat business. It is important to acquire new customers, but it is critical to keep your existing customer base happy. Not following up with a new customer is a shortsighted attitude toward selling, for it fails to consider the importance of developing and maintaining a customer for your company.

There are several ways that a salesperson can convert new customers into highly committed lifetime customers. Examples include (1) **building goodwill** by continually **adding value** to the product, (2) handling complaints in a timely and thoughtful manner, (3) processing requests for rush deliveries willingly and letting the customer know that the salesperson will do everything he or she can to make that request happen. However, it is just as easy for a salesperson to alienate a new customer by putting the focus on the short-term order and not the long-term activities that create a partnership. This can be done by (1) overpromising and underdelivering; (2) using exaggeration to get an order; and (3) blaming everyone else for problems. Exhibit 9.1 reviews relationship enhancers and detractors that can strengthen or destroy a relationship.

Relationship-oriented salespeople are creating bonds with their customers that will partially isolate them from competitive pressures or at least minimize the importance of easily altered and matched competitive variables such as price. This module explains the importance of follow-up to assess customer satisfaction. Next, harnessing technology to enhance follow-up and buyer-seller relationships is covered. This is followed by a discussion of why it is the salesperson's job to take action (i.e., proactive) before problems arise and not wait for complaints (i.e., reactive). Within the context of resolving complaints, a procedure to handle complaints is presented. This is followed by a discussion of the importance of collaborative involvement and working to add value for the buyer. Finally, the value of customer service is reviewed.

Following Up to Assess Customer Satisfaction

The importance of a diligent effort to maintain and enhance customer relationships is reflected in a survey of corporate buyers who were asked to identify the No. 1 activity of salespeople that annoyed them the most. Their response? "Lack of follow through."[1] Comments such as this indicate the emphasis on maintaining and enhancing customer relationships is definitely increasing.

John Haack, senior vice-president of marketing and sales for Ball-Foster (a glass container manufacturer), knows the importance of enhancing customer relationships as opposed to focusing solely on current sales. With such customers as

Anheuser-Busch, Quaker Oats, and Kraft, Haack says, "Making the sale is only the beginning. After that, you have to keep track of the process every step of the way. You have to make sure the product gets delivered on time and that everyone involved with the customer knows their customer's expectations." Haack continues, "Anybody can move product. I can go out and sell a ton of something, but if it's not right for that particular customer, it's just going to end up back on my doorstep as a major problem."[2]

Clearly, professional salespeople such as John Haack view their customer base as far too valuable an asset to risk losing it through neglect. In maintaining and enhancing customer relationships, salespeople such as Mary Grant in the opening vignette are involved in performing routine postsale follow-up activities and in enhancing the relationship as it evolves by anticipating and adapting to changes in the customers situation, competitive forces, and other changes in the market environment. Mary calls on 20 existing accounts per week. Only by doing this can she be sure that she is meeting her customers' needs.

Mary's objective in this step is to create a strong bond with her customers that will diminish the probability of her customers' terminating the relationship. In effect, she earns the business through a number of successive trials and strengthens her position as time passes through follow-up calls and by adding value.

Furthering this notion, Darrell Beaty of Ontario Systems (a collection software company) states, "We spend too much time and effort learning about our prospects to not follow through and assess satisfaction." Figure 9.1 demonstrates the time and commitment Ontario puts in to earn an order from a prospect. Darrell states, "We cannot be afraid to ask a customer, 'How are we doing?'" This practice should go on monthly, quarterly, and yearly. Sometimes, the salesperson will not like the answers that he or she gets from the customers. New customers generally feel special because they have received a lot of attention. Older customers may feel neglected because the salesperson has many new customers and cannot be as attentive as he

---

FIGURE 9.1   **Ontario Systems Call Strategy**

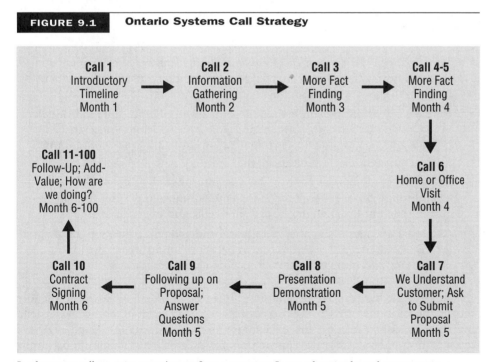

It takes many calls to earn commitment from a prospect. It can take months and even years to establish the trust needed to earn an order.

or she was previously. Routine follow-up questions, such as, "How are we doing?" can go a long way in letting a customer know the salesperson cares and is willing to make sure the customer is satisfied.

Harness Technology to Enhance Follow-Up and Buyer-Seller Relationships

While much attention has been given to the benefits and competitive advantages resulting from enhanced buyer-seller relationships, recent research indicates that there is still much room for improvement. Consider for example:

- Most Fortune 500 companies lose 50 percent of their customers in five years.[3]
- The average company communicates only four times per year with their customers and six times a year with their prospects.[4]
- It costs seven to ten times more to acquire a new customer than it does to retain an existing customer.[5]
- A 5 percent increase in customer retention can increase profits 25 to 125 percent.[6]

Indeed, building buyer-seller relationships is easier said than done. Building and nurturing customer relationships demands that salespeople do more than simply discover the buyer's needs and respond to them with a sales offering that resolves those needs. Relationships are formed over time through multiple buyer-seller interactions in which the seller wins the trust of the buyer. This emphasizes the importance of effective follow-up by the salesperson. As discussed in this module and illustrated in Figure 9.2, effective salesperson follow-up should include specific components designed to interact, connect, know, and relate with their customers.

- **Interact**   The salesperson acts to maximize the number of critical encounters with buyers in order to encourage effective dialogue and involvement between the salesperson and buyer.
- **Connect**   The salesperson maintains contact with the multiple individuals in the buying organization influencing purchase decisions and manages the various touch points the customer has in the selling organization to assure consistency in communication.
- **Know**   The salesperson coordinates and interprets the information gathered through buyer-seller contact and collaboration to develop insight regarding the buyer's changing situation, needs, and expectations.
- **Relate**   The salesperson applies relevant understanding and insight to create value-added interactions and generate relationships between the salesperson and buyer.

Salespeople have employed a variety of technology based salesforce automation tools in order to better track the increasingly complex combination of buyer-seller interactions and to manage the exchange, interpretation, and storage of diverse types of information. Among the more popular salesforce automation tools are the many competing versions of PC-based software applications designed to record and manage customer contact information. Applications such as ACT!, Maximizer, and

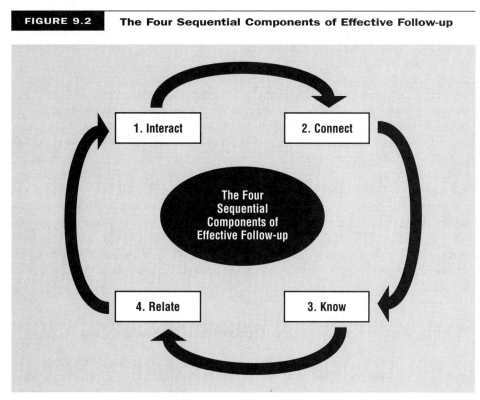

FIGURE 9.2   **The Four Sequential Components of Effective Follow-up**

Effective salesperson follow-up should include specific components designed to interact, connect, know and relate with their customers.

Goldmine enable salespeople to collect, file, and access comprehensive databases detailing information about individual buyers and buying organizations. In addition to providing explicit details about customers and the multiple individuals influencing purchasing decisions within any given account, these databases also provide an archive of the interactions and purchasing decisions taking place over time. Salespeople using these systems have found them to be invaluable in helping them track and better service their accounts in order to assure and enhance customer satisfaction. By better understanding every transaction and buyer-seller interaction, salespeople can be more effective in communicating with each individual customer throughout the lifetime of the account.

The advent of the Internet has allowed these customer-contact management tools to be enabled for use in multi-organization Intranets and Extranets. An Intranet is an organization's dedicated and proprietary computer network offering password controlled access to people within and outside the organization (e.g., customers and suppliers). Extranets are proprietary computer networks created by an organization for use by the organization's customers or suppliers and linked to the organization's internal systems, informational databases, and Intranet.

Internet activated and integrated with an organization's Intranet and Extranets, customer contact systems are transposed to full customer relationship management (CRM) systems. These systems dynamically link buyers and sellers into a rich communication network not previously possible. Salespeople and buyers have immediate, 24-by-7 access to one another and one another's organizations. Problems can be resolved online, routine ordering procedures can be automated, and information such as product brochures and spec sheets, inventory availability, price lists, and order status can be exchanged. Salespeople can use the Web to view everything that is relevant to any account. This can include information in the organization's databases (i.e., purchasing history, credit rating) as well as pertinent information such as news stories, stock prices, and research reports from sources outside the organization (Hoovers, Standard & Poor's, etc.).

These new customer relationship management systems enable salespeople to build and integrate multiple forms of customer information and create highly influential customer interactions that establish and reinforce long-term, profitable relationships. The benefits to salespeople learning to effectively use these advanced, integrated systems are self-evident. Every time a salesperson and buyer interact in a positive manner, the corresponding relationship is enriched. This enrichment translates to improved service levels, increased customer satisfaction, and enhanced revenues from loyal customers. The experience of Marriott Worldwide demonstrates the potential for salespeople adapting and using these integrated systems. Six months after Marriott's salespeople began using such a system, sales rose by 25 percent—all of which was attributed to the use of advanced salesforce automation enabling salespeople to track interactions with each customer and document each potential opportunity.[7]

Taking Action to Assure Customer Satisfaction

Exhibit 9.2 illustrates the partnership enhancement activities and the salesperson's responsibility that goes along with them. Specific relationship enhancement activities vary substantially from company to company but are critical to the success of building long-term relationships. These activities include

- Providing useful information
- Expediting orders and monitoring installation
- Training customer personnel
- Correcting billing errors
- Remember the customer after the sale
- Resolving complaints

EXHIBIT 9.2	Relationship Enhancement Activities
Partnership Enhancement Activities	*Salesperson Responsibility*
Provide useful information	• Relevant • Timely • High quality
Expedite orders/monitoring installation	• Track orders' status • Inform on delays • Help with installation
Train Customer Personnel	• Train even when contract does not call for it
Correct Billing Errors	• Go over all orders • Correct problem before customer recognizes it
Remembering the Customer after the Sale	• Set up a regular call schedule • Let customer know you'll be back
Resolve Complaints	• Preferably before they happen • Ask customer how he or she wants complaint resolved

FIGURE 9.3	Traditional versus Relational Sales Process

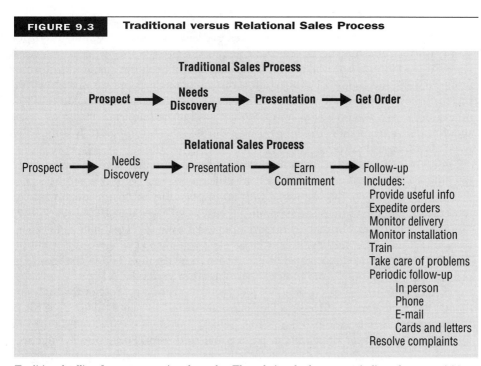

Traditional Sales Process

Prospect → Needs Discovery → Presentation → Get Order

Relational Sales Process

Prospect → Needs Discovery → Presentation → Earn Commitment → Follow-up
Includes:
Provide useful info
Expedite orders
Monitor delivery
Monitor installation
Train
Take care of problems
Periodic follow-up
In person
Phone
E-mail
Cards and letters
Resolve complaints

Traditional selling focuses on getting the order. The relational sales process indicated many activities must take place after the sale.

Traditional selling focused on getting the order. In a sense, the sales process was over once the order was signed. The salesperson's job was to focus on getting the next order and it was left to others in the organization to deliver and install the product. However, the relational sales process shown in Figure 9.3 indicates that many activities must take place after the sale, and it is the salesperson's responsibility to oversee and participate in all the follow-up activities. By being actively involved during this stage, the salesperson increases the odds that a long-term relationship will develop.

Providing Useful Information

Many buyers feel neglected once they place an order with a company. They were given a lot of attention before they placed the order, but once the order has been placed, the salesperson disappears. Once an economic relationship is established, the salesperson must continually provide timely, relevant, high-quality information to his or her customers. The job of educating the buyer never stops, and salespeople are responsible for updating customers and pointing out additional opportunities that will benefit them. By providing useful information, the salesperson is demonstrating commitment to the buyer. The salesperson is expressing the notion that he or she is in the relationship for the long term and he or she values the partnership. The salesperson should not only remember to provide information to the buyer but also to the secretaries, receptionists, department heads, and other influential members of the buyer's organization.

Several postsale follow-up methods can be used to provide useful information. The best way to provide useful information is by a personal visit. After the sale is made, it is critical to follow up personally and make sure the customer is completely satisfied with all the promises that have been made (e.g., delivery, installation done properly, courteous installers). This is the only strategy that provides face-to-face communication. When a salesperson takes the time to make a well-planned personal visit to follow up, he or she indicates to the prospect that he or she really cares. A good salesperson will use the follow-up call to keep the customer informed of new developments in the industry, new products, or new applications. Providing this information may bring about future sales. When a salesperson makes a follow-up call, he or she should always have an objective for the sales call. The salesperson should be sure not to stay too long with gossip sessions or chit-chat. It is the salesperson's job to add value.

An efficient option for providing useful information after a sale is by using the telephone. The telephone is a quick and efficient way to contact customers. The cell phone has provided salespeople with an opportunity to stay in touch with customers while on the road. A salesperson can easily make seven to 10 phone calls per hour, and the cost is minimal. Although a personal note to a customer is always appropriate, the telephone has the advantage of a two-way exchange of information. The phone can be used to verify delivery, inform the customer of any changes (e.g., price, delivery schedule), and check for problems in general.

E-mail is another way to stay in touch with a customer. Most individuals and companies have e-mail addresses. The salesperson has to make this part of his or her information-gathering process. When getting pertinent company and buyer information, the salesperson should also get e-mail addresses. Some buyers will check their e-mail and respond daily; others will not check and respond to theirs for weeks. The salesperson must determine which buyers like to use e-mail and make it part of his or her follow-up process when dealing with these customers.

Finally, a handwritten thank-you card to a customer is an inexpensive and convenient form of customer follow-up. It should always be used in conjunction with the other follow-up methods. The mail can also be used to send out new promotional material, information about new products, and trade publication articles that may be of interest to customers, and periodically, a salesperson could send his or her customers a short survey that asks "How are we doing?" Exhibit 9.3 summarizes the strengths and weaknesses of follow-up methods. Checking the customers' level of satisfaction might highlight an area of customer concern for the customers that the salesperson can take care of before it becomes a major problem.

EXHIBIT 9.3	Methods to Provide Useful Information	
Method	*Strength*	*Weakness*
1. Personal Call	Best for interactive face-to-face communication; view body language	Most time-consuming Most expensive Customers won't always see salesperson
2. Telephone	Can make 7–10 calls per hour Cell phones allow call to be made from anywhere Inexpensive Immediate feedback	May interrupt your customers Can't evaluate facial expressions
3. Mail	One more touch that lets the customers know you are thinking about them	Customers get a lot of mail Customer may not see it if secretary opens mail and tosses One-way communication
4. E-mail	Easy to get many touches Inexpensive Not time-consuming	Customer may not read e-mail every day One-way communication

---

PROFESSIONAL SELLING IN THE 21ST CENTURY

Follow Up and Follow Through

Stephanie Ulrich, sales representative for Hormel Foods, states,

Follow-up and follow-through are the most important things I do once I get a contract signed. I establish a follow-up schedule with each of my customers. They know when to expect to see me and how often. They have my cell phone number for emergencies.

I really take advantage of the fax, if I can give my customers special pricing for a weekend, I'll fax it in and follow it up with a phone call. I wouldn't be able to reach everyone personally. This way, all my customers get my best price, and they also know I am really working for them.

Brett Carrington, salesperson for Wallace, knows that personalized service is the best way to stay in touch with his customers. He states,

It is a lot easier to get a feel for what is going on with a buyer and his or her company if I can meet the buyer in person. Some customers can't take the time to see me. I now have e-mail addresses for more than 80 percent of my customers. They get at least one e-mail contact from me per week. My customers know that I check my e-mail daily and can send me messages and complaints. I follow up immediately. There are times when my customers are busy and can't take my phone call. Not only will I e-mail a response to their problem, but I will also fax them a hard copy. One of my customers wanted some numbers to show her boss, and I had a fax out in less than 20 minutes. I want my customers to know that I care.

Customer preference should determine the method of communication. The salesperson should find the methods that work with individual customers and stay with them. "Professional Selling in the 21st Century: Follow Up and Follow Through" gives two salespeople's opinions on the importance of follow-up and how they accomplish this.

Expediting Orders and Monitoring Installation

Generally, salespeople will set estimates on product delivery times. The salesperson must work to prevent a delay in delivery. The salesperson's job is to track the order status and inform the customers when there are delays. It is unpleasant to inform a buyer of a delay, but the information allows buyers to work around the inconvenience and plan accordingly. Waiting until the delivery date to announce a delay is inconsiderate and hurts the trust built between the salesperson and buyer.

Many problems with shipping and the delivery of an order are out of the salesperson's control. However, today's sophisticated tracking systems allow salespeople to track orders and find out what is causing the delay. The salesperson must keep the customer up to date on the delivery status and any possible delays.

Monitoring order processing and after-sale activities is critical to enhancing the relationship with a customer. Customers often have done a poor job of forecasting and end up expecting their salesperson to bring their emergency to a happy conclusion. Although it is not always possible to speed up orders, the salesperson should investigate and attempt to do everything in his or her power to help the customers. If the buyer sees concern on the salesperson's part and knows the salesperson is attempting to help the buyer, then the relationship will be strengthened, even if the order cannot be pushed through as quickly as the buyer had hoped.

Depending on the industry, salespeople generally do not help with installation. Nevertheless, some salespeople believe that it is in their best interest to supervise the installation process and to be available when customers have questions. Typically, installers do not have the same relationship with the customer and may not have the type of personality to deal with difficult situations. The salesperson can act as the buffer between the installation team and the customers.

Training Customer Personnel

Companies are always looking for ways to gain a competitive advantage. Once the order is placed, traditional salespeople are happy to get their commission or bonus and move on to their next conquest. Relationship managers understand the real work begins once the order is signed. Training customer personnel may or may not be included in the price terms of the agreement. Salespeople may use this to gain the competitive edge they need. For example, instead of only training one person as stated in the sales terms, the salesperson gladly trains three people for the same price. Adding value should always be a priority with any salesperson.

When the product is technical, customer training may require the assistance of the company trainer or engineer. The salesperson still has a key role as he or she knows the customer best and should serve as the facilitator to make sure all the parties have been properly introduced and started off in a positive manner. The salesperson should schedule the training sessions as conveniently as possible for the customer. Customer education is an integral part of the marketing strategy of Ontario Systems Corporation, a collections software company. What separates Ontario from its competitors is its ability to provide timely training and education for all its customers. Ontario knows service after the sale is crucial and that is why it provides an 800 telephone number for 24-hour service. Each year, Ontario strengthens its relationship with the customers by providing one week of training, seminars, and goodwill at their home office. Ontario understands the importance of the team approach to providing outstanding customer service. "Professional Selling in the 21st Century: Stay in Touch with Customers" describes Darrell Beaty's approach to managing customer service for his team and customers.

Correcting Billing Errors

Billing errors could turn into customer complaints if not found in a timely fashion and corrected. A salesperson should go over all orders and billing records to ensure

---

PROFESSIONAL SELLING IN THE 21ST CENTURY

Stay in Touch with Customers

Darrell Beaty, national account manager for Ontario Systems Corporation, understands the importance of staying in touch with his customers. He offers the following advice:

Always be a team player. Your success over the long haul depends on the efforts of different people within your organization (e.g., field engineers, technical support staff, customer service reps). Those people will go the extra mile for you and your accounts if you become a team player for them. I like to do special things for my teammates (e.g., buy pizza for lunch for the field engineers, bring in donuts for the customer service reps).

A good salesperson must also plan the service strategy. Brainstorm what it will take to delight your customer, then use all the resources you can to make sure it happens. The more carefully you plan, the more resources you will be able to tap to meet your goals. I must always be trustworthy and resolve problems promptly. It is critically important to continually provide my customers with worthwhile information. I have to let them know I am always thinking about them.

proper billing has been sent to the customer. A customer will know the salesperson has his or her best interest in mind if the salesperson corrects problems without being prompted by the customer.

Remembering the Customer after the Sale

Customer follow-up methods should be used to express appreciation for the purchase and to further develop the relationship after the sale. Poor service and lack of follow-up are consistently cited by customers as the primary reasons that buyers stopped buying. In one Wallace branch office, there is a saying that hangs above the door that states "Remember the Customer between Calls." Personal visits should be the primary method to follow up after the sale. It is the most costly but also the most effective. This method allows face-to-face, two-way communication. The customer's body language can also be observed. "An Ethical Dilemma" demonstrates a typical complaint a salesperson has to overcome.

An Ethical Dilemma

Tim Lyon of Advanced Computers has sold three personal computers to a small business in his hometown. He secured the order by offering a fair price and guaranteeing his customer that he could meet the delivery date of four weeks. Tim called his home office and was given the green light to sign the order with the delivery conditions. He was excited until the four-week delivery date had passed and his home office needed two more weeks before the PCs could be shipped. His customer was furious. What do you do if you are Tim? What else could Tim have done?

The telephone can also be used to follow up a sale. Most salespeople send a written follow-up thanking the customer for his or her business. The telephone can then be used to reinforce the written message. The customer can give verbal feedback, and the salesperson can ask questions and use probing techniques that cannot be used with written correspondence. It is important not to forget the customer after the sale.

Resolving Complaints

Complaints will never be completely eliminated by any company. Nevertheless, it is every company's hope that it can reduce the frequency of complaints. Complaints typically arise because the product did not live up to the buyer's expectations. Buyers complain for any number of reasons: (1) late delivery; (2) wrong order sent (e.g., too many, too few); (3) product performs poorly; or (4) nobody at the salesperson's company takes the buyer's problems seriously. See Exhibit 9.4 for a more comprehensive list of complaints.

Many times, the complaint is not the fault of the salesperson (e.g., late delivery, wrong order, product performs poorly). However, this is not a concern to the buyer as they expect the salesperson to resolve it. Traditional salespeople have been known to pass the blame when complaints arise. A salesperson would be better off to tackle the complaint by accepting responsibility and promptly fixing the problem. Salespeople get into trouble by overpromising what their product can do, being overly optimistic about delivery dates, and not being attentive to their customers when they do complain. "An Ethical Dilemma" discusses one manager's problems in getting her salesforce to follow up after the orders are signed. Many complaints can be avoided by giving the customers a reasonable expectation of what the product can do for them.

An Ethical Dilemma

Sandy Myers has set aside two hours per day when her sales staff is supposed to be out making calls on existing customers. She implemented this program because she noticed that they were getting orders but losing about 20 percent after three months. The first month of her new program has gone by, and she can tell her staff has not complied with her request. She reviewed the call reports and doubted anyone spent five minutes per day making follow-up calls, let alone two hours. She suspects her company's compensation program of straight commission may have something to do with her problem. What would you do if you were Sandy? If Sandy is right and the compensation program is the problem, can you blame her salesforce?

If periodic meetings are taking place between the buyer and seller after the sale, then in all probability, most of the important issues are being discussed. Salespeople must ask their buyers to be candid with them and encourage the buyer to discuss tough issues (i.e., late deliveries, damaged products), especially in areas where the salesperson's organization is providing less than satisfactory performance. Some buyers will not complain because they feel it won't do any good. Others won't complain because they feel the salesperson should be in tune with their problems or concerns and recognize these problems on their own. If a salesperson encourages **critical encounters** and acts accordingly to diffuse a situation where the buyer's expectations have not been met, then this will help with future meetings and sessions where critical encounters are discussed. If the salesperson does not act on these issues, then future meetings with the buyer will not uncover problem areas because the buyer is convinced nothing will be done to solve them.

Some salespeople tell the customer what he or she wants to hear to get the order and cannot deliver on the promises they made. Complaints can be avoided by being truthful when presenting a product's capabilities. Providing sales support can eliminate problems with late deliveries, wrong orders being sent, and the feeling that the salesperson does not care about the customer's complaints. The following section provides an outline on how to handle customer complaints.

EXHIBIT 9.4   **Typical Customer Complaints**

1. Late delivery
2. Damaged merchandise
3. Invoice errors
4. Out of stock—back orders
5. Shipped incorrect product
6. Shipped incorrect order size
7. Service department unresponsive
8. Product does not live up to expectations
9. Customer not informed on new developments
10. Customer's problems not taken seriously
11. Improper installation
12. Need more training
13. Price increase—no notice
14. Can't find the salesperson when needed

A Procedure to Handle Complaints

Customer complaints must be handled quickly and with great sensitivity. Customers do not care about all the problems the company is experiencing and the reasons why the salesperson is providing less than stellar customer service. The reason that relationship selling is such a critical part of retaining customers is because the salesperson must have an open communication line with the customer and encourage feedback, whether positive or negative. Most customers will not complain. The salesperson must have built the relationship to the point where buyers will not hesitate to speak their minds if they are unhappy about the service. If the customer does not complain, then the salesperson does not know what it is that he or she needs to fix. A general procedure for handling customer complaints follows.

Build the Relationship to the Point Your Customers Are Comfortable Complaining

Salespeople have been overheard saying to their customers, "If I only had known you were unhappy about our service, I could have fixed it." The buyer typically responds, "Well, I gave you enough signals, why weren't you more perceptive to the problems I was having when doing business with you?" The buyer and salesperson must work together to develop a trust so that whatever is on the mind of each, he or she feels comfortable about speaking up. Open communication channels are a must to good customer service. Companies today cannot be afraid to ask their clients, "How are we doing?"[8] Some companies are conducting 30-, 60-, and 90-day customer satisfaction follow-up visits after the sale. Beyond that, the salespeople maintain quarterly follow-up, even if only by phone! This at least tells the customer, "We are interested in you as a company and we want to service your account well."

Listen Carefully and Get the Whole Story

The salesperson must listen carefully to what is being said and what is not being said. Good salespeople let the customer know that they are happy the complaint has been brought to their attention. Chances are the customer will not complain again if he or she is made to feel uncomfortable with the initial complaint. The salesperson must be careful not to interrupt early in the discussion. The customer must be allowed to vent his or her frustration and calm his or her emotional state. Once the customer stops complaining, the salesperson may have to probe and ask follow-up questions to get the whole story. For instance, the buyer may have not told the salesperson whom he or she talked to at the salesperson's company about the problem, and this information may be helpful to the salesperson in solving the complaint. This is a good time to show empathy. The salesperson should let the buyer know that he or she is sorry for any inconvenience, that he or she is happy that the buyer brought the problem to his or her attention, and that the salesperson is anxious to resolve the problem and keep the buyer as a satisfied client.

Ask Customers How They Would Like Their Complaint Resolved

Many salespeople attempt to solve the complaint without understanding what the customer wants them to do. For example, a salesperson may reason that the customer last wanted a 20 percent discount to make things better. "Thus, I will offer this unhappy buyer the same thing." The salesperson may be surprised to find out the buyer wanted something totally different to resolve the problem. The salesperson cannot be afraid to ask the customer what it will take to make him or her happy. A salesperson could say something like, "Theresa, we value you and your company's business. I am sorry for the inconvenience we caused you. Can you, please, tell me what we can do to solve this problem and keep you as a satisfied customer?" Then, the salesperson must listen carefully. The buyer may simply want an apology. He or she may want a discount; still other buyers might ask for another product to be substituted until the regular shipment arrives. Salespeople typically find that the customer is not demanding as much as they thought that he or she might have, considering the circumstances of the complaint. The solution should center on what the customer wants and not what the salesperson thinks is appropriate.

Gain Agreement on a Solution

Once the salesperson hears what the customer wants, he or she must agree on a solution. Sometimes, the salesperson can do exactly what the customer asks. Other times, the buyer may be asking for an unrealistic solution. The salesperson's focus should always be on trying to do exactly what the customer wants. When that is not possible, the salesperson's message should concentrate on what he or she can do for the customer and do it in a timely manner.[9] The conversation might sound like, "Jim, I'm sorry for the inconvenience we caused you. Thanks for your suggestions on what we need to do to resolve the problem. Here are a couple of things we can do, which of these will work better for you …?" The salesperson is telling the buyer that he or she cannot do exactly what the buyer asked, but the salesperson can do the following. Good salespeople always focus on the positive.

Take Action—Educate the Customer

Once an agreement is reached, the salesperson must take action and solve the customer complaint in a timely fashion. The communication lines must be kept open to the customer (e.g., letting him or her know when the repair people will be arriving). When time permits, the repair work should be monitored and the customer kept up to date on progress.

If customers have unrealistic expectations of the services provided, then this would be a good time to educate the customers so they have realistic expectations of the services the company will provide. Some salespeople promise the moon to secure an order, and then let the customer down when the product does not perform up to expectations. This is not the way to develop a trusting relationship.

Follow Through on All Promises—Add Value

Whatever promises are made, good salespeople must make sure that they are kept, and this is a good time to go beyond what has been promised. Those salespeople who overdeliver what is promised will truly impress their customers and build stronger relationships faster than their competitors.[10] Adding value to what the buyer expects helps ensure repeat business down the road. Exhibit 9.5 summarizes the procedures to handle complaints.

EXHIBIT 9.5	General Procedure for Handling Complaints

1. Build relationship to the point the customer is comfortable complaining.
2. Listen carefully and get the whole story.
3. Ask the customer what he or she would like you to do.
4. Gain agreement on a solution. Tell them what you can do; don't focus on what you can't.
5. Take action; educate the customer so he or she has realistic expectations.
6. Follow through on all promises. Add value.

Maintaining Open, Two-Way Communication

Early in the selling process, the salesperson determines the specific needs of the buyer so that a good match can be made between the product's attributes and the needs of the buyer. This is done through effective questioning and listening with the buyer. Once the sale is made, the salesperson must continue to maintain open, two-way communication with the buyer. Periodic meetings with the buyer allow for this feedback. Collaborative discussion becomes the most effective tool when dealing with customers and their problems. If the customer believes the salesperson is sincere, listens carefully, and responds accordingly to his or her concerns, then an already trusting relationship will become stronger.

Expanding Collaborative Involvement

A salesperson's goal is to work with customers who have entered into a strategic alliance with the salesperson's firm. This is done by building trust over a long period of time. The salesperson should always be looking for ways to take the relationship to a higher level and a stronger bond. One way to accomplish this goal is to expand the collaborative involvement between the buyer's and salesperson's organization. The salesperson may take a group of engineers along on a sales call and introduce them to the buyer's engineers. It may be possible for the engineers to work together to enhance the product offering. Customers often know the strengths and weaknesses of the product they use and can provide some insight into how improvements can be made.

Another example of a company's attempt to expand **collaborative involvement** is to host its customers in a week-long series of seminars, training sessions, and social engagements to expand the relationship. Brainstorming sessions with the customers demonstrate a willingness to listen, show that the company cares, and often result in better ways to serve the customers. Any time the salesperson can involve additional personnel from the buyer's company during relationship building, chances are the relationship will become stronger.

Working to Add Value and Enhance Mutual Opportunities

To build mutually satisfying relationships between buyers and sellers, professional salespeople must work toward adding value and enhancing mutual opportunities for the customer. This can be done by reducing risk through repeated displays of the seller's ability to serve the customer. By demonstrating the willingness to serve the customer, the seller reduces the buyer's risk—both real and perceived. A good relationship is one that has few, if any, unpleasant surprises.

Salespeople must also establish high standards and expectations. Many relationships fail due to unmet expectations. The higher the customer's expectations, the better, provided the seller can meet or exceed those expectations. Salespeople should ensure that customer's expectations are reasonable, and continually work to improve performance.

Finally, salespeople must monitor and take action to improve customer satisfaction. Salespeople must never let up on this one. Doing so only invites competitor challenges. A good salesperson must always look for cracks in the relationship, and patch them before insurmountable problems occur. All relationships require work, and taking a good customer for granted is foolish. It should be remembered that the salesperson must continually add value to the relationship or run the risk of losing the customer.

Providing Quality Customer Service

Every salesperson is looking for a competitive edge to help him or her differentiate his or her products in the eyes of customers. Many of the products that a salesperson sells have essentially the same features and benefits as the competitors'. Chris Crabtree of Lanier once said, "A copier is a copier, is a copier. There is just no difference between what I have to offer and my competitors. We all charge about the same price. In fact, I can match any price my competitor puts on the table. That leaves only one attribute for me to differentiate on—service."[11]

More and more companies are turning to service quality as a strategy to acquire and maintain customers. A salesperson must be able to convince a customer that service is important, demonstrate service quality, and then maintain a high level of service over an extended period of time.

The problem is that every salesperson claims to provide outstanding service. The goal today is not to meet customer expectations but to exceed them. Salespeople will rarely be given a second chance to prove that they provide outstanding service if they do not get it right the first time.

> A sign in a small-town business reads, "Service is advertised....
> Service is talked about ...
> But the only time service really counts ...
> Is when it is delivered ...
> And we promise your experience with us will be outstanding."

Customers do not care about slogans and service claims until something happens to them. This is called a moment of truth. Each salesperson experiences daily moments of truth—brief moments that occur whenever a customer comes into contact with a salesperson, the training staff, installers, field engineers, or service personnel and has an opportunity to form an impression. These moments of truth are when the customer will determine if promises are being kept by the sales organization, and whether the salesperson truly cares about the customer or is simply an order getter!

There are four benefits of service enthusiasm that allow the sales organization to gain an advantage over its competitors.

First, reputation is an important part of any organization's ability to attract and keep new customers. Reputation allows a salesperson to distinguish himself or herself from the competition. A solid reputation tells customers that "you care" and will help a salesperson build a loyal relationship in his or her market. Reputations take a long time to establish and only one negative event to destroy.

Second, by providing good customer service the first time, an organization makes the profit that it needs to stay in business. Whenever mistakes are made (e.g., wrong order, short order delivered), service personnel have to sort out the problem and fix it. The result could lead to a lost customer. In any event, it does not take long to go into the red when people have to be added to fix problems. Efficient operations, cost savings, and doing things right the first time increase the chances for increased profits.

The third benefit of service enthusiasm is convenience. It is critically important to put the customer's convenience first. A salesperson must make it easy for his or her customers to discuss problems or complaints. Most customers are uncomfortable complaining. Customers generally will not complain if the salesperson does not encourage complaint behavior. The most dangerous customer to any business is a silent complainer. It is difficult for a salesperson to solve a problem if he or she is not aware of it. It is also dangerous if other customers hear this customer bad-mouthing the salesperson. It may influence other customers in how they feel about the salesperson.

Salespeople must design user-friendly feedback systems. Periodically inquiring about customer satisfaction can greatly enhance a customer's feelings toward a salesperson and his or her organization.

TWA, for instance, does not understand this principle. Its 800 number is a recording that tells customers to leave a voice mail or fax in the problem. Complaints, the caller is told, will be handled within 45 days!

Finally, service enthusiasm goes hand in hand with spirit. A customer can be turned on to an organization by meeting many caring "can-do" people. The spirit must start with an enthusiastic, service-minded corporate culture. The salesperson, sales manager, field engineer, installer, and CSR (customer service representative) must all have the same service enthusiasm to generate the benefits of service enthusiasm. That is why the salesperson must monitor and coordinate all the people who have access to the account to ensure that good customer service is taking place.

The most difficult aspect of customer service is the potential for inconsistency. For instance, field engineer A, who has a great understanding of service enthusiasm, may be called into an account early in the week. The customer is duly impressed. Three weeks later, the customer calls for help again. Field engineer A is out on another account, and field engineer B, who has little or no service skills, is sent in on the next call. Field engineer B is good at fixing the problem but has a hard time relating to customers; in fact, he is down-right cold! As a result of this unevenness, the customer's level of satisfaction decreases.

The inconsistency of customer service is a problem for every sales organization. By understanding the benefits of service enthusiasm and the rewards of proper spirit, the sales organization can ensure consistency and exceed customer expectations.

Customer Expectations

A salesperson must meet the needs of his or her customer. At a minimum, customers expect a warm and friendly salesperson. Buyers have enough things going on during their day that it would not be a plus to have to deal with a surly salesperson. Warmth and friendliness are the building blocks of a successful relationship.

Reliability is another attribute that buyers look for in choosing a salesperson with which to do business. Customers must have the confidence that the expected service will be delivered accurately, consistently, and dependably. Helpfulness and assistance are two more variables that buyers expect when working with a salesperson. Will the customer be able to find his or her salesperson when he or she needs to do so? Can the salesperson provide the speed and promptness needed by the customer? The salesperson can solve this issue by developing a regular call routine so that the customer knows when to expect the salesperson. Other customer expectations include follow-through as promised, empathy, and resolution of complaints, mistakes, or defects. The customer must know that if anything goes wrong, the salesperson will move in quickly and solve the problem. Exhibit 9.6 summarizes what customers expect from their salesperson.

EXHIBIT 9.6   **Customer Expectations of Salespeople**

---

1. Warmth and Friendliness
2. Reliability
3. Helpfulness/Assistance
4. Speed or Promptness
5. Assurance
6. Accuracy
7. Follow-through (as promised)
8. Empathy
9. Resolution of complaints, mistakes, or defects
10. Tangibles

EXHIBIT 9.7   **Checklist for Developing a Service Strategy**

Here are the questions that a salesperson must ask when developing a service strategy:
- What is our business?
- Who are our customers?
- What do our customers want and what is important to them?
- How are our customers' needs and perceptions changing?
- How are social, economic, and political factors affecting current and future customer needs and our ability to respond to them? How are competitors responding to these factors?
- How do customers rate us in terms of their expectations?
- What are we best known for?
- What do we do best?
- What can we do better?
- How can we position ourselves in the market to differentiate our services?

Developing a Service Strategy

Salespeople can calculate the lifetime value of one of their customers. Hershey Chocolate, USA, knows exactly how much candy it has sold at the Wal-Mart in Muncie, Indiana. It is easy for Hershey to calculate the loss if any customer decides to replace them. It is imperative for Hershey to provide the service level that each of its customers demands. Less than quality service can lead to the loss of a customer.

Developing a **service strategy** allows a salesperson to plan his or her actions for each of the customers. A service strategy asks a salesperson to identify his or her business and customers and what the customers want and what is important to them. The salesperson also has to determine how his or her customers' needs and perceptions are changing. The salesperson cannot be afraid to ask how the customers rate him or her in terms of their expectations. What does the salesperson's company do best and what can the organization do better? The salesperson, ultimately, must determine how to position his or her company in the market to differentiate its products and services. All this must be done while directing efforts against the competitors. Exhibit 9.7 is an example of a checklist for developing a service strategy.

Customer Service Dimensions

The most important **customer service dimension** is communication. Most problems arise because the customer was not informed of a change in plans (e.g., late delivery, price increase). Salespeople are extremely busy and many times do not have the time to communicate with all their customers. **Communication tools** such as e-mail can be used to quickly do mass communication to inform customers of these changes. Over time, the telephone and personal visits can be used to confirm that the customers are aware of the changes.

Another customer service dimension is **resilience.** Resilience is the ability of a salesperson to get knocked down several times a day by a customer's verbal assault (i.e., complaint) and get right back up with a smile and ask for more. A salesperson cannot lose his or her cool just because a customer does. A tired salesperson must treat late-afternoon, difficult customers the same way that he or she would treat an early-morning dilemma while he or she was fresh. They must both be treated well.

Finally, the most important customer service dimension is the motivation of a salesperson to service his or her customers. Salespeople must find time each day to deal with difficult customers and problems that exist. Ignoring these activities will not make them go away. Working diligently on behalf of the customer indicates to him or her that the salesperson truly cares about the partnership. If a salesperson has a complaint from a customer and gladly fixes it, the customer becomes a more committed customer.

Summary

1. **Explain how to follow up to assess customer satisfaction.** Salespeople cannot be afraid to ask their customers, "How are we doing?" Periodic follow-up is critical to long-term sales success. New customers generally feel special because they have received a lot of attention from the salesperson. Older customers may feel neglected because the sales rep has many new customers and cannot be as attentive as he or she was previously. Routine follow-up to assess "How are we doing?" can go a long way in letting a customer know that the salesperson cares and is willing to make sure he or she is satisfied.

2. **Explain how to harness technology to enhance follow-up and buyer-seller relationships.** Effective salesperson follow-up should include specific components designed to interact, connect, know, and relate with their customers.
   - **Interact** The salesperson acts to maximize the number of critical encounters with buyers in order to encourage effective dialogue and involvement between the salesperson and buyer.
   - **Connect** The salesperson maintains contact with the multiple individuals in the buying organization influencing purchase decisions and manages the various touch points the customer has in the selling organization to assure consistency in communication.
   - **Know** The salesperson coordinates and interprets the information gathered through buyer-seller contact and collaboration to develop insight regarding the buyer's changing situation, needs, and expectations.
   - **Relate** The salesperson applies relevant understanding and insight to create value-added interactions and generate relationships between the salesperson and buyer.

   Salespeople have employed a variety of technology based salesforce automation tools in order to better track the increasingly complex combination of buyer-seller interactions and to manage the exchange, interpretation, and storage of diverse types of information. Among the more popular salesforce automation tools are the many competing versions of PC-based software applications designed to record and manage customer contact information. Applications such as ACT!, Maximizer, and Goldmine enable salespeople to collect, file, and access comprehensive databases detailing information about individual buyers and buying organizations.

3. **Discuss how to take action to assure customer satisfaction.** Salespeople must follow up on specific relationship enhancement activities such as
   (a) providing useful information to their customers;
   (b) expediting orders and monitoring a successful installation;

       (c) training customer personnel;

       (d) correcting billing errors;

       (e) remembering the customer after the sale;

       (f) resolving complaints in a timely manner.

4. ***Discuss how to maintain open two-way communication.*** Periodic meetings with the buyer allow for feedback. Listening becomes the most effective tool when dealing with customers and their problems. The salesperson must encourage the buyer to be candid about his or her concerns and problems and to let the salesperson know when his or her needs are not being met. If the customer believes the salesperson is sincere, listens carefully, and responds accordingly to his or her concerns, then a trusting buyer-seller relationship can be built even stronger.

5. ***Explain how to encourage critical encounters.*** If periodic meetings are taking place after the sale between the buyer and seller, then in all probability most of the important issues are being discussed. If an agenda is planned for a meeting, then tough issues must be placed on it and not ignored. The buyer must be encouraged to discuss service areas that are not being met periodically. Otherwise, the salesperson will not know what needs to be fixed.

6. ***Discuss how to expand collaborative involvement.*** The easiest way to expand collaborative involvement is to get more people involved in the relationship from both the buyer's and seller's firms.

7. ***Explain how to add value and enhance mutual opportunities.*** The salesperson can enhance mutual opportunities by reducing risk for the buyer by repeated displays of outstanding customer service. The salesperson can also demonstrate a willingness to serve the customer over extended periods of time. The buyer needs to experience a willingness on the seller's part to go to bat for the buyer when things get tough.

Understanding Professional Selling Terms

- Building goodwill
- Adding value
- Monitor installation
- Expedite orders
- Two-way communication
- Interact
- Connect
- Know
- Relate
- Service strategy
- Customer service dimensions
- Communication tools
- Resilience
- Critical encounters
- Collaborative involvement

Developing Professional Selling Knowledge

1. How can a salesperson convert new customers into highly committed customers for life?
2. Why should a salesperson follow up to assess customer satisfaction?
3. Explain why the relationship enhancement activities are important.
4. What does a salesperson hope to accomplish by providing his or her customers with useful information after the sale?
5. Most salespeople are not trained in how to install their products. Why then should a good salesperson make it a point to oversee the installation process?
6. Why is it important for a salesperson to ask a buyer what he or she wants the salesperson to do when resolving the complaint?
7. Why should a salesperson encourage his or her customers to complain? Isn't this just asking for trouble?
8. Why is it important for a salesperson to gain agreement on a solution when dealing with a customer complaint?
9. Why do many salespeople seem to ignore after-sale activities that enhance the relationship?
10. Why is it important for a salesperson to establish expectations with a new customer?

Building Professional Selling Skills

1. This exercise explores potential points of added-value differentiation by comparing various facets of the subject company's market offering with those of a principal competitor. Find a salesperson who is willing to be interviewed. After reviewing the *Customer Benefits Worksheet* and *Points for Discussion* following this introduction, interview that salesperson to determine how his or her market offering (including the activities of the salesperson) compares with that of a specific competitor. Determine where the salesperson's offering has an advantage over the competition that results in added customer value. Based on your interview, complete the following *Customer Benefits Worksheet* and *Points for Discussion* pages.

Student Name: _____ Date: _____

Name of Salesperson Interviewed: _____

Names of Salesperson's Company: _____

Type of Product: _____

Customer Benefits Worksheet

Source of Benefit	Benefits of Company's Offering	Benefits of Competitor's Offering
The Product		
Services		
The Company		
The Salesperson		

Points for Discussion

1. Describe this salesperson's relationship-marketing role in creating added customer value. What does the salesperson do that adds value for the customer?

_____

_____

_____

_____

_____

_____

_____

_____

_____

2. What additional behaviors or activities, other than those already being performed, could the salesperson undertake that might further increase customer value?

_____

_____

_____

_____

_____

_____

_____

_____

_____

_____

3.   Why have these behaviors or services not been implemented?

_____

_____

_____

_____

_____

_____

_____

_____

_____

_____

2.   *Diary of Sales/Service Encounters*

Part A:

Keeping a Diary of Sales Encounters

Using the following preformatted worksheets, keep a sales/service diary for one month. Include all your encounters with salespeople, recording (1) the date, (2) where the sales encounter happened, (3) a factual description of what happened (i.e., the salesperson's attitude, behaviors, and so forth), (4) your reactions and attitudes (i.e., your perceptions, feelings, future intentions), and (5) did the salesperson provide or offer any follow-up activities to enhance the relationship?

Part B:

Written Report with Conclusion/Implications

At the end of one month, select two sales encounters from those in your diary—one encounter that you rated from good to outstanding and one that you rated from poor to terrible. Write a short report comparing the two encounters. Summarize each encounter, assess what went wrong as well as what went right, and develop conclusions and implications for salespeople relevant to relationship selling.

Part C:

Oral Presentation and Discussion

Based on your written report, prepare and deliver an oral presentation to the class. This oral presentation should be informative and emphasize your conclusions and implications for relationship selling.

Student Name: _____ Date: _____

Diary of Sales/Service Encounters

Encounter Date	Where	What Happened/Behaviors	Your Reactions/Attitudes
1.			
2.			
3.			
4.			
5.			
6.			
7.			
8.			
9.			
10.			
11.			
12.			

Making Professional Selling Decisions

CASE 9.1   *The Reluctant Salesforce*

Background

Gary Calling, sales manager for a large engineering firm, cannot get his salespeople into the field. He summarized his problem as follows:

1. Lack of outgoing calls or e-mails to prospects and customers;
2. Lack of planning on a daily basis;
3. No use of a follow-up program to generate additional customer contacts;
4. Lack of overall planning strategy for a particular customer or group of customers;
5. Reactive salesforce instead of proactive.

Current Situation

He thinks that his problem is that his staff is technical in nature and want to be thought of as experts, not salespeople. He goes on to say that his staff does great when the customers call them but cannot plan for sales opportunities. His reps say they are too busy with everything else to make outside calls.

Gary had the following conversation with his top salesperson, Ted (who happens to be his brother).

Gary: Ted, have you had any luck making new contacts?

Ted: Not really.

Gary: What's the problem?

Ted: What do you mean, man? What's the problem? I spend all day on the phone talking to our existing customers. They need me. I can't be out of the office all day. My customers would never be able to find me.

Gary: I'm not talking about being out of the office all day. I need you to spend one day per week following up on existing customers to build goodwill and another half-day per week looking for new business.

Ted: That sounds good, but I don't see how I can get that done. I am already overloaded.

Questions

1. What would you do if you were Gary?
2. Can you force your salesforce out of the building?

CASE 9.2   *Whatever It Takes to Get the Order*

Background

Roberta Thomas has seen the good life. Her company is paying high bonuses to bring in new customers. Roberta has earned more than $100,000 per year the past three years. Roberta has been given increasingly higher quotas to reach the past two years to reach her bonus. She feels her company is putting her in an awkward position. She wants to continue to reach her quota, but in doing so, she will spend more than 90 percent of her time trying to bring in new business. Just over two years ago, she spent half her time keeping her present customers satisfied. Her customers have been complaining about how little attention they receive. Roberta knows that she is not spending enough time with them. She brought her dilemma to her boss, Betty Barrett, who seemed less than sympathetic.

Current Situation

Their conversation follows:

Roberta: I am really having a problem with the quota I've been assigned this year.

Betty: Is that so? What is the problem?

Roberta: I think it is too high. I have to spend way too much time going after new business.

Betty: That is what we pay you to do; your job is to bring in new business.

Roberta: It was not that many years ago when I spent at least half of my time keeping my present customers happy. I enjoyed following up on them and building a strong relationship.

Betty: Times change, you know. We have to bring in new business or face the chance of laying some of you off.

Roberta: You can look over some of these phone messages I have received. These are some of our best customers, and they do not think we are taking very good care of them.

Betty: Roberta, we have a big contest going on, and I do not intend to lose it. You had better bring in your share of the new business to win or you will let down your entire branch.

Roberta could see she was not getting anywhere and changed the subject.

Questions

1. What would you do if you were Roberta?
2. What would you do if you were Betty?

N O T E S

MODULE 1

[1] Marjorie J. Caballero, Roger A. Dickinson, and Dabney Townsend, "Aristotle and Personal Selling," *Journal of Personal Selling and Sales Management* 4 (May 1984): 13.

[2] William T. Kelley, "The Development of Early Thought in Marketing," in *Salesmanship: Selected Readings,* ed. John M. Rathmell (Homewood, IL: Irwin, 1969): 3.

[3] Thomas L. Powers, Warren S. Martin, Hugh Rushing, and Scott Daniels, "Selling before 1900: A Historical Perspective," *Journal of Personal Selling and Sales Management* 7 (November 1987): 5. For additional review of personal selling from 1600 to the present era, see Robert Desman and Terry E. Powell, "Personal Selling: Chicken or Egg," in *Proceedings,* 13th Annual Conference of the Academy of Marketing Science, ed. Jon M. Hawes (Orlando, FL: 1989).

[4] Michael Bell, *The Salesman in the Field* (Geneva: International Labour Office, 1980): 1.

[5] Stanley C. Hollander, "Anti-Salesman Ordinances of the Mid-19th Century," in *Salesmanship,* 9.

[6] Ibid., 10.

[7] Jon M. Hawes, "Leaders in Selling and Sales Management," *Journal of Personal Selling and Sales Management* 5 (November 1985): 60.

[8] Charles W. Hoyt, *Scientific Sales Management* (New Haven, CT: George W. Woolson and Co., 1913): 3.

[9] Ibid., 4.

[10] Edward C. Bursk, "Low-Pressure Selling," *Harvard Business Review* 25 (Winter 1947): 227.

[11] "From Push to Pull: Why Market Forces Demand the Conceptual Sell," *Selling* (July–August 1995): 50.

[12] Synthesized from Thomas N. Ingram, "Relationship Selling: Moving from Rhetoric to Reality," *Mid-American Journal of Business* 11 (Spring 1996): 5; David W. Cravens, Emin Babakus, Ken Grant, Thomas N. Ingram, and Raymond W. LaForge, "Removing Sales Force Performance Hurdles," *Journal of Business and Industrial Marketing* 9, no. 3 (1994): 19; David W. Cravens, Thomas N. Ingram, and Raymond W. LaForge, "Evaluating Multiple Sales Channel Strategies," *Journal of Business and Industrial Marketing* (Summer/ Fall 1991): 37.

[13] Michele Marchetti, "The Cost of Doing Business," *Sales and Marketing Management* (September 1999): 56.

[14] "Here's to the Winners," *Sales and Marketing Management* (July 1999): 70.

[15] Kevin J. Corcoran, Laura K. Petersen, Daniel B. Baitch, and Mark F. Barrett, *High Performance Sales Organizations* (Chicago, IL: Irwin, 1995): 152.

[16] "Here's to the Winners," 64.

[17] Michele Marchetti, "A Sales Pro Tries to Energize HP," *Sales and Marketing Management* (September 1999): 15.

[18] Kevin R. Fitzgerald, "What Makes a Superior Supplier?" *Velocity* (Spring 1999): 22.

[19] Thomas N. Ingram and Charles H. Schwepker Jr., "Perceptions of Salespeople: Implications for Sales Managers and Sales Trainers," *Journal of Marketing Management* 2 (Fall/Winter 1992–93): 1.

[20] Thomas N. Ingram, "Relationship Selling: Moving from Rhetoric to Reality," *Mid-American Journal of Business* 11 (Spring 1996): 5.

[21] "Here's to the Winners," 66.

[22] Michael J. Swenson, William R. Swinyard, Frederick W. Langrehr, and Scott M. Smith, "The Appeal of Personal Selling as a Career: A Decade Later," *Journal of Personal Selling and Sales Management* 13 (Winter 1993): 51.

[23] Marchetti, "The Cost of Doing Business," 57.

[24] Steven P. Brown, Thomas W. Leigh, and J. Martin Haygood, "Salesperson Performance and Job Attitudes," in *The Marketing Manager's Handbook,* 3rd ed., ed. Sidney J. Levy, George R. Frerichs, and Howard L. Gordon (Chicago: The Dartnell Corporation, 1994): 107.

[25] *Occupational Outlook Handbook,* 1998–99 ed. (Washington, DC: U.S. Department of Labor, 1998).

[26] Emin Babakus, David W. Cravens, Ken Grant, Thomas N. Ingram, and Raymond W. LaForge, "Removing Salesforce Performance Hurdles," *Journal of Business and Industrial Marketing* 9, no. 3 (1994): 19.

[27] See Herbert M. Greenberg and Jeanne Greenberg, *What It Takes to Succeed in Sales* (Homewood, IL: Dow-Jones Irwin, 1990).

[28] James M. Comer and Alan J. Dubinsky, *Managing the Successful Sales Force* (Lexington, MA: D.C. Heath and Co., 1985): 5; Brown et al., "Salesperson Performance," 107.

[29] Babakus et al., "Removing Salesforce Performance Hurdles," 19.

[30]Rosann L. Spiro and Barton A. Weitz, "Adaptive Selling: Conceptualization, Measurement, and Nomological Validity," *Journal of Marketing Research* 27 (February 1990): 61.

[31]Bruce K. Pilling and Sevo Eroglu, "An Empirical Examination of the Impact of Salesperson Empathy and Professionalism and Merchandise Salability on Retail Buyers' Evaluations," *Journal of Personal Selling and Sales Management* 14 (Winter 1994): 45.

[32]Lyndon E. Dawson, Jr., Barlow Soper, and Charles E. Pettijohn, "The Effects of Empathy on Salesperson Effectiveness," *Psychology and Marketing* (July/August 1992): 297.

[33]Andy Cohen, "Here's to the Winners," 60.

[34]Kevin J. Corcoran, Laura K. Petersen, Daniel B. Baitch, and Mark F. Barrett, *High Performance Sales Organizations* (Chicago: Irwin Professional Publishing, 1995): 77.

[35]Arun Sharma and Rajnandini Pillai, "Customers' Decision-Making Styles and Their Preference for Sales Strategies: Conceptual Examination and an Empirical Study," *Journal of Personal Selling and Sales Management* 16 (Winter 1996): 21.

[36]Victoria Davies Bush and Thomas N. Ingram, "Adapting to Diverse Customers: A Training Matrix for International Marketers," *Industrial Marketing Management* (Spring 1996): 373.

[37]"And the Surveys Say," *Personal Selling Power* (October 1995): 55.

MODULE 2

[1]Adapted from Jagdish N. Sheth, Banwari Mittal, and Bruce I. Newman, *Customer Behavior: Consumer Behavior and Beyond* (Fort Worth, TX: The Dryden Press, 1999); and Jagdish N. Sheth, Bruce I. Newman, and Barbara L. Gross, *Consumption Values and Market Choice: Theory and Application,* (Cincinnati, OH: South-Western Publishing Co., 1991).

[2]Bixby Cooper, Cornelia Drodge, and Patricia Daughtery, "How Buyers and Operations Personnel Evaluate Service," *Industrial Marketing Management,* (February 1991): 81–85.

[3]Michael A. Humphreys, and Michael R. Williams, "Exploring the Relative Effects of Salesperson Interpersonal Process Attributes and Technical Product Attributes on Customer Satisfaction," *Journal of Personal Selling and Sales Management,* 16 (Summer 1996): 47-58; and Michael A. Humphreys, Michael R. Williams, and Ronald L. Meier, "Leveraging the Total Market Offering in the Agile Enterprise," *ASQ Quality Management Journal,* 5 (1997): 60–74.

[4]Wesley J. Johnston and Thomas V. Bonoma, "The Buying Center: Structure and Interaction Patterns," *Journal of Marketing* (Summer 1981): 143–156.

[5]"Business-to-Business E-commerce Penetration, Projected Growth Higher than Current Estimates," in "News & Analysis," http://PropertyandCasualty.com (December 21, 1999).

[6]Barton A. Weitz and Kevin D. Bradford, "Personal Selling and Sales Management: A Relationship Marketing Perspective," *Journal of the Academy of Marketing Science* 27 (Spring 1999): 241–254.

[7]Jakki Mohr and John R. Nevin, "Communication Strategies in Marketing Channels: A Theoretical Perspective," *Journal of Marketing* (October 1990): 36–51.

[8]Tom Davis, "Effective Supply Chain Management," *Sloan Management Review* (Summer 1993): 36.

MODULE 3

[1]Sherry Kilgus, "Building Trust into High Level Alliances," *NAMA Journal* 34, (Winter 1998).

[2]Ibid.

[3]John E. Swan and Johannah Jones Nolan, "Gaining Customer Trust: A Conceptual Guide for the Salesperson," *Journal of Personal Selling & Sales Management* V, 2 (November 1985): 39.

[4]Robert F. Dwyer, Paul H. Schurr, and Sejo Oh, "Developing Buyer-Seller Relationships," *Journal of Marketing* 51 (April 1987): 11.

[5]This was the concluding point of the symposium on trust held by the National Account Management Association at Wake Forest University, September 24–26, 1997.

[6]Source: Interview with Missy Rust, Glaxo-Welcome, February 13, 2000.

[7]Petersen, "Consultative Selling: A Qualitative Look at the Salesperson Credibility Requirements," *AMA Educator Proceeding Enhancing Knowledge Development in Marketing* 8 (1997): 224.

[8]Ibid.

[9]Source: Interview with Doug Lingo, Hoechst Marion Roussel Pharmaceutical, May 23, 1997.

[10]Source: Interview with Darrell Beaty, Ontario Systems Corporation, February 29, 2000.

[11]Thomas Ingram, Scott Inks, and Lee Mabie, *Sales and Marketing Executive Certification Study Guide* (1994).

[12]Source: Interview with Jenny Osborne, Eli Lilly, November 15, 1999.

MODULE 4

[1]S. D. Morgen, *Selling with Integrity: Reinventing Sales through Collaboration, Respect, and Serving* (San Francisco, CA: Berrett-Koehler Publishers, Inc., 1997).

[2]R. L. Jolles, *Customer Centered Selling* (New York: The Free Press, 1998).

[3]Ibid.

[4]Neil Rackham, *Spin Selling* (New York: McGraw Hill, 1988).

[5]Thomas Ingram, Tubs Scott, and Lee Mabie, *Certification Study Guide* (New York: Sales and Marketing Executives International, 1994): 44–46.

[6]B. Kimball, *Successful Selling* (Chicago: American Marketing Association, 1994), 53; and S. B. Castleberry and C. D. Shepherd, "Effective Interpersonal Listening and Personal Selling," *Journal of Personal Selling and Sales Management* 13, (Winter 1993): 35–49.

[7]T. N. Ingram, C. Schwepker Jr., and D. Hutson, "Why Salespeople Fail," *Industrial Marketing Management*, 21, (1992): 225–230.

[8]R. P. Ramsey, and R. S. Sohi, "Listening to Your Customers: The Impact of Perceived Salesperson Listening Behavior on Relationship Outcomes," *Journal of the Academy of Marketing Science*, 25 (Spring 1997): 127–137.

[9]L. Barker, *Listening Behavior* (Englewood Cliffs, NJ: Prentice-Hall, 1971): 30–32.

[10]S. B. Castleberry and C. D. Shepherd, "Effective Interpersonal Listening and Personal Selling," *Journal of Personal Selling and Sales Management* 13, (Winter 1993): 36.

[11]L. K. Steil, L. L. Barker, and K. W. Watson, *Effective Listening: Key to Your Success* (Reading, MA: Addison-Wesley Publishing Company, 1983); and R. P. Ramsey and R. S. Sohi, "Listening to Your Customers: The Impact of Perceived Salesperson Listening Behavior on Relationship Outcomes," *Journal of the Academy of Marketing Science* 25 (Spring 1997): 127–137.

[12]J. C. Mowen and M. Minor, *Consumer Behavior* (New York: Macmillan Publishing Co., 1997).

[13]G. P. Thomas, "The Influence of Processing Conversational Information on Inference, Argument Elaboration, and Memory," *Journal of Consumer Research* 19 (June 1992): 83–92.

[14]R. A. Avila, T. N. Ingram, R. W. LaForge, and M. R. Williams, *The Professional Selling Skills Workbook* (Fort Worth, TX: The Dryden Press, 1996): 83.

[15]R. A. Peterson, M. P. Cannito, and S. P. Brown, "An Exploratory Investigation of Voice Characteristics and Selling Effectiveness," *Journal of Personal Selling and Sales Management* 15 (Winter 1995): 1–15.

[16]Ibid.

[17]R. F. Kantin and M. W. Hardwick, *Quality Selling through Quality Proposals* (Danvers, MA: Boyd & Fraser Publishing Co., 1994): 65–70.

[18]J. Conlin, "The Write Stuff," *Sales & Marketing Management* (January 1998): 71–75.

MODULE 5

[1]S.R. Covey, *The 7 Habits of Highly Effective People,* (New York: Simon & Schuster, 1989).

[2]B. Kimball, *AMA Handbook for Professional Selling* (Chicago: American Marketing Association and Lincolnwood, IL: NTC Business Books, 1994).

[3]W. Ferguson, "A New Method for Routing Salespersons," *Industrial Marketing Management* (April 1980): 171–178; "Planning a Road Trip?" *An Executive Guide to Sales and Marketing Technology,* a supplement to *Sales and Marketing Management* (June 1996): 39; E. Strout, "Charting a Course," *Sales and Marketing Management* (August 1999): 46–53.

[4]For a good discussion of selling technology, see D. Peppers and M. Rogers, "Marketing's New Direction: How Campaigns Are Becoming Faster and More Precise through Automation," *Sales and Marketing Management* (March 1999): 48–54.

[5]For a comprehensive and comparative guide to sales and marketing automation systems, technology, and software, see http://www.salesandmarketing.com/more.

[6]E. Babakus, D. W. Cravens, K. Grant, T. N. Ingram, and R. W. LaForge, "Removing Salesforce Performance Hurdles," *Journal of Business and Industrial Marketing* 9, 3 (1994): 19–29.

[7]J. Attaway, M. Williams, and M. Griffin, *The Rims-QIC Quality Scorecard,* (Nashville, TN: The Quality Insurance Congress, 1998, 1999).

[8]James Champy, "Selling to Tomorrow's Customer," *Sales and Marketing Management* (March 1999): 28.

[9]S. R. Covey, *The 7 Habits of Highly Effective People* (New York: Simon & Schuster, 1989).

MODULE 6

[1]Robert F. Gwinner, "Base Theory in the Formulation of Sales Strategy," *MSU Business Topics* (Autumn 1968): 37.

[2]Malcolm Fleschner, "How to Sell New Products," *Selling Power* (July/August 1999): 23.

[3]This section on consultative selling is based on Kevin J. Corcoran, Laura K. Petersen, Daniel B. Baitch, and Mark F. Barrett, *High Performance Sales Organizations* (Chicago: Irwin, 1995): 44.

[4]Malcolm Fleschner, "We Want to Be the Biggest Small Company Around," *Selling Power* (April 1999): 48.

[5]Jon M. Hawes, Kenneth E. Mast, and John E. Swan, "Trust Earning Perceptions of Sellers and Buyers," *Journal of Personal Selling and Sales Management* 9 (Spring 1989): 1.

[6]Interview by the authors with Blake Conrad, sales representative with Centurion Specialty Care.

[7]Francy Blackwood, "Out of the Cold," *Selling* (May 1996): 22.

[8]Dana Ray, "Confront Call Reluctance," *Personal Selling Power* (September 1995): 46.

[9]Thomas W. Leigh and Patrick F. McGraw, "Mapping the Procedural Knowledge of Industrial Sales Personnel: A Script-Theoretic Investigation," *Journal of Marketing* 53 (January 1989): 16.

[10]Warren Burger, "Shopping Survival Skills," *Stereo Review* (February 1990): 70.

[11]Thomas N. Ingram, Michael D. Hartline, and Charles H. Schwepker Jr., "Gatekeeper Perceptions: Implications for Improving Sales Ethics and Professionalism," *Proceedings of the Academy of Marketing Science* (1992): 328.

[12]Theodore Levitt, *Industrial Purchasing Behavior: A Study in Communications* (Boston: Division of Research, Harvard School of Business, 1965).

[13]Francy Blackwood, "Building a Record," *Selling* (April 1996): 22.

[14]Franco DiCarlo, "An Eye for What Customers Buy," *Selling* (April 1995): 68.

[15]Hawes, Mast, and Swan, "Trust Earning Perceptions," 7.

[16]For more on the ADAPT questioning model, see Ramon A. Avila, Thomas N. Ingram, Raymond W. LaForge, and Michael R. Williams, *The Professional Selling Skills Workbook* (Fort Worth, TX: The Dryden Press, 1996): 109.

MODULE 7

[1]Source: Personal interview with Kim Lucas, Ikon Office Solutions, October 22, 1999.

[2]Source: Interview with Gwen Tranguillo, Hershey Chocolate, USA, November 3, 1999.

[3]Source: Interview with Thomas Avila, Davis and Davis, May 4, 1999.

[4]Source: Interview with Mark Thomas, United Insurance Agency, Muncie, IN, September 20, 1998.

[5]Source: Interview with Garry Robbins, Indiana Energy, September 20, 1997.

[6]Source: Interview with Frank Flanagan, Honeywell, March 20, 1998.

[7]Source: Personal Interview with Kristen Solik, Walker Group, January 15, 1998.

APPENDIX 7

[1]D. W. Merrill and R. H. Reid, *Personal Styles and Effective Performance* (Radnor, PA: Chilton Book Company, 1981).

MODULE 8

[1]Source: Interview with Steve Pidgeon, June 11, 1998.

[2]Source: Interview with Chris Crabtree, Ikon Office Solutions, June 22, 1999.

[3]Mandy Albright, Glaxo-Welcome, October 15, 1999.

[4]SMEI Accreditation Institute, 1994.

MODULE 9

[1]Source: *Purchasing*, November 27, 1997: 65

[2]Source: Personal Interview with John Haack, Ball-Foster, April 19, 2000.

[3]Marketing, Inc., in *Customer Relationship Management: Transforming Transactions into Relationships* (2000), NCR.

[4]NCDM, in *Customer Relationship Management: Transforming Transactions into Relationships* (2000), NCR.

[5]Yankee Research, in *Customer Relationship Management: Transforming Transactions into Relationships* (2000), NCR.

[6]Reichheld, Frederick F., *The Loyalty Effect*.

[7]Denise D. Jackson, Director of Marketing Operations, Marriott Worldwide, "All-time SalesLogix Sales Leaders," *Sales and Marketing Management* (March 2000): 29.

[8]"The Best Offense Is a Great Defense Personal Selling Power," *Trade Journal* (September 1994): 56.

[9]"Consistent Success in an Inconsistent World: Solid Customer Relationships Are the Key," *Selling Power* (May 1996): 28.

[10]"At Your Customer's Service: The True Test of a Salesperson's Value Comes after the Sale," *Selling Power* (May 1996): 58.

[11]Source: Personal interview with Chris Crabtree, Lanier Office Products, September 23, 1997.

CREDITS

MODULE 1

Exhibit 1.2: Excerpted from Sales and Marketing Executives International Certified Professional Salesperson Code of Ethics (Cleveland: Sales and Marketing Executives International, 1994). Reprinted by permission of SME International at 800-999-1414.

Exhibit 1.3: *Occupational Outlook Handbook, 1998–99 ed.* (Washington, DC: U.S. Department of Labor, 1998).

MODULE 2

Professional Selling (p. 27): The Quality Insurance Congress and The Risk and Insurance Management Society, *The 1999 Quality Scorecard Detailed Report*, Nashville: The Quality Insurance Congress.

An Ethical Dilemma (p. 30): "Prudential Insurance Settlement," CNN.com, January 19, 1999, 7–8. Retrieved April 9, 2000 from the World Wide Web: cnn.com/US/9901/19/scouts.01.

Figure 2.4: Adapted from Michael Humphreys and Michael Williams, "Exploring the Relative Effects of Salesperson Interpersonal Process Attributes and Technical Product Attributes on Customer Satisfaction," *Journal of Personal Selling and Sales Management* (Summer 1996): 47–58.

Professional Selling (p. 45): Nancy Rutter and Owen Edwards, "Ready to Ware: Software and Hardware, That Is," *Forbes ASAP*, April 5, 1999: 30–32.

MODULE 3

Professional Selling (p. 61): L.B. Gschwandtner and Gerhard Gschwandtner, "Balancing Act: By learning how to balance two basic drives—the need to close with the need to develop relationships—every salesperson can become a star," *Selling Power*, June 1996, 24. Updated June 15, 1999.

Exhibit 3.5: American Marketing Association, Chicago, Illinois.

Exhibit 3.6: SMEI Accreditation Institute, The University of Memphis, 1994.

Exhibit 3.7: SMEI Accreditation Institute, The University of Memphis, 1994.

MODULE 4

Figure 4.3: L.K. Steil, L.L. Barker, and K.W. Watson, *Effective Listening: Key to Your Success* (Reading, MA: Addison-Wesley Publishing Co., 1983): 21.

Exhibit 4.7: L. K. Steil, L. L. Barker, and K. W. Watson, *Effective Listening: Key to Your Success* (Reading, MA: Addison-Wesley Publishing Co., 1983): 72–73.

Exhibit 4.8: Adapted from R. M. Rozelle, D. Druckman, and J. C. Baxter, "Nonverbal Communication," in O. Hargie, Ed., *A Handbook of Communication Skills* (London: Croom & Helm, 1986), 59–94; and T. Alessandra and R. Barrera, *Collaborative Selling* (New York: John Wiley & Sons, Inc., 1993), 121–122.

Exhibit 4.9: R. F. Kantin and M. W. Hardwick, *Quality Selling through Quality Proposals* (Danvers, MA: Boyd & Fraser Publishing Co., 1994), 65–70.

Exhibit 4.10: Adapted from A. C. Lowander, "How to Write Good (Uh, We Mean Well)," in "The Write Stuff," *Sales & Marketing Management* (January 1998): 73.

Building Professional Selling Skills, Exercise 1: D. Bone, *The Business of Listening: A Practical Guide to Effective Listening* (Crisp Publications, 1988), 30–31.

MODULE 5

Exhibit 5.5: T. Ingram, R. W. LaForge, R. Avila, C. H. Schwepker, and M. Williams, *Sales Management: Analysis and Decision Making* 4 ed. (Fort Worth, TX: The Dryden Press, 2001).

Figure 5.7: Adapted from S. R. Covey, *The 7 Habits of Highly Effective People* (New York: Simon & Schuster, 1989).

MODULE 6

Exhibit 6.1: Ramon A. Avila, Thomas N. Ingram, Raymond W. LaForge, and Michael R. Williams, *The Professional Selling Skills Workbook* (Fort Worth, TX: The Dryden Press, 1996), 20.

Exhibit 6.2: Adapted from D. Forbes Ley, *The Best Seller* (Newport Beach, CA: Sales Success Press, 1986).

Exhibit 6.3: Adapted from A. J. Dubinsky, "A Factor Analytic Study of the Personal Selling Process," *Journal of Personal Selling and Sales Management* 1, no. 1 (Fall–Winter, 1980–81): 28. Used with permission.

Exhibit 6.4: Tri-State Advertising Co. Inc., Warsaw, Indiana, as printed in Tweed Robinson and Mark L. Boos, "Get 'Em while They're Hot," *Marketing Tools* (June 1996): 67.

Exhibit 6.6: John I. Coppett and William A. Staples, *Professional Selling: A Relationship Approach,* 2 ed. (Cincinnati, OH: South-Western Publishing Co., 1994): 220.

APPENDIX 7

Exhibit 7A.1: Growmark Inc., 1998.

Exercise for Appendix 7: D. W. Merrill and R. H. Reid, *Personal Styles and Effective Performance* (Radnor, PA: Chilton Book Company, 1981); and G. L. Manning and B. L. Reece, *Selling Today: An Extension of the Marketing Concept* (Boston, MA: Allyn and Bacon, 1995).

MODULE 8

Professional Selling (p. 215): Adapted from Helen Berman, "To Close Sales—Ask Questions," *Personal Selling Power,* (March 1991): 48–49. Adapted October 20, 1999.

COMPANY INDEX

NAME INDEX

SUBJECT INDEX